COMMENTARIES FOR BIBLICAL EXPOSITORS

An Annotated Bibliography
of Selected Works

Revised and Enlarged 1993

by
Dr. James E. Rosscup
Professor of Bible
The Master's Seminary

GRACE BOOK SHACK
Sun Valley, California

Published by Grace Book Shack
13248 Roscoe Blvd., Sun Valley, California 91352

Library of Congress Cataloging-in-Publication Data

Rosscup, James E.

Commentaries for Biblical expositors: an annotated bibliography of selected works / by James E. Rosscup.— Rev. and enl.

Originally published in 1966 and was later revised in 1983.

ISBN 1-883973-00-7

1. Bible—Commentaries — Bibliography.
2. Bibliography — Best books — Bible. I. Title.

Z7770.R67   1993   [BS491.2]   016.2207

GRACE BOOK SHACK
Sun Valley, California

PRINTED IN U.S.A.

ACKNOWLEDGMENTS

*I would like to express my deep appreciation to God for His strength
and to others who made this book possible.*

*First my immeasurable gratitude to my wife, Mildred,
who graciously supported me in the many hours of study.*

*Thanks, also to the scholars who wrote supporting words — John MacArthur, Jr.,
Dick Mayhue, Cyril Barber, Harold Hoehner, and Walter Kaiser, Jr.*

*Thanks to those who spent many hours typing the manuscript — Nancy Martin,
Amy Osmus, Carole Milam, and a former student of mine, John Metcalf.*

Thanks to Floyd Votaw for his capable assistance as librarian.

*Gratitude is also due to Stephen Wheeler, Director of Grace Bookshack,
who cheerfully carried out the many phases of production
to bring this book to fulfillment.*

— Jim Rosscup

TABLE OF CONTENTS

Foreword by John MacArthur vii

Preface by Dr. Cyril J. Barber ix

Recognized Limitations of the Bibliography...1

Rating Commentaries on Bible Books...3

Commentaries on the Whole Bible...16
      Synthetical 16
      Analytical 22

Commentaries on the Old Testament 31
      Synthetical 31
      Analytical 33

Commentaries on the Pentateuch 34

Individual Commentaries on Old Testament Books...37
      Genesis..37
      Exodus...49
      Leviticus..56
      Numbers 61
      Deuteronomy 65
      Joshua..70
      Judges..75
      Ruth...78
      Samuel...81
      Kings..85
      Chronicles...88
      Ezra, Nehemiah, Esther 91
      Job...97
      Psalms 102
      Proverbs 109
      Ecclesiastes 113
      Song of Solomon 117
      Isaiah...121
      Jeremiah..127

Lamentations 134
Ezekiel 136
Daniel 141
Minor Prophets 150
    General Works 150
    Individual Works 156

General Commentaries on the New Testament 181
    Greek 181
    English...183

Background Works and Special Studies in the Gospels.................187

Commentaries on Individual New Testament Books 191
    Matthew...191
    Mark 203
    Luke 208
    John 212
    Acts 221
    Romans 227
    First Corinthians 240
    Second Corinthians..246
    Galatians 251
    Ephesians..256
    Philippians..261
    Colossians...267
    First and Second Thessalonians 270
    Pastoral Epistles 274
    Philemon...278
    Hebrews...279
    James...286
    First Peter..291
    Second Peter...295
    The Johannine Epistles 297
    Jude 301
    Revelation 303

FOREWORD

By John MacArthur
Pastor, Grace Community Church
President, The Master's Seminary

Anyone who is committed to the exposition of Scripture knows the tremendous challenge of the study that faces him: the need to reconstruct the historic setting, deal with the language, maintain a consistent theological relationship with the rest of Scripture, unravel the difficult and obscure portions and make all of that study produce a work that is both profound and practical.

I'm convinced that trying to do all of that alone is nothing short of foolish. You need some friends; men who have more insight than you in their various areas of expertise, men whom the Holy Spirit has illuminated, men whom time has proven to be gifted, excellent interpreters of Scripture. Where can one find such a group to work with, such an enlightened, insightful, wise group of friends? I have found such a group of friends with whom I meet every week on the pages of their commentaries. In fact, I probably spend more time with them than I do with any other group. They are my teachers providing the benefit of past illumination and all the Holy Spirit-directed insights of centuries and decades past and present.

I have found commentaries are vital for several reasons. They interpret a given passage in the larger book framework so that there is always recognition of the compelling matter of context. Secondly, they give me the benefit of seeing how each text fits into the author's theological frame of reference; that is, how Calvinists, Arminians, Lutherans, etc. interpret passages. This helps me work through all the arguments that might be made in each given interpretation. Thirdly, commentaries help with the difficult sections. And fourthly, they speed up the process of cross-referencing by suggesting related passages. Time saved, scholarship tapped, illumination shared, problems solved, these and more are the benefits of having such friends. Who wouldn't want to be able to access the best of Christian biblical interpretation throughout the centuries and up to the present in a short time?

Having said all that, there are more commentaries in print than one could or should read. Since time and money is of the essence and there is little benefit to be gained from collecting or muddling through inept discussions, every expositor is in desperate need of help in selecting the right commentaries. Dr. Jim Rosscup becomes for us the friend who helps us choose our other friends. This annotated bibliography of commentaries is so foundational and so necessary that no student of Scripture who intends to exposit it accurately and effectively should begin to select his commentary friends until he has spent time first with my friend, Jim Rosscup and come through his careful evaluation of the available commentaries on all the books of the Bible.

No man could ever accumulate this information without unrelenting diligence lasting over three decades. This is a treasure and you need to learn to first make friends with it and it will introduce you to the other friends who will enrich your life and the lives of those who hear you.

PREFACE

By Dr. Cyril J. Barber
Author, The Minister's Library

When George Barna conducted his poll to determine American attitudes and mores—a poll that was later published in **What Americans Believe** (Ventura, CA: Regal, 1991)—he uncovered some startling facts. He found, for example, that blacks are more spiritual than whites, and are far more inclined to practice their beliefs.

Barna also learned that only 36% of those calling themselves Christians read a single Christian book during the previous year.

When seeking to determine what Americans deemed to be important, family and health topped the list, with leisure time and friends coming second. Church attendance and reading the Bible did **not** come in third, for only about 50% of those calling themselves Christian found them to be necessary to support their beliefs.

The conclusion reached after interpreting the results of his survey led Barna to make the following comment: While the Bible may be the book most frequently bought (and nearly all homes had at least one copy), it continues to be the least read of any book available today.

These troubling facts recall to mind the situation of the northern tribes of Israel after the division of the kingdom. The Lord, speaking through one of His prophets, said:

"My people perish for lack of knowledge ..." (Hosea 4:6).

Jeroboam I (931-910 B.C.) had consecrated as priests any who wanted to buy their way into this office, and as a result there arose a body of individuals who were untaught in the Scriptures and the history of their people. They were blind leaders of the blind. That is why God, speaking this time through Amos, said:

"Behold the days are coming when I will send a famine on the land, not a famine for bread or a thirst for water, but rather for hearing the words of the Lord" (Amos 8:11).

And that seems to sum up the way things are in our land today. History has repeated itself. The example set for all who minister the Word of God faithfully is to declare to the Lord's people "the whole counsel of God" (Acts 20:27 AV).

But how is this to be achieved?

Those in the ministry, as well as those preparing for it, need to become people of "the Book." And this is where Professor James Rosscup's annotated bibliography is so helpful. For as long as I have known him (i.e., for the past 30 years) he has been a diligent student of the Scriptures. His knowledge of Bible, and of Bible commentaries and related works, is exemplary in evangelical circles. Those students fortunate enough to study under him should make the most of every opportunity and learn from him.

And they, together with those not as fortunate, should avail themselves of this bibliography and attempt whenever possible to acquire the books Dr. Rosscup has recommended.

Dr. Rosscup has condensed a lifetime of personal research into these pages. His comments are judicious and his recommendations reliable. Happy, therefore, are those who will emulate his example and become students of **"the Book"**!

Obviously a small library of several hundred commentaries cannot be acquired overnight. Those entering the ministry would do well to plan their preaching and secure in advance those books that they will need to use as a part of their sermon preparation. In this way, and over time, their library can grow.

One of the greatest problems facing us in this "information intensive age" is the need to bring people and resources together. I trust that, in the providence of God, what Dr. Rosscup has incorporated into this bibliography will be a means of achieving this goal. To that end I commend this work to the present generation of pastors, as well as to those who are "ministers-in-the-making."

RECOGNIZED LIMITATIONS
OF THE BIBLIOGRAPHY

I. **It is selective.**

    A.   Not all helpful works relating to Bible exposition are included. For example, the bibliography contains few and in some cases no books on such areas as Bible geography, archeology, manners and customs, history, chronology, pseudepigrapha and apocrypha, versions, alleged discrepancies or problem texts, etc. Scores of specialized works in systematic and biblical theology are of immeasurable help in Bible exposition, but these are not noted here. Then there are the invaluable helps in dictionaries, encyclopedias, works on certain limited portions of Scripture (i.e., like Marcus Rainsford on John 17, <u>Our Lord Prays for His Own</u>; Erich Sauer, exposition of Hebrews 12 in his work <u>In the Arena of Faith</u>, etc.), books on specialized subjects like Bible miracles, parables, types, humor, plants, birds, women, promises, the Flood, the Law, the Tabernacle, characters like Abraham, Moses, Elijah, Paul, Peter, the speeches (as in Acts), the cities of the New Testament (William Ramsay's, Merrill Unger's and Colin Hemer's works, etc.). Only a few of such books are included.

    B.   Not even all helpful commentaries are included. The list is very selective in this sense and could be greatly expanded. There are various reasons for omitting works which may be deemed important by some who may read the list. First, the compiler of the bibliography was not seeking to be absolutely exhaustive but to serve the practical purpose of suggesting helpful works for expositors who are seeking to build their libraries. The demand has been so incessant that it was the arranger's opinion that a reasonable list could be made available. Second, some works are not included because, while helpful in themselves, they make no special contribution beyond the commentaries which are listed. Third, it is readily acknowledged that the field is so vast that the compiler may not be aware of some works which <u>should</u> be included. Fourth, some works of great value have undoubtedly been left out inadvertently. Fifth, there has been no attempt to include a large number of Puritan or other reprints. Many are expositions of books and have been recommended highly in lists by such men as Cyril Barber and Charles Spurgeon.

C.   Not any work later than 1992 is included with an annotation.

D.   Not all editions have been indicated. For example, a foreign edition may be listed although there may also be an American edition. Further, the date, place, and publisher indicated do not necessarily represent the latest or current publication. New editions of some works are continually appearing.

II.   It is succinct.

Though an annotation is given for each work, comments are brief in varying degrees. Some books do not receive the fuller entries of which they are worthy. And it is expected that in any such list there will be disagreement among readers as to the relative helpfulness of any given work.

RATING COMMENTARIES ON BIBLE BOOKS

The rating is in three categories: (1) detailed exegetical works which may include much technical material; (2) competent expositional surveys, and (3) more predominantly devotional efforts which can include some exposition and, at times, handling of interpretive problems. The rating is based on the reviewer's estimate of how well writers explain the text we have. Works which go aside into speculative theories rather often negative toward a real explanation of the text that is before most readers here, however painstaking their scholarship is in technical matters, may be left out on occasion.

Detailed Exegetical	*Expositional Survey*	*Devotional Flavor*
Genesis		
1. H. C. Leupold	1. J. J. Davis	1. W. H. Griffith-Thomas
2. V. Hamilton (only chs. 1-17 so far)	2. A. P. Ross (CAB)	2. J. Phillips
3. G. Wenham	3. R. Youngblood	3. D. Barnhouse
4. J. Sailhamer	4. D. Kidner	4. A. W. Pink
5. H. Stigers		
Pentateuch		
	1. J. Sailhamer	
	2. H. Wolf	
	3. H. Livingston	
	4. C. H. Bullock	
Exodus		
1. W. Kaiser	1. J. J. Davis	1. B. Ramm
2. N. Sarna (Lib.)	2. R. Youngblood	2. A. W. Pink
3. B. Childs (Lib.)	3. R. A. Cole	3. F. B. Meyer
4. C. Keil/F. Delitzsch	4. J. Hanna (<u>BKC</u>)	
Leviticus		
1. R. K. Harrison	1. R. L. Harris	1. A. Bonar
2. G. Wenham	2. L. Goldberg	2. S. Schultz
3. J. Milgrom (Lib.)	3. D. Kidner	

	Detailed Exegetical	*Expositional Survey*	*Devotional Flavor*

Numbers

1. G. Wenham	1. R. Allen	1. J. Philip
2. R. K. Harrison	2. S. Maarsingh	
3. J. Milgrom (Lib.)	3. D. Kidner	
4. G. Gary (Lib.)		

Deuteronomy

1. P. Craigie	1. R. K. Harrison	1. S. Schultz
2. J. A. Thompson	2. J. Deere	
3. S. Driver (Lib.)		
4. J. Ridderbos		

Joshua

1. M. Woudstra	1. J. J. Davis	1. D. Davis
2. R. Boling/	2. C. Goslinga	2. F. Schaeffer
G. Wright (Lib.)	3. P. Enns	3. R. K. Hughes
3. J. Bright (Lib.)	4. A. Cohen	4. A. Johnson
	5. D. Campbell	5. F. B. Meyer
	6. A. W. Pink	

Judges

1. L. Wood	1. P. Enns	1. C. Barber
2. A. Cundall/	2. C. Goslinga	2. D. Davis
L. Morris	3. D. Lindsey	3. J. Hercus
3. G. Moore (Lib.)	4. J. J. Davis	4. F. B. Meyer

Ruth

1. E. F. Campbell (Lib.)	1. P. Enns	1. C. Barber
2. A. Cundall/L. Morris	2. J. J. Davis	2. J. V. McGee
3. D. Atkinson	3. R. L. Hubbard, Jr.	3. F. B. Meyer
4. A. R. S. Kennedy	4. C. Goslinga	4. H. Moorhouse

I, II Samuel

1. R. P. Gordon	1. J. C. Laney	1. F. B. Meyer
2. C. Keil	2. E. Merrill	2. C. Barber
	3. L. Wood	
	4. J. J. Davis/J. Whitcomb	
	(Hist. of Isr.)	
	5. J. C. Baldwin	

Detailed Exegetical	Expositional Survey	Devotional Flavor

I, II Kings

1. R. Patterson/	1. L. Wood (IUM)	1. R. Dilday
H. Austel	2. T. Constable	2. F. B. Meyer
2. C. Keil	3. J. J. Davis	3. L. Wood (Elijah)
3. S. DeVries (Lib.)		
4. J. A. Montgomery (Lib.)		

I, II Chronicles

1. J. B. Payne	1. E. Merrill	1. M. Wilcock
2. J. Myers (Lib.)	2. J. Sailhamer	
3. C. Keil	(brief)	
4. H. G. M. Williamson (Lib.)		

Ezra/Nehemiah

1. F. Fensham	1. J. C. Laney	1. J. Boice (Neh.)
2. E. Yamauchi	2. D. Kidner	2. G. Getz (Neh.)
3. J. Blenkinsopp	3. J. C. Whitcomb	3. D. Campbell (Neh.)
4. J. Myers (Lib.)	4. J. G. McConville	4. C. Swindoll (Neh.)
5. C. Keil	5. J. Martin	5. C. Barber (Neh.)
6. H. Williamson (Lib.)	6. H. A. Ironside	

Esther

1. E. Yamauchi	1. J. Baldwin	1. H. A. Ironside
2. C. A. Moore	2. J. G. McConville	2. J. V. McGee
3. L. B. Paton, ICC	3. J. Whitcomb	
(Lib.)	4. J. Martin	

Job

1. F. Andersen	1. E. Smick	1. A. Blackwood, Jr.
2. J. E. Hartley	2. R. B. Zuck (BKC,	2. R. Stedman
3. N. Habel	also EvBC)	3. D. Atkinson
4. R. Gordis	3. R. B. Zuck (SWJ)	
5. A. B. Davidson		
6. E. C. S. Gibson		
7. F. Delitzsch		

Psalms

1. J. van Gemeren	1. A. P. Ross	1. C. Spurgeon (6 vols.,
2. D. Kidner	2. W. G. Scroggie	3 vols., or 1 vol.)
3. H. C. Leupold		2. J. Phillips
4. J. J. S. Perowne		3. J. R. W. Stott
5. P. Craigie, M. Tate,		4. E. C. Olsen
L. Allen		5. R. Alden
6. J. A. Alexander		

	Detailed Exegetical	Expositional Survey	Devotional Flavor

Proverbs

1. D. Kidner	1. R. L. Harris	1. J. Draper, Jr.
2. A. P. Ross	2. S. Buzzell	2. E. Woodcock
3. F. Delitzsch	3. R. Alden	3. W. Mouser
4. W. McKane (Lib)		4. G. Santa (rev.,
5. G. Lawson		C. Bridges)

Ecclesiastes

1. J. Wright	1. W. Kaiser	1. D. Kidner
2. H. C. Leupold	2. M. Eaton	2. C. Swindoll
3. E. Hengstenberg	3. D. Glenn	
4. C. D. Ginsburg	4. L. Goldberg	

Song of Songs

1. G. L. Carr	1. J. Deere	1. H. A. Ironside
2. R. Gordis	2. P. Patterson	
3. M. Pope (Lib)	3. C. Glickman	
4. D. Kinlaw		

Isaiah

1. G. Grogan (Premill)	1. J. Martin (Premill)	1. H. A. Ironside
J. Oswalt (Amill)	2. W. E. Vine (Premill)	
E. Young (Amill)	3. G. C. Morgan (Premill)	
2. H. Leupold (Amill)	4. D. Garland (Premill)	
3. F. Delitzsch (Amill)		

Jeremiah

1. C. Feinberg (Premill)	1. C. Dyer (Premill)	1. John Guest
J. Thompson (Amill)	2. I. Jensen (Premill)	2. D. Kidner
W. Holladay (Lib)	3. G. C. Morgan	
2. R. K. Harrison (Amill)	4. F. Huey, Jr.	
3. T. Laetsch (Amill)	5. A. W. Streane	
4. J. Calvin (Amill)		

Lamentations

1. R. K. Harrison	1. C. Dyer	1. W. Kaiser, Jr. (could
2. D. Hillers	2. I. Jensen	fit in col. two)
	3. D. Kent	2. F. Schaeffer
	4. A. W. Streane	

	Detailed Exegetical	*Expositional Survey*	*Devotional Flavor*

Ezekiel

1. C. Feinberg (Premill)
   C. Keil/F. Delitzsch
   (Amill)
   W. Zimmerli (Lib)
2. W. Eichrodt (Lib)

1. R. Alexander (Premill)
1. J. Taylor (Amill)
2. C. Dyer (Premill)
3. P. Enns (Premill)

Daniel

1. L. Wood (Premill)
   E. Young (Amill)
   J. Montgomery (Lib)
2. J. Walvoord (Premill)
   J. Goldingay (Amill)
   N. Porteous (Lib)
3. H. Leupold (Amill)

1. J. Pentecost (Premill)
2. R. Culver (Premill)
3. J. Whitcomb (Premill)
4. J. Baldwin (Amill)

1. J. Phillips/
   J. Vines (Premill)
2. D. Campbell (Premill)
3. W. Criswell (Premill)

Minor Prophets Overall

1. T. Laetsch (Amill)
   R. Chisholm, Jr.
   (Premill)
2. J. Calvin (Amill)
   C. H. Bullock (Premill)

1. C. Feinberg (Premill)
2. BKC I and EBC entries (Premill)
3. J. Boice (Premill)
4. P. Fink (Premill, Liberty BC)

Hosea

1. F. Andersen/D.
   Freedman (Amill)
   H. Wolff (Lib)
2. D. Stuart (Amill)
   J. L. Mays (Lib)
3. C. Keil (Amill)

1. J. Riggs (Premill)
2. C. Feinberg (Premill)
3. R. Chisholm, Jr.
   (Premill)
4. D. Garland (Premill)
5. D. Hubbard (Premill)
   P. Fink (Premill)

1. D. Kidner
2. G. C. Morgan
3. H. A. Ironside

Joel

1. R. Patterson
   (Premill)
   H. Wolff (Lib)
   D. Stuart (Amill)
2. T. Finley (Premill)
3. C. Keil (Amill)

1. R. Allen (Premill)
2. C. Feinberg (Premill)
3. P. Fink (Premill)
   D. Hubbard (Premill)

	Detailed Exegetical	Expositional Survey	Devotional Flavor

Amos

	Detailed Exegetical	Expositional Survey	Devotional Flavor
	1. T. Finley (Premill)	1. C. Feinberg (Premill)	1. J. Motyer
	S. Paul (Lib)	2. D. Sunukian (Premill)	
	D. Stuart (Amill)	3. D. Garland (Premill)	
	2. T. McComiskey	4. P. Fink (Premill)	
	(Premill?)	D. Hubbard (Premill)	
	F. Andersen/		
	D. Freedman (Lib)		
	3. H. Wolff (Lib)		
	J. L. Mays (Lib)		

Obadiah

	Detailed Exegetical	Expositional Survey	Devotional Flavor
	1. T. Finley (Premill)	1. B. Beyer (Premill)	
	H. Wolff (Lib)	2. C. Feinberg (Premill)	
	D. Stuart (Amill)	3. P. Fink (Premill)	
	2. C. Keil (Amill)		

Jonah

	Detailed Exegetical	Expositional Survey	Devotional Flavor
	Cf. "MP Overall"	1. J. Hannah	
	1. D. Stuart (Amill)	2. J. Kohlenberger	
	2. C. Keil (Amill)	3. J. Walton	
		4. C. Feinberg	
		5. P. Fink	

Micah

	Detailed Exegetical	Expositional Survey	Devotional Flavor
	1. T. McComiskey	1. J. Riggs (Premill)	
	(Premill?)	2. J. Martin (Premill)	
	B. Waltke (Amill)	3. C. Feinberg (Premill)	
	2. D. Stuart (Amill)	4. P. Fink (Premill)	
	H. Wolff (Lib)		

Nahum

	Detailed Exegetical	Expositional Survey	Devotional Flavor
	1. W. Maier (Amill)	1. J. Kohlenberger (Premill)	
	2. R. Patterson (Premill)	2. E. Johnson (Premill)	
	3. O. Robertson (Premill)	3. C. Feinberg (Premill)	
		4. P. Fink (Premill)	

Habakkuk

	Detailed Exegetical	Expositional Survey	Devotional Flavor
	1. O. Robertson (Premill)	1. C. Feinberg (Premill)	1. D. M. Lloyd-Jones
	2. R. Patterson (Premill)	2. C. Barber (Premill)	
	3. T. Laetsch (Amill)	3. R. Blue (Premill)	
	4. J. Calvin (Amill)	4. P. Fink (Premill)	

Detailed Exegetical	*Expositional Survey*	*Devotional Flavor*

Zephaniah

1. O. Robertson (Premill)   1. J. Hannah (Premill)   1. R. Allen (Premill)
2. R. Patterson (Premill)   2. C. Feinberg (Premill)
3. T. Laetsch (Amill)   3. C. Barber (Premill)
4. J. Calvin (Amill)   4. P. Fink (Premill)
    C. Keil (Amill)

Haggai

1. P. Verhoef (Premill)   1. H. M. Wolf (Premill)
2. J. Heflin (?)   2. C. Feinberg (Premill)
3. J. Baldwin (Amill)   3. F. Lindsey (Premill)
4. D. Petersen (Lib)   4. P. Fink (Premill)
5. T. Laetsch (Amill)
6. J. Calvin (Amill)
    C. Keil (Amill)

Zechariah

1. K. Barker (Premill)   1. J. C. Laney (Premill)
    H. C. Leupold (Amill)   2. H. Heater (Premill)
    D. Petersen (Lib)   3. F. Lindsey (Premill)
2. C. Feinberg (Premill)   4. P. Fink (Premill)
    M. Unger (Premill)
    J. Calvin (Amill)
3. J. Baldwin (Amill)
    D. Baron (Premill)

Malachi

1. P. Verhoef (Premill)   1. H. M. Wolf (Premill)   1. G. C. Morgan (Premill)
2. B. Glazier-   2. C. Feinberg (Premill)
    McDonald (Evan.?)   3. C. Blaising (Premill)
3. W. Kaiser, Jr. (Premill)   4. P. Fink (Premill)
4. J. Baldwin (Amill)

Matthew

1. J. Broadus (Amill)   1. H. Kent   1. W. H. Griffith-Thomas
    W. D. Davies/   (Premill disp.)   (Premill disp.)
    D. Allison (Lib)   2. R. H. Mounce   2. H. A. Ironside
    D. Carson (Premill)   (Amill)   (Premill disp.)
2. W. Hendriksen (Amill)   3. R. France (Amill)
3. J. MacArthur   4. S. Toussaint (Premill disp.)
    (Premill disp.)   5. L. Barbieri (Premill disp.)
      6. R. V. G. Tasker (Amill)
    Watch for David Turner (Premill)

	Detailed Exegetical	*Expositional Survey*	*Devotional Flavor*
Mark			
	1. W. Lane	1. R. A. Cole	1. R. K. Hughes
	2. H. Anderson (Lib)	2. R. Wolff	2. K. S. Wuest
	R. Guelich (Lib)	3. W. Wessel, <u>Expositors BC</u>	
	3. C. E. B. Cranfield		
	4. W. Hendriksen		
	5. D. Hiebert		
	6. V. Taylor		
	7. H. B. Swete		
Luke			
	1. I. H. Marshall	1. L. Morris	1. M. Wilcock
	2. F. Godet	2. J. Martin, BKC II	2. W. H. Griffith-
	3. A. Plummer (Lib.)	(Premill disp.)	Thomas
	4. W. Hendriksen	3. M. Tenney	(Premill disp.)
	5. J. Fitzmyer (Lib.)	4. W. Liefield	
	6. N. Geldenhuys		
John			
	1. R. E. Brown (Lib)	1. J. C. Laney	1. J. Phillips
	2. D. Carson	2. H. Kent	2. J. Boice
	3. F. F. Bruce	3. M. Tenney	3. R. K. Hughes
	4. L. Morris, NIC	4. E. Blum, BKC II	
	5. W. Hendriksen		
	6. B. F. Westcott		
	7. R. Schnackenburg, 3 vols.		
Acts			
	1. F. F. Bruce, NIC	1. H. Kent	1. J. Stott
	1. E. Haenchen (Lib)	2. S. Toussiant	2. J. Phillips
	2. R. N. Longenecker	3. G. E. Ladd	3. H. A. Ironside
	3. I. H. Marshall	4. C. C. Ryrie	
	4. J. B. Polhill		
	5. S. Kistemaker		
	6. E. Harrison		
	7. R. Rackham		

Detailed Exegetical	*Expositional Survey*	*Devotional Flavor*

Romans

1. C. E. B. Cranfield (2 vols)	1. L. Morris	1. W. H. Griffith-Thomas Life Application
2. D. Moo (Rom. 1-8)	2. J. MacArthur	Bible Commentary
3. W. Sanday/ A. Headlam	3. A. J. McClain	2. R. K. Hughes
4. J. Murray	4. J. Stifler	3. A. Johnson
5. W. Hendriksen	5. R. Haldane	4. D. M. Lloyd-Jones
6. E. Harrison	6. W. Newell	5. H. A. Ironside
	7. J. Witmer	6. D. G. Barnhouse

I Corinthians

1. G. Fee	1. S. L. Johnson (Wyc. BC)	1. D. Prior
2. A. T. Robertson/ A. Plummer	2. W. H. Mare	2. H. A. Ironside
3. C. K. Barrett	3. J. MacArthur	3. G. C. Luck
4. R. C. H. Lenski	4. L. Morris or R. G. Gromacki	
5. H. Conzelmann (Lib)	5. R. B. Hughes	
	6. D. Lowery, BKC II	
	7. C. Hodge	
Watch for S. Kistemaker		

II Corinthians

1. C. K. Barrett	1. H. Kent	1. A. B. & W. D. Spencer
2. P. E. Hughes	2. R. G. Gromacki	2. A. T. Robertson, The Glory of The Ministry
3. A. Plummer	3. C. G. Kruse	3. H. A. Ironside
4. V. P. Furnish (Lib)	4. D. Lowery, BKC II	4. Paul Barnett
5. C. Hodge	5. C. Hodge	
6. F. W. Danker	6. R. V. G. Tasker	
7. M. Harris		

Galatians

1. E. D. Burton	1. H. Kent	1. J. Stott
2. J. B. Lightfoot	2. R. A. Cole	2. D. Hubbard
3. F. F. Bruce	3. D. Guthrie	3. L. Strauss
4. R. Fung	4. R. G. Gromacki	4. H. A. Ironside
5. R. Longenecker		
6. W. Hendriksen		
7. J. Eadie		

Detailed Exegetical	Expositional Survey	Devotional Flavor

Ephesians

Detailed Exegetical	Expositional Survey	Devotional Flavor
1. Andrew Lincoln	1. H. Hoehner, BKC II	1. J. Stott
2. T. K. Abbott	2. J. MacArthur	2. R. K. Hughes
3. F. F. Bruce	3. H. Kent	3. H. A. Ironside
4. Markus Barth (Lib)	4. A. S. Wood	4. L. Strauss
5. W. Hendriksen	5. D. M. Lloyd-Jones	5. R. Paxson
6. B. F. Westcott		
7. J. Eadie		
Watch for H. Hoehner, longer work		

Philippians

Detailed Exegetical	Expositional Survey	Devotional Flavor
1. G. Hawthorne	1. R. Mounce	1. P. Rees
P. T. O'Brien	2. H. Kent	2. J. Motyer;
2. J. B. Lightfoot	3. D. M. Lloyd-Jones,	J. D. Pentecost
3. Ralph P. Martin, NCB	2 vols.	3. F. B. Meyer
4. W. Hendriksen		4. G. King
5. F. F. Bruce		5. H. A. Ironside
6. M. Sivla		6. K. S. Wuest
7. F. W. Beare (Lib)		7. J. G. Thomas
8. M. R. Vincent		(Phil. 4)

Colossians

Detailed Exegetical	Expositional Survey	Devotional Flavor
1. P. T. O'Brien	1. R. G. Gromacki	1. R. K. Hughes
2. T. K. Abbott	J. MacArthur	2. R. C. Lucas
3. F. F. Bruce or	2. E. E. Ellis	3. W. H. Griffith-Thomas
S. L. Johnson	3. C. Vaughan	
4. Ralph P. Martin	4. N. T. Wright	
5. J. B. Lightfoot		
6. W. Hendriksen		
7. E. Lohse		
8. M. Harris		

Philemon

Detailed Exegetical	Expositional Survey	Devotional Flavor
1. P. T. O'Brien	1. J. MacArthur	1. R. K. Hughes
2. J. B. Lightfoot	2. N. T. Wright	2. H. A. Ironside
3. F. F. Bruce	3. E. Deibler, BKC II	3. R. C. Lucas
4. W. Hendriksen		
5. R. P. Martin		
6. M. Harris		
7. M. R. Vincent		

	Detailed Exegetical	*Expositional Survey*	*Devotional Flavor*

I Thessalonians

	Detailed Exegetical	*Expositional Survey*	*Devotional Flavor*
	1. R. L. Thomas (Premill disp.)	1. T. Constable (Premill disp.)	1. H. A. Ironside (Premill disp.)
	2. F. F. Bruce (Premill)	2. J. Stott (Amill)	
	3. I. H. Marshall (Amill) D. E. Hiebert (Premill disp.), revised	3. J. Walvoord (Premill disp.) 4. C. C. Ryrie (Premill disp.)	
	4. L. Morris (Amill)		
	5. E. Best (Amill)		
	6. W. Hendriksen (Amill)		

II Thessalonians

	Detailed Exegetical	*Expositional Survey*	*Devotional Flavor*
	1. R. L. Thomas (Premill disp.)	1. J. Stott (Amill)	1. H. A. Ironside (Premill disp.)
	2. F. F. Bruce (Premill)	2. J. Walvoord (Premill disp.)	
	3. I. H. Marshall (Amill) D. E. Hiebert (Premill disp.), revised	3. C. C. Ryrie (Premill disp.)	
	4. L. Morris (Amill)		
	5. E. Best (Amill)		
	6. W. Hendriksen (Amill)		

I Timothy

	Detailed Exegetical	*Expositional Survey*	*Devotional Flavor*
	1. J. N. D. Kelly	1. H. Kent	1. G. King
	2. C. K. Barrett	2. D. Guthrie	
	3. J. E. Huther	3. T. Lea	
	4. W. Hendriksen		
	5. R. C. H. Lenski		
	6. G. Fee		
	7. G. W. Knight		

II Timothy

	Detailed Exegetical	*Expositional Survey*	*Devotional Flavor*
	1. J. N. D. Kelly	1. H. Kent	1. G. King
	2. C. K. Barrett	2. J. Stott, Guard The Gospel	2. G. Getz
	3. J. E. Huther	3. D. Guthrie	
	4. W. Hendriksen	4. T. Lea	
	5. G. Fee		
	6. R. C. H. Lenski		
	7. G. W. Knight		

	Detailed Exegetical	Expositional Survey	Devotional Flavor

Titus

	Detailed Exegetical	Expositional Survey	Devotional Flavor
	1. J. N. D. Kelly	1. H. Kent	1. G. Getz
	2. C. K. Barrett	2. D. Guthrie	
	3. J. E. Huther	3. H. Griffin, Jr.	
	4. W. Hendriksen		
	5. G. Fee		
	6. R. C. H. Lenski		
	7. G. W. Knight		

Hebrews

	Detailed Exegetical	Expositional Survey	Devotional Flavor
	1. F. F. Bruce	1. L. Morris (EBC)	1. A. Murray
	2. S. Kistemaker	2. J. MacArthur	2. W. H. Griffith-Thomas
	3. B. F. Westcott	3. R. E. Brown	3. K. S. Wuest
	4. P. E. Hughes	4. H. Kent	
	5. W. Lane (WBC)	5. W. Lane (NIBC)	
	6. D. Hagner	6. J. Owen, 1 vol. abridgement of 8	
	Watch for S. L. Johnson	7. D. Guthrie	

James

	Detailed Exegetical	Expositional Survey	Devotional Flavor
	1. P. Davids	1. H. Kent	1. Life Application Bible Commentary
	2. J. B. Mayor	2. S. Kistemaker	
	3. C. L. Mitton	3. R. Wolff	2. G. King
	4. J. Adamson	4. R. V. G. Tasker	3. J. Motyer
	5. Sophie Laws (Lib)		
	6. D. E. Hiebert, revised		
	7. R. P. Martin		
	8. D. Moo		

I Peter

	Detailed Exegetical	Expositional Survey	Devotional Flavor
	1. E. G. Selwyn	1. C. E. B. Cranfield	1. R. Leighton
	2. J. N. D. Kelly	2. R. H. Mounce	2. F. B. Meyer
	3. P. Davids	3. I. H. Marshall	3. K. S. Wuest
	4. J. R. Michaels	4. A. M. Stibbs	
	5. C. Bigg	5. E. Blum	
	6. W. Grudem	6. R. Raymer	
	7. S. Kistemaker		
	8. D. E. Hiebert, revised		

	Detailed Exegetical	*Expositional Survey*	*Devotional Flavor*

II Peter

1. J. N. D. Kelly	1. R. H. Mounce	1. D. M. L.-Jones
2. J. B. Mayor	2. M. E. Green	2. K. S. Wuest
3. R. Bauckham (Lib)	3. C. E. B. Cranfield	
4. C. Bigg	4. E. Blum	
5. D. E. Hiebert		

I John

1. R. E. Brown	1. J. Stott	1. R. E. O. White
2. D. Burdick	2. S. Kistemaker	2. K. S. Wuest
3. S. Smalley	3. C. C. Ryrie, <u>Wyc BC</u>	
4. I. H. Marshall	4. R. Cameron	
5. B. F. Westcott		
6. A. E. Brooke		

II, III John

Same as I John

Jude

1. J. N. D. Kelly	1. M. E. Green	1. J. MacArthur
2. J. B. Mayor	2. S. Kistemaker	
3. W. Jenkins	3. C. E. B. Cranfield	
4. D. E. Hiebert	4. E. Blum	
5. R. Bauckham	5. R. Wolff	
6. G. Lawlor		
7. A. Plummer		

Revelation

1. R. L. Thomas (Premill disp.) W. Hendriksen (Amill) H. B. Swete (tech.) D. Chilton (Postmill)	1. J. F. Walvoord (Premill disp.) 2. J. B. Smith (Premill disp.)	1. J. Stott (Rev. 2-3) 2. W. Newell (Premill disp.) 3. M. Wilcock (Amill)
2. I. T. Beckwith (Amill) D. Clark (Postmill)	3. L. Morris (Amill) 4. J. A. Seiss (Premill)	
3. R. H. Mounce (Amill)	5. G. E. Ladd (Premill)	
4. G. R. Beasley-Murray (Amill)	6. C. Colclasure (Amill)	

COMMENTARIES ON THE WHOLE BIBLE

I. SYNTHETICAL

This section relates to commentaries of a more general, synthetical, survey-type treatment.

Baxter, J. Sidlow. Explore the Book. 6 volumes. Grand Rapids: Zondervan, 1960. Also available unabridged in 1 volume, 1966.

Here is one of the best syntheses in lucid exposition by an outstanding and beloved Bible conference teacher of England who has had a wide ministry in the United States. There is a helpful overall view of each book in the Bible. The 1,600 page work is the result of more than 30 years of preaching. His treatment of Zechariah is very fine, and he is exceptionally good on Ephesians also.

The Beacon Bible Commentary. 10 volumes. Kansas City, MO: Beacon Hill, 1964—1968.

This major work of the Nazarene Church offers its readers a paragraph by paragraph (but not always verse by verse) study of Scripture with the King JamesVersion text printed in bold face type. Though there is considerable use of the Hebrew and Greek, the commentary is primarily calculated to be an aid to the average layman. Among the top scholars in the Nazarene Church who contributed to the commentary are Drs. Ross Price (Isaiah) and Paul Gray (Jeremiah) of the Point Loma College (Nazarene).

The Bible Speaks Today. Downers Grove, IL: IVP, 1986ff.

Here are volumes attempting to give survey expositions of Bible books in a lucid way that explains passages concisely, deals with some problems, and seeks to show the practical import of principles. Writers often draw on considerable scholarly help for a competent evangelical product. Joyce Baldwin does The Message of Genesis 12-50 (1986). Derek Kidner contributes Love to the Loveless (Hosea) and A Time to Mourn and a Time to Dance (Ecclesiastes). Michael Wilcock is fairly helpful on Chronicles, John Stott very good on Galatians and Ephesians, R. C. Lucas vital on Colossians and Philemon, etc. For lay readers and pastor-teachers desiring a readable tracing of the chain of thought, the volumes often offer much that refreshes.

Bible Study Commentary. **Grand Rapids: Baker, 1969—**

This is a popular, usually brief set of evangelical commentaries designed for lay people but offering simple, quick surveys even for preachers, leaders of Bible groups, etc. The authors are well-known scholars, for the most part: Leon Wood (Daniel), Alan F. Johnson (Revelation), Leon Morris (Hebrews), Howard F. Vos (1, 2 Samuel), etc. Competence in aware scholarship is wedded with simplicity in synthesis, with comments of worth on some of the main problem texts.

Brown, Raymond, et al, editors. **The New Jerome Biblical Commentary.** **Englewood Cliffs, NJ:** **Prentice Hall, 1990.** **1,475 pp.**

After 22 years this update of the Jerome Biblical Commentary has appeared to account for recent learning. It offers some of the cream of Roman Catholic scholarship on commentary and special articles on topics such as the Pentateuch, Wisdom literature, Prophetic scripture, apocalyptic, Hebrew poetry, apocryphal sources, Dead Sea scrolls, other Jewish literature, text and versions, modern Old Testament criticism, biblical archaeology, and religious institutions of Israel. It is about 60 per cent a replacement.

Bruce, F.F., General Editor, The International Bible Commentary. **1 volume.** **Revised edition.** **Grand Rapids: Zondervan, 1986.** **1st published in 1979 as The New Layman's Commentary.**

The old edition of this evangelical work used the RSV, the new version the NIV. Some of the writers on books are: Genesis (H. L. Ellisen), Psalms (Leslie Allen and John W. Baigent), Jeremiah (Donald Wiseman), Ezekiel (F. F. Bruce), Matthew (Ellisen again), Romans (Allen again), Hebrews (Gerald Hawthrone), Revelation (Bruce again). The book has introductory articles on the Old Testament and the New Testament and updates each 1979 article's bibliography. The product is aimed at lay people. It skips some verses and often is too thin. There is some focus on leading problem verses, as Isaiah 7:14.

Carter, Charles W. (Ed.) **The Wesleyan Bible Commentary.** **6 volumes.** **Grand Rapids:** **Baker.**

Wesleyan scholars highly respected in nine evangelical denominations contributed to this attempt to make relevant in the 20th century scene the traditions of John Wesley and Adam Clarke. It is done with spiritual flavor and aware scholarship. Three volumes deal with Old Testament, three with the New Testament.

Darby, John N. **Synopsis of the Books of the Bible.** **2nd edition.** **NY:** **Loizeaux, 1950.**

Brief surveys of all 66 books (Genesis, pp. 20-83; Exodus, 84-143, etc.). Darby seeks only to give a short synopsis of the main subjects in each book, often so cursory it is of little use except as the most elemental summary for a beginner. The conviction is premillennial, as in Isaiah 64-65, Jeremiah 31-32, 33, Ezekiel 45-47, Daniel 2, 7, Rev. 3:10, chapter 20, etc.

Eason, Lawrence. <u>The New Bible Survey</u>. Grand Rapids: Zondervan, 1963.

A 544-pp. popular-level evangelical work written as a survey for beginning students of Scripture which provides much helpful material for teachers. It is very useful.

Elwell, Walter, editor. <u>Evangelical Commentary on the Bible</u>. Grand Rapids: Baker, 1989. 1,229 pp.

The one-volume work is designed to help those without technical training understand, an aim already fulfilled by several commentaries which also were not done for scholars. Writers from many viewpoints are included, with no aim at unity (p. viii). Some of the better writers are: Genesis and Ezekiel (Victor Hamilton), Leviticus and Ezra/Nehemiah (Louis Goldberg), Joshua and Judges (Andrew Bowling), Ruth (R. K. Harrison), I and II Samuel (Herbert Wolf), Proverbs (R. K. Harrison), James (Douglas Moo), and Johannine Epistles (James B. DeYoung).

Halley, H. <u>Halley's Bible Handbook</u>. Revised edition. Grand Rapids: Zondervan, 1992. 860 pp.

A much-used older evangelical handbook bringing together a brief commentary on Bible books, some key archaeological findings, historical background, maps, quotes, etc. It is helpful to a lay Bible teacher, Sunday School leader, or pastor looking for quick, pertinent information on a Bible book. This is the 72nd printing somewhat revised. Halley packed in much information. Unger's is better overall, but that is not to say that Halley's will not provide much help on basic information.

Henry, Carl F. H. <u>The Biblical Expositor</u>. 3 volumes. Philadelphia: Holman, 1960.

Sixty-five conservative scholars teamed up to produce this work which has brief outlines and general surveys of the Bible books. Authors are men like H. C. Leupold, Edward J. Young, Merrill C. Tenney and Merrill F. Unger. It is a good, broad synthesis, authored by outstanding men.

Ironside, Henry A. <u>The Ironside Collection (Joshua to Revelation)</u>. Neptune, NJ: Loizeaux, 1987-89.

A famous Bible teacher much sought after a few decades back continues to minister after his departure, as A. C. Gaebelein, A. W. Pink, W. H. Griffith-Thomas and others. He is staunchly evangelical, showing good broad surveys based on diligent study, practical turns, even choice illustrations. In prophecy he is premillennial dispensational. The series now reprinted offers Joshua, Ezra, Nehemiah, Esther, Psalms, Proverbs, Song of Solomon, Isaiah through Malachi (various volumes), Matthew-Revelation (again different volumes). Many preachers have found that Ironside works, read along with heavier books on details of exegesis, help them see the sweep of the message and prime their spirits for practical relevance.

Liberty Bible Commentary, edited by Jerry Falwell et al. Nashville: Thomas Nelson, 1983. 2,721 pp.

Liberty Baptist issued this evangelical work on the whole Bible. Some contributors are: S. R. Schroder (Genesis), James Borland (Exodus), Paul Fink (Minor Prophets) and Charles Feinberg, visiting lecturer (Revelation). It is frequently cursory but does have good surveys, handles some problems well, and offers a premillennial perspective on long-range prophecy as in the Major Prophets, Minor Prophets, Matthew 24-25, the Thessalonian Epistles, and Revelation.

Luck, G. Coleman. The Bible Book by Book. Chicago: Moody, 1991.

A brief, simple but capable lay person's look at the historical outline and synthesis of each book by a long-time Moody Bible Institute professor. It is evangelical and premillennial. Sometimes it is fair, although overall J. Sidlow Baxter's Explore the Book offers more survey help.

MacDonald, William. Believer's Bible Commentary. Revised edition. Edited by Arthur Farstad. 2 volumes. Nashville: Thomas Nelson, 1990.

This work, originally issued in 1983, is conservative and premillennial, written to help teachers, preachers and people in every walk of life with different views, explanation and application. The 2-column format runs verse by verse for the most part, usually in a helpfully knowledgeable manner, and there are several special sections such as "Prayer" in Acts and "Legalism" in Galatians. The premillennial view is evident on Acts 1:6, 3:20, Romans 11:26, Galatians 6:16, Revelation 20, etc.

Mays, James L. editor, Harper's Bible Commentary. San Francisco: Harper & Row, 1988. 1,326 pp.

Eighty-two scholars of the Society of Biblical Literature provide introductory essays and commentaries. The work's essays deal with such topics as reading and interpreting the Bible, Old Testament context, context of Apocrypha and New Testament, how the Bible relates to literature of the ancient near east and the Greco-Roman era, Jewish interpretation, and introductions to sections of the Bible such as Psalms and Wisdom, with a bibliography ending each. The work is shot through with leanings to a JEDP theory on some Old Testament books, Canaanite religious ideas, the view that Genesis 1-2 give two creation accounts, etc.

Morgan, G. Campbell. An Exposition of the Whole Bible. Westwood, NJ: Revell, 1959.

Morgan deals with the Bible chapter by chapter, with nearly 300 words on each. He devotes 400 pages to the Old Testament, 150 to the New Testament. It is a stimulating broad evangelical coverage of Scripture, if the reader is looking for synthesis rather than detail. Morgan was a master expositor in the early part of this century. Some of the effort is so general it is of little help except to those looking for sketchy treatment. It is evangelical and premillennial. Morgan is better in such works as The Crises of the Christ.

A New Catholic Commentary on Holy Scripture. **Edited by Reginald Fuller et al. Camden, NJ:** **Thomas Nelson and Sons, 1969.** **1,363 pp.**

The work includes more than 30 introductory essays to Old Testament, New Testament and main sections, and surveys of all Bible books by Catholic scholars. Readers can see how Catholics explain passages, especially those where they often differ from Protestant writers on certain doctrines.

New American Commentary. **Cf. under New Testament section.** **Only some N. T. vols. out so far.**

Phillips, John. **Bible Explorer's Guide.** **Neptune, NJ:** **Loizeaux, 1987.** **274 pp.**

This general introductory work, evangelical in nature, has two sections, Hermeneutics and Helps. Under the first are 22 divisions such as studying Words, Figures of Speech, Culture, Context, Types, Parables, Prophecy, Devotional Rule, Application, Christ the Ultimate Key, etc. The section deals with a quick survey of the Bible, summary of Bible history, symbols, helpful books, etc. Phillips is well-known for his Exploring the New Testament series of clear, practical expositions of key books such as John and Romans. He is premillennial.

Richards, Lawrence O. **The Teacher's Commentary.** **Wheaton:** **Victor Books, 1987.** **1,110 pp.**

This is an evangelical effort by a Dallas Seminary graduate to survey each book of the Bible and provide special material to help teachers of Sunday Schools, Bible study groups, and pastors teach on different sections. The special features are material to illustrate and apply, definitions of biblical and doctrinal terms, background, maps and charts, and teaching suggestions. Coverage of sections is very broad synthesis, picking out some key points and skipping a lot. Psalms 74-150 are given five and a half pages, Proverbs 10-31 and Ecclesiastes dealt with similarly, etc. Readers can be deeply agitated at how much is by passed. The work is set up in 2 columns with very readable type.

Scroggie, Graham. **Know Your Bible.** **2 volumes.** **Old Tappan, NJ:** **Revell.**

The evangelical volumes are divided between the Old Testament and New Testament and include introductions and outlines for each book of the canon. The comments are pithy in the Scroggie tradition.

Smith, F. LeGard. **The Narrated Bible in Chrological Order** **(NIV).** **Eugene, OR: Harvest House, 1984.**

An evangelical professor at Pepperdine University in Los Angeles sought to arrange the Bible in sequence. He uses black print for Bible verses, red for frequent explanatory synopses, very frequent headings that pin-point concisely the subject of a paragraph, etc. Smith is also known for Out on a Broken Limb

(Harvest House, 1986), answering Shirley MacLaine's New Age book <u>Out on a Limb</u>, and <u>Crystal Lies</u> (Vine Books, 1989), another response to New Age ideas.

Unger, Merrill F.   The New Unger's Bible Handbook.   Revised by Gary N. Larson. Chicago: Moody, 1984.   720 pp.

A former Professor of Old Testament at Dallas Seminary, evangelical writer of many scholarly books, did this in his late years. He has sections on each Bible book, archaeology, Major Prophets, Minor Prophets, between the testaments, the four gospels, epistles of Paul, how the Bible came to us, Bible statistics, outline of church history, creation stories, Ur of Abram's day, Egypt, Assyria, the Chaldean empire, demonism, miracles, Bethlehem, Dead Sea scrolls, Corinth, Ephesus, Rome, etc. The work includes more than 20 charts and 30 maps and has color sections. Unger has good material at some points in surveying passages, dealing with certain problems, etc., and handles the long-range prophecies in a premillennial way. Often he is very cursory.

Walvoord, John F. and Roy Zuck (eds.).   Bible Knowledge Commentary.   2 volumes. Wheaton: Victor Books, 1983-1985.

A work entirely by Dallas Seminary faculty aiming at a consistent theology, conservative and premillennial. Contributors write on every verse or group of verses, use Hebrew and Greek expertise, deal with problem passages, and provide historical settings. The work will no doubt vary in quality from book to book as some of the contributors are from departments of biblical expertise and some not. Most books are done well in a concise yet well-informed manner. Notable exceptions are the treatments of Hebrews and John's Epistles, which have strange, different twists on verses.

Wesley, John.   John Wesley's Commentary on the Bible.   Grand Rapids: Francis Asbury Press of Zondervan Publishing House, 1990.   612 pp.

Wesley (1703-1791) originally published <u>Explanatory Notes on the New Testament</u> (1755) and had 3 volumes on the Old Testament (1765-66), 3,682 pp., all told. Here now is a one-volume condensation by G. R. Schoenhals, who for ten years had been editorial director of the Free Methodist Publishing House. Wesley drew a lot of help from works of his day such as Matthew Henry, Matthew Poole, and John Bengel (New Testament). Wesley adds much from his pastoral concern. He felt that Henry's work (6 large volumes) was too long, heavy and expensive for the common person (p. 8). The editor, seeing that Wesley's own work would today cost more than $100, did the abridgement! He left out the Bible text, some of the technical material, and other things to trim the work to about one-sixth.

II. ANALYTICAL

Commentaries here are of a more detailed, specific nature in discussing the text of Scripture.

The Anchor Bible, ed. by W. F. Albright and D. N. Freedman. NY: Doubleday, 1964—

Several volumes are out in this basically liberal work. The format includes an introduction, original translation, notes and commentary. Speiser's work on Genesis (1964) is an example. Though rejecting the unity of Genesis, he has a lucid translation and notes which abound in rich grammatical, philological and historical value. However, the work sometimes lacks spiritual illumination. The series was conceived with a plan to include Catholic, Jewish, and Protestant authors. There is a wealth of information and fine documentation of rich sources. Some of the work is outstanding, e.g. Jacob Myers (I, II Chronicles and Ezra-Nehemiah), Raymond Brown (John), etc.

Barnes, Albert.   **Barnes' Commentary on the Bible.**   **Grand Rapids:**   **Baker, 1975rp.**

This includes 16 volumes on the Old Testament, 11 on the New Testament. The New Testament part of this old work was first published in 1832-1851. Various authors contributed. It is evangelical and amillennial. Also see the Kregel reprint (1966) in 1 volume of 1,776 pages on the New Testament. Often the explanations of verses are very worthwhile.

Bewer, Julius A. (Ed.).   **Annotated Bible Series.**   **NY:**   **Harper, 1949—**

This is a critical approach by liberal men who use the King James Version throughout.

Bible Student's Commentary.   **Grand Rapids:**   **Baker, 1981—**

This is an effort of Baker to offer a translation of the Korte Verklaring, a well-respected conservative commentary among the Dutch in various parts of the globe as early as the 1930's with an updating in some instances in the 50's and 60's. The set is prepared for lay readers without knowledge of Hebrew and Greek, and little grasp of critical issues. Baker has edited the NIV text into the commentary. Even scholars have a healthy respect for the usually solid explanation and exegetical insights reflected here. Some of the contributors are G. Charles Aalders (Genesis, 2 volumes) and A. Noordtzij (Leviticus; Numbers).

Black, M. and H. H. Rowley (eds.).   **Peake's Commentary on the Bible.**   **New York: Thomas Nelson, 1962.**

The new Peake's has some contributions by good scholars (usually liberal) that are especially helpful at points, e. g. Krister Stendahl (Matthew), C. F. D. Moule (Colossians) and C. E. B. Cranfield (I Peter), as examples. One has to remember the theological perspective that shows up in certain critical presuppositions, as in Matthew, but finds much good comment informed by careful study and wide reading. The old Peake's was edited by Arthur S. Peake (NY: Thomas Nelson and Sons Ltd., 1919, new addition 1937).

The Broadman Bible Commentary. Edited by Clifton J. Allen et al. 12 volumes. Nashville: Broadman Press, 1969.

Evangelical work from a Southern Baptist press, for ministers and lay people, using the RSV. It holds the high reliability of Scripture but sometimes buys into "priestly" material theory etc. in the pentateuch (I, 109, 120 etc.). It says "there is no way that the days of Genesis 1 can be held to 24 hours" (I, 121). But it upholds the trustworthiness of the material as tradition that is true, as Genesis 2:4bff. The work favors an amillennial view (volume 12, p. 350).

Bullinger, E. W. The Companion Bible. 6 volumes. London: Lamp. One-volume edition is now available in the United States, 1964.

By a church of England clergyman who produced the famous Critical Lexicon and Concordance to the Greek New Testament. When Bullinger died in 1913, the Companion Bible was completed only up to the middle of John. His followers finished the work with comments from his prolific writings elsewhere. The name comes from the fact that a wide margin is left to be a companion to the text, and the work is intended to be the Bible reader's companion. Bullinger was an ultra-dispensationalist, but his system does not usually shine through noticeably in the work. The C. B. is not especially helpful today because so many other works are better.

Calvin, John. Calvin's Commentaries. 22 volumes. Grand Rapids: Zondervan, 1979rp.

Calvin was not only a great theologian but also a great expositor, and his insight into Scripture contributed to his grasp of doctrinal truth. His commentaries are deep in spiritual understanding, usually helpful on problem passages, and refreshing in a devotional sense to the really interested reader. He usually offers good help on a passage. The present work skips Judges, Ruth, Samuel, Kings, Chronicles, Ezra, Nehemiah, Esther, Job, Ecclesiates, Song of Solomon, II and III John and Revelation. Calvin is amillennial on long-range prophecy, but in other respects usually has very contributive perception on passages and doctrinal values edifying to the believer. He also can be very wordy, but the serious and patient glean much.

The Cambridge Bible Commentary. Cambridge: University Press, 1965.

Several volumes are now out in this set which follows the New English Bible translation. The Cambridge Bible Commentary is aimed more at the general reader, with comments which are exegetical but brief. The brevity renders it less valuable to the student who wants a more thorough study which he can obtain elsewhere. There is little original contribution.

Clarke, Adam, 1760-1832. <u>A Commentary and Critical Notes</u>. **6 volumes. NY: Eaton and Mains (n.d.).**

This old, conservative Wesleyan Methodist work is good devotionally and aggressive for righteous living. Laypeople can find it still valuable today. It is Arminian in viewpoint and thus helpful, for example, in showing the reader how this approach deals with texts involving the eternal security question. The work contains much background material from many sources on all books of the Bible.

Ellicott, Charles J., 1819-1905. <u>Commentary on the Whole Bible</u>. **8 volumes. Now published in 4 volumes. Grand Rapids: Zondervan, 1959.**

Though often scanty, the work edited by a brilliant scholar is sometimes very helpful. Ellicott was an Anglican bishop. The New Testament part is more valuable. The work dates back to 1897 and is verse by verse, consisting of 2,292 pp. Ellicott was an outstanding Anglican conservative scholar of the 19th century in England. He also wrote critical commentaries on Galatians, Ephesians, Philippians, Colossians, Thessalonians and Philemon. Different scholars here contributed on different scripture books. Famous names included are George Rawlinson (Exodus), H. D. M. Spence (I Samuel), E. H. Plumptre (Isaiah, Jeremiah, Lamentations, Acts, 2 Corinthians), W. Sanday (Romans, Galatians), Alfred Plummer (2 Peter, Jude), etc. A one-volume condensation edited by John Bowdle is available (Zondervan, 1971, 1,242 pages).

<u>Everyman's Bible Commentary</u>. Chicago: Moody Paperback, 1960ff.

These are less expensive, concise evangelical expositions by such men as Hiebert on I Timothy, Pfeiffer on Hebrews, Coder on Jude, and Ryrie on Revelation. In prophecy it follows a premillennial pattern.

Gaebelein, Arno C., 1861-1945. <u>The Annotated Bible</u>. **9 volumes. NY: <u>Our Hope Magazine</u>, 1913-1921. Also published by Loizeaux.**

This dispensationally-oriented work is not verse-by-verse, but deals with the exposition on a broader scale, treating blocks of thought within the chapters. Cf. also Arno C. Gaebelein, <u>Gaebelein's Concise Commentary on the Whole Bible</u> (1 Volume, Neptune, NJ: Loizeaux, 1985), the Annotated Bible revised. The author was a popular evangelical Bible teacher of the first part of the century, much like H. A. Ironside in his diligent but broad, practical expositions of Bible books. Gaebelein was premillennial and dispensational, and editor for many years of <u>Our Hope</u> magazine.

Gaebelein, Frank E., ed. <u>The Expositor's Bible Commentary</u>. **12 volumes. Grand Rapids: Zondervan, 1979—1992.**

The top general work of scholarly evangelicalism by 72 writers from several countries who hold to divine inspiration and premillennialism (for the most part). They use the NIV. The Associate Ed. is J. D. Douglas, and consulting Eds. are Walter C. Kaiser, Jr., Bruce K. Waltke, James Boice and Merrill C. Tenney. The work represents study abreast of recent literature, issues and views in exposition. Some very skilled, established scholars are among the contributors, men on introductory matters such as Gleason Archer, Jr., G. W. Bromiley, Donald Guthrie, R. K. Harrison, Carl Henry, Harold Hoehner, Walter Kaiser, Bruce Metzger, Roger Nicole, Robert L. Saucy, Bruce Waltke, Andrew Walls, Donald Wiseman, and Edwin Yamauchi. Scholars on New Testament books are such men as M. C. Tenney (John), R. N. Longenecker (Acts), James Boice (Galatians), Homer Kent, Jr. (Philippians), Robert L. Thomas (Thessalonians), D. E. Hiebert (Titus), Leon Morris (Hebrews), Edwin Blum (I, II Peter, Jude), and Alan Johnson (Revelation).

Gill, John. Gill's Commentary. 6 volumes. Grand Rapids: Baker, 1980 from 1852-1854 edition (London: William Hull).

Gill (1697-1771), a pastor of England, wrote these which are two-column pages, ca. 900-1,000 pages per volume. Originally they were 9 volumes, folio. He also wrote Body of Divinity, 3 volumes, and several other volumes. His commentary is evangelical, wrestles with texts, is often wordy and not to the point but with worthy things for the patient who follow the ponderous detail and fish out slowly what his interpretation of a text is. He feels the thousand years in Revelation 20 cannot begin until after the conversion of the Jews and the bringing in of the fullness of the Gentiles and destruction of all antiChristian powers (volume 6, p. 1063) but in an amillennial sense of new heavens and new earth coming right after Christ's second advent (1064-65), and the literal thousand years of binding at the same time. He feels the group that gathers against the holy city at the end of the thousand years is the resurrected wicked dead from the four quarters of the earth (i.e. from all the earth, etc. (1067)).

Grant, F. W., 1834-1902. The Numerical Bible. 5 volumes. NY: Loizeaux, 1894-1903.

This premillennial-dispensational work gives good expository notes, but they are irregular. It omits several poetic books of the Old Testament. There is a stress upon the significance of numbers in Scripture. Grant also authored a book called The Numerical Structure of Scripture (Loizeaux, 1899).

Guthrie, D. et al. The Eerdman's Bible Commentary, i.e. New Bible Commentary Revised. 3rd edition. 1 volume. Grand Rapids: Eerdmans, 1970. 1,310 pp.

An evangelical updating (since the 1st edition, 1953, 1,119 pages) of the New Bible Commentary edited by F. Davidson et al. Some of the best known commentators are: O. T. Allis (Leviticus), Gleason Archer, Jr. (Micah), Joyce Baldwin (Ruth, Esther), G. R. Beasley-Murray (Ezekiel, Revelation, etc.), F. F. Bruce (Judges, Acts, Thessalonian Epistles, etc.), R. K. Harrison (Deuteronomy), Derek Kidner (Isaiah, amillennial), Meredith Kline (Genesis), I. H. Marshall (Luke), R. P. Martin (Romans, Ephesians), Leon Morris (John's Epistles), etc. In the revision, 37 commentaries on books are by different scholars, and five articles are new.

Extensive revision occurs in other respects, and the work uses the RSV rather than the KJV.

Henry, Matthew, 1662-1714. <u>Commentary on the Whole Bible.</u> **6 volumes. Revell. Now out in one-volume abbreviated form edited by Leslie F. Church, Zondervan, 1961, and other more recent one-volume editions.**

This evangelical work, devotional in character, has been in constant demand for about 280 years. Its insight into human problems is great, but it often does not deal adequately with problems in the text. The one-volume form eliminates the Biblical text and is thus less bulky. It has sold very well. The late Wilbur M. Smith, internationally noted Bible teacher, seminary professor and lover of books, tabbed this "The greatest devotional commentary ever written" (cover, 1 volume edition). Henry was born in a Welch farmhouse, studied law, and became a Presbyterian minister near London. He wrote this commentary in the last 13 years before he died at 52 in 1714. The first of six volumes was published in 1708. He completed through Acts, and the rest of the New Testament was done by 14 clergymen (p. ix, 1 volume edition). Another 1 volume edition, unabridged but in 3 columns and small but clear print, is <u>Matthew Henry's Commentary on the Whole Bible</u> (Peabody, MA: Hendrickson, 1991, 2,485 pages).

Hubbard, David A. and Glenn W. Barber, gen. eds. <u>Word Biblical Commentary.</u> **Waco, Texas: Word Books, Publisher, 1982—**

This recent sometimes liberal, sometimes evangelical work, with many volumes already out, projects 52 volumes and an imposing list of around 50 scholars, many of them internationally known. The Old Testament editor is John D. W. Watts, the New Testament editor Ralph P. Martin. Each contributor prepares his own translation of the biblical text and fits his exegesis to this, yet makes the technical, scholarly matter understandable and relevant for seminary students (in some places more advanced ones) and pastors as well as professional scholars and teachers. The introductions and commentaries on individual books are done in fairly good detail, even with well-organized excursuses on larger problems and lengthy bibliographies of books and journal literature. For the verse by verse comment, Hebrew or Greek words or phrases are printed and the explanation of their sense follows. Often, good detail is devoted to different views on the sense of a passage, e.g. F. F. Bruce on I Thessalonians 4:4, whether <u>skeuos</u> ("vessel") means a man's wife or his body. Other contributors are such names as Gordon Wenham (Genesis, 2 volumes); Peter C. Craigie (Psalms 1-50; Marvin Tate, Psalms 51-100, and Leslie Allen, 101-150); G. R. Beasley-Murray (John); James D. G. Dunn (Romans); Ralph Martin (2 Corinthians, James); Richard Longenecker (Galatians); Robert Mounce (Pastoral Epistles.); Wm. Lane (Hebrews), etc. The venture varies on different books as is true of any set of such breadth.

The International Critical Commentary (ICC). **Edinburgh: T. & T. Clark, 1885-1964.**

This usually liberal work was begun in 1885 under the editorial supervision of C. A. Briggs, S. R. Driver and Alfred Plummer. The intention was to provide for English readers a Bible commentary equal in scholarship to the critical German productions of that day. The emphasis is critical and philological. Volumes have now been produced on all Old Testament books, and among better ones available are: Kings (Montgomery); Ezekiel (Cooke); Judges (Moore) and Daniel (Montgomery). In the New Testament, the better works are: Luke (Plummer); Romans (Sanday and Headlam; recently replaced by Cranfield's 2 volumes); Galatians (Burton); First Corinthians (Robertson and Plummer); St. Peter and St. Jude (Bigg). The technical nature of the work renders it more helpful to the trained expositor, especially in detailed problems. In quality it varies. Recently Davies and Allison have two often highly helpful volumes out on Matthew 1-18 with a third yet to appear.

The Interpreter's Bible. **12 volumes, ed. George Arthur Buttrick, et al.** **NY: Abingdon, 1952-57.**

A great amount of money was poured into this series which is beautifully printed and has elaborate, often very informative introductions. The work has more than 11,000 pages. It is very liberal. Actually much good material that is presented can be equalled in other commentaries such as the Expositor's Bible Commentary with more done in a satisfying way. But the set has exercised a wide influence over ministers in the United States. Cf. also Layman, Charles M., Editor of The Interpreter's One-Volume Commentary on the Bible (1-volume, Nashville: Abingdon Press, 1971. 1,386 pp.). This too is a liberal work of brevity by seventy scholars who are Protestant, Roman Catholic, and Jewish, compared with the multi-volume Interpreter's Bible that takes up passages more at length. One also finds articles on historical, literary, linguistic, geopgraphical, archeological and theological areas as related to biblical interpretation, from liberal perspectives.

Jamieson, Robert, A. R. Fausset, and David Brown. **A Commentary on the Old and New Testaments.** **6 volumes.** **Grand Rapids: Eerdmans, 1961.** **1,591 pp.**

This is a helpful old set of 1863 for laypeople and pastors to have because it usually comments at least to some degree on problems. Though terse, it provides something good on almost any passage, phrase by phrase and is to some degree critical in nature. It is evangelical. There is also a 1-volume edition, briefer at some points (Grand Rapids: Zondervan, 1961). Especially in its multi-volume form this is one of the old evangelical works that offers fairly solid though brief help on many verses. Spurgeon said, "It contains so great a variety of information that if a man had no other exposition he would find himself at no great loss if he possessed this and used it diligently" (Commenting and Commentaries, p. 3). It is primarily of help to pastors and lay people looking for quick, though usually somewhat knowledgeable treatments on verses.

Lange, John Peter, 1802-1884. <u>Commentary on the Holy Scriptures</u>. **12 volumes. Grand Rapids: Zondervan, 1871-1874.**

The treatments of books within this evangelical set vary in importance. Generally, one finds a wealth of detailed commentary, background, and some critical and exegetical notes. Often, however, there is much excess verbiage that doesn't help particularly. On the other hand, it usually has something to assist the expositor on problems and is a good general set for pastors and serious lay people, though it is old.

Maclaren, Alexander, 1826-1910. <u>Expositions of Holy Scripture</u>. **25 volumes but now in 11 volumes without abridgement. Grand Rapids: Eerdmans, 1959.**

This evangelical work is both homiletical and expository and is often very good homiletically but weaker otherwise. Helpful in discussing Bible characters, it is weak in prophecy at times because of allegorization. It is not really as valuable today as some other sets for the serious Bible student. The expositions are in the form of sermons.

Morgan, G. Campbell, 1863-1948. <u>The Analyzed Bible</u>. **10 volumes. NY: Revell, 1907-1911.**

Morgan was an evangelical master at surveying a book and giving its message within a brief compass. He introduces each book with a chart giving an analysis and synthesis. Revell put it out in a one-volume form in 1959 (see Synthetical), and it is adequate to have the one-volume work, since Morgan is broad in his treatment anyway.

<u>The New Clarendon Bible</u>. **Oxford: Oxford University Press, 1963—**

This commentary, also not finished, uses the NEB as its translation like the CBC, but is aimed at a higher intellectual level. Thus it is more technical than the CBC.

Nicoll, W. Robertson (Ed.). <u>The Expositors Bible</u>. **26 volumes. NY: A. C. Armstrong, 1903.**

Though this work is generally helpful on historical background, it is often not of great assistance on the original text or problem passages. It skips over these many times. It is generally conservative, but not always. The value is greater on some books because the authors have done an excellent work: Kellogg on Leviticus; Blaikie on Joshua and I, II Samuel; Plummer on the pastorals, James and Jude. Some sections are by radical liberals, for example George A. Smith on Isaiah and the Minor Prophets. By and large, the student will do better to use a detailed set like The Expositor's Bible Commentary plus individual best works on the different Bible books or sections of Scripture.

Parker, Joseph, 1830-1902. <u>The Peoples Bible</u>. **28 volumes. NY: Funk and Wagnalls, 1888.**

This work, now called <u>Preaching Through the Bible</u> (Baker Book House), is rich in its applications and exhortations, though often not particularly helpful for the reader who is looking for exposition that stays right with the text. Treatment of the texts is sermonic.

Pfeiffer, Charles and Everett Harrison (Eds.). <u>The Wycliffe Bible Commentary</u>. 1 volume. Chicago: Moody, 1990rp of 1962 edition. 1,525 pp.

Conservative and premillennial scholars here have been experts in their fields. The work contains brief introductions and attempts to give a verse-by-verse exposition, though it does skip over some verses. The treatments vary with the authors, but as a whole it is a fine one-volume commentary for pastors and students to use or give to a layman. Outstanding sections include, for example: Whitcomb on Ezra-Nehemiah-Esther; Culver on Daniel; Ladd on Acts; Harrison on Galatians; Johnson on I Corinthians; and Ryrie on the Johannine Epistles.

<u>The Pulpit Commentary</u>. **Edited by H. D. M. Spence and Joseph S. Exell.** 23 volumes. Grand Rapids: Eerdmans reprinted various dates, 1950's -1970's.

Many authors contributed to this work that had the aim of giving preachers material on introduction, verse by verse exposition, a section on homiletics, and a section of collected homilies (outlines, etc.) by various preachers, which can stimulate thought. It moves through one small section of Bible verses after another.

<u>The Seventh-day Adventist Bible Commentary</u>. **Edited by Francis D. Nichol et al.** 7 volumes. Washington, D. C.: Review and Herald Publishing Association, 1953-76.

These are large volumes by 34 writers (Volume I, on Genesis-Deuteronomy is 1,120 pages, 2 columns). General essays appear on such topics as the languages, manuscripts and canon of the Old Testament, science and a literal creation, evidences of a global flood, archeology, daily life in the Patriarchal Age, chronology, etc. The commentaries are extensive. Genesis is pp. 201-487, Exodus 491-689, etc. Ellen G. White's comments are sprinkled in sections throughout as supplements.

<u>The Twentieth Century Bible Commentary</u>. **Edited by G. Henton Davies et al.** Revised edition. 1 volume. NY: Harper and Brothers, 1932, 1955. 571 pp.

Designed for ministers, Sunday school leaders, Bible teachers and lay people, this sometimes liberal, sometimes evangelical work (cf. contributors, pp. vii-viii) has general articles and extremely brief commentaries such as Genesis (24 pp. 2 columns). Parts of the pentateuch are assigned to the "priestly" or some other alleged strand of writing centuries later.

<u>The Wesleyan Bible Commentary</u>. **Edited by Charles W. Carter, et al.** 6 volumes. Grand Rapids: Eerdmans, 1967.

Devotes 3 volumes to Old Testament and 3 to New Testament, upholding views within the Wesleyan theological frame of reference, as of John Wesley and Adam

Clarke. It is evangelical, expositional, Arminian, practical, homiletical and devotional. More than 20 scholars of the United States wrote it, coming from the Church of God, Church of the Nazarene, Evangelical United Brethren, Free Methodist, Friends, Methodist, Missionary Church Association, Pilgrim Holiness and Wesleyan Methodist. It is written for the average minister, Sunday School leader and teacher, Bible teacher, college professor, student and Christians in general. The commentary is 2 columns in format. It deals with some problems but not others, as the supposed high totals in Numbers 2. It has much good summary and upholds a high view of Scripture's reliability. Sometimes one writer was asked to do too much, as on Joshua-Job.

COMMENTARIES ON THE OLD TESTAMENT

I. SYNTHETICAL

Benware, Paul N. <u>Survey of the Old Testament</u>   (Everyman's Bible Commentary).
Chicago: Moody, 1988.   267 pp.

> A Professor of Bible and Theology at Moody Bible Institute and more recently Trinity Evanglical Divinity School gives brief, sweeping surveys. For a quick lay person's glimpse it is helpful, and well-done, but it does not deal with as much or provide nearly the help of the works by Baxter, Scroggie, Unger or Wood.

The Daily Study Bible (OT).   Philadelphia: Westminster Press, 1981ff.

> Various scholars join efforts to cover the Old Testament for the general public in a way similar to William Barclay's 17-volume Daily Study Bible on the New Testament. Portions of the Old Testament are divided off for daily readings and comments. The work is liberal, and also amillennial on prophecy. Evangelicals who for briefer expositional treatments use the Bible Study Commentary (Zondervan) or Everyman's Bible Commentary (Moody) will not find a lot here that adds to the picture.

Jensen, Irving L. <u>Jensen's Survey of the Old Testament</u>.   Chicago: Moody, 1991.

> A broad evangelical look at key things about each Old Testament book — background, outline, theme and synthesis with reading lists and charts. Cf. also Jensen's New Testament survey.

Merrill, Eugene A. <u>Historical Survey of the Old Testament</u>.   Nutley, NJ: The Craig Press, 1966.

> A good brief evangelical survey to give a person quick perspective, especially helpful for introductory, beginning study. Merrill stops on some problem areas to state his view and reasons. For example, he believes that Melchizedek in Genesis 14 is the preincarnate Christ.

Schultz, Samuel. The Old Testament Speaks. **NY: Harper and Row, 1960.**

This is an excellent general survey of Old Testament backgrounds and arguments of books. The evangelical author was then abreast of illuminating archaeological discoveries and shows that he has read broadly to devote to this work an exacting type of scholarship. Though brief, he is helpful on some problem passages like Joshua 10, the account of the long day, and Judges 11, the problem of whether or not Jephthah actually offered his daughter as a sacrifice. It is a good general work to possess.

Scroggie, W. Graham, 1877-1958. The Unfolding Drama of Redemption. **3 volumes. London: Pickering and Inglis Ltd., 1957.**

This evangelical master of synthesis has produced a well-organized survey of Bible books which is valuable to the student who is seeking to work his way through for his own knowledge of the Bible or for a series of messages or lessons covering the sweep of the Old Testament. His survey stops at the end of Acts.

Unger, Merrill C. Unger's Commentary on the Old Testament. **2 volumes. Chicago: Moody Press, 1981.**

The former head of the Department of Old Testament and Semitics at Dallas Seminary wrote this work of 2,090 pp. shortly before his death. Volume one covers Genesis—Song of Solomon, volume two the rest of the Old Testament. A somewhat detailed introduction is given for each book, looking at the title, author, date, canonicity, problems modern critics discuss, the basic theme, and a detailed outline. In the commentary, Unger writes section by section, commenting on what he regards as the key expositional issues, using Hebrew words at times, historical background, and context. We see the view of a well-known conservative and premillennial dispensational scholar on many a text, sometimes very helpful and other times cursory and general by the nature of the broad range of the study.

Wood, Leon J. Survey of Israel's History. **Grand Rapids: Zondervan, 1970. Revised 1986 by David O'Brien.**

This is one of the most rewarding surveys available from the standpoint of giving a survey and yet pausing on key problem areas to state a well-considered view and specific supports marshalled briefly. It is firmly evangelical.

II. ANALYTICAL

Cohen, A.   Soncino Books of the Bible.   14 volumes.   Bournemouth, Harts, England: Soncino, 1945-61.

These volumes represent the best in popular, orthodox Jewish scholarship, though the editors come from all three schools of Judaism. The Hebrew text is printed and a commentary is given, though actual Hebrew exegesis is sparse. The order of pages naturally accords with the Hebrew text, running from right to left. A good brief introduction is presented for each book, and these are generally conservative in outlook (see Slotki on Isaiah for a notable exception). Tradition plays a large role, hence the use of views by Rashi, Kimchi and other former Jewish scholars. Since it is Judaism's best, concise work, it is valuable to have if the student can afford it. Much of the historical background information is somewhat helpful. One of the better works is Ezekiel, written by Fisch.

Keil, C. F. and Franz Delitzsch.   Commentary on the Old Testament.   25 volumes. Grand Rapids: Eerdmans, 1950.

This is the best older, overall treatment of a critical nature on the Old Testament Hebrew text verse by verse and is a good standard work to buy. The student can buy parts or the whole of this series. Sometimes it is evangelical, at other times liberal ideas enter.

Old Testament Library.   Philadelphia: Westminster Press, 1985ff.

A scholarly series steeped in critical issues, views and reasoning that does not please firm evangelicals with its aspects of liberalism. It can be helpful on verses but too often is not. Some volumes are more profitable in explaining passages along lines conservatives can value, as Joseph Blenkinsopp frequently on Ezra-Nehemiah. But many of the entries will have their greatest usefulness among quite liberal readers. Examples are G. von Rad on Genesis and Deuteronomy, and Robert P. Carroll on Jeremiah.

COMMENTARIES ON
THE PENTATEUCH

Hamilton, Victor P. <u>Handbook on the Pentateuch</u>. **Grand Rapids: Baker, 1982. 496 pp.**

Hamilton is Professor of Religion at Asbury College with an M. A. and Ph. D. from Brandeis University. This is a one-volume exposition that can serve as a text for an English Bible college survey course. He has done his survey with a good grasp of what is vital for comment, an awareness of different main views on certain problems, and a very readable style. He is evangelical in his conclusions, as on the unity of Genesis 1-2, and follows many evangelicals on the Messianic thrust of Genesis 3:15. His lists for further reading at the ends of chapters provide many sources from a wide knowledge of commentaries and journals but focus on only the last ten years before his book, include mostly liberal works, and at times overlook key evangelical sources.

JPS Torah Commentary. New York: Jewish Publication Society, 1989—1993.

These recent commentaries are surveys as Nahum Sarna's on Genesis and Exodus and Baruch Levine's on Leviticus or massive as Jacob Milgrom's on Numbers (520 pp.). Thorough study in a wide range of sources is poured into the effort, especially in Milgrom's work, and one sees how scholarly Jews explain passages. There is more depth of detail than in the Soncino Series and use of recent writings. Jeffrey Tigay's work on Deuteronomy, set for 1993, was not yet available for this review. The commentaries are liberal but on many points the explanations contribute, viewing what is said in a helpful light. One learns much about Jewish background and customs.

Livingston, G. H. <u>The Pentateuch in Its Cultural Environment</u>. **Grand Rapids: Baker, 1987. 2nd edition. 322 pp.**

A readable, comprehensive, well-respected evangelical work by a professor of Old Testament at Asbury Theological Seminary since 1953. Livingston discusses peoples of the ancient near east (Sumerians, Assyrians, Amorites, Egyptians, Hyksos, Hittites, Philistines, Canaanites and others). He also writes of relevant ancient scripts, literature (compared with the Pentateuch), concepts, practices, schools of thought on Pentateuchal studies, Mosaic authorship, Dead Sea scroll relevance, the JEDP theory, literary criticism, form criticism, canonical criticism, etc. The final chapter (10) deals with canonization of the Pentateuch and factors related to this. Indices of subjects and scripture verses help readers locate specific discussions.

Mackintosh, C. H. <u>Genesis to Deuteronomy, Notes on the Pentateuch.</u> **Neptune, NJ: Loizeaux, 1989. 912 pp.**

This is a one-volume edition of an old evangelical devotional work. It has some value at times, especially for lay readrs yet is not to the point as much with pertinent material as W. H. Griffith-Thomas on the pentateuch (also old) and John Sailhamer's recent introductory survey.

Sailhamer, John H. <u>The Pentateuch as Narrative. A Biblical-Theological Commentary.</u> **Grand Rapids: Zondervan, 1992. 522 pp.**

An associate professor of Old Testament, Trinity Evangelical Divinity School, offers an introduction to the Pentateuch (1-79) looking at background, authorship, sources, literary form, structure, purpose, theology, basic principles etc. Later he provides a fairly detailed, well-outlined survey of each book section by section, for example Genesis (81-240), and Exodus (241-322). He is concerned with style and structure so as to relate details to their context. He not only connects parts and surveys what is said but deals with leading problems such as Genesis 1:1-2, 6:2, 4 (sons of God), etc. He handles the Hebrew skillfully, is usually lucid and has a high evangelical view of the integrity and unity of accounts. He is steeped in awareness of literature on issues as reflected in footnotes, some of which are quite substantial. If one does not agree with Sailhamer on everything, this still is, overall, one of the most adept, informative books on the Pentateuch and will prove very helpful for teachers, pastors and students. Sailhamer in an appendix lists together all the commands of the law in various categories and gives examples where Jesus and New Testament writers adduce the principles (482-516). He is insightful on many verses, for example the validity of a Messianic reference in Deuteronomy 18:18 (456). For further detail on Genesis, one can go to Sailhamer's commentary in <u>The Expositor's Bible Commentary</u>.

Wolf, Herbert. <u>An Introduction to the Old Testament Pentateuch.</u> **Chicago: Moody Press, 1991. 276 pp.**

Wolf is associate professor of Old Testament, Wheaton Graduate School. He provides an evangelical discussion on introductory aspects such as the fivefold division of the Pentateuch, unity, impact on other Old Testament and New Testament books, theology (God, man, salvation, the Messiah, faith, atonement, covenants), the Samaritan Pentateuch, literary characteristics, and Moses' significance. He argues for Moses as the main author and for the unity of the Pentateuch. Then he deals with each of the five books. In Genesis, he discusses key problems in 1:1—2:3, sons of God in 6:2, 4, the extent of the flood and other issues. Wolf sometimes gives various views, as on the length of "day" in Genesis 1, but it is not easy to find where he states a definite preference (84-88). The same is true in lengthy comments on sons of God (97-100). He would often be more helpful if, when he introduces a question, he finally concludes with some clear preference. An example where he does do this is his decision that the exodus occurred early (148). There are fine discussions of several problems, such as the much-attacked numbers for Israel as in Numbers 2 (148-51). Overall the book is well worth the reading, though surveys of Pentateuchal books are briefer than Sailhamer's. A good bibliography appears (223-61). Indices of subjects, authors and scriptures also offer help.

INDIVIDUAL COMMENTARIES ON OLD TESTAMENT BOOKS

I. GENESIS

In any case where commentaries on a book of the Pentateuch are sparse, the notes by W. H. Griffith-Thomas, Through the Pentateuch Chapter By Chapter (Eerdmans) will be a warm devotional help. Cf. also Barnhouse, Boice, Calvin, etc. One may use the I.C.C. work here by Skinner for a liberal treatment. Speiser's volume in the Anchor Bible series is also liberal but at times helpful in exegesis and background. Better commentaries old and recent from the conservative and other standpoints are:

Aalders, G. Charles. Genesis (Bible Students Commentary). 2 volumes. Grand Rapids: Zondervan, 1981. 311 + 298 pp.

Zondervan has been issuing English translations of the top evangelical commentary in Dutch dating from the 1930's and 40's, a 62-volume set called Korte Verklaring der Heilige Schrift. It is designed for lay readers but is so well done in detail that it is of substantial benefit to teachers up to the seminary level too. It is Reformed, and in the English effort uses the NIV. Aalders is clear, deals with problems usually well, explains most verses quite adequately, and defends at length Mosaic authorship and the infallible truth in the Pentateuch (pp. 1-41, cf. p. 40). He sees 1:1 as an absolute statement of original creation, sees no gap in 1:2, is non-committal about the length of the days except to say these are not twenty-four-hour days. "Sons of God" in 6:2, 4 are humans, and Aalders devotes a detailed look at views. He views the flood as universal. The work is well worth the time.

Baldwin, Joyce G. The Message of Genesis 12-50 (The Bible Speaks Today). Downers Grove, IL: IVP, 1986. 224 pp.

This is not a commentary per se but a well-organized, popularly readable exposition in a devotional vein, with refreshingly conceived lessons applied to life today. Using the RSV, Baldwin deals with faith, patience, etc., stimulating readers in rich paths. She provides helps on geography, customs, and other areas, and shows, for example, how Abraham's responses are like Christians' today. The book shows a considerable use of scholarly literature in the footnotes.

Barnhouse, Donald G. <u>Genesis, A Devotional Commentary</u>. **2 volumes in 1. Grand Rapids: Zondervan, 1973. 208 + 250 pp.**

Provocative principles drawn by a famous Bible teacher and radio voice a few decades back. As to devotional lessons in Genesis, this book rates just behind W. H. Griffith-Thomas. It is suggestive of points for preachers, and rewarding for laypeople. Boice is a tie with it or third, though more recent.

Boice, James M. <u>Genesis, An Expositional Commentary</u>. **3 volumes. Grand Rapids: Zondervan, 1982-87.**

Broad exposition, not verse by verse. The long-time pastor of 10th St. Presbyterian, Philadelphia chooses doctrinal and practical emphases, which can help a Christian grow by seeing how to apply truths. Boice can be very helpful or can read in meanings that some will doubt are in Genesis, such as seeing the pact between Abraham and Abimelech as teaching on church and state matters (pp. 206-11).

Brueggemann, Walter. <u>Genesis</u> **(Interpretation). Atlanta: John Knox Press, 1982. 384 pp.**

This is by the Professor of Old Testament, Columbia Theological Seminary, Decatur, GA. Using the RSV, he does an exposition with the belief that Genesis arose from diverse narratives from many times and places (p. 2). He leans a lot on commentaries in critical areas. He subjectively assigns some material to J and P and follows von Rad in placing Joseph material in the tenth century (pp. 6-7) and some portions in exilic days. While there is a lot of insight at times, the work is often an exercise in speculation which gets in the way of seeing what the text itself says without Brueggemann's encrusted theory. He assumes, for instance, that 1:1—2:4 uses older creation stories and cosmologies from Egypt and Mesopotamia composed in the sixth century to address exiles (p. 24). Claims of Genesis 1-2 are not to be taken as literal to say what happened but only to witness to us of God's lordly intent (p. 26). Historic or literal reality disappears beneath disclaimers that leave one mystified as to why the text says what it says about a fall of humans or gives an account of how evil came into the world or death entered (41-42). He feels that Paul in Romans 5 draws conclusions not founded in the Genesis text (42). The book is an exercise in how a liberal mind construes things quite differently.

Bush, George. <u>Notes, Critical and Practical on the Book of Genesis</u>. **2 volumes. NY: Newman and Ivison, 1852; rp Minneapolis: Klock & Klock, 1976.**

Spurgeon used this in his day though he said that Bush plagiarized. The exposition, however, is thorough and cautious, based on the Hebrew text, with the English text rendered at the top of the page. Bush is not one to dodge problem passages and usually is very helpful. He seeks to discover the motives and the movement behind events, and gives good applications. He was Professor of Hebrew and Oriental Literature at New York City University.

Calvin, John. <u>Genesis</u> **(Geneva series). 2 volumes in 1. Carlisle, PA: Banner of Truth Trust, 1975rp. 523 pp.**

This was first issued in Latin in 1554 and in English in 1578. It has no outline but is verse by verse. Much space is used printing English and Latin translations side by side before the comments. Calvin usually has something quite helpful, so this is profitable reading. He sees 1:1 as summing up original creation, <u>ex nihilo</u>; 1:2 is the initial, shapeless and empty or incomplete state that is formed and filled in 1:3ff. Days are twenty-four hours. The Trinity is reflected upon in 1:26; 4:1 does not state it so, but Calvin thinks Cain and Abel were twins; sons of God in Chapter 6 were men of the godly line; the flood was universal; 49:10 refers to the Messiah, etc.

Candlish, Robert S. <u>Exposition of Genesis</u>. **Wilmington, DE: Sovereign Grace, 1972. Reprint, two volumes in one.**

This was rated by Spurgeon, <u>Commenting and Commentaries</u> (past century) as then "the work on Genesis". There are 72 chapters in lecture form. Candlish believes in a young earth but alas, the universal fatherhood of God. His work is often helpful in spite of some peculiarities.

Cassuto, Umberto. <u>From Adam to Noah</u> **(I) and** <u>From Noah to Abraham</u> **(II). 2 volumes. Jerusalem: Magnes Press, 1961.**

This Jewish scholar covers thirteen chapters only, fluctuating between good and weak in his helpfulness explaining salient points. He is often good, but not consistently enough to rank with the top commentaries.

Cummings, Vera. <u>Noah's Ark: Fact or Fable?</u> **San Diego: Creation Science Research Society, 1971.**

This book traces various trips to the Mt. Ararat region in search of an ark; gives intriguing accounts of some who have allegedly either seen an ark or traces of it in that area; and stirs the reader with the question of whether or not Noah's ark might yet be discovered. A more recent work on this same subject is John W. Montgomery's <u>The Quest For Noah's Ark</u>. It examines the attempts in history to find the ark, tells of his own experiences in the quest, and discusses biblical matters relating to the ark.

Custance, Arthur. <u>Without Form and Void</u>. **Brockville, Canada: Privately published, 1970.**

The author published this book after nearly thirty years of special study. He presents evidence favoring the gap view in Genesis 1:2 correlated from many sources. In recent times this is the most detailed effort arguing for a gap. Fields' work below answers it in detail from a no-gap view.

Davis, John J.   Paradise to Prison.   Grand Rapids: Baker, 1976.

This is an excellent, well-documented and readable survey on some of the key passages and problems in Genesis. It does not discuss verse by verse but does hit crucial areas such as views on the time of creation, whether there was a gap in Genesis 1:1, 2, what the days of Genesis 1 mean, key problems of Genesis 3, whether the flood was local or universal, who were the "sons of God" in Genesis 6, and so on throughout. Davis is helpful in that he usually comments on main issues and reflects careful thinking as well as reading awareness of scholarship on the areas. He is a staunch evangelical Old Testament scholar, teaching at Grace Theological Seminary, Winona Lake, Indiana. This work, the one by Allen Ross (Creation and Blessing), and a more recent work on the narrative of Genesis by John Sailhamer are the best three broad scholarly surveys of Genesis.

Delitzsch, Franz, 1813-1890.   A New Commentary on Genesis.   2 volumes. Edinburgh: T. & T. Clark, 1899.

The author holds to the documentary hypothesis but does not deny the uniqueness of Genesis or minimize the significance and authority of its message. He is careful in the Hebrew and deals with the problems, providing much to aid the expositor.

Epp, Theodore.   Commentary on Genesis.   4 volumes.   Lincoln, NE: Back to the Bible Broadcast, 1970-72.

These are 4 paperback volumes of 190, 219, 357 and 143 pp. The volumes cover Genesis 1-3, 4-11, 12-36, and 37-50. They are conservative and devotional exposition aimed at the general reader. Epp has some rich spiritual lessons on faith in the lives of the patriarchs and in Joseph's experience. He does not subscribe to a gap theory in 1:2, posits a recent creation, explains the "sons of God" in 6:2 as the godly human line, has a universal flood, and a premillennial understanding of God's covenant intentions. The work is primarily of help to laymen needing a simple explanation easy to follow.

Epp, Theodore.   Joseph: God Planned It For Good.   Lincoln, NE: Back to the Bible Broadcast, 1971.

The author, who wrote several helpful books, should be included here because this work is a rich survey of leading moments in the life of Joseph and in Genesis 37-50. Those studying this portion of Genesis will find it a contribution to their understanding of the way God faithfully works in the lives of His own. Cf. also, on Joseph, works by John Hercus, George Lawson, Martin Luther (2 volumes) and F. B. Meyer, for example.

Fields, Weston W.   Unformed and Unfilled.   Nutley, NJ: Presbyterian and Reformed, 1976.

A detailed evaluation and critique of Arthur C. Custance's Without Form and Void, based on Fields' Th. D. dissertation in Old Testament at Grace Theological Seminary, Winona Lake, Indiana. He argues at length against a gap in relation to

Genesis 1:2 and favors a recent creation of the earth, with twenty-four-hour days and with 1:1-5 speaking of the creative work during the first day. He holds to a universal flood geology. He has brought into a systematic presentation a wealth of details from rather wide research that enter into a competent discussion of the issues.

Filby, F. A.   The Flood Reconsidered.   Grand Rapids: Zondervan, 1970.

He lucidly argues that the Flood was local but destroyed all mankind, those not aboard the Ark.

Garrett, Duane.   Rethinking Genesis.   Grand Rapids: Baker, 1991.   273 pp.

This is a conservative array of evidence vs. the documentary hypothesis and critical theories seeing Genesis as latedated and disunified. The author concludes the book was written during the Exodus period (cf. p. 237).

Gibson, John C. L.   Genesis (Daily Bible Study Series).   2 volumes.   Philadelphia: Westminster, 1982.

He assumes sources J, E, P and composition centuries after the patriarchal and wilderness periods by re-tellers of folk tales (p. 1). The Genesis stories are not a source for factual material on such things as the origin of the universe (p. 11). Yet he believes that real historical events lie behind the passed on stories, but seems to exclude chapters 1-11 from what is "based on things that actually happened" (p. 13). One has to skip through Gibson's material to pick up where he goes on with the text and is to the mark after much that is not to the point. He assumes that ancient Hebrews held to a flat earth (p. 29).

Hamilton, Victor P.   The Book of Genesis, Chapters 1-17 (NICOT).   Grand Rapids: Eerdmans, 1990.   522 pp.

This first of 2 volumes has a very informative introduction of around a hundred pages surveying the history of critical theories and not arriving at a firm view of authorship. He gives twenty-five pages of bibliography. On some problems he is detailed, as in examining interpretive issues such as days in Genesis 1. He is thorough on the meaning of verses in view of biblical usage of words, context, and Near Eastern literature in which he is steeped. Overall it is a standout commentary along conservative lines, even covering many subjects relevant to Genesis. Some of what he writes in the introduction will be readily grasped only by scholars; others will be guessing and re-reading to figure things out, if they are patient. The author is not able to decide on which view about "sons of God" (6:2, 4). One will have to search to decide where he explains if the Flood was local or universal. The explanation at times is very good, at other times falls short of really illumining a passage, as on the ritual ceremony in Genesis 15. But so much data is given that the reader is bound to receive much to think about.

Harbach, Robert C. **Studies in the Book of Genesis.** Grandville, MI: Grandville Reformed Church Publication Committee, 1986. 938 pp.

A long-time Reformed pastor gives a conservative, thorough explanation of verses, interacting knowledgeably with scientific disciplines but in cases of tensions favoring Scripture (he has a high view of it). He opts for original creation in 1:1-2, no gap in 1:2, twenty-four-hour days, a creation date of Adam around 6,000 B. C., and is opposed to evolutionary theory. He defends Mosaic authorship. Very often he is helpful on normal questions readers have passage by passage, and is clear. He is non-dispensational (p. 45).

Hercus, John. **Pages from God's Casebook.** Downers Grove, IL: IVP, 1962.

Some arresting comment on Joseph that is pertinent to 20th century life.

Jacob, Benno. **The First Book of the Bible, Genesis.** New York: KTAV Publishing-House, 1974.

Translated but reduced in length by about 2/3 from the 1932 German edition, Das Erste Buch der Tora, Genesis ubersetzt und eklaert (Berlin: Schocken verlag). The English product is 357 pp. Jacob was a Jewish scholar, often helpful on seeing things from the standpoint of what the text itself means. In the abbreviated English work, much valuable philological explanation was cut out, as well as details that argued against a documentary approach to Genesis.

Keil, C. F. and Franz Delitzsch. **The Pentateuch.** Cf. Commentaries on the Old Testament, Analytical.

Kidner, Derek. Genesis. Wheaton: Tyndale House, 1968.

It is evident that much study lies behind this concisely stated commentary in the Tyndale series. Kidner has packed in a lot of understanding of word meanings, movements of thought in different parts of Genesis, customs, God's purposes, and relationship to other parts of Scripture. It is a solid but brief work.

Kikawada, Isaac M. and Arthur Quinn. **Before Abraham Was.** Nashville: Abingdon Press, 1985. 144 pp.

Two who believed in the documentary hypothesis show how patterns of structure in Genesis 1-11 convinced them of the unity of these chapters and writing by one person. They argue that the same phenomena run through all of Genesis and the Pentateuch.

Kline, Meredith G. "Genesis," New Bible Commentary Revised, ed. D. Guthrie, et al. Grand Rapids: Eerdmans, 1970, pp. 70-114.

Famous professor of Old Testament, Gordon-Conwell Theological Seminary, favors Mosaic authorship, defends historical reliability of events (cf. p. 80) and the unity of the material in opposition to the documentary hypothesis. He is conservative in views. He takes the days of Genesis 1 as figurative for ages, 49:10 as looking on to the Messiah, etc.

Klotz, John. Genes, Genesis and Evolution. **St. Louis: Concordia, 1955.**

A man who is both a scientist and minister has written this work. He knows the main arguments used by those taking evolutionary views and shows that they are not the last answer. Conservative and clear-cut in his own convictions, he shows the inconclusive nature of many of the dating methods used by science in figuring the age of the earth and man. However, some have charged him with failing to understand the nature of the evidence at some points and thus drawing improper conclusions from it (cf. Richard S. Beal, Jr., Eternity Magazine, February, 1956, p. 30). Another charge is that he has misrepresented certain authors he cites, though not necessarily intentionally, by quoting them out of context rather than objectively.

Law, Henry. Christ is All. The Gospel in Genesis. **London: Banner of Truth Trust, 1961. Reprint.**

Evangelical on typology, frequently very good in suggestiveness for expositors.

Lawson, George. The History of Joseph. **Carlisle, PA: Banner of Truth Trust, n. d. Reprint of 1807. 12 volumes. Cf. 1972 edition, Edinburgh, Banner of Truth.**

Here are many stimulating lessons for the spiritual life, some of them dated. If one is preaching in a series of Joseph, the book can be very helpful in priming the pump. Lawson expounds each verse in Genesis 37-50 with vital truths for Christian life. A person looking for a very detailed discussion here will appreciate the book as well as Martin Luther's 2 volumes (of eight on Genesis) that deal with 37-50. Cf. also on Joseph sources listed under Theadore Epp, plus John Hercus (Pages From God's Case Book. Downers Grove, IL: IVP, 1962).

Leupold, H. C. Exposition of Genesis. **2 volumes. Grand Rapids: Baker, 1990 reprint.**

In this very thorough, monumental work on Genesis, the author is conservative and uses the original Hebrew constantly. He considers carefully most major truths of the book and uses the grammatical-historical method. This is one of the most valuable works to have on Genesis. It came out originally in 1942.

Luther, Martin. Luther's Commentary on Genesis. A New Translation **by J. Theodore Mueller. 2 volumes. Grand Rapids: Zondervan, 1958. Also cf.** Lectures on Genesis, **8 volumes. Ed. J. Pelikan. Saint Louis: Concordia, 1965.**

A great Lutheran scholar and man active in missionary writing did this translation (he authored John G. Paton, Great Missionary to Africa, etc.). At the beginning of the first day God created a shapeless mass or lump of earth with fog and water (1:1,2). This He later fashioned and adorned and also put into it the light, which was an as yet imperfect light that He completed on the fourth day. One has to plod amidst much detail to search out what kind of "day" Luther means, but on p. 34 (citations are from Zondervan publication), he says the six were natural days. The serpent is a literal animal the Devil used as an agent (65). Luther is refreshing in saying of things God has not revealed, concerning which men ask questions, that we ought not judge God or ask an account of what He does or permits, but accept His will and be clay in the Potter's hands (65). Luther defends the estate of marriage in Genesis 4:1 against papists who he says condemn the marital communion of husband and wife as unclean. Eve in 4:1 believed "I have the Man, the Lord," meaning the Redeemer of 3:15. The "sons of God" in Genesis 6 are male descendants of the godly line, who lapsed from the true religion into sin with unions with the daughters of the wicked. Luther's compassion shows as in chapter 7 where the flood caught away men and other creatures, and Moses perhaps "could not describe these things without tears in his eyes" as he saw them "without hope and help, only to be destroyed." There is a great amount of material that explains pertinent questions very relevantly to the serious reader. Two volumes deal with the fourteen chapters on Joseph in great detail (in the 8 volume set).

Mackintosh, C. H. <u>Genesis to Deuteronomy. Notes on the Pentateuch.</u> **Neptune, NJ: Loizeaux Bros., 1972rp.**

This is a one-volume reprint of the six-volume C. H. M. work of 1880. Mackintosh frequently has devotionally refreshing insights and is mainly helpful at times from that standpoint. Personally, I find that W. H. Griffith-Thomas' <u>Genesis</u> is more to the point and touches on the main devotional lessons in a very systematic, outlined fashion.

Morris, Henry M. <u>The Genesis Record.</u> **Grand Rapids: Baker, with Creation Life Publishers, 1976.**

A verse by verse work of over 700 pp. by a strongly committed evangelical scholar. Morris deals with many of the difficulties in normal exposition—views of creation, whether 2:19 and other details in chapter 2 contradict the sequence in chapter 1, the "sons of God" in chapter 6, the extent of the flood, the prophecy of Noah, etc. He makes a special attempt to deal with scientific questions in chapters 1-11, since that has been the area of his life-long primary focus, and has a heavy emphasis on universal flood geology and a recent creation perspective. He was a coauthor with John Whitcomb of <u>The Genesis Flood</u>. Many laymen have regarded this as one of the most helpful and readable works. Cf. also <u>The Revelation Record</u>, on the Apocalypse, by the same author.

Petrie, George L. <u>Jacob's Sons.</u> **New York: Neale Publishing Co., 1910.**

Evangelical lectures that can help an expositor on Jacob's last words to his sons in Genesis 49 before he died.

Phillips, John. <u>Exploring Genesis.</u> **Chicago: Moody Press, 1980.**

A good expositor from the Moody Bible Institute Extension Department gives a well-organized, often provocative survey of the meaning, with principles made evident for application. Phillips' works on many of the Bible books in recent years have been a help to preachers and laypeople. He is conservative, clear, and often has a very good outline of a passage.

Pink, Arthur W. <u>Gleanings in Genesis</u>. Chicago: Moody (n. d.).

This conservative, premillennial work has good application and devotional spirit. It is often of help in tracing out prophecies fulfilled and unfulfilled, but some feel that Pink sees too many types. A weak element is that it does not deal so exhaustively with most passages as does Leupold. It is not based on the Hebrew text.

Ramm, Bernard. <u>The Christian View of Science and Scripture</u>. **Grand Rapids: Eerdmans, 1971 paperback reprint of 1954 work.**

This is not actually a commentary, but a work dealing with supposed tensions between Scripture and science. Ramm is well-read and penetrating in his discussions so that the reader is deeply stimulated. However, some of Ramm's conclusions are not tenable in the opinion of many conservatives—for example, his pictorial revelatory day view in Genesis 1, his view of progressive creationism, and his local flood idea. But he has discussions of these areas which at least seek to deal with the problems as he sees them. He is helpful on many other areas like Joshua's so-called long day (Joshua 10) and Jonah and the great fish.

Ross, Allen P. <u>Creation and Blessing</u>. **Grand Rapids: Baker, 1988. 744 pp.**

This is a major contribution, growing out of immense study in relevant literature of recent times dealing with ancient literature. Ross does a broad exposition section by section, not verse by verse, and handles major problems with adept awareness of views and discussion of arguments. It is a valuable scholarly work in surveying issues and literature that deals with them. Also cf. his "Genesis," <u>Bible Knowledge Commentary</u>, Volume 1, eds. J. F. Walvoord and Roy B. Zuck. Wheaton, IL: Victor Books, 1983.

Sailhamer, John. "Genesis," <u>The Expositor's Bible Commentary</u>, **Volume 2, ed. Frank Gaebelein and R. P. Polcyn. Grand Rapids: Zondervan, 1980.**

This Genesis contribution to the commentary is by the Associate Professor of Old Testament and Semitic Languages, Trinity Evangelical Divinity School, Deerfield, IL. It is a very good conservative work verse by verse, with insights from a wealth of literature from the ancient Near East that throws light on details and their relevance in their connections. Sailhamer shows much on competency, conciseness, clarity, and is frequently perceptive on the applicational relevancy.

Schaeffer, Francis A. <u>Genesis in Space and Time</u>. **Downers Grove, IL: Inter-Varsity Press, 1972.**

These chapters give a survey (not verse by verse study) of Genesis 1-11 with particular attention devoted to such matters as: showing the literal historicity of the events and persons in answer to many modern theologians, commenting with conviction of the meaning of without form and void (1:2), the alleged contradiction of chapter 1 by chapter 2, the chronology of chapters 5 and 11, the sons of God in 6:2, whether the flood was universal or only local (he feels universal), etc. He relates the truths here solidly to other Scripture and has helpful discussions of such areas as the image of God, marriage, sin, redemption, the genealogies, and the confusion of tongues at Babel.

Stigers, Harold G. <u>A Commentary on Genesis</u>. **Grand Rapids: Zondervan, 1976.**

A detailed work by an evangelical which moves verse by verse and is thorough on many of the problem passages. It is geared more for the rather serious student and is a good contribution. Laymen might consider it slow reading because of its length on many of the verses.

Stock, Eugene. <u>Lesson Studies From the Book of Genesis</u>. **London: Religious Tract Society, n. d.**

This has some good insights and illustrations on certain lessons in Genesis. For expositors it is especially helpful, and laypeople will receive an uplift in reading it.

Thomas, W. H. Griffith. <u>Genesis</u>. **Grand Rapids: Eerdmans, 1960. 507 pp.**

This work is good in tracing the argument and showing connections between chapters. It is devotional and gives suggestions for meditation at the ends of the chapters. Applications are usually good. It is an excellent book to put into the hands of a layman who is not ready to grapple with the minutia of exegesis, but who is serious about his Bible study. It is also good for the preacher and teacher.

Vos, Howard. <u>Genesis</u> **(Everyman's Bible Commentary). Chicago: Moody, 1982. 174 pp.**

A simple, broad survey by a conservative who tends to give some good comments but at times not nail down his view to explain a matter (cf. his survey of four views on days in Genesis 1, then leaving the matter hanging, and not commenting on how long God rested in 2:1-3; or his not choosing a preference on "sons of God" in Genesis 6 after a shallow consideration of issues). However, in a concise treatment he does touch on many of the problems.

Waltke, Bruce K. <u>Creation to Chaos: An Exegetical Study of Biblical Cosmology</u>. **Portland: Western Conservative Baptist Seminary, 1974.**

Lectures on Genesis 1-2 compared with Mesopotamian creation accounts. Waltke argues a gap before 1:1, not between 1:1 and 1:2.

Westermann, Claus. <u>Genesis: A Commentary</u>. **Translated from German. 3 volumes. Minneapolis: Augsburg Publishing House, 1984-86.**

The 3 volumes came out covering Chapters 1-11, 12-36 and 37-50. In more than 1,500 pages, a form critical scholar discusses critical matters on the text and also word meaning, history, theology, all in immense detail. Cf. his one-volume condensation in <u>Genesis, A Practical Commentary</u> (Eerdmans, 1987. 338 pp.). The latter, for about one-seventh the cost, focuses on Westermann's own convictions in much briefer, simpler form, without the technical comments. While one can by careful discrimmination glean out much that is profound and helpful in the 3 volumes, some statements will puzzle many. One is his idea that the God of the fathers is not the same as the God of Israel (p. 107). Often the work is of help to the scholar, whether often in the commentary or considerably in the bibliography (though most entries are German works and few are evangelical). Textual comments and summaries on the history of interpretation of some parts (Genesis 14, 15, 16, etc.) are informative. Westermann thinks Genesis 37-50 was from a separate, independent writing that later was composed during the era of David and Solomon and assembled into a unity with Genesis. The work is often disconcerting to the conservative in its low view of the authority of the text, and often opposes conservative views. It has a large amount of material theorizing how the text came into the form we now have. It rejects original sin in Genesis 3.

Wenham, G. J. Genesis 1-15 (Word Biblical Commentary). Waco, TX: Word Books, 1987. 406 pp.

Wenham gives much readable and good information on the Hebrew text, word study, exegesis and insightful exposition. He is somewhat freed from traditional critical views and holds to historicity of events and persons. He does not deny different strands of literary composition may have led to the Genesis we know, but is skeptical toward this. He places his stress on the canonical text as a unity. Despite this, many conservatives wonder what kind of evangelical he is when he uses J and P, not clearly explaining how his usage departs from the intent usually involved in these designations. His claims that certain P material, so-called, was earlier or later than J material will be regarded as arbitrary and speculative.

Whitcomb, John C. and Henry Morris. The Genesis Flood. Grand Rapids: Baker, 1971 paperback reprint of 1961 work. 518 pp.

A theologian formerly from Grace Seminary (Whitcomb) and a civil engineer at Christian Heritage College near San Diego (Morris) combined their efforts to produce this carefully documented work in defense of a world-wide flood. They have assembled the evidences in a masterful fashion, dealing seriously with both Scriptural and scientific data. The book represents the results of years of research in areas relating to the flood and careful study of hundreds of books, journals and papers available in many libraries. They integrate the basic scientific factors, as they see them, into the flood account in Genesis. It is the most impressive book on the flood problem by the conservative side. See also the well-documented book, The Biblical Flood and the Ice Epoch, by Donald Wesley Patten (Seattle: Pacific Meridian Publishing Co., 1966).

Wood, Leon J. Genesis, A Study Guide. Grand Rapids: Zondervan, 1975. 152 pp.

A staunch conservative offers a quick survey in basic information, often resolving main problems briefly. He leaves open the length of the days in Genesis 1, employs a detailed outline, and primarily assists lay readers and students looking for a terse review. A fine, brief evangelical survey of the main flow of the book, with a number of quite helpful comments on problem areas most readers want to see discussed. Among the briefer works this is one of the best.

Young, Davis A. Creation and Flood: An Alternative to Flood Geology and Theistic Evolution. Grand Rapids: Baker, 1977. 217 pp.

A good statement by an evangelical who believes in age days in Genesis 1 and an old earth. The son of Edward J. Young, Davis has his Ph. D. in geology from Brown University, B. S. E. in Geological Engineering from Princeton University, and M. S. in Minerology and Petrology from Pennsylvania State University. He argues against the flood geology in such a work as Henry M. Morris and John C. Whitcomb, The Genesis Flood, believing that a study of the rocks shows a much older earth than the fairly recent creation they champion. He holds an age-day view of the "day" concept in Genesis 1, arguing that the Genesis account only focuses on the chief or climactic events that were finished on each of the days. The days overlap. In appraising Young's position, one might find help from some of his critics' reviews (cf. Charles A. Clough and Louis E. Fredericks, "Creationist Science: A Challenge from Professor Young," 20 pp., Clough, Lubbock Bible Church, 3202 34th St., Lubbock, TX, 79410; Henry M. Morris, "The Day-Age Theory Revisited," Institute of Creation Research Impact Series, No. 55, 2716 Madison Avenue, San Diego, California 92116).

Young, Edward J. Studies in Genesis One. Philadelphia: Presbyterian and Reformed Publishing Co., 1964; also In The Beginning, Genesis 1-3 and the Authority of Scripture. Carlisle, PA: Banner of Truth Trust, 1976; and Genesis 3, A Devotional and Expository Study. Carlisle, PA: Banner of Truth Trust, 1966.

All three books present careful discussion of issues within the passages they treat, grappling with views and reasons and offering much to conservative readers. The work on Genesis 3 deals with the matter verse by verse.

Youngblood, Ronald. The Book of Genesis. An Introductory Commentary. Grand Rapids: Baker, 1991. 2nd edition.

This is extensively revised from the first edition in 2 volumes (chapters 12-50 in 1976 and 1-11 in 1980). It is a broad exposition by the Professor of Old Testament, Bethel Theological Seminary, West. A brief introduction (pp. 9-18) upholds Mosaic authorship and a date between 1445-1405 B. C. Youngblood sees no gap in 1:2, days of chapter 1 partly in literary order and partly in chronological, and favors science's claim that man-like creatures were on earth five million years ago (p. 46) but man in the Adamic race in a covenant relation with God at a more recent date. He favors the human view of "sons of God" in Genesis 6 and concludes the flood was local. He offers a fairly good, very readable survey of Genesis, but it is not as valuable overall as the work by John Davis or the ones by Ross and Sailhamer.

II. EXODUS

Atkinson, Basil F. D.   <u>The Book of Exodus</u> (The Pocket Commentary of the Bible). London: Henry E. Walter, n. d.

Somewhat in the way A. W. Pink has done, he moves verse by verse pointing out explanation, principles and applications. He is helpful quite often but not one of the best.

Bimson, J. J.   <u>Redating the Exodus and Conquest.</u>   Sheffield, England: University of Sheffield, 1978.

A case reasoning that archaeological data points better to a 15th century B. C. invasion of Canaan than a 13th century date. He shows a competent grasp of information.

Boyd, E. H.   <u>The Gospel in Exodus.</u>   Cleveland: Union Gospel Press, 1919.

Boyd selects verses and ideas and gives illustrations that often stimulate helpfully for messages. Sometimes he contributes well, sometimes he is rather flat.

Bush, George.   <u>Notes, Critical and Practical on the Book of Exodus.</u>   Boston: Henry A. Young & Company, 1841, 1856.   2 volumes.   Reprint.   Minneapolis: Klock & Klock.

As on Genesis, Bush is very helpful in his careful evangelical commentary here.

Calvin, John.   <u>Harmony of the Last Four Books of the Pentateuch.</u>   Grand Rapids: Eerdmans, n. d.

The Geneva theologian/expositor is richly profitable on the many laws he believes correlate with the ten commandments (he felt that the many are facets of the ten at the core). Drawing from here and there, he has much to say. The index at the close helps the one who keeps using it. Still, particular developments in sections and chapters of the Pentateuch are not always drawn in to show how things fit together.

Childs, Brevard S.   <u>The Book of Exodus: A Critical, Theological Commentary</u> (Old Testament Library).   Philadelphia: Westminster, 1974.   659 pp.

Childs was Professor of Old Testament, Yale University. He has a mere four-page introduction, and is committed to a subjective form-critical, traditio-historical idea of strands of compositions going through a redaction process. He says he intends to explain the final, canonical text for the church's good, yet assumes and frequently brings in much on redactional strands from literary critics, and appears subjective and questionable. Each section begins with a bibliography. The textual and philological notes can be quite helpful. But Childs calls in question the historical veracity of details as Exodus relates them (cf. p. 11). Still, the immense learning provides detailed discussions that aid the reader to look at matters from various angles and see what others regard as problems and possibilities. The work is more suitable for scholars or intense, advanced students who have discernment to weigh what is good and what is subjective theory pressed in. Though often liberal in its critical decisions, this work is frequently perceptive theologically to a discerning student who is maturely capable of gleaning the good and leaving the bad without being misled. In some ways its good points make it a serious example of an attempt at theological exegesis.

Clements, Ronald E. Exodus (Cambridge Bible Commentary). Cambridge: University Press, 1972.

He comments on the NEB text for pastors, students in schools and laypeople. He takes them often to speculative theories of strands of material, J, E, D, P. All the materials in this construction are supposedly from centuries after events they purport to describe. Clements has many references to them, assuming mere theory as fact. Typical of many works, he dates the exodus late (p. 7). He skips some verses; the commentary often is piecemeal and does not actually explain much (cf. 1:15 and its context, p. 14). At 3:2 he feels fire in the bush is a sign of God's presence, but does not discount natural explanations (p. 20). In 4:24-25, Clements is unable to represent to readers that the Lord really met Moses, as the text witnesses, for he supposes that this has to be out of harmony with the context. His own idea is in his judgment better: some evil power of the desert attacked Moses (p. 31). Much comment, however, is beneficial if one weighs things with discernment and keeps in mind Clements' liberal perspective; he sifts the good from the other.

Cole, R. Alan. Exodus. Downers Grove, IL: IVP, 1973. 239 pp.

A good commentary reflecting a breadth of reading and awareness of good scholarship, in the Tyndale Old Testament Commentary series. It is one of the better brief works.

Davies, G. Henton. Exodus: Introduction and Commentary (Torch Bible Commentary). London: SCM, 1967. 253 pp.

A preface and lengthy Introduction (11-55) concludes that not all material in Exodus is from Moses' day. It gives a survey of scholarly opinion, and thinks much bare fact does appear in the account (p. 29). The plagues were historical, the exodus was late, the two and a half million in the exodus is too high a figure (p. 41), and he endorses J, E, P documents in a redactional process (48, 53-55). The commentary is frequently fairly good, frequently explains little (1:1-6; 1:15-22), intersperses subjective theory about which redactional strand is involved (this interrupts the flow of thought, cf. p. 75) and pulls in highly unnecessary suggestions at times (the firstborn theme in Exodus 4 does not occur again until after 11:4, so the sequence is from 4:22f. to ch. 11, and chs. 5-10 are a series of parentheses (p. 76)). Overall, this work ranks far down the line in getting at what Exodus itself is saying, even if it has good material at many spots.

Davis, John J.   Moses and the Gods of Egypt.   Grand Rapids: Baker, 1972.   331 pp.

Here is a series of chapters on highlights of Exodus, reflecting a good grasp of historical backgrounds, customs, the divine message in Exodus, and the like. Davis has been establishing himself solidly as a very competent and widely studied writer on various parts of the Old Testament. He is on the faculty of Grace Theological Seminary, Winona Lake, IN.

Driver, S. R.   The Book of Exodus.   Cambridge: University Press, 1911.

This work in the Cambridge Bible series is another careful work in Hebrew exegesis with helpful comments on matters of historical background and word meanings. It helps on problems, though Driver was liberal.

Durham, John I.   Exodus (Word Biblical Commentary).   Waco, TX: Word Book, 1987.   516 pp.

He furnishes much help on textual and exegetical details, customs, etc., and often has good comments in explaining verses as they stand. However, he uses higher critical assumptions in such a way that he casts doubt on or denies reliability of details. He recognizes that the final form of the text which we have is what needs to be explained, but does not think that such matters as chronological references of when things happened are accurate. He provides lengthy lists of sources but gives little attention to conservative studies. No doubt his work will be primarily of assistance to liberal readers, despite the WBC being billed as an evangelical work.

Ellison, H. L.   Exodus (Daily Bible Study Series).   Philadelphia: Westminster, 1982.

Surprisingly, barely over a page of introduction precedes a commentary on the RSV set up under brief captions such as "The Burning Bush." He dates the exodus late. Much space is used just printing the RSV, and it breaks up continuity. He assumes the midwives lied, and says apart from the last plague "there is nothing supernatural in the plagues on Egypt" (p. 40). He deems it probable that when Moses thrust a piece of wood into Marah's waters, "nothing miraculous was intended" (85). Yet to him the manna and the water out of the rock were supernatural (90, 92). Quite a bit of the survey is helpful, even if one is perplexed here and there by Ellison's unnecessary conclusions.

Erdman, Charles R.   Exodus.   Grand Rapids: Eerdmans (n. d.).

This is only a brief, survey work. Its value to the expositor lies in its helpfulness in giving the sweep and movement of Exodus. It is not of help down in the trenches of exegesis.

Feinberg, C. L.   "Tabernacle," Zondervan Pictorial Encyclopedia of the Bible, Volume 5, pp. 572-83.   Grand Rapids: Zondervan, 1975.

Excellent well-organized survey of main facets of information about the Tabernacle, showing awareness of views and cogent reasons for conservative perspectives.

Getz, Gene.   Moses: Moments of Glory...Feet of Clay.   Glendale, CA: G/L Publications/Regal, 1976.

Simple character portraits with principles for ministers and laypeople today. Refreshing, stimulating.

Gispen, W. H.   Exodus (Bible Student's Commentary).   Grand Rapids: Zondervan,

Translated from conservative Dutch work of 1951, dating back to a 1932-39 work. Reformed in orientation, with fairly good detail explaining texts but at times with references that are not really pertinent to a point. Gispen takes an early date of the exodus and other evangelical views.

Gooding, D. W.   The Account of the Tabernacle.   Cambridge: University Press, 1959.

A well-regarded work using the LXX text as a basis and exercising perception.

Hyatt, J. P.   Commentary on Exodus (New Century Bible).   Greenwood, SC: Attic Press, 1971.

A thorough-going liberal belief in J, E, P, R [the latter, he says, is a Deuteronomic redactor] pervades the introduction and commentary. So Exodus is not primarily a historical record but a deposit of traditions, he says (p. 37). Yet the narrative, professing to be history, "rests upon a solid core of historical happening" (38). "It is not possible, however, for us now to disentangle all the historical and legendary elements in this book" (38). He rejects an early date for Israel's exodus, favoring a 13th century exit (43). The comments verse by verse are often good, though the reader has to be prepared to read of inconsistencies, contradictions, etc. in Hyatt's opinion. The narrative of Moses' birth (2:1-10) is, he says, legend, not history, and compares with myths and legends as of stories about Hercules, Romulus, Cyrus, etc. (62). He cites as striking the similarity between Moses being put in an ark on the water and Sargon in the mid 3rd century B. C. whose mother placed him in a basket of rushes on a river where he was rescued by royalty (62). Hyatt here, as in other places, mentions helpful detail, e.g. Josephus' account of Moses' father having a vision of how Moses would deliver his people, and Philo's details of Moses' lavish education (63). In Exodus 12, no attempt is made to see aspects of the Passover as typical of Jesus Christ. He rejects the 600,000 figure for men in 12:37, Numbers 11:21 and the similar 603, 550 in Numbers 1:46 as not credible and supposes the correct number is a few thousand, exaggerated by Israelite tradition (139). Hyatt has many such ideas, often put forth by liberals, but also frequently good information helpful to those who take a more approving view of the text. As a liberal work, it is a good commentary and shows good use of recent scholarly literature.

Kaiser, Walter C., Jr.   "Exodus" (Expositor's Bible Commentary), ed. Frank Gaebelein and R. P. Polcyn.   Volume 2.   Grand Rapids: Zondervan, 1990.

Conservative, Kaiser has fine verse by verse elucidation that shows keen awareness of and help on problems as well as the flow of the book. He is profitable in matters of context, word study, exegesis, background, customs, etc., and uses a wealth of scholarly literature to furnish further benefit. It is a firm evangelical effort.

Keil, C. F. and Franz Delitzsch. <u>The Pentateuch</u>. **Cf. on Commentaries on the Old Testament, Analytical.**

Kidner, Derek. <u>Hard Sayings</u>. **Grand Rapids: Eerdmans, 1972.**

Concise comments on Old Testament moral teaching, often as related to the ten commandments. Sometimes provocative for Christian nourishment and growth, and a stimulant for expositors, done by a keen scholar.

McCarthy, Dennis. <u>Old Testament Covenant</u>. **Nashville: John Knox Press, 1972.**

The reader will find much here in discussion of Old Testament laws and the ten commandments, with a lot pulled together.

MacGregor, J. <u>Exodus</u>. **Edinburgh: T. & T. Clark, 1909.**

A brief evangelical work that often has excellent comments on settings for episodes.

Meyer, F. B. <u>Devotional Commentary on Exodus</u>. **Grand Rapids: Kregel, 1978. 476 pp.**

This is a reprint of an old classic, 2 volumes in 1. Meyer, who did the refreshing books on characters in Genesis and other Bible books, was a great English expositor known for his close walk with God, his stimulating spiritual life works, and preaching; he takes Christians through Exodus passage by passage. He organizes lessons to point out timeless principles which frequently are insightful and gripping. Many paragraphs are headed by boldface statements showing the subject.

Moorehead, W. G. <u>Studies in the Mosaic Institutions</u>. **New York: Revell, 1893.**

Excellent evangelical studies especially on the tabernacle.

Murphy, James G. <u>A Critical and Exegetical Commentary on the Book of Exodus</u>. **Boston: W. H. Holliday, 1868.**

A careful Hebrew exegetical work by the professor of Hebrew in Belfast.

Noth, Martin. <u>Exodus</u> (Old Testament Library). **Philadelphia: Westminster, 1962. 283 pp.**

A highly regarded work among scholars pursuing literary composition theories and late-dating. Noth holds that the Pentateuch cannot be by one writer, Moses, due to what he regards as the assured results of scholarly study (p. 12). He subscribes to subjective J, E, P strands (12-18), and says his commentary deals with the final form, yet has frequent recourse to aspects of his hypothesis. Comments sometimes offer real meat, at other times have scarcely anything beyond generality which one can already see in the verses. Noth says parts of the narrative may have been grafted on artificially in a later composition by a redactor. Much speculative opinion posits editorial strands that were not in the original telling. We often get more of Noth's theory than substantial explanation of the text. He supposes contradictions, such as Moses being presented as a firstborn child in Exodus 2, then presently having an older sister (p. 25). To him, similar rescue stories shaped Israelite minds to make up a Moses story like these (27) to intermingle with whatever in the passage may have historically happened. The "story of the plagues has no real purpose . . ." (68). One often feels that things which can be seen meaningfully are being manipulated to suit the commentator's opinion. Conservative readers with perception and maturity can alertly find much good help amidst all of this. The work is an example of a scholar sitting in judgment over the Scripture, often bringing into question the veracity.

Phillips, A.   Ancient Israel's Criminal Law.   New York: Schocken, 1970.

He devotes more detail to exegesis than Kidner's work. One can glean much here by patient study.

Pink, Arthur W.   Gleanings in Exodus.   Chicago: Moody (n. d.).

Like his work on Genesis, this book is devotional in thrust and quite voluminous (384 large two-column pages, well over 700 pages in an ordinary book). If one is doing a detailed study of Exodus to present messages to a congregation, this is a good book to consult for stimulating thoughts as well as applications and exhortations. Pink overdoes some types.

Ramm, Bernard L.   God's Way Out. Finding the Road to Personal Freedom through Exodus.   Ventura, CA: Regal Books, 1984, 1987.   166 pp.

Simple, clear, running commentary, not verse by verse, centered on God's attributes and work, types of Christ and His church, New Testament truth related to Exodus, and application to life today. Ramm has intriguing chapter titles, sweeping surveys rich in connections to life now, notes on word meanings, and refreshment that warms the heart. Chapter 4 on Moses' excuses and God's answers is entitled, "God Can Use Even You." The popular-level survey is adept in simplifying a long book into three very manageable points, Divine Redemption, Divine Morality (The Law), and Divine Worship. Its contribution is in the synthesis, the perspective that copes with so much detail.

Sarna, Nahum M.   Exodus (Jewish Publication Society Torah Commentary).   New York: JPS, 1991.   278 pp.

A Jewish effort that quite often furnishes definite help in its straight-forward approach. Sarna uses the Massoretic Hebrew text side by side with the JPS rendering into English at the top and his commentary on the last half or three-quarters of the large pages. Footnotes come in sections at the end of the commentary. Sarna is cogent with word meanings, customs, resolution of problems and giving possibilities briefly. He favors a late exodus. He cites scholarly literature without the constant intrusion of theories of literary strands. At times fairly good detail sums up matters, as on "flowing with milk and honey" (3:8; p. 16). The commentary is excellent on some texts, such as 6:3, 7:11, and 11:5. Some miracles passages are given a natural explanation, as Moses using a piece of wood to render Marah's water drinkable, e.g., the water filtered through porous wood, straining impurities (p. 84). By contrast, the manna is said to have no naturalistic explanation (p. 89). Among excursuses at the end, No. 2 is a fine citation of different abandoned hero stories sometimes cited at Exodus 2, with an evaluation that the account of Moses is markedly different in several details (267-68).

Soltau, Henry W.   The Holy Vessels and Furniture of the Tabernacle.   Grand Rapids: Kregel, n. d.   Also The Tabernacle, The Priesthood, and the Offerings. Christian Publications, 1965.

He is often helpful on typology, giving insightful attention to connections with the New Testament. Cf. also C. W. Slemming's books: These are the Garments, and Made According to Pattern, which go into much detail on priestly clothing and tabernacle furniture.

Stamm, J. J. and M. E. Andrew.   The Ten Commandments in Recent Research. London: SCM, 1967.

The authors provide considerable exegesis of the text and therefore help on details.

Watson, Thomas.   The Ten Commandments.   Edinburgh: Banner of Truth Trust, 1976 rp   (cf. also his works on The Beatitudes and The Lord's Prayer, also A Divine Cordial, on Romans 8:28).

A popular London preacher in Puritan times wrote this exploration of the commandments in depth. Many insights are helpful for preaching, also a section on the law and sin, and the way of salvation. In the latter discussion, Watson deals with faith, repentance, the word, baptism, the Lord's Supper, and prayer, relating each to salvation and Christian commitment. He also has a section on infant baptism. The portion on the Lord's Supper covers the subject from various angles.

Youngblood, Ronald, F.   Exodus.   Chicago, IL: Moody Press, 1983.

Youngblood of Bethel Theological Seminary (West) in San Diego has written this helpful 144-pp. paperback for the Everyman's Bible Commentary Series. He divides Exodus into twelve great theses: Persecution, Preparation, Confrontation, Plagues, Passover, Redemption, Journey, Covenant, Law, Tabernacle, Priesthood and Renewal. His introduction shows that he is well-versed in the "documentary hypothesis," and he argues forcibly for Mosaic authorship of Exodus. He does, however, appear to be significantly less conclusive about a Mosaic authorship of either Genesis/Pentateuch. He adopts the more traditional evangelical date of writing (1445 B.C.) and defends it admirably. Youngblood also shows familiarity with Egyptian culture and setting. The volume is practical enough for the preacher and "Hebrew" enough for the seminary student. Youngblood's treatment of the nine plagues as three threes, and his desire to couch these in some form of scientific credibility is one of his debatable points. Additionally, he views the Red Sea crossing as the lesser possibility, and opts for the common idea "sea of reeds" which he locates further to the north. Chapters 19-24 of Exodus are dealt with under the general theme of "Covenant." Youngblood's entries under "Temple" and "Priesthood" are also excellent. They are descriptive enough so that even the novice can grasp the full ramifications of Jewish temple culture. Conclusion: On the whole a fine work by a conservative scholar, but it does require critical reading. —Jan Sattem

III. LEVITICUS

Allis, Oswald T. **"Leviticus," in** New Bible Commentary Revised, **ed. D. Guthrie et al. Grand Rapids: Eerdmans, 1970, pp. 140-67.**

A good, brief commentary by a skilled conservative Old Testament scholar. He takes Mosaic authorship, and for this in the same volume cf. J. W. Wenham, "Moses and the Pentateuch," pp. 41-43, and E. J. Young, "History of the Literary Criticism of the Pentateuch," 38-40.

Bamberger, Bernard J. Leviticus **(The Torah, A Modern Commentary). New York: Union of Hebrew Congregations, 1979. 417 pp.**

A Jewish scholar who has subscribed to liberal theories. He says that the first half of Leviticus "contains much that is not relevant to our times" (xv). He assumes multiple authorship, discrepancies that show the book is a composite from various sources (xviii-xix), writing as late as the exile and post-exilic days, though with redactors preserving without change much of what was earlier. He says that the central tabernacle with its highly organized sacrifice system must have been added later since it is, to him, "completely inappropriate to desert conditions" (xix). He uses the Jewish Publication Society translation into English, revised in 1967. Sections of commentary are prefaced with general introductions as chapter 1 has six pages on sacrifices in ancient times. Comments are often very helpful, but usually terse, and some verses are skipped. He gives only one view for why Nadab and Abihu were consumed in Leviticus 10, but in a section called "Gleanings" presents other views (p. 85). Often he sheds light by reviewing explanations in history, as on reasons for dietary laws in Chapter 11 (pp. 90-91). There also is a good section on dietary laws in Jewish history (91-92) and in Reformed Judaism (93-94). The work has a wealth of help at times on Jewish interpretation and also on views in general.

Bonar, Andrew, 1810-92. <u>A Commentary on the Book of Leviticus</u>. **Grand Rapids: Zondervan, 1959; now Grand Rapids: Baker, 1978.**

This is a reprint of a work which Spurgeon described as "very precious." Bonar treats the text in an expository and practical way, with critical notes. He is thoroughly conservative, and rich in application. Many regard this as the best older work on Leviticus from a conservative writer.

Bush, George. <u>Notes, Critical and Practical, on the Book of Leviticus</u>. **New York: Newman and Ivison, 1852, rp by James and Klock Christian Publishing Co., Minneapolis, 1976.**

Bush has works on Genesis, Exodus, Leviticus, Numbers, Joshua and Judges, all reprinted in recent years. His work on Leviticus is often helpful along the same lines as on Genesis and Exodus (cf. remarks in this bibliography).

Chapman, A. T. and Streane, A. W. <u>Leviticus</u> **(Cambridge Bible for Schools and Colleges). New York: Putnam, 1914.**

Though old, this is still good for exegesis and comments on many of the problems.

Erdman, Charles R. <u>The Book of Leviticus</u>. **NY: Revell, 1951.**

This is a synthesis which helps the student find his way through the many details of Leviticus with an understanding of the flow of thought or argument.

Goldberg, Louis. <u>Leviticus: A Study Guide Commentary</u>. **Grand Rapids: Zondervan, 1980.**

Goldberg is Professor of Theology and Jewish Studies at Moody Bible Institute. His introduction is very evangelical, he supplies a detailed outline at the outset, and has clear, well-standardized syntheses of sections as well as helpful comments on each sub-section that help an expositor. Unlike such a commentator as Snaith, he shows a relation to typology and does it sanely. He also pauses to point out principles for believers today. At various points he provides lists of suggestions for further pertinent study or reflection on key areas or questions. This is a good, brief commentary that gives insight on the chief details and can stimulate an expositor.

Harris, R. Laird. "Leviticus" (<u>Expositor's Bible Commentary</u>), **ed. Frank Gaebelein and R. P. Polcyn. Volume 2. Grand Rapids: Zondervan, 1990.**

The Professor of Old Testament, Covenant Theological Seminary, is conservative, contributing on the panorama the introductory sections give on scholarly discussion and views, as well as verse by verse detail fitted in its historical context of the wilderness era.

Harrison, R. K. <u>Leviticus. An Introduction and Commentary</u> (Tyndale OTC). Downers Grove, IL: IVP, 1980. 252 pp.

Highly-regarded among conservatives, the book upholds veracity of many matters. Harrison draws from his expertise in ancient studies. Some believe that he does not give dietary details their due in explaining much as hygienic. He argues for Mosaic authorship and usually is very helpful on how sections fit and how verses can be explained reasonably.

Jukes, Andrew. <u>The Law of the Offerings</u>. London: James Nisbet, 1870.

This famous work deals exclusively with Leviticus 1-7, explaining the offerings and the laws regulating them. Devotional in character.

Keil, C. F. and Franz Delitzsch. <u>The Pentateuch</u>. Cf. Commentaries on the Old Testament, Analytical.

Kellogg, S. H. <u>The Book of Leviticus</u>. In the Expositors Bible. NY: A. C. Armstrong and Son, 1903; rp by Klock & Klock, 1978.

This lucid broader work is one of the best theologically on Leviticus. It deals perceptively with some questions not touched upon by Bonar. However, it is weak on application.

Kidner, Derek. <u>Leviticus, Numbers, Deuteronomy</u> (Scripture Union Bible Study Books). Grand Rapids: Eerdmans, 1971. 92 pp.

This is a preparation for laypeople's daily segments of Bible reading. An outline of each book runs throughout, and comments on each chapter are about a half page or more. Brevity prevails, and he has done a fine job in this to get to the gist of things for those who desire a quick look and survey.

Kurtz, J. H. <u>Sacrificial Worship of the Old Testament</u>. Grand Rapids: Baker, 1980. Reprint of a work first appearing in 1863.

Kurtz has long been a help on details on sacrifice at the tabernacle and how this met needs of Israelites. Its usability led Baker to make it available again.

Levine, Baruch A. <u>Leviticus</u> (Jewish Publication Society Torah Commentary). NY: JPS, 1989. 284 pp.

Assumes stages of redaction and different segments from various times (xxx). An extended introduction (31 pp.) synthesizes the structure (1-16, manuals of practical address to priests; 17-27, priests' teachings to the other people). It also has a good survey on the critical method and problems scholars think they are resolving. Levine includes notes at the ends of the introduction, commentary, and a special section on "Leviticus in the Ongoing Jewish Tradition," and at the end excursuses such as "The Meaning of the Dietary Laws," "The Sabbath," "The Annual Festivals," etc. The commentary verse by verse is sometimes brief, sometimes detailed, beneath the Hebrew Massoretic text and JPS English translation set side by side. Levine is excellent on word meaning, helpful on exegesis and customs (such as salt used in sacrifices, p.13; honey used or not used, p. 12). He cites a plethora of scholarly literature for perception on some matters. Often he gives several views, as on the nature of the offense by Aaron's sons (chapter 10; p. 59).

Milgrom, Jacob. Leviticus 1-16 (Anchor Bible). NY: Doubleday, 1991. 1163 pp.

This work is very impressive in its command of the subjects and scholarly literature helpful on them. Often Milgrom takes views conservatives will appreciate. He argues at length for the ancient rooting of material called priestly, and the reasonableness of seeing Aaron and his line of priests as historical. His commentary often cites from medieval Jewish exegetes who have been much passed over by scholarship in general. He also draws from scholars of the past century and a half, such as Kalisch, Driver, Noth, Snaith, Wenham, Harrison and Levine (cf. his lengthy bibliography, pp. 69-128). A translation and broad introduction precedes sections, then Milgrom gives "Notes" which deal exhaustively with verses (9 pp. on 1:1, etc.). He explains problems, such as prohibiting leaven and honey and including salt (2:11-13) and the reason Nadab and Abihu were struck down in the midst of service in 10:1 (cf. p. 598 and pp. 633-35 where he cites twelve views of rabbis). He goes into much detail on why some foods, as pork, were prohibited (cf. his verse by verse commentary plus special sections, 691-742). Few stones are left unturned. At the end are indices of subjects, terms, authors, sources in Scripture, Apocrypha/Pseudepigrapha, Qumran, Versions, Targums, Rabbinics, etc.

Noordtzij, A. Leviticus (Bible Student's Commentary). Grand Rapids: Zondervan, 1982. 280 pp.

Cf. Aalders under Genesis. Though this is an evangelical series and Noordtzij is conservative on much, he posits the Mosaic origin of some material and much later origin of other material (pp. 12, 189). The publisher's note at the outset alerts readers to the mixed bag. But on many details the author writes against the Wellhausen school, and says it makes much of Leviticus "deliberate deceit" (11). On many passages he is quite helpful and has a high view of the integrity, a good study of problems, etc. Read with alertness and discernment the work yields a lot of solid benefit.

Noth, Martin. Leviticus, A Commentary (Old Testament Library). Philadelphia: Westminster, 1965. 208 pp.

As on Exodus, Noth offers much solid material explaining verses with basic information conservatives will find usable. But again he depends on a theory of literary compostitions according to scholarly guesswork and subjective reasoning. He admits scholars vary. The commentary is often terse but usually has some help. Readers need to be alert to discern where Noth is delivering speculation from his sources agenda and not the text itself. He is often clear, but sometimes unclear and incomplete, as when he leaves vague why leaven, prohibited in 2:11-

13, is permitted in 7:13 (p. 61). On 23:17 he is a bit more helpful on leaven's allowance.

Pfeiffer, Charles F. <u>The Book of Leviticus: A Study Manual.</u> **Shield Bible Series of paperbacks. Grand Rapids: Baker, 1957.**

Though brief and concise, this work by a noted conservative scholar of recent times is quite helpful in gaining a perspective and a direction through the myriad details.

Schultz, Samuel. <u>Leviticus: God Among His People</u> **(Everyman's Bible Commentary). Chicago: Moody, 1983. 141 pp.**

This teacher for forty-one years at Wheaton College says, "Leviticus may be the most neglected book in the Old Testament" (p. 7). He provides fairly good introductory remarks (pp. 7-32). Chapter 2, next, leaps on to 8:1-10:20, "God Among His People." Then Chapter 3 switches back to 1:1-7:38. Why not recognize God among His people in Exodus 40, then move right on to Leviticus 1:1? From 11:1 on, Schultz keeps to the Leviticus sequence. He writes clearly, simply, explaining main aspects in a conservative vein and showing how they relate to today in principle. Some things are left unclear, as a reference to G. J. Wenham explaining uncleanness laws on food (Leviticus 11) as symbolical, stemming from a social anthropologist's study, but not defining what the symbolical meaning in that view is (p. 72). However, much of the book is to the point, even if brief.

Snaith, Norman H. <u>Leviticus and Numbers</u> **(The Century Bible). Camden, New Jersey: Thomas Nelson and Sons, 1967.**

He works on a foundation of non-Mosaic authorship, rather groups of authors from different centuries a la Robert Pfeiffer, Otto Eissfeldt, etc. This is a foregone conclusion with him. So, writers of P read back details of the Ezra temple into the ancient tabernacle of the wilderness (p. 28), etc. Many contradictions are seen in the account which have been reconciled well by others. From this standpoint it is disconcerting to come expecting explanations of the text and be met by various theories (assumptions) of different, supposed inconsistencies according to radical ways of construing things. Yet Snaith does, of course, have many helpful details on word meanings. Many verses are skipped over in comments. The reader is plunged into detail verse by verse without introduction of a kind that synthesizes or gives the sweep of sections or compares the offerings in Leviticus for perspective. Often details are interspersed to tell readers of similar or comparable practices among other peoples. Typological reference to the New Testament is missing. Occasionally Snaith gives helpful illustrations, e.g. on Leviticus 4:2, sinning "unwittingly": like "a devout Jew of modern times involved in a breakdown of transport on the Eve of the Sabbath so far from home that he must break the Sabbath rule concerning making a journey" (p. 41; cf. also 12:1-8, p. 90). He is not afraid to sit in judgment, as in 4:7 where to his notion putting blood on horns of the altar is "a wholly animistic way of thinking" (p. 43). The story of Nadab and Abihu being rejected (Leviticus 10) has to be, in his scheme, a late story of post-exilic times to justify why these two and their descendants had no place in the priesthood, and show the rights of the accepted Aaronic priesthood (p. 75). He appears to accept the idea that the holy devouring fire on Nadab and Abihu in Leviticus 10 is a primitive idea that should be discounted today as in liberal, humanistic belief (p. 76). He often perceives the point of an episode, as the two goats on the Day of Atonement (p. 112). Things many regard as types are not related to possible antitypes in the New Testament, as the great offerings, the Day of Atonement, manna. Snaith cannot grasp how God showed Himself to be holy in Numbers 20:13 unless it be in "might and awesomeness" (p. 276).

Wenham, Gordon J.   The Book of Leviticus (NICOT).   Grand Rapids: Eerdmans, 1979.

Sparkling, inviting and generally convincing effort at showing the modern meaning and relevance of Leviticus, based on the legitimate and inherent meaning of the text. Displays a minimum of "reaching," and a real respect for the canonical text. Indispensable for preaching or teaching, and rewarding for personal (serious) study. —Dan Phillips

IV. NUMBERS

Allen, Ronald B.   "Numbers" (Expositor's Bible Commentary),   Volume 2, ed. Frank Gaebelein and R. P. Polcyn.   Grand Rapids: Zondervan, 1990.

A Professor of Old Testament at Western Conservative Baptist Seminary, Portland, OR, has provided this excellent conservative introduction, verse by verse commentary handling problems adeptly (such as the high numbers), and pointing out theological truths.

Budd, Philip J.   Numbers (Word Biblical Commentary).   Waco: Word Books, 1984. 409 pp.

Budd accepts a J, E, D, P scheme of literary sources, regarding Genesis—Joshua as put together by priestly writers in the sixth to fifth centuries B. C., writing to enhance their own concerns and meet problems of their day. Budd takes very little in the various incidents to be trustworty history (xxvi-xxxi, etc.); it rather is tradition on which scholars can pronounce. If one wants to read on past and fairly current critical judgment on Numbers, and profit from extensive bibliography, and stick with sometimes ponderous discussions of scholars' opinions, he can learn much here. But much is relevant only to a time centuries later than the wilderness wanderings. For example, Korah's rebellion (Numbers 16), in Budd's judgment, addresses a power struggle in post-exilic days between Zadokite and Levite priests. Much of the commentary furnishes examples of the commentator's theories pressed upon Numbers, this being more pervasive than an illumination of the book in a wilderness setting in which conservatives believe it more naturally fits. The discerning student who is rightly oriented to the wilderness setting of the book can profit much from understanding fine word study, exegesis etc. to relate to that and not later times where Budd places things.

Bush, George. <u>Notes, Critical and Practical on the Book of Numbers.</u> **Boston: Henry A. Young Co., 1858.**

The author shows the same serious, careful work that characterizes his books on other parts of the Pentateuch. See earlier annotations.

Gray, George G. <u>A Critical and Exegetical Commentary on Numbers</u> (ICC). **Edinburgh: T. & T. Clark, 1912.**

This is a detailed commentary relevant to the serious student who desires help on problem passages as well as general help throughout the book. See earlier comments on the I.C.C.

Harrison, R. K. <u>Numbers</u> (Wycliffe Exegetical Commentary). **Chicago: Moody, 1990. 452 pp.**

Harrison's introduction is well-done in surveying main areas of scholarly debate. Though he sees different literary sources compiled into our present book, among these Balaam's oracles (Numbers 22-24) from a non-Israelite source but valid, he does hold to the historicity of accounts as coming from eye-witnesses during the wilderness trek. Moses, he feels, exercised supervision over these and contributed some material himself (pp. 22-23). The commentary often shows a well-read scholar who is skilled in bringing in material that throws light on texts exegetically, historically, culturally, etc. Harrison is not ready, as Gispen and some others, to assume that the numbers of Israelites are correct, but wants more information before making a judgment (45-47). By and large he is very accepting of the passages as they stand, and free of tendencies to explain them away.

Huey, F. B., Jr. Numbers (<u>Bible Study Commentary</u>). **Grand Rapids: Zondervan, 1981. 115 pp.**

The work on Exodus in this series is also a fairly good survey. Here, the Professor of Old Testament, Southwestern Baptist Theological Seminary, Fort Worth, has a detailed outline which he follows well. He gives a summation of seven views on the numbers being allegedly too high (pp. 9-11). One wishes Huey stated the theme of Numbers distinctly at the outset. Sometimes he lacks clarity. He calls Moses' striking the rock in Exodus 17 "the parallel experience" with his striking a rock in Numbers 20 (p. 72). These were at different times and places, not strictly parallel. In the same discussion he gives as different scholars' views six different aspects of Moses' sin, which are not views and which can all be true together. Still, this is for the most part a good brief look at Numbers.

Jensen, Irving L. <u>Numbers, Journey to God's Rest-land</u>. **Chicago: Moody, 1964. Paperback.**

This is a brief but good evangelical survey exposition.

Keil, C. F. and Franz Delitzsch. <u>The Pentateuch</u>. **Cf. under Commentaries on the Old Testament, analytical.**

As in their other works in this Old Testament set, the authors are careful in the exegesis of the Hebrew text.

Kidner, Derek. Cf. on Leviticus.

Maarsingh, B. <u>Numbers</u>. **Grand Rapids: Eerdmans, 1987. 221 pp.**

This is lucid, brief, vigorous in tackling and explaining words, phrases and many issues with a learned grasp of text, exegesis, ancient customs, etc. Yet the author remains practical and has a freshness to spark application and growth. Lay readers and even advanced students can profit from the survey.

MacRae, A. A. "Numbers," <u>The New Bible Commentary</u>. **Edited by F. Davidson, A. M. Stibbs and E. F. Kevan. Grand Rapids: Eerdmans, 1953.**

This is a more concise discussion of Numbers by a well-known conservative scholar of recent times who was president of Faith Theological Seminary and a member of the editorial committee for the revised Scofield Reference Bible of 1967.

Milgrom, Jacob. <u>Numbers</u> **(JPS Torah Commentary). NY: JPS, 1990. 520 pp.**

As on Leviticus, Milgrom delves in rich detail; there are 331 pages of commentary, and 77 excursuses (pp. 335-513) usually one to three pages long. Topics of the latter are such as "The Census and its Totals," "Adultery...," "Repentance in the Torah and the Prophets," and "The Copper Snake," etc. Each chapter of commentary is followed by copious, helpful notes, some lengthy and reflecting wide reading in relevant literature. Notes on excursuses also have notes at the end of the section. Frankly, notes would be more handy if placed on pages in the commentary or right with an excursus. Milgrom draws much from medieval exegetes and gives sketches on 17 of these (pp. xlii-xlv). The section on theological and anthropological matters has good summary comments about God, intercession, etc. While the commentary is concise it is often contributive on crucial points. At times Milgrom champions a high view of the unity and integrity of passages. Not all will agree when he sees the Dathan and Abiram story in Numbers 16 as from a separate story not originally a part of the Korah episode (Excursus 39).

Noordtzij, A. <u>Numbers</u> **(Bible Student Commentary). Grand Rapids: Zondervan, 1983. 304 pp.**

This translation from the Dutch is at most points a very able treatment of the text, word study, background, and relation to other Scripture. Sometimes it is too thin on a verse, at other times exegetical detail is rewarding. The writer brings enormous reading and awareness to his comments on issues, and often has special details on episodes (20:2-12; 21:4-9, etc.). Pastors and students as well as serious lay readers will appreciate much of it. The publishers warn readers that Noordtzij, while in most places sound, has strange ideas at times. For example, he writes of God's law keeping an Israelite "from inhaling through his mouth and nose further demonic influences" (p. viii). He also lacks a bibliography, footnotes, and an overall doctrinal orientation in his introduction. He loses the flow of the book in details. He claims that instructions for camp format and order of march in Numbers 2 could not possibly have been given originally in the present form. For the number of men and names of leaders are out of place in such initial instructions (p. 12). Many will wonder how this naturally follows. Yet he often defends traditional views against critical theories.

Noth, Martin. <u>Numbers, A Commentary</u> **(Old Testament Library). Philadelphia: Westminster, 1968. 258 pp.**

Cf. his works on Exodus and Leviticus; much the same applies here. He holds to late compostition from various traditions, seeing confusion and lack of order, varied styles and methods which rule out a single authorship. To him it is self-evident that Numbers has repeated factually contradictory ideas in passages, and he sees no need for exhaustive proof (p. 4). His assumptions on which source a given part was from frequently intrude on explanationss of passages. If, however, one patiently stays with the book, he can sift out much that is of help and leave much that is unconvincing, arbitrary conjecture. Conservatives may feel, for example, that it is far more reasonable to see the bronze serpent idea as continued by Israelites to the time of 2 Kings 18:4 than to say, with Noth, that "the later existence of the `bronze serpent' . . . was certainly the reason for the telling of the plague . . . in the wilderness . . ." (p. 157). On the beneficial side, Noth often presents several views and a good discussion of how a problem can possibly be resolved, for example the high numbers of Chapter 1 (21-23). The work will offer help at times to the advanced student who has discernment and skill in weighing matters.

Philip, James. "Numbers" (The Communicators Commentary). Waco: Word Books, 1987. 364 pp.

Philip has long been a bright light for the evangelical faith in Scotland, pastoring the Holyrood Abbey Church in Edinburgh. Using good sources and explaining the text conservatively, he also shows practical applications to people today.

Plaut, W. Gunther. <u>Numbers</u> **(The Torah, A Modern Commentary). New York: Union of American Hebrew Congregations, 1979. 366 pp.**

He also did the commentary on Genesis in this series. There he says many things against the veracity of Genesis, for example Genesis gives Israel's history "not, perhaps, as it was but as it ought to have been" (xviii). Abram's experience of God promising him Canaan "will not pass as historic `fact,' (yet) its reality was accepted by generations . . . and, for them, validated their possession of the land" (xix). Many verses of Genesis are not really explained, or are given liberal comments, or are just skipped, as most of the verses in Genesis 3 are. The finest value of the commentary for those taking a high view of scriptural integrity is its frequent examples of how a liberal mind thinks on verses, and also the rabbinic comment brought in helpfully at times.

In Numbers again he is brief and skips verses (as 1:4, 16-46; 1:5-15 receive seven lines) or is too brief to take up issues in any adequate way. Special notes, usually one to a section, do go into some problems or define issues, as "The Census Figures" (pp. 18-19). Plaut is not certain but favors viewing the word elef, "thousand," as a tribal contingent; so, Reuben's 46,500 would be 46 elefs, = a total of 500 men (p. 18, cf. 272). Each section ends with "Gleanings," citations from rabbinic sources or modern scholars, explanations of points, etc. Sometimes really key points, such as the cruciality that one look if he would live in Numbers 21, are passed over. At many points this is fairly good Jewish commentary, but very spotty and not anything near the helpfulness of Milgrom's impressive work.

Snaith, Norman H. (cf. on Leviticus)

Wenham, Gordon J. Numbers (TOTC). Downers Grove: InterVarsity Press, 1981.

For its brevity, a superb commentary in lifting out the legitimate meaning of the text and applying it to the contemporary reader in a crisp, thoughtful and reverent manner. Good, solid treatments of the significance of the rituals and dietary laws, fair (but not always satisfying) treatment of most problems. Indispensable for preaching or teaching, an excellent aid for understanding. —Dan Phillips

V. DEUTERONOMY

Craigie, Peter C. The Book of Deuteronomy (NICOT). Grand Rapids: Eerdmans, 1976. 424 pp.

Scholarly study of the text, based on analysis of the Hebrew and cognate languages, written in an attitude of faith and aimed at a broad (but serious) audience. Craigie notes and capitalizes on the book's similarity in structure to second-millennium ancient Near East vassal treaties, and holds the authorship to be Mosaic, finished by Joshua. Includes an 86-page introductory section, with a nine-page section on the theology of the book. Craigie, Associate Professor of Religious Studies at the University of Calgary, is inclined toward a Mosaic date or shortly after, agreeing with M. Kline. He usually shows good awareness of views and recent books and articles (cf. his select bibliography, pp. 69-72). He even furnishes in Appendix III a "Concordance of Principal Qumran Manuscripts Relating to Deuteronomy" (pp. 84-86). The comments verse by verse are quite good, but sometimes lacking in detail on views and arguments (e.g. on 18:15, the conviction that the passage is "prophetic in foreshadowing another Prophet . . . namely, Jesus" (p. 39), but with little discussion). — Dan Phillips

Deere, Jack S. "Deuteronomy" (Bible Knowledge Commentary), Volume I, ed. John F. Walvoord and Roy B. Zuck. Wheaton: Victor Books, 1983, pp. 259-324.

Conservative work showing experise in scholarly literature and handling of Hebrew exegesis, history, customs, etc. Deere provides help on synopses of sections and also the verse by verse explanation an expositor needs.

Driver, S. R. A Critical and Exegetical Commentary on Deuteronomy (ICC). NY: Scribner's, 1902.

Though liberal, the author is helpful in details if the student is aware of critical theories and can read discerningly.

Harrison, R. K. "Deuteronomy," New Bible Commentary Revised, ed. D. Guthrie et al. Grand Rapids: Eerdmans, 1970, pp. 201-29.

This is a very good evangelical work by a skilled Old Testament scholar. He favors Mosaic authorsip, but thinks Chapters 32-34 were added shortly after Moses' death, partly by Joshua (Moses' death) and partly by Eleazer (p. 203). Restricted by space, Harrison offers a helpful, concise commentary that contributes on most verses and problems.

Hillers, Delbert R. Covenant: The History of a Biblical Idea. Baltimore: Johns Hopkins, 1969.

This 188-pp. book is useful as an introductory survey of the covenant idea in the Old Testament and extra-biblical literature. Deuteronomy is dated late, whereas Kline (Treaty of the Great King) sees it as early.—-Dan Phillips

Keil, C. F. and Franz Delitzsch. The Pentateuch.

See annotation under Old Testament sets, Analytical.

Kline, Meredith. By Oath Consigned. Grand Rapids: Eerdmans, 1968.

This is a kind of sequel to the idea of a covenant in Treaty of the Great King (1963). Kline believes there is a treaty idea all through the Bible with the ordeal or self-malediction occurring with the forming or the renewing of a covenant. He develops circumcision (Old Testament) and baptism (New Testament) as ordeal rituals. Circumcision pointed on to Christ's death—a cutting off of God Himself in Christ, as he sees it. —Dan Phillips.

Kline, Meredith. Treaty of the Great King. Grand Rapids: Eerdmans, 1963.

A competent scholar wrote this book which most reviews hailed as an epochal work. Also see Kline's commentary on Deuteronomy in The Wycliffe Bible Commentary (Moody Press, 1962). The author investigates the relevance of recently discovered treaties of great kings to understanding the nature of the

Decalogue and the covenant in Deuteronomy. He wrestles with the statements of higher criticism. It is conservative.

Mayes, A. D. H. <u>Deuteronomy</u> **(New Centrury Bible Commentary). Grand Rapids: Eerdmans, 1981. 416 pp.**

This is by a lecturer in Hebrew and Semitics, University of Dublin. He is liberal, and his work is highly regarded by many. His exegesis is thorough and he has much excellent data on word meaning, background, etc., plus a good bibliography (pp. 9-23) and a lengthy introduction with a 3-page outline (27-108). As many he is persuaded that Deuteronomy is part of a larger deuteronomic history of Israel running through 2 Kings, a history finalized during the exile. He theorizes that particular verses were written later, according to his opinion. He feels Levites of the Jerusalem temple (p. 107) give the distilled teaching, so the historical background is there, not in the wilderness (81-82). Still, much of the verse by verse commentary has basic, explanatory material which conservative users with discernment can fit into the time of Moses and not in exilic days with Mayes. Mayes sees in 18:15 nothing of messianic connection, and has no reference to the New Testament use of it.

McCarthy, Dennis J. <u>Old Testament Covenant: A Survey of Current Opinions</u>**. Richmond, VA: John Knox Press, 1972. 108 pp.**

This little book (89 pp. plus a 19-pp. bibliography) gives a good survey of views and developments among scholars in this field up to the time of writing (cf. good review by Walter C. Kaiser, Jr., <u>JETS</u>, XV, Fall, 1962, 241-42).

Miller, Patrick D. <u>Deuteronomy</u> **(Interpretation series). Louisville: John Knox Press, 1990. 253 pp.**

This is a sweeping exposition with essays on structure, motifs and sections in the book and not a verse by verse discussion. Miller, Professor of Old Testament Theology at Princeton Theological Seminary, follows the line of many in thinking final redaction took place during Josiah's career. However, here he does not devote much time to this but has many helpful perceptions on the meaning of the text we have. His well-organized work aims to help teachers, preachers and students by commenting on the RSV translation. Synopses at the outset of chapters orientate readers to the setting and how the section of Deuteronomy fits in the book and what the structure of this unit is, in Miller's opinion. At times Miller serves up such arbitrary ideas as: "It is highly unlikely that we have here an accurate historical report of words and actions by Moses on the plains of Moab" (p. 25). However, the book draws spiritual life lessons which are quite worthwhile (cf. chs. 38-40, for example). It just will not set well with conservatives to be told that the concern for possession of the land in Deuteronomy is because the book was done centuries later than the wilderness era when Israel was in danger of being uprooted from the land (44). Even then, Miller has many helpful things summarized about the land (44-52).

Ridderbos, J. Deuteronomy (Bible Students Commentary). **Grand Rapids: Zondervan, 1984. 318 pp.**

This work is frequently quite helpful, sometimes valuable in dealing with verses in a concise, competent, direct exegesis based on obvious wide knowledge. Ridderbos is conservative, discussing but finding Wellhausian theory as to authorship and unity invalid; he argues that Moses was the author, with a few sections or parts by editorial work after Moses "under God's special providence" (p. 22). On many matters the commentary is satisfactory, getting at vital things fully enough for many teachers, preachers and diligent laypeople.

Schneider, Bernard N. Deuteronomy—A Favored Book of Jesus. **Grand Rapids: Eerdmans, 1970. 163 pp.**

This is an attempt to show the close tie between Jesus' teachings and Deuteronomy (a book quoted or alluded to ca. 90 times in the New Testament). Schneider says the emphasis in Deuteronomy is on God's love for His people. Moses poured out his heart telling the people of Israel the message of love God had given (p. 11). A reader looking not for a detailed commentary but for a book setting forth section by section the vital spiritual truths of Deuteronomy that are relevant today as in Moses' day will find many stimulating things here.

Schultz, Samuel J. Deuteronomy, The Gospel of Love. **Chicago: Moody Press, 1971.**

This is in The Everyman's Bible Commentary series. It provides a good, brief explanation with a clear outline. Like Schneider, Schultz shows that God's love is the heart of this book by Moses the lawgiver.

Thompson, J. A. Deuteronomy: An Introduction and Commentary (Tyndale Old Testament Commentary). **Downers Grove, IL: IVP, 1974.**

A helpful verse by verse work abreast of recent scholarship on many of the issues in Deuteronomy for the more serious reader. Thompson believes that the book is not authored by Moses, yet much of it goes back to the time of Moses. But "the present Deuteronomy represents the end-point of subsequent revisions both in language and in form," and is derived from "the re-application of the great principles of the covenant at Sinai to the changing conditions of a new age, be it that of Samuel, or Solomon, or Hezekiah, or Josiah" (pp. 46-47). The material is mostly from Moses' day and Israel's situation then. But it has been retouched to serve the needs of later generations in Israel. Cf. an evangelical evaluation of Thompson's concessions to critical scholarship along this line in Meredith G. Kline, review, Westminster Theological Journal, 39 (Fall, 1976), 168-70. Deuteronomy, to Thompson, shares in the pattern of the ancient form of a Near Eastern treaty (covenant). He does not interpret some things literally, e.g. the 40 days of Moses receiving the law could mean an indefinite time (p. 140). Though some conclusions run against the grain for one who holds to inerrancy,

Thompson in general says things consistent with a rather high view of the Bible, and evinces a scholarship of depth and breadth.

von Rad, Gerhard. <u>Deuteronomy, A Commentary</u> **(Old Testament Library). Philadelphia: Westminster, 1966.**

Well-regarded in much of the scholarly community, though among conservatives of occasional help only to more advanced students. The author holds to a complicated history of different compositions and, like many, subjectively picks and chooses as he will. Priestly and Levitical composers centuries after the wilderness period sought "to make the old cultic and legal traditions relevant for their time" (p. 23). These men fictionalized the idea that the sermons were spoken to Israel in Moab (28) when in actuality, as von Rad sees things, they were directed to Israel's needs centuries later. One can sift out much good explanation of what certain details mean, but he is often met by an intermeshing of theory about which parts are from the early days and which from the exile. The commentary is not verse by verse; it broadly gathers sometimes many verses into a paragraph or two, and often with more comment on von Rad's personal construction of things than on the canonical text. He deals only glancingly with the messianic possibility of 18:15, and without referring to the New Testament text. Quite frankly, despite the stature of von Rad to many, this work does not adequately enough get down to the straight-forward business of explaining passages in a way conservatives will regard as probable from the evidence—at least not often enough.

Weinfeld, Moshé. <u>Deuteronomy 1-11</u> **(Anchor Bible). NY: Doubleday, 1991. 458 pp. lst of 2 volumes.**

Serious, skilled students will find much help here on the details of text, meaning of words and phrases, history, etc., as well as bibliography. The introduction brings together much thought on literary-critical, legal, historical and theological matters. The list of journal articles runs nearly 36 pages. Much of the material is assigned to centuries later than Moses (p. 13). Many readers will feel that his reasons are arbitrary, yet may appreciate seeing how such a case may be built. While much benefit can be laboriously gleaned from individual verse notes, some will wish there could be better synthesizing orientation before the plunge into the many details. It is not easy to keep the book's movement in view due to the fragmented nature of the minute aspects, and so the work seems primarily of help to the very patient, advanced user. Often, Weinfeld furnishes very worthwhile comments on problems, such as whether to take as literal or figurative the binding of the words on the hand and on the forehead (6:8; pp. 341-42).

VI. JOSHUA

Boling, Robert G. and Wright, G. Ernest. <u>Joshua: A New Translation with Notes and Commentary</u> (Anchor Bible). NY: Doubleday, 1982. 580 pp.

This is thorough and in many places good help for indepth students who already have a background in Pentateuchal and conquest studies and want a laborious study. Much in the notes will not be meaningful for those without such preparation and a high motivation. Liberal assumptions are frequent, the introduction is wordy but highly informative (pp. 1-110), the bibliography is 19 pages, and there is considerable aid on philology, archeology, customs, and the text. Gleaning much from details, the student can lose the sweep of the book and not see the forest for the trees. At times the authors assume things where other explanations are possible. They say the two scouts went to Rahab's place and "Probably the narrator intends to titillate by reminding readers of an immediate symbiosis between military service and bawdy house" (p. 145). Sometimes one finds a different view from the norm: destroying Achan's family with him was probably not because of complicity or solidarity in guilt but due to peril of contamination that could spread to hurt others (225, 228).

Bright, John. <u>The Book of Joshua, Introduction and Exegesis</u> (Interpreter's Bible), Volume 2. Nashville: Abingdon Press, 1953. Pages 540-673.

Bright shows breadth in his introduction, surveying issues and scholarly discussion. He is concise and often provides good information on verses, and one will soon take note of his liberal approach. More advanced students will find a good amount of assistance here.

Bush, George. <u>Notes, Critical and Practical on the Book of Joshua.</u> NY: Ivison, Phinney and Company, 1862. Reprint. Minneapolis: Klock & Klock, 1981.

See annotations under Genesis, Exodus and other Pentateuchal works.

Butler, Trent C. <u>Joshua</u> (Word Biblical Commentary). Waco: Word Books, 1983. 304 pp.

The diligently prepared bibliography on each passage can be of much help, yet one sees infrequent awareness of conservative literature. Readers need to realize that Butler is not evangelical in the traditional sense of the word, despite the series' claim to be evangelical. He buys into a system that posits that material not historical fact is meshed with things that may be true, written during exilic times (pp. 99, 117, 125). The book is taken up with concerns burdening the believing community during the exile. Some things are concocted in order to further truth; Butler believes in an inspiration in which clashing traditions blend after the passage of time as God's Word. Still, his bibliographies can aid a serious researcher, and textual notes put forth considerable assistance.

Campbell, Donald. "Joshua," in <u>Bible Knowledge Commentary</u>, editors John F. Walvoord and Roy B. Zuck. Volume I. Wheaton: Victor Books, 1983, pp. 325-71.

A skilled Bible expositor for many years and more recently President of Dallas Theological Seminary gives a lucid, perceptive brief commentary drawn from careful study. He is helpful on synopsis that keeps the flow of the book in view and also in details of many verses—word meaning, customs, how problems may be resolved, and how things fit. Cf. also his book on Joshua, <u>No Time For Neutrality</u> (Wheaton: Victor Books, 1981, 143 pp.), with more application and illustration.

Cohen, A. <u>Joshua and Judges</u> (Soncino Series). London: Soncino Press, 1950. 333 pp.

The Hebrew text is given side by side with the Jewish Publication Society English translation in a 2-column format with the commentary below. The writer sees the writing as being by a contemporary eye-witness, Joshua, with a unity of purpose. Joshua wrote all but a few later additions. The comments are fairly good quite frequently, but most of the time are concise. Sensitivity of the writer to main things needing explanation makes the work rather helpful a good percentage of the time. To him, the sun standing still can be seen as a miracle or explained by natural phenomena.

Davis, Dale R. <u>No Falling Words. Expositions of the Book of Joshua.</u> Grand Rapids: Baker, 1988. 204 pp.

These 21 expositions are by a former Professor of Old Testament at Reformed Theological Seminary. Davis furnishes evangelical material to help preachers blend sound exegesis, theological substance, interesting exposition and practical application. Davis groups his chapters under Entering the Land (Joshua 1-4), Taking it (5-12), Possessing it (13-21), and Retaining it (22-24). He uses creative chapter titles. The book title comes from 21:45 (cf. 23:14). The studies are not on every verse but key portions out of each chapter, done in a very readable style. At times footnotes cite good sources and add important help. Overall the book is a good survey of Joshua that preachers or lay people can enjoy. It has many ideas to provoke sermons and point to application.

Davis, John J. <u>Conquest and Crisis. Studies in Joshua, Judges, and Ruth.</u> Grand Rapids: Baker, 1969. 176 pp.

These evangelical studies provide very helpful and pertinent background material as well as a survey of the main elements in the passages. He is particularly helpful on some of the main problem passages.

Enns, Paul. <u>Joshua</u> (Bible Study Commentary). Grand Rapids: Zondervan, 1981. 145 pp.

A very fine conservative survey, well-organized, summarizing sections well and explaining most verses awarely, making good suggestions on many of the problems expositors face. Often on problems, as the sun in Chapter 10, he discusses serveral views and documents well.

Goslinga, C. J. Joshua, Judges, Ruth (Bible Students Commentary). Grand Rapids: Zondervan, 1986. 558 pp.

This is substantial conservative commentary, Joshua running through page 195, Judges to 510, then Ruth. Goslinga gets down to business explaining in a straight-forward way. He argues in ten steps that the book is a unit by a contemporary of Joshua, possibly Phinehas (pp. 11-19). He sees no true contradictions (19-26) and favors an early exodus date. Judges, though recounting events of more than three hundred years, is drawn into a unity by a governing thread (198, 205, 214-17). Samuel or someone under his influence wrote Judges. Goslinga gives much space to chronological problems of Judges (223-35). He looks fairly at arguments for two views of what Jephthah did to his daughter and cautiously concludes that either is possible (391-96). Ruth, he decides, was written during Solomon's reign (cf. 4:7). Verses in the books are handled with deep reverence for the integrity, diligent work to offer help, and energy to set forth spiritual lessons.

Gray, John. Joshua, Judges and Ruth (New Century Bible). Greenwood, SC: Attic Press, 1967. 435 pp.

A liberal work from which one can carefully gather many helps on details of word meaning, customs, etc. But Gray follows many in assuming a composition centuries after alleged events, before 586 B. C., and a post-exilic redaction (p. 2). He often does not hold to historical accuracy but feels accounts were created later (19, 31, 37, 360-61, etc.). Subjectivity abounds in his preferences of what may be reliable and what may not. He imagines inconsistencies where many diligent students will not think his judgment reasonable or necessary (cf. p. 53), and often regards his own doubts as better than what the book says (cf. his comments on great hailstones in 10:11). Only more advanced students will be persevering to sift through his assessments of which supposed compositional tradition appears at a given point. In Judges 11 he takes the view that Jephthah offered his daughter in death but does not look at views. Likewise many other problem verses are not explained (14:4; 16:3, forty miles, etc.). At times, however, he mentions views (cf. Ruth 3:4, "uncovered his feet,") so that readers are made more aware of how a verse has been seen.

Hughes, R. Kent. Living on the Cutting Edge: Joshua and the Challenge of Spiritual Leadership. Westchester, IL: Crossway Books, 1987. 172 pp.

A warm, popular, broad exposition dealing with some chapters in Joshua. Hughes often has good insights on analogies from Israel's victories for growth and victory today, through God's strength. He shows traits for effective leadership. Most lessons are good. One that disappoints is, "Rahab's lie was a stupendous act of true faith" (p. 37). Well, yes, she lied, and yes, she did have faith. But who says it is necessary to make the lie a part of faith or faith a part of the lie? Cf.

also page 38: Hughes conveys the idea that a Christian musters faith out of a glass. In actuality, when we wrongly persuade ourselves that we have to clutch at certain means to come by faith, true faith is not generated by human fallacy but by the Lord, using means He can endorse, His Word etc. He can use us even though we fail Him by leaning on false means and tracing our effectiveness to those means, wrongly. Overall, the book is usually quite helpful for preaching or just for devotional aims.

Johnson, Alan F. <u>Thirty Days to Spiritual Power</u>. **Wheaton: Tyndale House, 1975.**

In thirty brief sections Johnson of Wheaton College (a past national president of Evangelical Theological Society) competently seeks to capture the main spiritual lessons of Joshua and Judges. He moves usually but not always chapter by chapter. He seeks to point out the relevance for life today. The book triggers many profitable thoughts for the lay reader or for the Christian worker feeding his life and preparing messages.

Meyer, F. B. <u>Choice Notes on Joshua - 2 Kings</u>. **Grand Rapids: Kregel, 1985. 221 pp.**

Meyer (1847-1929) published this originally in 1895. He left a big witness as a Christian, husband and expositor on the spiritual life. Here he is clear, simple, to the point, and practical in application. The book is especially suited for pastors, Sunday School teachers and laypersons. Sometimes he overdoes things, as in seeing Hittites and confederates as depicting "The evil habits of the old past" (p.12). Yet in many cases he is apt, as using Gideon to show the need to look to God for adequacy. He sees Saul as unsaved, having the Spirit on him but not in him (103).

Miller, J. M. and Tucker, Gene M. <u>The Book of Joshua</u> (**Cambridge Bible Commentary**). **Cambridge: U.P., 1974. 206 pp.**

Two associate professors of Old Testamemnt at Emory University use the NEB. Liberals, they assume a long literary history of traditions, with contradictions (pp. 10-11), finally compiled ca. 550 B. C. (5). "Much of the material is too late to be very reliable" (12). Pages 7-14 sum up reasons they will not comment on the book as reliable history. Their commentary is only on clusters of verses generally, having some good insights, some assumptions which fault the biblical record but which are not really required by it, etc. Many expositors will feel they can get far more help from works by Davis, Enns, Wood, the <u>Expositor's Bible Commentary</u>, etc., which deal with Joshua in a dependable and fair way.

Pink, Arthur W. <u>Gleanings in Joshua</u>. **Chicago: Moody, 1964.**

This is a good devotional work on Joshua, though his study of types is overdrawn.

Rawlinson, George.   Joshua: His Life and Times.   NY: Revell (n. d.).

Here is a valuable work to have because it is very good from the historical standpoint.

Redpath, Alan.   Victorious Christian Living.   Westwood, New Jersey: Revell, 1955.

Though not exegetical or scholarly, this work will be a blessing to laymen and also to a pastor, teacher, or Christian leader in some other capacity. It is popular in its thrust and written by a well-known and beloved speaker at Bible conferences as well as former pastor of the Moody Memorial Church in Chicago. He skips around, dealing only with certain verses, and writes in a sermonic style.

Schaeffer, Francis.   Joshua and the Flow of Biblical History.   Downers Grove: IVP, 1975.

The man who led the L'Abri Fellowship in the Swiss Alps shows that the book is a bridge between the Pentateuch and the rest of Scripture. The rest is in continuity with the first five books. Continuities that go on are the written book, God's power, and the supernatural leader. Schaeffer shows how "alive" the text is by drawing lessons that can apply now as well as in the time of Joshua's conquest. This is a conservative, refreshing, absorbing flow of comment through Joshua. It is a companion volume to his Genesis in Space and Time. His style is somewhat sermonic at times in dealing with major characters and incidents. He highlights central truths in each chapter of Joshua. A good book to prime personal study and home Bible studies.

Scroggie, W. Graham.   Joshua in the Light of the New Testament: The Land and Life of Rest.   Grand Rapids: Kregel, 1981.

This reprint of the 1950 edition shows a life of faith that rests in an inner peace drawn from the sufficiency of God and lived out in a life of costly effort that triumphs. Scroggie (1877-1958) pastored in Halifax, Sunderland, Edinburgh and Spurgeon's Tabernacle in London. He also was a teacher and spiritual life speaker at Bible conferences, known for diligently-studied expositions. He is best remembered for his three volume Unfolding Drama of Redemption and his gold mine called Guide to the Gospels. Here he is profitable in organizing some key lessons based on Joshua. Originally a series of Bible readings at the English Keswick Conference, this is another warm devotional treatment of Joshua.

Soggin, J. A.   Joshua, A Commentary (Old Testament Library).   Philadelphia: Wesminster Press, 1972.   245 pp.

This liberal book follows generally-accepted theory that late dates the Book of Joshua to a composition centuries after the conquest. Soggin casts much denial on Joshua having the place in leading Israel in a unified conquest as the book shows. To Soggin, this is "a fictional construction" (p. 17); for Joshua's exploits were read back into things so as to have a well-known representative in Israel's history (18). Often Soggin imposes contradictions on the text which many will not consider necessary. For example, he has 1:10-13 teach a peaceable conquest, then 1:4ff a military thrust (33). It seems to strain his credulity that a prostitute would put herself at such risk with her own people in Joshua 2 (40). The Ark, he feels, could not have been used so early in conquering Jericho (87). He is skeptical about the numbers of Israelites in 7:5 (104), and feels the address in Joshua 23 is derived from the one in Chapter 24 (227). Yet his massive scholarship often has really helpful explanation, as regarding the flat roof where the scouts hid (41). In Joshua 10 he refers to ancient accounts of a god helping warriors win by delaying the sun's setting, as well as further views, but favors a miracle in the biblical case (123). He has a commanding grasp of views on some of the passages, at least from liberal works such as Noth's, and shows the problems many find in all the passages.

Wood, Leon J. A Survey of Israel's History. **Grand Rapids: Zondervan, 1986. Revised, enlarged by David O'Brien from 1970 ed.**

Chapter 8 surveys the Joshua period succinctly but very helpfully in conservative style, dealing with main problems such as the long day and providing frequently good footnotes. Another fine survey of conservatives is by John J. Davis & John C. Whitcomb, Israel, A Commentary on Joshua—2 Kings (Grand Rapids: Baker, 1989, 542 pp.). The latter work combines three former books, Conquest and Crisis, The Birth of a Kingdom and Solomon to the Exile. The section on Joshua, as the other parts, offers comments that pull together main truths and seek to assist on main problems even to the extent of giving views and reasons.

Woudstra, Marten H. Joshua **(New International Commentary of the Old Testament). Grand Rapids: Eerdmans, 1981. 396 pp.**

A conservative effort that may well be the best overall commentary on Joshua so far, this holds to a possible authorship in Joshua's day or that of the elders who outlived him (p. 13). He argues for unity of composition even if with sources and brings immense scholarly awareness and use of recent literature to his commentary verse by verse. He explains matters in a careful vein kept in key with a high view of the book's reliability, so he is quite helpful to conservatives while maintaining a readability that serves teachers, pastors, and laypeople.

VII. JUDGES (cf. also on Joshua)

Barber, Cyril J. Judges, A Narrative of God's Power. **Neptune, NJ: Loizeaux Brothers, 1990. 293 pp.**

A well-organized, conservative exposition arising out of much study and skill in showing how alive biblical passages are. The Dale Davis book is fairly good, but this one is even better overall, although Barber does not see impropriety in some of Samson's episodes with women as he interprets the texts differently. Barber uses captivating headlines for sections, a vivid flow, arousing descriptions, analogies, illustrations, and applications. He deals with many problems awarely, using notes that sometimes are rather lengthy and meaty. Like Davis, he is competent, thought-provoking, and often sharp in exposing the timeliness of the book for life today.

Blaikie, William. Judges. In The Expositors Bible. **NY:** Loizeaux, Inc. (n. d.).

This is not a verse by verse commentary but a work with helpful character studies, since Judges is predominantly a series of lives.

Boling, R. G. Judges: Introduction, Translation and Notes **(Anchor). Garden City, NY: Doubleday, 1975. 339 pp.**

The "Notes" sections have much help in textual, exegetical and philological areas to explain passages. The work is liberal, claiming that later priestly editors finalized it in exilic days (pp. 32, 34). Boling assumes strands of material as if established fact. Comments on which alleged strand a passage is assigned to must be weighed by conservatives (63, etc). Boling offers very thin help on some problems, as Jephthah's fulfilling of his vow, or how 14:4 or 15:4 can be resolved, etc. He has a long introduction acquainting readers with scholarly thought (3-45), a selective bibliography (43-45), and is quite helpful on some verses, more usable to the trained student who can discerningly choose what is good and leave what is misleading.

Bruce, F. F. "Judges" in New Bible Commentary Revised, **ed. D. Guthrie et al. Grand Rapids: Eerdmans, 1970.**

A brief, evangelical commentary by the renowned scholar who always has much that helps.

Burney, C. F. The Book of Judges. **London: Rivingtons, 1920.**

This, like the commentary by Moore, is a minute study of the text verse by verse from a critical standpoint. It is later than Moore.

Bush, George. Notes, Critical and Practical on the Book of Judges. **NY: Ivison, Phinney and Co., 1844. Rp Minneapolis: Klock & Klock, 1981.**

See comments earlier on his works.

Cohen, A. Cf. on Joshua.

Cundall, Arthur and Leon Morris. Judges and Ruth. **Wheaton: Tyndale House, 1968.**

This is a competent Tyndale Old Testament commentary even though somewhat brief. It enables the student to get at the meaning of the books more readily than the more detailed works. The writers pack a lot of expertise into verses.

Davis, Dale R. <u>Such A Great Salvation.</u> **Grand Rapids: Baker, 1990. 227 pp.**

A flowing, popular conservative exposition that can be suggestive for pastors on individual messages or series. Davis deals with problems in footnotes. He keeps the vital message foremost and points out the relevance to today. The book is usually refreshing to help one grow in grace. Davis keeps spotlighting the beauty of God. Cf. also his book on Joshua.

Davis, John J. **Cf. his book listed under Wood on Joshua, and cf. the Wood book as well.**

Both have very good survey material from a conservative standpoint, helpful on synopsis and problem passages.

Enns, Paul. <u>Judges</u> **(Bible Study Commentary). Grand Rapids: Zondervan, 1982. 148 pp.**

If one wants down to business exposition, well-organized, with keen sensitivity to providing help on problem texts, this is a very good, brief conservative work by a clear, diligent student. It almost always goes right to the point, deals with pertinent questions, and always upholds a high view of the passages as being the Word of God.

Goslinga, C. J. **Cf. on Joshua.**

This, too, is a fine conservative commentary on Judges, usually quite solid and helpful.

Hercus, John. <u>God is God.</u> **London: Hodder, 1971.**

In a book moving like a fast-paced novel, Hercus grips readers with God's action in the episodes. He shows how alive and provocative the passages are with principles to apply and writes in an arresting style. The book is most usable as a refresher for pastors and a nourishment for laypeople wanting help in worship. A brief, modern effort to retell the stories of Judges in a captivating way and show how God is involved.

Lewis, Arthur. <u>Judges and Ruth</u> **(Everyman's Bible Commentary). Chicago: Moody, 1979. 128 pp.**

Though not as contributive as the work by Enns, also concise, this will help pastors with a quick review and provide material for Bible class teachers and laypeople. At times, the generalizing such as on Jephthah's vow offers no real explanation, yet he is better on some hard verses as 14:4, even if always brief.

Lindsey, F. Duane. **"Judges," in** <u>Bible Knowledge Commentary</u>**, ed. John F. Walvoord and Roy B. Zuck, Volume 1. Wheaton: Victor Books, 1983.**

Dallas Seminary faculty member gives a knowledgeable survey providing assistance on many of the normal problems pastors and Bible class teachers encounter in the book.

Meyer, F. B.   Cf. on Joshua.

Moore, George F.   A Critical and Exegetical Commentary on Judges (ICC).   NY: Scribners, 1901.

This is a thorough study of the text and is valuable from the historical and philological standpoint. It is among the better works in the I.C.C. series, though liberal in approach.

Soggin, J. Alberto.   Judges: A Commentary (Old Testament Library).   Philadelphia: Westminster, 1981.

This is part of the Westminster Old Testament Library series. Writing from the perspective of recent higher critical conviction, Soggin handles passages with awareness of a broad spectrum of views, even by conservative Christian scholars. In each section he offers a bibliography, translation, discussion of textual and philological points, and his commentary. Liberal work along similar lines to his book on Joshua (cf. on Joshua).

Wood, Leon J.   Distressing Days of the Judges.   Grand Rapids: Zondervan, 1975. 434 pp.

This is an outstanding work by a firm evangelical scholar. The book discusses in detail many of the key problems expositors need help on in the book. It provides solid help in understanding the main aspects of most sections. It is one of the most valuable books on the period of the judges and on character sketches of the main judges.

VIII. RUTH (cf. also Joshua and Judges)

Atkinson, David.   The Wings of Refuge: The Message of Ruth.   Downers Grove, IL: InterVarsity Press, 1983.   128 pp.

Atkinson, Chaplain of Corpus Christi College at Oxford in England has written this paperback for the Bible Speaks Today series. The author has set out to acquaint the readers with the overpowering concept of "providence." He reflects an awareness of liberal criticisms of the book, but offers little defense in the areas of authorship, dating, or time and place of writing. He prefers a 12/11th century B. C. setting, making Ruth a contemporary of the period of the Judges. At the same time, however, Atkinson does entertain the thoughts that pre-Deuteronomic ideas are present within the book. Thus, critical matters are not the author's primary concern. Atkinson has written a volume which will aid the Bible student/pastor in his appreciation for the "providence" motif. —Jan Sattem

Barber, Cyril J.   Ruth, A Story of God's Grace.   Neptune, NJ: Loizeaux Brothers, 1989.   198 pp.   Originally Ruth, An Expositional Commentary.   Chicago: Moody, 1983.

As on Judges, this conservative is creatively lucid in a way many pastors, students and laypeople in general will value. This time he has nine chapters, furnished with footnotes placed at the end, some having substantial added help drawn from wide reading. A section on critical studies (pp. 131-47) takes up authorship, date, unity of the genealogy in Chapter 4 with the rest of the book, and themes. Good illustrations appear at times. Barber usually touches briefly on problems, such as in defending the chastity of Boaz and Ruth in lying near one another, and explains customs.

Campbell, E. F.   Ruth: A New Translation with Introduction, Notes and Commentary (Anchor Bible).   NY: Doubleday, 1975.   189 pp.

A highly regarded work steeped in knowledge on words, often discussed in detail. A long introduction informs the reader of issues, and the verse by verse commentary offers much on exegesis. One is provided with a wealth of information from many sides and can be steeped in the scenes. Campbell, however, will not meet with some conservatives' approval in some matters, such as feeling that the genealogy (4:18-22) was not a part of the original book but appended later (172-73).

Cox, Samuel.   The Book of Ruth.   London: The Religious Tract Society, 1922 revised edition.

A devotional work, this is also helpful in Hebrew word studies and in explaining difficult passages. It is conservative.

Cundall, Arthur E. and Leon Morris.   Judges and Ruth (Tyndale Old Testament Commentary).   Downers Grove, IL: IVP, 1968.

These are fine commentaries based on a great breadth of reading. Some views favored, however, do not reflect that proper weight has been given to evidence, e. g. they hold a late date of the exodus (28-29) and understand I Kings 6:1 (480 years) as representing twelve generations of 40 years, not a strictly accurate number (31). Cundall has a stimulating discussion of moral problems raised by the book of Judges (41-45), using Samson as an example. Both commentators provide a competent verse by verse explanation. Often they defend against attacks on the reasonableness of details. —Jan Sattem in part.

Davis, John J.   Cf. Wood on Joshua.

Enns, Paul.   Ruth (Bible Study Commentary).   Grand Rapids: Zondervan, 1982. 75 pp.

He deals with Ruth as with Joshua and Judges (cf. those books). This is a fine conservative, concise commentary.

Goslinga, C. J.   Cf. on Joshua.

Gray, John.   Cf. on Joshua.

Hals, Ronald.   The Theology of the Book of Ruth.   Philadelphia: Fortress Press, 1969.

Here is an exhaustive work, mediating, sometimes good and sometimes weak where he imagines things in passages beyond the evidence. Overall it has many helps. A thorough, insightful discussion of theological aspects, though some will feel that Hals sees more than there is in some details. The book is not a commentary but is frequently of great help to expositors.

Hubbard, Robert L., Jr.   The Book of Ruth (New International Commentary on the Old Testament).   Grand Rapids: Eerdmans, 1988.   317 pp.

The Professor of Hebrew at Denver Theological Seminary holds that the book dates from Solomon's era, to which the genealogy of Ruth 4 brings matters, and is a unity including 4:18-22. In detail verse by verse Hubbard is thorough and knowledgeable, documents well, sizes up issues from several angles, is skilled as to customs, and is adept in literature relating to the book. He writes primarily for pastors and laypeople.

Kennedy, A. R. S.   The Book of Ruth.   NY: Macmillan Co., 1937.

A person able to use the Hebrew text will benefit from this careful study that furnishes much information and insight.

Leggett, Donald A.   The Levirate and Goel Institutions in the Old Testament with Special Attention to the Book of Ruth.   Cherry Hill, NJ: Mack Publishing Co., 1974.

A specialized investigation that the diligent student may wish to consult for depth on customs in the Book of Ruth and how they worked.

Lewis, Arthur.   Cf. on Judges.

Mauro, Philip.   Ruth, The Satisfied Stranger.   NY: Revell, 1920.

Vigorous Bible study suggestive for expositors looking for possibilities in applying the truth. Conservative.

McGee, J. Vernon.   Ruth, The Romance of Redemption.   Findlay, OH: Dunham (n.d.).

In the opinion of the compiler, this is quite a fine expository work on Ruth. It is detailed and well footnoted. The author was pastor of the Church of the Open Door in Los Angeles, 1949-1971, before entering full-time radio and Bible conference ministry.

Meyer, F. B.   Cf. on Joshua.

Moorhouse, Henry. <u>Ruth, the Moabitess.</u> **Chicago: Revell, 1881.**

Many times the old works have much value, as here. This work is devotional and practical, by a preacher Dwight L. Moody liked to hear.

Myers, J. M. <u>The Linguistic and Literary Form of the Book of Ruth.</u> **Leiden: E. J. Brill, 1955.**

Scholarly study, often with much help on the subject of the title. The advanced student, even many pastors who study much, can find substantial benefit here.

Wood, Leon J. **Cf. on Joshua.**

IX. I AND II SAMUEL

Ackroyd, Peter R. <u>The First Book of Samuel</u> **(Cambridge Bible Commentary). Cambridge: U. P., 1971. 238 pp.**

This is much the same as his work on the second book of Samuel (cf. that entry).

Ackroyd, Peter R. <u>The Second Book of Samuel</u> **(Cambridge Bible Commentary). Cambridge: U. P., 1977. 247 pp.**

An attempt to meet general readers' needs. The approach is mildly critical. Ackroyd has a clear writing style and often is of help on the reading of a given text, historical setting, customs and explanation of the passage. The work is cursory.

Anderson, A. A. <u>2 Samuel</u> **(Word Biblical Commentary). Waco, TX: Word Books, 1989. 302 pp.**

Conservatives will find much to aid them here in meticulous exegetical detail and giving of different views, all done quite readably. One is soon aware, however, of the nonconservative perspective, as in supposing errors as to historical fact, misstatements, and portions ineptly inserted by an exilic redactor (cf. pp. 118-19, 132, 161, 168 etc.). Users will have to use the work with much carefulness but can glean heavy profit from places where he contributes well. Anderson is Honorary Fellow in theology, University of Manchester, England. His introduction takes up theories of composition that specialized scholars can follow completely. Many things said in Samuel are attributed to the artistic skill of the author, and one gains the impression that to Anderson they are not historically reliable (xxxiv, etc.). The form/structure/setting sections have much that can help evangelicals and much that gives liberal slants based on ideas of theoretical sources. Careful advanced students can sift out much and leave much. Like Klein's work on I Samuel, the flow is broken in many ways, so the use of the commentary for any but specialist students will be slow plodding.

Baldwin, Joyce C. 1 and 2 Samuel: An Introduction and Commentary (Tyndale Old Testament Commentary). Grand Rapids: Eerdmans, 1988. 299 pp.

A concise, competent, clear evangelical work using various sources, elucidating most passages well and showing their theological and practical relevance then and now.

Barber, Cyril J. and Carter, John. I Samuel, Always a Winner. A Bible Commentary for Laymen. Glendale, CA: G/L Publications, 1977. 160 pp.

Sunday School or Bible class teachers and laypeople in general can gain good ideas on how to present material, how to explain some of the main customs and resolve certain problems. The book is simple, well-organized, refreshing for a series of Bible readings in devotional times, but also has frequent things that stimulate for preaching.

Blaikie, William. Samuel. 2 volumes (The Expositors Bible). NY: A. C. Armstrong, 1903.

Historically helpful, the work offers rich character studies.

Cummings, John. Sabbath Morning Readings on the Old Testament: The First and Second Books of Samuel. London: Arthur Hall, Virtue, 1859.

These are Sunday morning expositions on characters and events. They are suggestive in sermonic material.

Davis, John J. Cf. on Joshua, under Wood.

Driver, S. R. Notes on the Hebrew Text and the Topography of the Books of Samuel. Oxford: Clarendon Press, 1913. 2nd edition.

This liberal work is a detailed discussion of Hebrew philology and textual criticism in Samuel. It is for the student who can use his Hebrew well.

Faulstich, E. W. Historical Harmony of the Hebrew Kings. Spencer, IA: Chronology Books, 1986. 304 pp.

The author says he will defend the Bible text vs. rationalism (pp. 2-3). His plan is in using a computer printout of astronomical events and matching things up with these dates from ancient Near Eastern literature. He assumes that biblical numbers are reliable because scribes were under the auspices of God and exacting in writing such detail. Cf. also James D. Newsome, Jr., ed., A Synoptic Harmony of Samuel, Kings, and Chronicles, with Related Passages from Psalms, Isaiah, and Ezra. Grand Rapids: Baker, 1986. 275 pp. This is an English harmony setting texts side by side, using the RSV but basing work on the Massoretic text from I Samuel 31 through 2 Chronicles 36 (cf. also Wm. D. Crockett, A Harmony of the Books of Samuel, Kings and Chronicles. Grand Rapids: Baker, 1985 rp of 1951 ed.). Newsome's layout is easier to use. In cases of tension Newsome suggests possibilities. Many will regard it as a weakness that the harmony is in texts as given in Scripture, not necessarily in actual chronology of events in the books.

He does not take up the issue of problems as the chronology in these biblical chapters. Cf. also John H. Hayes and Paul K. Hooker, <u>A New Chronology for the Kings of Israel and Judah and its Implications for Biblical History and Literature</u>. Atlanta: John Knox, 1988. 112 pp. These writers from Emory University reject co-regencies, antedating and emendations. They say that the regnal years for Israel and Judah were dated from the first Fall New Year festival when a king was on the throne (this switched from Tishri to Nisan in Josiah's reign), and they use only Massoretic Text numbers. They offer their own explanations for numbers being inconsistent. Big problems persist at several reigns (pp. 23, 28, 33, 74 and others). Work by Thiele (cf. under Kings) has long been regarded well by many conservatives.

Gordon, R. P.   <u>1 and 2 Samuel: A Commentary</u>.   Grand Rapids: Zondervan, 1986. 375 pp.

This generally high-regarded work offers much assistance verse by verse, using the RSV. The author comments a lot on the Hebrew text as to exegesis, word study, dealing with problems, etc.

Klein, Ralph W.   <u>I Samuel</u> (Word Bible Commentary).   Waco, TX: Word, 1983. 307 pp.

A detailed work that often assumes liberal, hard-to-follow ideas positing literary strands from various sources in the book. Klein feels that some accounts cannot be harmonized (xxx). Theories of textual criticism will be a frequent problem for many evangelicals, and much is unclear except to specialists. Still, a lot in the general summary explanations of passages is helpful for the patient and shows how things fit. For more advanced scholarly use the many lists of literature on sections can offer aid, and notes on technical matters in verses specify word meanings, readings, etc. The reader, however, will meet with many liberal perspectives. For the most part the helpful flow of I Samuel bogs down even for serious students in the mixture of explanation and heavy material or theory from Klein's critical system.

Kirkpatrick, A. F. (ed.)   <u>The First Book of Samuel</u> (Cambridge Bible for Schools and Colleges).   Cambridge: University Press, 1911.

Originally published in 1880, this work takes the book as written not by Samuel but by some compiler who used several sources-chronicles of Samuel (chs. 1-24), Nathan and Gad and also writings in the school of prophets. It is taken to have been put together soon after the beginning of the Divided Kingdom. There is a detailed outline at the beginning, good surveys of the life and work of Samuel, the prophetic order, Saul and David, a commentary that touches on most of the main points, and helpful appendices on such topics as the Lord of hosts, Philistines, and exterminations by the Israelites.

Laney, J. Carl. **First and Second Samuel.** **Chicago, IL:** **Moody Press, 1982.** **132 pp.**

Laney, an assistant professor of Biblical literature at Western Conservative Baptist Seminary and more widely known for his volume The Divorce Myth, traces the lives of Samuel, Saul and David. This 1982 update for Moody Press's Everyman's Bible Commentary Series is a surprisingly resourceful paperback. Laney argues tersely for a 722 B. C. date for the Fall of Samaria. Thus, he prefers a time of writing for I & II Samuel sometime during or immediately following David's lifetime. He dates the dividing of the kingdom as 931 B. C. Regarding textual matters, Laney does not overlook the lacuna of I Samuel 13:1 as he states that great benefit can be gleaned from the LXX in a study of these two books. One interesting sidelight is his citation of the "dynastic defense" motif evident in I Samuel 15 and II Samuel 8, a setting apparently not unlike a 13th Century Hittite tradition. Laney's discussion of God's will in I Samuel 8:21, 22 is quite helpful. In I Samuel 28 the treatment of the Witch of Endor is thorough. He concludes that God caused Samuel himself to appear. In II Samuel 7, Laney sheds light on the covenant by picturing its threefold nature. Laney's maps and graphics are well-placed and worthwhile. His treatment in II Samuel 24 of the two-sided nature of David numbering God's people is also worthy of attention. This is a well researched and supported volume. There are few volumes on I & II Samuel which could claim to be more helpful on expositional matters. —Jan Sattem

McCarter, P. Kyle Jr. **I Samuel: A New Translation with Introduction and Commentary** (Anchor Bible). **NY:** **Doubleday, 1980.** **475 pp.**

McCarter writes this liberal work out of an immensely broad awareness of scholarly literature (cf. his 14-pp. bibliography, textual notes and informed way of handling many of the problem texts). He goes after the meaning of a passage, seeks to reach defensible conclusions, provides one of the best recent, up-to-date commentaries for more advanced students needing technical help on I Samuel, and is conversant with critical studies. Cf. also his work II Samuel, also in the Anchor Bible (553 pp.). He is Professor of Religious Studies at the University of Virginia.

Merrill, Eugene. **"I and II Samuel,"** **Bible Knowledge Commentary,** **ed. John F. Walvoord and Roy B. Zuck.** **Volume I.** **Wheaton:** **Victor Books, 1983.**

Professor of Old Testament at Dallas Theological Seminary surveys both books with conservative expertise, dealing with Hebrew meaning, problems, customs, etc. He has a high view of inspiration and a good use of literature relevant in the area.

Meyer, F. B. **Cf. under Joshua.**

Vos, Howard F.   1, 2 Samuel (Bible Study Commentary).   Grand Rapids: Zondervan, 1983.   166 pp.

Vos was Professor of History and Archaeology, King's College, Briarcliff Manor, New York. In this conservative work he gives a long outline at the outset, then incorporates this in his survey of 1 and 2 Samuel. For many Bible teachers, preachers, and lay people the exposition helpfully sums up what is said and some implications. It offers brief explanation of some main problems, such as the number judged at Beth Shemesh in I Samuel 6:19ff. and how to fill in the number of Saul's years in 13:1.

Wood, Leon J.   Cf. under Joshua.

X. KINGS

Constable, Thomas.   "I and II Kings," in Bible Knowledge Commentary, ed. John F. Walvoord and Roy B. Zuck.   Volume I.   Wheaton: Victor Books, 1983.

Constable shows awareness of Hebrew word meanings, has much good exegesis and judicious comments on many of the verses, even if brief. On several problem areas he offers helpful data, and reflects awareness of literature. This is a contributive conservative effort.

Davis, John J.   Cf. Joshua, under Wood.

DeVries, S. J.   I Kings (Word Biblical Commentary).   Waco: Word Books, 1985.   286 pp.

This is a rather well-studied work offering frequent help on word meaning, views on problems, background, customs, etc. Used by conservatives who exercise discernment and see better possibilities for a high view of biblical accuracy at some points, it can be of considerable help. Cf. on Chronicles.

Dilday, Russell H.   "1, 2 Kings," in The Communicator's Commentary.   Waco: Word Books, 1987.   512 pp.

The president of Southwestern Baptist Theological Seminary in Fort Worth, Texas has given a thoroughly studied, clear, well-illustrated and applied work that furnishes rich assistance to an expositor. Dilday frequently gives different views on an issue and includes many footnotes with further sources for added help.

Gray, John.   I & II Kings.   London: SCM Press, 1964.

This is an attempt to provide a fresher technical, liberal commentary than the work of Montgomery which preceded it by 13 years. It uses works of the German form critical approach.

Hendricks, Howard. Elijah. Chicago: Moody, 1972.

Here are expository messages by one of America's long-time noted spiritual life speakers, a professor at Dallas Theological Seminary. Hendricks developed these lessons in Bible conference ministry, making them practical to effect change. They are suggestive for preachers and devotionally stimulating for any readers.

Hobbs, T. R. 2 Kings (Word Biblical Commentary). Waco: Word Books, 1985. 388 pp.

He places the writing in the early part of the captivity by one writer, and is thorough on literature pertaining to 2 Kings as well as on matters of text, exegesis and theology. Students can glean considerable material that is worthwhile.

Jones, G. H. 1 and 2 Kings. 2 volumes (New Century Bible). Grand Rapids: Eerdmans, 1984. 666 pp.

This liberal work is steeped in ponderous scholarly literature (cf. a long bibliography) and has an introduction of around 85 pages which pulls readers abreast of discussion and views up to the early 1980's, heavily so in liberal circles. Jones sees discrepancies between the Greek tradition and the Massoretic Text. He does not accept co-regencies as E. Thiele does to harmonize kings' reigns. Rather he uses basically K. T. Anderson's system of taking MT figures, consulting the LXX at some points, concluding some contradictions, etc. His own opinion picks and chooses arbitrarily what he wishes to regard as historically accurate and what he thinks is fictionalized addition (cf. 2 Kings 18-20, pp. 556-95).

Knapp, Christopher. The Kings of Judah and Israel. NY: Loizeaux, 1956.

The author, who served as an evangelist in the Bahamas and a missionary to Honduras, Central America, has given here a biography of each king in Judah and Israel. He traces the characteristics and accomplishments of each reign. In each case, he draws together all of the Bible references to the king's reign, gives the names of prophets ministering in his day, and presents a key verse which summarizes that reign in a nutshell. He has good sketches of the kings.

McNeely, Richard I. First and Second Kings. Chicago, IL: Moody Press, 1978.

McNeely, formerly Professor of Biblical Studies at Biola University, has written a readily understandable account (158 pp.) of events and kings in these books. McNeely's style allows the reader to be drawn into the milieu. He divides the book into seven areas, focusing on major kings and occurrences. In abbreviated treatments McNeely attempts most chronological reconciliations. He advocates the schema of Edwin Thiele. This addition to the Everyman's Bible Commentary is helpful to new believers and laymen in a Bible study or Sunday school format. — Jan Sattem

Meyer, F. B. Cf. on Joshua.

Meyer, F. B.   Elijah and the Secret of His Power.   Chicago: Revell, n. d.

Perceptive on many of the devotional principles, and often refreshing.

Montgomery, J. A.   A Critical and Exegetical Commentary on the Book of Kings. NY: Scribners, 1951.

In an area of Scripture not frequently studied by Christians or made the source of sermons, Montgomery has provided a detailed work of a critical nature. A part of the I.C.C., it is often noted by conservative scholars as among the best single volumes in the entire set. The archaeological material throwing light on the era of the monarchy and the divided kingdom, plus the philological study, make the book very helpful.

Patterson, R. D. and Hermann J. Austel.   "1 and 2 Kings," Expositor's Bible Commentary,   Volume 4, ed. F. Gaebelein and R. P. Polcyn.   Grand Rapids: Zondervan, 1988.

Staunch conservative work very well done in detail verse by verse, handling problems, using a wide range of relevant literature. The reader finds both the regular commentary and the notes sections packed with pertinent information.

Pink, A. W.   The Life of Elijah.   Grand Rapids: Zondervan, 1956;   also Gleanings from Elisha.   Chicago: Moody, 1972.

Rich devotional thoughts, frequently, on the character and situation of each prophet.

Thiele, Edwin R.   The Mysterious Numbers of the Hebrew Kings.   Grand Rapids: Zondervan, 1983,   revision of 1951 and 1965 eds.

This is not a commentary but is very important since it is an outstanding work on the problems of chronology during the kings period. It is not an easy book to read because of the involved and intricate nature of working through seeming discrepancies of dates in the Biblical record and because of the many citations the author must make from ancient sources. But, for the serious student, it is an indispensable work.

Wallace, Ronald.   Elijah and Elisha. Expositions from the Books of Kings. Grand Rapids: Eerdmans, 1957.

As in his works on New Testament parables and miracles, Wallace is lucid on themes, principles, etc.

Wood, Leon J.   Cf. on Joshua.

Wood, Leon J.   Elijah, Prophet of God.   Des Plaines, IL: Regular Baptist Press, 1968.

A careful, informed evangelical scholar writes with great benefit on themes and applications, and helps on problem passages.

Wood, Leon J.   <u>Israel's United Monarchy</u>.   Grand Rapids: Baker, 1979.

Wood develops material surveying the kings, explaining difficult passages, and pointing out pertinent truths that are of value.

XI. CHRONICLES

Ackroyd, Peter R.   <u>I and II Chronicles, Ezra and Nehemiah</u>.   London: SCM Press, 1973.

Liberal, using redaction criticism quite a lot. Perceptive and advanced students can sift out much that is of worth on the meaning of verses or pericopes.

Braun, R. L.   <u>I Chronicles</u> (Word Biblical Commentary).   Waco: Word Books, 1986. 312 pp.

As one becomes accustomed to this series, he knows he will find much usable detail on the text, aspects of exegesis, customs, geography, and theological focus. He also comes to realize the contrast, at some points, with conservative convictions about the historicity of matters, and wisely gleans out what is worthwhile.

DeVries, Simon J.   <u>1 and 2 Chronicles</u> (Forms of the Old Testament Literature Series). Grand Rapids: Eerdmans, 1989.   439 pp.

Such a work will show serious readers advanced in theological training how a scholar has done a form-critical analysis. One also will see discusssion on the history of such study. The work probes the structure, genre, setting and aim of each section, according to the opinion of DeVries, which the conservative student may find of value or pass up for what he regards as a more defensible view. Such study can be very insightful at times but also can be quite arbitrary and subjective.

Dillard, Raymond B.   <u>2 Chronicles</u> (Word Biblical Commentary).   Waco: Word Books, 1987.   323 pp.

Cf. Braun for I Chronicles. Much the same comment is fitting here. One can feel he has a gold mine on many details of verse meaning and on bibliography, yet be aware of a less than conservative way of handling many things.

Ellison, H. L.   "1 and 2 Chronicles," in <u>New Bible Commentary Revised</u>, ed. D. Guthrie et al.   Grand Rapids: Eerdmans, 1970.

Ellison is limited to pp. 369-94. Like Cundall on Ezra and Nehemiah, he argues unity with Ezra and Nehemiah and a date around 400-340 B. C. (p. 369). He assumes that many problems in numbers arose from textual corruption, poor transmission of the text of Chronicles, and other explanations. Overall his commentary is a fair, concise work that often provides some help of an evangelical nature.

Elmsley, W. A. Leslie. The Books of Chronicles, With Maps, Notes and Introduction. Cambridge: University Press, 1916. Second Edition.

This edition follows the first edition by W. E. Barnes in 1899. Elmsley incorporates much of the same material but at some points gives improved wording or even additional material enlarging on the subject. Liberal views show in certain places, but the commentary is quite helpful in general.

Kelly, William. Lessons on the Books of Chronicles. Oak Park, Illinois: Bible Truth Publishers, 1963.

This work is sketchy (only 109 pp.) but helpful for a general, quick survey. As is to be expected, there can be no discussion of many problems.

McConville, J. Gordon. Chronicles (Daily Study Bible). Edinburgh: Saint Andrews Press, 1984. 270 pp.

Generally conservative in outlook, this displays a firm grip on the data, aiming at looking at things in their setting during the kings period and applying principles to life now. He does not sidestep problems, such as a million dead (2 Chr. 14:9ff.). The RSV is printed in space that, for those with Bibles, would be better used for even more comment.

Merrill, Eugene. "I and II Chronicles," in Bible Knowledge Commentary, ed. John F. Walvoord and Roy B. Zuck. Volume I. Wheaton: Victor Books, 1983.

Conservative scholar from Dallas Theological Seminary deals with the passages knowledgeably, showing good awareness of relevant literature and handling many of the problems at least with some help.

Myers, Jacob M. I Chronicles. Introduction, Translation and Notes (Anchor Bible). NY: Doubleday, 1965.

Myers argues that the Chronicler wrote in the Persian period (ca. 538-333 B. C.), more precisely ca. 400 B. C. (p. LXXXIX). Ezra is a possibility, as language, literary mannerisms and interests are like those in the Ezra memoirs (Ezra; Nehemiah), but Myers leaves the matter there. In the commentary section, he gives his own translation, then brief notes on problem words, finally his comments on the more crucial issues in a chapter or part of a chapter. Myers does not always explain differences between statements, as in II Samuel 21:19 where Elhanan killed Goliath and I Chronicles 20:5 where Elhanan slew the brother of Goliath. Myers briefly offers just enough to leave one somewhat puzzled (p. 136, on v. 5). But cf. Gleason Archer, Encyclopedia of Bible Difficulties, pp. 178-79, for further possible resolution of the problem. Myers, though often willing to take accounts in Chronicles as reasonable, sometimes assumes "obvious legendary accretions and embellishments" even if in his opinion "the nucleus of the story may be taken as historical" (p. 147), as in the census episode of I Chronicles 21. The back inside jacket of the volume says, "I Chronicles is to be neither accepted as a faithful narrative of the Davidic period nor dismissed as a forceful, imaginative recreation of that history. It must be taken as an important clue to the biblical process" (cf. also his II Chronicles, xx, xxiv-xxxii). He says in II Chronicles (p. xxxii): "... within the limits of its purpose, the Chronicler's story is accurate wherever it can be checked, though the method of presentation is homiletical. The only valid objection to the foregoing statement could be the numbers which, by any interpretation, are impossibly high. This fact perhaps more than any other has made the chronicler's work suspect." Liberal but sometimes moderately so, Myers defends the genealogical lists at many points as trustworthy history, whereas such scholars as Wellhausen had viewed them as fabrications. Myers does, however, disconcertingly make some statements that negate his claims about reliability, leaving the reader wondering about consistency. He looks at the numbers (statistics) as exaggerated in some cases but upholds them on occasion. He tries to offer suggestions for what he regards as high numbers. In archeological confirmation of various points in the books, he is profitable sometimes. He dates Chronicles-Ezra-Nehemiah around 400 B. C., answering critics who place these books about 330 B. C. or later. In his opinion, the same Chronicler composed all three books at the same time. He has contributed the Ezra-Nehemiah commentary to The Anchor Bible series as well.

Myers, Jacob M. II Chronicles (Anchor Bible). NY: Doubleday, 1965.

This is done along the same lines as his work on I Chronicles.

Payne, J. Barton. "1 and 2 Chronicles," in Expositor's Bible Commentary, Volume 4, ed. F. Gaebelein and R. P. Polcyn. Grand Rapids: Zondervan, 1988.

Another competent conservative treatment of the text, its exegesis and problems. Payne and Merrill advocate a high view of the integrity of history in the books and offer plausible solutions where there are difficulties. Their outlook is quite different from many on the books.

Sailhamer, John. First and Second Chronicles. Chicago, IL: Moody Press, 1983.

Sailhamer, formerly of Biola College and Bethel Seminary and more recently of Trinity Evangelical Divinity School, has written this 116-pp. paperback for the Everyman's Bible Commentary. Historically, I and II Chronicles are often overlooked by biblical commentators. This volume will add little to knowledge in the field. Sailhamer has recounted the important events and persons in these books in a rather cursory and simplistic fashion. Little problem solution is even broached and citation of Hebrew for support or exegesis is quite scanty. This volume due to its brevity and simplicity will benefit the new believer and those unfamiliar with the historical position and flow of Chronicles. —Jan Sattem

Wilcock, Michael. The Message of Chronicles (The Bible Speaks Today). Downers Grove: IVP, 1987. 288 pp.

An evangelical approach that defends conservative views on a number of the problems, feeling there are no errors. Wilcock sometimes delightfully applies the meaning to life today, and writes with clarity. He assists readers to see why material is used where it is, how it fits a need there, etc. Wilcock is vicar of St. Nicholas Church, Durham, England. For principles and for the movement in Chronicles this is a worthwhile book.

Williamson, H. G. M.   1 and 2 Chronicles (New Century Bible Commentary). Grand Rapids: Eerdmans, 1982.   428 pp.

Some regard this as the top work on textual, literary-critical discussion. Much help is here on meanings of verses at times, drawn carefully from a wealth of learning and various sources. However, Williamson sees historical inaccuracies at many points, and conservative users will wisely deal with it in a very watchful judgment.

Wood, Leon J.   Cf. on Joshua.

XII. EZRA—NEHEMIAH—ESTHER

Anderson, Stanley E.   Nehemiah the Executive.   Wheaton: Van Kampen, 1954.

The author has not done an exposition of Nehemiah, but has given a collection of selected applications which are suggestive for a preaching series.

Armerding, Carl.   Esther.   Chicago: Moody, 1955.

Here is another good evangelical survey-type book on the message of Esther.

Baldwin, Joyce. C.   Esther: An Introduction and Commentary (Tyndale Old Testament Commentary).   Downers Grove: IVP, 1984.   126 pp.

A frequent, respected contributor to this series, she presents careful research on setting, text, exegesis and related matters such as customs, with good notes. The work is evangelical, but some will think it strange that Baldwin says some details "continue to seem improbable" (p. 24).

Barber, Cyril J.   Nehemiah.   New York: Loizeaux Bros., 1976.

This is a clear, practical evangelical effort to do exposition and at the same time point out principles from the life of Nehemiah to help Christians be more organized in handling their lives and business today. The work grew out of a 26-week laymen's Bible class series geared to shoe leather living, but shows much study.

Blenkinsopp, Joseph.   Ezra-Nehemiah, A Commentary (Old Testament Library). Philadelphia: Westminster, 1988.   366 pp.

He upholds the view that Ezra-Nehemiah gives a continued account of 1 and 2 Chronicles and are authored by the chronicler, an individual or a school. He also holds traditional views such as Ezra coming in 458 B. C., Nehemiah in 445. Often he is good verse by verse, and he includes a bibliography for each section, his translation, textual notes and a fairly thorough commentary. "The chronicles of Nehemiah" (1:1) he takes as referring to Nehemiah as subject, not author. He is saturated with the literature about the era.

Boice, James M.   Nehemiah: Learning to Lead.   NY: Revell, 1988.   219 pp.

One of America's famous expository pastors (10th St. Presbyterian Church, Philadelphia) issues a call to pattern life after Nehemiah's style of leadership. He brings out traits and shows how they can be relevant today, writing lucidly and using illustrations at times. His work is suggestive for expositors, also provocative for spiritual growth in usefulness to God.

Campbell, Donald K.   Nehemiah: Man in Charge.   Wheaton: SP Publications, Victor Books, 1979.   119 pp.

A long-time Bible professor at Dallas Theological Seminary, and most recently president, weaves lucid explanation of the book with choice illustrations. As a highly readable survey, it is helpful to both lay person and a pastor or Sunday School teacher seeking a clear tracing of the flow of the book plus a focus on key traits that made Nehemiah a good leader. Comments are well organized and truth applied relevantly to highlight many of the main lessons of Nehemiah. Preachers can get good ideas here, and any readers be built up.

Clines, D. J. A.   Ezra, Nehemiah and Esther (New Century Bible Commentary).   Grand Rapids: Eerdmans, 1984.   342 pp.

A concise work of deep study, usually with a well-organized explanation with support and references pointing to further help.

Cohen, A.   "Esther," in The Five Megilloth.   London: Soncino, 1946.

Concise commentary on many of the salient points of Esther showing Jewish concern to explain the text meaningfully. Much of the work is very helpful to conservative expositors.

Cundall, A. E.   "Ezra and Nehemiah," in New Bible Commentary Revised, ed. D. Guthrie et al.   Grand Rapids: Eerdmans, 1970.

Restricted to pp. 395-411, Cundall uses his space well. He favors unity with Chronicles as one composite history and advances a summary of the main points of controversy over the relationship of Ezra and Nehemiah (395-97). He deals with the critical theory which rejects the traditional position and does not concur that the Chronicler has confused the order of the books (397). In some number problems, he assumes copyist errors, as in Ezra 1:9-11 (399). Overall it is a terse work offering help many a time.

Fensham, F. C.   The Books of Ezra and Nehemiah (New International Commentary on the Old Testament).   Grand Rapids: Eerdmans, 1982.   288 pp.

An evangelical effort knowledgeably rich in exegesis with a firm grasp of Hebrew, matters of introduction, and solid explanation of many of the verses. He shows a more meaningful grip on the relationship of the material in Ezra and Nehemiah than Williamson, and is better overall.

Getz, Gene. <u>Nehemiah, A Man of Prayer and Perseverance</u>. **Ventura, CA: G/L, Regal Books, 1981.**

Author of several books of Bible characters (Abraham, Moses, etc.), Getz clearly elucidates principles on prayer and patience in a book with thirteen references to prayer. A good conservative effort that can fan fires of prayer in laypeople and stir pastors and Bible teachers to more faithfulness in this area.

Hess, Margaret. <u>Esther: Courage in Crisis</u>. **Wheaton: Scripture Union/Victor Books, 1980.**

The writer sketches a good character picture of Esther in a way that can be life-changing for other women and Christians in general. She does this competently against the clarified background of the crisis.

Huey, F. B., Jr. "Esther," in <u>Expositor's Bible Commentary</u>, **Volume 4, ed. F. Gaebelein and R. P. Polcyn. Grand Rapids: Zondervan, 1988.**

Detailed conservative comment on verses, taking up views and reasons on problem verses. This has quite a bit to offer.

Ironside, H. A. <u>Notes on Ezra</u>. **NY: Loizeaux, 1946.**
_____. <u>Notes on Nehemiah</u>. **NY: Loizeaux (n.d.).**
_____. <u>Notes on the Book of Esther</u>. **NY: Loizeaux, 1921.**

Though Ironside does not get into the detail of the text, he does give a practical exposition on a wider scale in popular fashion. He shows how the message is alive, and at times has good illustrations.

Kidner, Derek. <u>Ezra & Nehemiah</u> **(Tyndale Old Testament Commentary). Downers Grove: IVP, 1979.**

A fairly brief but model exposition, very good for rich historical background and treatment of problems in chronology and harmony, as well as profiles of the major characters. Included are solid appendices treating the questions of sources, the identity of Sheshbazzar, chronology, the book of the law, and a superb (if brief) discussion of Ezra-Nehemiah as history, concluding that "there is no merit in putting up memorials to the prophets we dismember" (p. 174) (Dan Phillips). Kidner has frequent logical defenses against the way the documentary hypothesis links Ezra and "P." He defends the biblical order Ezra, then Nehemiah and argues that a different order faces problems that are bigger. He shows a high view of the text and a deep grasp of how to defend it against skepticism.

Kitto, John. <u>Solomon and the Kings</u> (Volume IV of <u>Daily Bible Illustrations</u>). New Testament: Robert Carter, 1851.

These are short devotional sketches of characters, institutions and events important in the Biblical narrative. It is included here because the area is otherwise more sparse in devotional literature of value.

Laney, J. Carl. <u>Ezra and Nehemiah</u> (Everyman's Bible Commentary). Chicago: Moody, 1982.

A keen conservative scholar has contributed a well-studied and clear work in concise form. Laney is adept in context, word study, synopsis, customs, etc. and knows how to get at the main points, deal with some of the problems, and explain things reasonably.

Luck, G. Coleman. <u>Ezra and Nehemiah</u>. Chicago: Moody, 1961.

A brief work helpful to the expositor interested in the flow of thought and highlights in these books. It is in the Moody paperback series.

Martin, John. "Ezra," also "Esther," in <u>Bible Knowledge Commentary</u>, ed. John F. Walvoord and Roy B. Zuck. Volume I. Wheaton: Victor Books, 1983.

A diligent, lucid exposition of both books by a former expositor in the Bible Department at Dallas Theological Seminary. Works like these and the ones here by Huey, Fensham, Laney, McConville, Whitcomb and Yamauchi provide quite a lot for conservative expositors.

McConville, J. Gordon. <u>Ezra, Nehemiah and Esther</u> (Daily Study Bible). Philadelphia: Westminster, 1985. 198 pp.

Books in this series differ greatly in whether liberal or conservative. The present commentator as on Chronicles reaches views quite often that staunch evangelicals (in the way this has traditionally been understood) will appreciate. Ezra came to Jerusalem in 458 B. C., Nehemiah in 445, and both took part in Nehemiah 8-10, 12. McConville assumes that events in Esther are historically reliable. Though at so many points too brief, this is a refreshing, warm, and good commentary done clearly and using historical/archaeological help to shed light.

McGee, J. Vernon. <u>Exposition of the Book of Esther</u>. Wheaton: Van Kampen, 1951.

This is a good popular evangelical treatment of the book originating as a series of Sunday evening sermons.

Moore, C. A. <u>Esther: Introduction, Translation and Notes</u> (Anchor Bible). NY: Doubleday, 1971. 118 pp.

Highly thought of in many scholarly circles, this is competent on the text, exegesis, history, culture and matters of introduction (in regard to surveying views current in literature). It offers much help.

Myers, Jacob M.   Ezra-Nehemiah (Anchor Bible).   Garden City, NY: Doubleday, 1965.

A faculty member of the Lutheran Theological Seminary in Gettysburg, PA has written this highly-respected work after years of study. He sets well the background of the captivity in Babylon, the situation in Judah, the returns to Jerusalem. On the period of Ezra, Myers inclines to Albright's proposal that Ezra came in the thirty-seventh year, even after Nehemiah began, ca. 428 B. C., not earlier in 458 B. C. as the seventh year in 7:7, 8 suggests (thirty-seventh year, not seventh) (p. xxxvii). He shows some opinion in rabbinic and other ancient sources for Ezra-Nehemiah being one book, other evidence to make it separate. He feels that Nehemiah's memoirs were placed as an appendix with the larger corpus of the Chronicler, even if Nehemiah's coming preceded Ezra's (xli). To him the possible preference is Pavlovsky's theory that Ezra came with Nehemiah unofficially on his second tour in Jerusalem and was a key man in reforms. Later when Nehemiah desired it, Ezra came again to Jerusalem with kingly authority, heading a group of exiles from Babylon. He dealt with the problem of mixed marriages, then wrote a history (Chronicles and Ezra 1-6). One of his followers later contributed material from the work of Ezra and Nehemiah from various preserved sources (xlviii). Myers' idea of sources for the books involves a commitment to a JEDP theory. He dates the completion of the main work by the Chronicler ca. 400 B. C. The list of high priests (Nehemiah 12) does not include later priests (page lxx.) The commentary is at times fairly sparse and hit or miss verse by verse with some verses passed over. Such a verse as Ezra 7:10 receives little comment. Not much is attempted on drawing out spiritual life lessons based on the comments. Yet there is a wealth of data that explains and shows a competent grasp of Jewish conditions, word meanings, etc. Myers provides a five and a half page list of commentaries, other books, and articles (lxviii-lxxxiii).

Patton, L. B.   A Critical and Exegetical Commentary on the Book of Esther (ICC). Edinburgh: T. & T. Clark, 1908.   339 pp.

Though old, this still is a rich larder of information on details of word meaning, exegesis, history, etc. It is liberal in perspective but contributes much help if gleaned wisely.

Redpath, Alan.   Victorious Christian Service: Studies in the Book of Nehemiah. Westwood, NJ: Revell, 1958.

This is a lucid application of the content for the modern day Christian and his service. It is sermonic in style and incomplete in coverage.

Swindoll, Charles R.   Hand Me Another Brick.   Nashville: Thomas Nelson, 1978.

One of America's top Evangelical Free Church pastors (Fullerton, CA) gives challenging expositions of main lessons in Nehemiah, with illustrations and ways to apply the truth. Pastors, Bible teachers and laypeople in general will find pointed principles to refresh their spiritual lives and direct them in service.

Vos, Howard F.   Ezra, Nehemiah and Esther (Bible Study Commentary).   Grand Rapids: Zondervan, 1987.   191 pp.

Brief exposition from a conservative who is professor of history and archaeology, King's College, Briarcliffe Manor, New York. Vos surveys fairly well, providing help especially for lay readers who want a simple, quick study and pastors or Bible teachers needing a panoramic look and some concise help on some of the problems.

Williamson, H. G. M.   Ezra, Nehemiah (Word Biblical Commentary).   Waco, TX: Word Books, 1985.   417 pp.

Highly respected in the general scholarly community, this indeed does furnish help, often detailed, on many matters like word study, background, customs, and views on problems. He treats the books as essentially from the fifth century B. C., brought together fully by 300 B. C., and a literary unit. He believes the composer may have been misled by a mistaken identification of Sheshbazzar and Zerubbabel. He dismays conservatives at times by subjectively seeing so much material in Ezra and Nehemiah as fragmented (cf. for instance p. 309). Yet he is somewhat conservative at times, fairly includes evangelicals in his bibliography, etc.

Whitcomb, John C.   "Ezra," "Nehemiah," and "Esther" in The Wycliffe Bible Commentary.   Chicago: Moody, 1962.

The author, for many years Professor of Old Testament at Grace Theological Seminary in Winona Lake, Indiana has distinguished himself by co-authoring The Genesis Flood with Henry Morris and by his own work Darius the Mede. His commentary here shows the same painstaking research into historical matters as well as Hebrew meanings. See also his bibliography at the end of each book.

Whitcomb, John C.   Esther: Triumph of God's Sovereignty.   Chicago, IL: Moody Press, 1979.

Whitcomb has written this fine 128-pp. paperback for the Everyman's Bible Commentary. He includes a helpful bibliography along with charts and time-line illustrations. The chronology of Esther is dealt with in detail. The author uses nine chapters to discuss ten chapters of Esther. He uses a verse by verse format. Whitcomb's introductory remarks are very good but regrettably brief. Throughout the volume he counters two major detractors to the historicity and canonicity of Esther (Patton, ICC, 1908; Moore, Anchor Bible, 1977). Whitcomb dates Esther prior to the palace destruction at Susa in 435 B. C. He, like others, hypothesizes that perhaps a Diasporan Jew authored this work. His comments on the difference between canonicity and theological understanding are worthy of note. Whitcomb's approach to historicity itself makes valuable reading. The author equates Ahasuerus (486-465 B. C.) with Xerxes aka. Khshayarsha. Whitcomb's work here is especially valuable for its concern for the interplay between secular and sacred history. Conclusion: Outstanding approach and treatment. —Jan Sattem

Wright, J. Stafford. **The Date of Ezra's Coming to Jerusalem.** London: Tyndale, **1958.**

Not a commentary, this study is an assist in discussing the problem and views as background preparation for expositors and scholars.

Yamauchi, Edwin. **"Ezra, Nehemiah," in** **Expositor's Bible Commentary,** **Volume 4, ed. F. Gaebelein and R. P. Polcyn.** **Grand Rapids:** **Zondervan, 1988.**

A conservative investigation with plentiful help on text, word meaning, history, culture, etc. Yamauchi cites from a wide swing of scholarly literature. He is sometimes concisely helpful on differences in numbers between Ezra and Nehemiah (cf. also on the numbers Gleason Archer, Encyclopedia of Bible Difficulties. Grand Rapids: Zondervan, 1982, pp. 229-30).

XIII. JOB

Andersen, Francis I. Job (TOTC). **Downers Grove:** **InterVarsity Press, 1976.**

Andersen has provided one of the best modern and informed expositions of the text of Job, displaying intimate familiarity with the Hebrew and cognate languages and literature (as well as referring to a broad range of English literature). He utilizes a good, almost conversational style and closely analyzes the text. Not all evangelicals will be pleased with Andersen's cyclical theory of composition (which he sees as reaching completion by 750 B. C., although he allows that composition could have occurred any time between Moses and Ezra). This is a valuable aid to exposition. —Dan Phillips. He dates Job during Solomon's reign. On problem texts he gives views, as on 19:23-27, where he believes Job refers to a real meeting with God after death, though does not feel there is a full statement of a faith in bodily resurrection here (this point has been much debated). The verse by verse commentary is good most of the time, and Andersen is quite abreast of modern research on the book. —J. E. Rosscup.

Archer, Gleason L., Jr. **The Book of Job: God's Answer to the Problem of Undeserved Suffering.** **Grand Rapids:** **Baker, 1982.**

Occasioned in part by the death of a pastor friend due to lymphoma, this study provides a very helpful blend of solidly-based exposition and relevant personal application. Archer often comments by way of re-phrasing the speeches interpretively, making use of the Hebrew in (a rather odd system of) transliteration. Holding to the early dating (between 1876-1445 B. C.) of the book and historical background to the contents, Archer's exposition is sober and helpful for preaching, personal study, or even for counseling. —Dan Phillips

Ball, C. J. The Book of Job. Oxford, 1922.

An example of a liberal scholar's detailed discussion that sometimes tries to rewrite a text (cf. on 19:23-27). But it is one of the fine liberal works on Job.

Barnes, Albert. Notes on the Old Testament, Explanatory and Practical, Job, 2 volumes. Grand Rapids: Baker, 1950.

Among old, respected series much used by pastors and Bible teachers, Barnes ranks well. His work on Job is one of the best in the set. Many good commentaries have appeared since his day, but Spurgeon as an expositor felt, "The student should purchase this work at once, as it is absolutely necessary to his library" (Commenting on Commentaries, p. 75).

Blackwood, Andrew, Jr. A Devotional Introduction to Job. Grand Rapids: Baker, 1959.

Expositors can find provocative devotional principles drawn from Job. Usually these are well-done and of real service to speakers, especially those preparing for a series.

Bullock, C. Hassell. An Introduction to the Poetic Books of the Old Testament. Chicago: Moody Press, 1979.

A well-organized general evangelical introduction to wisdom in the Old Testament, how the poetic books relate to wisdom, wisdom in the ancient near East and in the apocrypha; theology in the Old Testament wisdom books (God, Man, emphases on retributive justice, universalism, and law), and immortality in wisdom and the Psalms; the Book of Job; the Psalms, Proverbs; Ecclesiastes; and the Song of Solomon. The book has a 14-page bibliography, subject index, author index, and Scripture index.

Clines, David J. A. Job 1-20 (Word Biblical Commentary). Dallas, TX: Word Books, 1989. 501 pp.

In many texts this is careful in handling details of text, syntax, views and reasons. Clines' grasp and use of scholarly writings enriches his effort, which seems of a conservative nature in many passages. He sees the story set in patriarchal times, but a writer between the seventh and second centuries B. C. using compositions from centuries before (a view that many will feel problematic). While so often productive on many aspects, Clines is a big disappointment in concluding on a key text, 19:25, that Job's redeemer is not God but Job himself in a personified plea, however that can be, which is not altogether clear.

Davidson, A. B. The Book of Job. Cambridge Bible. Cambridge: University Press, 1903.

This is a detailed investigation of the text verse by verse and has much to offer.

Delitzsch, Franz. The Book of Job. 2 volumes. Grand Rapids: Eerdmans, 1949.

See earlier comments on Keil and Delitzsch.

Dhorme, E.   A Commentary on the Book of Job.   Translated by Harold Knight. Nashville: Nelson, 1967.

The work, first published in 1926, is massively detailed in introduction (224 pp.), though often too scanty on exegesis of the Hebrew. No serious extended scholarly study should be done without the use of such a study. For Dhorme excels in setting forth the book's plan and movements so that the reader is made aware of the pattern, coherence, and development of the drama so as to grasp the unity and what is going on in different parts as relating to the overall sweep. Dhorme's references to Hebrew are for the technically trained.

Ellison, H. L.   From Tragedy to Triumph: The Message of the Book of Job.   London: Paternoster Press, 1958.

This is not a lengthy study nor a commentary verse by verse (only 127 pp. including R. V. text which is reproduced). But it is an interesting character description of the friends of Job and an effort to portray how they would appear in 19th century church life.

Garland, F. David.   Job (Bible Study Commentary).   Grand Rapids: Zondervan, 1971.   107 pp.

Garland has done a creditable work in putting together help summarizing sections and going into some details of verses. He gives conservatives a fairly quick-moving commentary that touches competently even though briefly (usually) on problems.

Gibson, Edgar C. S.   The Book of Job.   London: Methuen, 1919.

This book in the Westminster Series is one of the most profitable commentaries on Job.

Gordis, Robert.   The Book of Job: Commentary, New Translation and Special Studies. NY: KTAV, 1978.

A 602-pp. work of very fine calibre by a professor of Bible and religion at Jewish Theological Seminary, New York City and a well-known scholar in the wisdom literature. He gives a very detailed exegesis, reflecting wide awareness of ancient and recent studies. He presents the Hebrew text and an English rendering. Often he argues against emendations or subjective re-ordering of the text (but cf. his own re-arranging of 26:5-14 after chapter 25 etc.). He climaxes the work with 42 additional notes on relevant topics and problem texts in the book. This is one of the more helpful works of recent times.

Habel, Norman C.   The Book of Job: A Commentary (Old Testament Library). Philadelphia: Westminster, 1985.   586 pp.

This is widely regarded as outstanding on many aspects, usually showing high respect for the text and also the unity of the book (i.e. the prologue, epilogue and material between these, in a narrative plot). He has a good grasp of the Hebrew and its poetic and literary details as well as theological motifs. He does think that some speech material in the third cycle has been misplaced (p. 37), and subjectively shuffles segments to suit his own ideas. To him, Job's redeemer in Chapter 19 is a celestial being (cf. 16:19) who will be his advocate before God after death. Habel takes a postexilic date of writing (42). He views the Elihu portion as fitting and even is persuaded that Elihu is the arbiter Job longed for in 31:35. Habel skillfully comments on literary devices such as parallelism, irony, word plays, etc. He was for some years Professor of Old Testament, Concordia Theological Seminary, Saint Louis. He does much to guide readers to the theological message of Job.

Hartley, John E.   Job (New International Commentary on the Old Testament). Grand Rapids: Eerdmans, 1988.   591 pp.

It is good to see this firmly evangelical work. This is evident in many places. However, Hartley is subjective and without real necessity in shuffling Job 27:13-23 to Chapter 25, etc. Generally, his careful handling of the text, syntax, views and reasoning constitute this one of the best conservative works on Job.

Kent, H. H.   Job, Our Contemporary.   Grand Rapids: Eerdmans, 1957.

A fairly good and sometimes stimulating study, with much to suggest relevance to people today.

Morgan, G. Campbell.   The Analyzed Bible.   Volume V.   NY: Revell, 1909.

This is a good synthesis which helps to trace the developing thought of the book of Job. A detailed outline is given.

Rowley, H. H.   Job (New Century Bible).   London: Oliphants, 1970.

This liberal work is helpful primarily for its evidence of Rowley's wide reading and various views on problems. It is not one of the better overall commentaries verse by verse. Cf. also Rowley's chapter on approaches to Job in From Moses to Qumran (London, 1963).

Smick, Elmer B.   "Job," in Expositor's Bible Commentary (Volume 4), ed. Frank Gaebelein and R. P. Polcyn.   Grand Rapids: Eerdmans, 1988.

Smick is Professor of Old Testament Language and Literature, Gordon-Conwell Theological Seminary. Steeped in his area's scholarship, he provides a good introduction showing that Job is superior to all other literature in philosophical and theological depth (p. 844). He argues the reasonableness of seeing one man as the author, inspired by God, in the 2,000—1,000 B. C. period, and events of the book in the patriarchal era (847, 853). His bibliography is extensive (871-75; and much reference appears throughout to scholarly literature). After careful exegesis he sees the possibility of Job's personal, bodily resurrection in 19:25-27 (cf. 943). The Elihu speeches of Chapters 32-37 are seen to be in unity with and to serve a valid role with the rest of the book (998). Overall this is a very insightful and competent commentary by a conservative.

Stedman, Ray C. Expository Studies in Job: Behind Suffering. **Waco: Word Books, 1981.**

Good practical insights into the biblical message to meet people's needs. Sometimes interpretations do not satisfy, such as saying that behemoth and leviathan of chapters 40, 41 are symbolic and not literal animals, and Stedman's idea that leviathan symbolizes the world which is against the godly. The 216-pp. book of expository sermons has much that is commendatory in simple, popular fashion that reflects the drama of suffering as quite real.

Zuck, Roy B. Job. **Chicago, IL: Moody Press, 1978.**

Zuck, a Biola University graduate, Associate Academic Dean and Associate Professor of Bible Exposition at Dallas Theological Seminary, has written this 192-pp. paperback for the Everyman's Bible Commentary. Written in thirteen chapters for use in Sunday school, this volume assumes a thoroughly orthodox position with reference to all critical areas. In addition, Zuck reckons a patriarchal time setting (perhaps akin to Terah's time?). One helpful section is Zuck's treatment of chapters 20 and 21 and the repartee between Zophar and Job. Zuck views the grand purpose of the book as dealing with motives behind worship. He sees its solemn lesson in the futility of criticizing God's ways. This volume is recommended for home Bible studies and Sunday school. —Jan Sattem

Zuck, Roy B. "Job," in Bible Knowledge Commentary, **ed. John F. Walvoord and Roy B. Zuck (Volume I). Wheaton: Victor Books, 1983.**

A fine conservative survey with help on many key verses, help of a kind that reflects painstaking and competent study. Zuck also writes very clearly and summarizes well.

Zuck, Roy B. Sitting with Job: Selected Studies on the Book of Job. **Grand Rapids: Baker, 1992.**

Here are thirty-four chapters (sketches) by different scholars on key sections or topics in Job—men such as R. Laird Harris, Francis Andersen, Norman Habel, Don Carson, etc. Zuck himself writes on 19:23-29 and on Chapter 28. The book offers comments with high expertise on subjects that an expositor can find very instructive in the midst of preparing for in individual message or a series.

XIV. PSALMS

The commentary by Moll in the Lange series is one of the best in that 12-volume set. In addition:

Alden, Robert. Psalms. 3 volumes. Chicago: Moody, 1974-76.

This has some good comments as a conservative work but artificially assigns the psalms to three categories of Christian living, Songs of Devotion (1-50), Dedication (51-100) and Discipleship (101-150). Comments tend to be extremely brief for quick reading laypeople.

Alexander, J. A. The Psalms. 2 volumes. Philadelphia: Presbyterian Board of Education, 1850.

This is one of the more thorough older exegetical works on the Hebrew text. It represents a re-working of the famous commentary on Psalms by E. Hengstenberg.

Anderson, A. A. The Book of Psalms (New Century Bible). 2 volumes. London: Oliphants, 1972.

An exegetical treatment which often is helpful, by a liberal. It is one of the better recent liberal works from the standpoint of detailed commentary.

Anderson, B. W. Out of the Depths. Philadelphia: Westminster, 1974.

He treats sample psalms from each of the types scholars generally recognize since works by H. Gunkel (as The Psalms, Philadelphia: Fortress Press, 1967) and Sigmund Mowinckel (The Psalms in Israel's Worship, New York: Abingdon, 1962). He looks at doctrinal aspects and makes applications, some of which are quite worthwhile.

Armerding, Carl. Psalms in a Minor Key. Chicago: Moody Press, 1973.

Here is a series of brief, rich, simple, practical and stimulating chapters by a great Bible teacher (he taught at Wheaton College) on selected psalms. Many of the psalms are not usually treated in books on selected psalms, such as Psalms 3, 4, 5, 6, 12, 13, etc. But some better-known psalms are also included, e. g. 51, 73, 90. Armerding touches on many of the spiritual highlights in a lucid manner that will help a growing Christian and be thought-provoking to a pastor-teacher or other speaker.

Barth, C. Introduction to the Psalms. London: Blackwell, 1966.

This little book by a liberal author provides a general survey of approaches to the Psalms by critical scholarship up to the mid-1960's.

Bonhoeffer, Dietrich.   Psalms: The Prayer Book of the Bible.   Translated by James Burtness.   Minneapolis: Augsburg Publishing House, 1970.

Jesus' disciples asked Him, "Teach us to pray," and Psalms is the book that shows how to pray, how Jesus desires men to pray. His "Lord's prayer" (actually the disciples' prayer) summarizes all the prayers of the Bible. Bonhoeffer presents prayer as the heart's conversation with God in this small 86-page book. He discusses prayer in relation to such things as the Law, suffering, guilt, enemies, and daily victory.

Bridges, Charles.   Exposition of Psalm CXIX: As Illustrative of the Character and Exercises of Christian Experience.   London: Seeley, Jackson, and Halliday, 1859.

This is a classic of detail on the psalm, with much rich, solid and provocative discussion that deeply feeds the serious heart. It first appeared in 1827 and continues to be published. Bridges (1794-1869) has a way of relating the truth to other parts of Scripture and to the spiritual life that reflects a profound grasp of things. He is wordy, leaving few stones unturned, but there are many veins of gold beneath the stones. The famous interpretation of details in the longest psalm is mingled with suggestions for self-examination, prayer and other stimulating devotional material. An 8-pp. index of subjects at the end is helpful at times in locating a discussion.

Bridges, Charles.   Psalm 119, An Exposition (Geneva series).   Carlisle, Pa: Banner of Truth Trust, 1987rp of work first issued in 1827.   490 pp.

Cohen, A.   The Psalms.   London: Soncino, 1945.

A Jewish scholar gives brief comments, which often are quite good in capturing the essence.

Craigie, Peter, Marvin E. Tate and Leslie Allen.   Psalms (Word Biblical Commentary).   3 volumes.   Waco, TX: Word Books, 1983ff.

Craigie did 1-50, Tate 51-100 and Allen 101-150. In his part, Craigie also includes an introduction covering many aspects of discussion such as the literary and poetic form of individual psalms and the New Testament use of the psalms and pertinency to life today. He does not consider any psalm originally messianic, and of course many will disagree with this. Allen is good on the form, structure, setting, and problems of the psalms, even excellent on many matters, but believes in a Deuteronomistic tradition and is arbitrary for many users in his ideas, at times, of literary sources. On individual verses, the work is frequently a rich contribution on word meaning, text, basic exegesis, customs, etc. and one can learn or review much.

Crim, Keith R.   The Royal Psalms.   Richmond: John Knox, 1962.

This 123-pp. study is a sometimes helpful exposition of psalms that pursue the theme of kingship. He treats 2, 18, 20, 21, 45, 72, 89, 101, 110, and 144. The work is of special interest where the student is seeking to grasp where detail relates to a past, historical king of the days in which the psalms were written, or refers on predictively to Jesus Christ. At the beginning, Crim devotes 54 pp. to "kingship in Ancient Israel", and at the end 3 pp. to "Messianic Psalms." Crim has been influenced considerably by writers before him of liberal persuasions, such as Hermann Gunkel ("Psalmen", in Die Religion in Geschichte und Gegenwart, Vol. 4, 1st edition 1913, 2nd edition 1927); Gunkel and J. Begrich, Einleitun in die Psalmen, 1933, pp. 140-71, quite comprehensive in Old Testament aspects; A. R. Johnson, Sacral Kingship in Ancient Israel (Cardiff: University of Wales Press, 1955), H. J. Kraus, Die Konigsherrschaft Gottes im Alten Testament, Tübingen, J. C. Mohr, 1951; A. Bentzen, King and Messiah; Helmer Ringgren, The Messiah in the Old Testament; Sigmund Mowinckel, He That Cometh.

Dahood, Mitchell. Psalms I, II, III (Anchor Bible). Garden City, NY: Doubleday, 1966-71.

A major contribution of Dahood is his philological material based on recent discoveries in Ugaritic. Sometimes it is helpful in throwing light on word meanings according to ancient usage. Dahood believes, for example, that many texts in the Psalms show expectation of life after death, and uses philological arguments. A problem with his approach is that he carries the point to an extreme, and finds life after death in many texts where it is not clearly there, as even evangelical Old Testament scholars have said (cf., for example, the evaluation of Bruce K. Waltke, review of Dahood's Psalms I, in Bib. Sac. 123 (1966), 176; for more detail Elmer Smick, "The Bearing of New Philological Data on the Subjects of Resurrection and Immortality in the Old Testament," Westminster Theological Journal, 31 (1968-69), 12-21). However, finding life after death in some of the Psalms can be defended and has been firmly believed by many in such texts as 16:9, 10; 49:15; 73:24f, etc.

Davis, John J. The Perfect Shepherd (Psalms 23). Grand Rapids: Baker, 1979.

Superb treatment and good example of caring, responsible evangelical scholarship. Davis analyzes the Hebrew text, and draws on his own experiences with shepherds in the area of Palestine, and applies the text practically to the modern reader. — Dan Phillips. Davis is well-known for several works, for example his Paradise to Prison, Moses and the Gods of Egypt and Biblical Numerology, all very helpful. He teaches in the Old Testament at Grace Theological Seminary, Winona Lake, IN.

Dickson, David. Psalms. 2 volumes in 1. Carlisle, PA: Banner of Truth Trust, n.d.

Though this is a very old work, reprinted, it is heavily laden with richness that edifies in explaining the text and making truth clear. It is well worth the time, even if dated in parts.

Goldingay, John. <u>Songs From A Strange Land. Psalms 42-51</u> (The Bible Speaks Today). **Downers Grove: IVP, 1978.**

The author was a lecturer in Old Testament at St. John's College, Nottingham. He offers a fresh rendering of each psalm, interprets it as showing man's response to God as helper, comforter, king and redeemer, and points out the relevance to spiritual life now. His outline is clearly stated in headings and covers many of the vital aspects of life in a captivating exposition. The main headings are: "God has forgotten me" (42, 43); "God helps us" (44); "If God is King" (45, 47); "If God is with us" (46, 48, 50); "But God will Ransom" (49); "Will God Forgive?" (51). The treatment on 51 is worth the price of the book: repentance faces up to sins, recognizes sin, appeals to God's love, pleads for forgiveness, longs for spiritual renewal, looks forward to testimony, and offers the sacrifices for which God looks.

Hay, D. M. <u>Glory at the Right Hand. Psalm 110 in Early Christianity.</u> **Society of Biblical Literature Monograph Series, No. 18. Nashville/New York: Abingdon Press, 1973.**

This grew out of a Yale doctoral dissertation (1965). It provides a survey of how Psalm 110 was interpreted by ancient Jews and early Christians up to the 4th century, also a discussion of Christian references to the Psalm. For in-depth study of 110, this is quite enlightening and helpful.

Hubbard, David A. <u>Psalms for All Seasons.</u> **Grand Rapids: Eerdmans, 1971.**

Brief homiletically arranged studies of key psalms with good relevance to life today (Psalms 1, 2, 7, 8, 9, 14, 16, 23, 32, 40, 45, 49, 51).

Keller, Philip. <u>A Shepherd Looks at Psalm 23.</u> **Grand Rapids: Zondervan, 1970.**

Many are the books on Psalms 23. Cf., among many, John J. Davis, F. B. Meyer and Haddon Robinson. Yet Keller has much to offer on insights into phrases in the shepherd imagery, as well as refreshing illustrations that can be provocative of interesting preaching or teaching.

Kidner, Derek. <u>Psalms 1-72 and Psalms 73-150</u> (2 volumes) **(Tyndale Old Testament Commentary). Grand Rapids: Eerdmans, 1973-75.**

A good study by a leading evangelical, providing a reasonably detailed commentary, though too brief in many cases as well. This is one of the better works in recent times and on many points shows an in-depth grasp of things (cf. also his fine work on Proverbs).

Leslie, E. A. <u>The Psalms.</u> **NY: Abingdon-Cokesbury Press, 1949.**

Greatly influenced by the form-critical approach pioneered by Hermann Gunkel and developed further by Sigmund Mowinckel, Leslie has produced a commentary on the Psalms which classifies the individual psalms into categories according to the <u>Sitz im Leben,</u> i. e. the actual situation in life which gave impulse to the original writer. (For discussion of this approach, see A. R. Johnson, "The Psalms," in The Old Testament and Modern Study, edited by H. H. Rowley, Oxford University-Press, 1956). There is merit in this approach, but these scholars are liberal in their theological moorings. Leslie's commentary itself is a rather sweeping synthesis which, though well written, does not get down into the issues of exegesis enough to be of great help.

Leupold, H. C.   Exposition of the Psalms.   Minneapolis: Augsburg, 1959. 1,010 pp.

This Lutheran, amillennial commentary refers to the original text, gives attention to the background and has good introductions to the Psalms. It is one of the better works on Psalms in regard to providing competent, pertinent material of a serious nature to the pastor, teacher, or layman.

Lloyd-Jones, D. Martyn.   Faith on Trial. Studies in Psalm 73.   Grand Rapids: Eerdmans, 1965.   125 pp.

The famous successor of G. Campbell Morgan in London's Westminster Chapel, also famous for many outstanding books, deals in deeply perceptive and practical ways with profound problems God treats here. Why do the ungodly prosper? Why does He allow suffering? He seeks to show that true joy is realized only in a person's conscious sense of God's presence. This is one of the finest books I have ever read on a psalm in the area of deep insight into life and how God's Word helpfully guides us in right attitudes of trust. Some of Lloyd-Jones' other great books are Studies in the Sermon on the Mount, Spiritual Depression, and commentaries on Romans and Ephesians.

Longman, Tremper III.   How to Read the Psalms.   Downers Grove: IVP, 1988. 166 pp.

An evangelical work showing the main types of psalms, aim of the psalm titles, Davidic authorship, lines of covenant thought, messianic themes, relevance of psalms in the ministry of Jesus, charm of the psalms for us, parallelism, etc. Longman looks in detail at Psalms 30, 69, and 98 as examples. This is a good recent general introduction on certain main issues about the psalms, and reads well.

Manton, Thomas.   Psalm 119.   3 volumes.   Edinburgh: Banner of Truth Trust, 1990.   Originally in 1680.   1,685 pp.

This reprint gives 190 sermons based on a verse by verse study. Though the old classic has much insight it does not get down to the text enough. It is highly devotional, sometimes with inductive control but frequently without any. Another devotional work is the famous classic on Psalm 119 by Charles Bridges, which is even better known to many.

Meyer, F. B.   The Shepherd Psalm.   Grand Rapids: Kregel, 1991.   139 pp.

A master of devotional writing gives many perceptive thoughts on the believer and the Shepherd.

Mowinckel, Sigmund. The Psalms in Israel's Worship. **2 volumes. Oxford: Blackwell, 1962.**

Taking the "type-critical" approach in classifying the Psalms, Mowinckel follows in the train of Hermann Gunkel of Germany. There is much here for the more detailed and discerning conservative student because the two volumes offer an encyclopedia of information about the Psalms and the history of their interpretation at many points. However, the higher critical viewpoint is assumed and many of his conclusions are unacceptable. This is not a commentary, but a discussion of various facets in the Psalms.

Olsen, Erling C. Meditations in the Book of Psalms. **Neptune, NJ: Loizeaux Bros., 1941.**

This work, now in its second printing (1975), devotes about 4-6 pp. to each psalm. There is much practical wealth and illustration in the author's comments (formerly broadcasted), which are richly suggestive for emphases in messages. For example, in Psalm 1, we are not to spend all our time just meditating on the Word, but become busily involved as Jesus was in the lives of others, p. 3. This, however, is not a book that helps in grappling with problem verses; it simply helps a preacher or teacher come down to earth.

Perowne, J. J. Stewart. The Book of Psalms. **2 volumes in 1. Grand Rapids: Zondervan, 1976. Rp of 1878 ed. Zondervan issued 1966 ed. also, 2 volumes; and cf.** Commentary on the Psalms. **2 volumes in 1. Grand Rapids: Kregel, 1989rp.**

Distinguished among 19th century works on Psalms, this model 1864 work by a competent Anglican Hebrew scholar has much that is detailed and discerning along evangelical lines. Perowne has a fine introduction though it lacks findings of the past century. He shows, among other things, that the psalmist often went far beyond himself in statements and projected his thought prophetically to Christ. In most cases the verse by verse commentary solidly explains the text. Perowne often shows the unity between a Psalms statement and New Testament truth.

Phillips, John. Exploring the Psalms. **5 volumes. Neptune, NJ: Loizeaux, 1985-88.**

One of America's fine Bible expositors, from Moody Bible Institute's extension department, gives more of his lucid work (he has works on several books of the Bible). His outline for each psalm is intently alliterated, though it seems apt in many cases at least. The exposition is broad and sweeping, with many statements that seize the reader's mind and heart. Due to the clarity and flow, this would be suggestive for preachers and also refreshing for any Christian to use in daily worship times, reading his Bible and then the comments on given verses.

Plumer, William. Psalms (Geneva series). Carlisle, PA. Banner of Truth Trust, 1990rp of work originally from 1867. 1210 pp.

A discussion which is quite helpful to the expositor who is seeking to get at the actual meaning of each verse. It cross-references carefully with other relevant passages.

Robinson, Haddon. Psalm Twenty-Three. Chicago: Moody, 1968.

A scholar of Gordon-Conwell Theological Seminary has turned excellent expository preaching on Psalm 23 into this series of devotional chapters. The material reflects keen insight into shepherd customs behind the phrases and then crystal clear relating of the truth to the spiritual realm of believers today.

Ross, Allen P. "Psalms," in Bible Knowledge Commentary, ed. John F. Walvoord and Roy B. Zuck. Volume I. Wheaton: Victor Books, 1983.

Outstanding grasp of things, explanation from many sides, conservative clarity and knowledge of the literature brought together. The reader gains much insight here, as in Ross's work on Proverbs in the Expositor's Bible Commentary or his survey on Genesis, Creation and Blessing. He helps users follow the structure, see word meanings, customs, parallelism, and other parts of the study, shedding a lot of light.

Scroggie, W. Graham. The Psalms. Westwood, NJ: Revell, 1965.

This is an excellent synthesis on each of the 150 Psalms, with homiletical outlines, choice quotes and concise glimpses of the thought. A sentence title is given to each psalm.

Spurgeon, Charles H. The Treasury of David. 3 volumes. Grand Rapids: Zondervan, 1975. Rp of 7 volume 1889 work; there is also a 6-volume ed. from London: Marshall, Morgan & Scott, 1957.

In this very detailed exposition, the London pulpit master dealt with each verse, giving a wealth of illustration, practical comment, and preaching hints. Spurgeon shows that he read widely in the best literature of his day, gleaning out rich quotes. On any given verse one can expect to find exposition or quotes looking at it from various angles. The devotional flavor is excellent. Here is a suggestive source for preacher or teacher and much wealth for general readers, though readers must go elsewhere for word studies and exegesis to supplement their own personal exegetical study. There is also a condensation of the Treasury which cuts out about two-thirds of it, leaving much of the richness (David Otis Fuller, Psalms by Spurgeon. Grand Rapids: Kregel, 1976. 703 pp.). The condensation is a help to the busy who want to get at the hub of things quickly.

Stott, John R. W. Selected Psalms and Canticles. London: Hodder & Stoughton, 1971. Chicago: Moody, 1988.

Here is a brief but excellent exposition of several key Psalms by one who has come to be known for his stimulating articulations of favorite Bible passages.

The Moody edition of 127 pages has many color pictures to illustrate psalms. Stott deals lucidly with Psalms 1, 8, 15, 16, 19, 22-24, 27, 29,32, 34, 40, 42-43, 46, 51, 67, 73, 84, 90-91, 95, 98, 100, 103, 104, 121-123, 125, 127, 130-31, 133, 139, 145 and 150.

van Gemeren, W. A. "Psalms," in Expositor's Bible Commentary, Volume 5, ed. **Frank Gaebelein and R. P. Polcyn. Grand Rapids: Zondervan, 1991.**

The writer provides a good introduction on key aspects of the study, also a good bibliography (pp. 39-47). His own list of titles gives the subjects of each of the 150 psalms (48-51), and he offers a detailed commentary, in 880 pages. He gives an introduction for each psalm, discussing main aspects to orientate readers. He deals with problems in verse by verse study and in special appendices. In some psalms he copiously lists sources before moving on. The Hebrew word study and grammatical remarks are quite helpful. This is an outstanding commentary, showing some of the best of evangelical expertise.

Weiser, Artur. The Psalms, A Commentary, Translated by H. Hartwell. London, 1962.

A lucid, liberal commentary of some detail which sometimes reaches rather evangelical conclusions (cf. on 16:9-11; 49:15; 73:24 etc.). Weiser has a lot of stimulating insight.

XV. PROVERBS

Aitken, Kenneth T. Proverbs (Daily Bible Study). Philadelphia: Westminster, 1986. 264 pp.

Though Aitken late-dates the present form of Proverbs to fifth/fourth century B. C., he furnishes many insights of value on possible renderings of phrases. He looks at Proverbs 1-9 in sequence, then in 10-31 switches to a topical method, dealing with the scoffer, drunkard, liar and other characters. He also devotes parts to honoring parents, old age, false witnesses, sadness vs. gladness, prayer, etc. All in all it is a very profitable work, and time will be spent well here.

Alden, Robert L. Proverbs. A Commentary on an Ancient Book of Timeless Advice. Grand Rapids: Baker, 1983.

Alden is Professor of Old Testament at Denver Conservative Baptist Seminary, and also author of a 3-volume commentary on the Psalms. The present work is based on specialized study into canonical wisdom literature. The commentary deals in capsule style with each verse based on analysis of the Hebrew, but mentions the Hebrew words only occasionally. Alden seeks to relate the message to 20th century life.

Arnot, Wm. Studies in Proverbs. **Grand Rapids: Kregel, 1978, rp of 1878 work. 583 pp.**

These homilies were originally issued in 1857 as Illustrations of the Book of Proverbs, later as Laws from Heaven for Life on Earth (1878). There is much rich material, but Arnot skips Proverbs 7 and 21, and various verses in the other chapters. The work is famous for the grasp of spiritual truths and the easy-flowing style.

Bridges, Charles. An Exposition of the Book of Proverbs. **Grand Rapids: Zondervan, 1959. Reprint.**

Originally issued in 1850, this conservative work is still valuable. Spurgeon called it the best book on Proverbs in his day. About one page, sometimes more, is devoted to each proverb. There is some good exposition, and the emphasis of the work is mainly practical. Cf. Santa for one-volume edition.

Buzzell, Sid S. "Proverbs," in Bible Knowledge Commentary, **ed. John F. Walvoord and Roy B. Zuck. Volume I. Wheaton: Victor Books, 1983.**

A former teacher at the Dallas Theological Seminary has done this concise, clear, adept work. He shows a fine grasp of Hebrew exegesis and word meaning, use of context where it is pertinent, parallelism, customs, etc. The pastor, other church worker or layperson who uses this for preparation to speak or to live in God's values will benefit much.

Cohen, A. Proverbs **(Soncino series). London: Soncino, 1946.**

Comments are very much the same as on the Psalms. It is a fairly good terse commentary, just not nearly one of the best.

Delitzsch, Franz. The Proverbs of Solomon **(2 volumes). Grand Rapids: Eerdmans, 1950. Reprint.**

From the standpoint of Hebrew exegesis and careful detailed scholarship this is very good.

Draper, James T., Jr. Proverbs: The Secret of Beautiful Living. **Wheaton: Tyndale House, 1971.**

A clear, concise, refreshing book at many points, offering some good help especially to laypersons and stimulation to expositors.

Harris, R. Laird. "Proverbs," in Wycliffe Bible Commentary, **ed. C. Pfeiffer and E. F. Harrison. Chicago: Moody, 1962.**

A competent, well-studied and often contributing treatment by a top Old Testament conservative scholar. One of the best brief commentaries, offering considerable insight.

Ironside, H. A. <u>Proverbs</u>. **NY: Loizeaux, 1952.**

Selected proverbs are expounded practically with the author's usual warmth, illustration, and insight into spiritual living.

Jensen, Irving. <u>Proverbs</u>. **Chicago: Moody Press, 1982.**

In the Everyman's Bible Commentary series, this is a 116-page simple layman's help geared to provoke application to life. Several charts and a detailed outline printed at the outset and followed in the sweeping survey help in this. Of course many verses are passed over, but the survey draws many things together in perspective and can be a catalyst used along with more detailed works in preparation to preach or teach or just to enjoy a brief sketch that can refresh.

Jones, Edgar. <u>Proverbs and Ecclesiastes</u> **(Torch Bible Commentary). London: SCM Press Ltd., 1961.**

The Professor of Hebrew and Old Testament at the Northern Congregational College, Manchester, England did this. He feels that some parts of Proverbs linked with Solomon's name may be due to Solomon, but the majority of the material comes from later times (8th to 3rd centuries). In his view Solomon did not write Ecclesiastes; rather more than one teacher in the wisdom school wrote parts of the book, taking the pseudonym of Solomon ca. 250 B. C. Verse by verse this is usually a fair, though quite concise commentary touching on some of the most crucial aspects and based on use of modern critical scholarship on the liberal side. The brevity results in passing over many verses with generalized comments too sparse to be of serious help (cf. Prov. 3:5, 6; 22:6). His lists of sources do not reflect use of <u>evangelical</u> works available when he wrote.

Kidner, Derek. <u>Proverbs</u>. **Downers Grove, IL: InterVarsity, 1972.**

Many reviews have been enthusiastic about this evangelical work. It offers a wealth of brief comments on the Proverbs and an especially helpful section on various key subjects and what the proverbs as a whole say about these themes. It is one of the most stimulating treatments of Proverbs from the standpoint of offering to-the-point relationships to our experience today.

Kidner, Derek. <u>The Wisdom of Proverbs, Job and Ecclesiastes</u>. **Downers Grove: IVP, 1985. 175 pp.**

An introduction to wisdom writings, touching on themes, and treating readers to recent thought on wisdom literature. He looks at the biblical material alongside apocryphal wisdom sources and parallels in ancient Near Eastern works. He often helps on proverbs that seem to clash, and has insights on how to view the ones that generalize and do not work in some cases. Chapters of this evangelical effort deal with Old Testament wisdom literature, Proverbs, Job, Ecclesiastes, recent thought and evaluation of higher critical studies, and the correlation of Proverbs, Job and Ecclesiastes in certain ways. Three appendices treat each Old Testament wisdom writing in relation to Near Eastern works. Kidner also shows comparisons and differences between Ecclesiasticus, Wisdom of Solomon and the Old Testament books. Cf. Bullock under Job for another outstanding study of the Old Testament poetic literature.

Lawson, George. Exposition of Proverbs. **Grand Rapids:** **Kregel, 1980 rp of 1829 ed.**

Lawson was a Scottish clergyman (1749-1820) who learned exegesis at the University of Edinburgh and later became Professor of Theology there for 33 years as the successor of John Brown. His 890 pages here are not of a critical nature but seek only to explain the verses with simple, practical, judicious comments flavored with pertinent quotes, illustrations or thoughts that suggest illustrations. His definition of the fear of the Lord in 1:7 is choice, and he gives good food for counsel in 3:5, 6; 4:18; 6:25, 26; 7:6-27; 8:14-32 applied to Christ; 22:6; 26:4, 5; 31:10 ff., and many others. This has to rate as one of the most helpful older works in reference to the main task of explaining the sense of verses, usually quite well.

McKane, William. Proverbs. A New Approach. **Philadelphia:** **Westminster, 1970.**

This liberal work provides a wealth of material on philological connections with Proverbs and can make the serious reader really think about the meaning of phrases. McKane is highly regarded, and his work well-respected as one of the better commentaries by a critical scholar.

Mouser, William E., Jr. Walking in Wisdom. **Downers Grove:** **IVP, 1983.**

A fairly lucid book that can prime the thought and set it running in productive paths as one prepares a message, or as any Christian seeks help from wise counsel.

Nicholls, Benjamin E. The Book of Proverbs. **London:** **Rivingtons, 1858.**

Not verse by verse but very good in comparing Scripture with Scripture. There is a very fine section on the methods of interpreting various proverbs.

Ross, Allen P. "Proverbs," in Expositor's Bible Commentary **(Volume 5).** **Ed. Frank Gaebelein and R. P. Polcyn.** **Grand Rapids:** **Zondervan, 1991.**

This is an outstanding conservative effort (pp. 881-1134). Ross, who has written also well in Genesis and Psalms, has a good introduction concluding with a three page list of key literature. He includes a very helpful index of topics (897-903) before the commentary to facilitate finding exact subjects discussed. He draws richly from wide reading in noted sources to pour much help into many of the verse comments, and is helpful on main views and aspects that are pertinent (cf. on the wife in 31:10-31).

Santa, George F.   A Modern Study of Proverbs.   **Milford, MI: Mott Media, 1978. 752 pp.**

Actually this is a revision of the famous commentary by Charles Bridges (1794-1869). It replaces the archaic English in a direct, clear vocabulary of today. Still, Santa clings fast to Bridges' meaning.

Stuart, Moses.   A Commentary on the Book of Proverbs.   **NY: Dodd, 1852.**

Written by a Hebrew scholar, this commentary offers an extensive introduction of 134 pages and is a useful, profitable work.

Woodcock, Eldon.   Proverbs.   **Grand Rapids: Zondervan, 1988.   237 pp.**

A Dallas Theological Seminary graduate and Professor of Bible at Nyack College in New York deals with key topics such as wisdom (Hebrew words for this, folly, righteousness, and wickedness), fear, human relationships (adulterous woman, wife, family circle, speech), counsel for a work ethic, and other subjects. Rightly heeded, the principles Woodcock clearly sets forth can lead to true success. The book is of special benefit to laypeople in a series of devotional times but can prime the pump for preachers too.

XVI. ECCLESIASTES

Barton, G. A.   Ecclesiastes (ICC).   **Edinburgh: T. & T. Clark, 1908.**

A detailed commentary on textual and linguistic matters by a liberal scholar. In serious study of the book it is one of the most helpful on technical areas.

Bullock, C. Hassell.   Cf. on Job.

This is outstanding in giving a well-organized survey of main issues relating to interpreting the book. It also has a rich exposition of several of the sections. Teachers and church workers preparing to speak on Ecclesiastes would wisely acquaint themselves with this material before going ahead.

Crenshaw, James L.   Ecclesiastes (Old Testament Library).   **Philadelphia: Westminster, 1987.   192 pp.**

This is liberal, an illustration of human rationalism at work on Scripture. In many cases the Duke University scholar in Old Testament wisdom material is contributive in giving views and reasons by other writers on particular passages. Yet in many ways he is very disappointing. To him, Ecclesiastes has no reasoned structure but is randomly brought together (cf. p. 47). Theologically the work is of little help. Crenshaw sees a pessimistic approach in which life has no meaning (25, 34, 53 etc.), and a positive outlook is downplayed (20). He brings his own rationalization to explain away verses about fearing God (102, 184, 190). He rejects "Remember your creator" (12:1), feeling that it must be "your wife" so as to suit the context (184-85).

Delitzsch, Franz. "Ecclesiastes," in Keil and Delitzsch series.

Though old, this is in many ways a productive work offering considerable help on word meaning, connections of sections, views, etc.

Eaton, Michael A. Ecclesiastes (Tyndale Old Testament Commentary). Downers Grove: IVP, 1983. 159 pp.

A carefullly measured work that is usually very helpful, by an English Anglican. He holds the author is not Solomon but two persons who put themselves in Solomon's sandals to speak from his stance, so the date is unresolved. The theme is to advocate faith in a good God, who is in control and invests life with meaning and purpose, as distinguished from futility without Him. Eaton has much of benefit on introduction, word studies and problem passages.

Fredericks, Daniel C. Qoheleth's Language. Re-evaluation of its Nature and Date. Lewiston, PA: Edwin Mellen Press, 1988. 301 pp.

This examines past explanations and concludes that the Hebrew has evidences of being pre-exilic, not post-exilic as critical scholars usually hold.

Ginsburg, C. D. The Song of Songs and Coheleth. NY: KTAV Publishing House, 1970rp of 1857 work.

A famous Jewish commentary with much to offer on what the text says, what it means, etc. It is one of the better older works with help on exegesis, customs, views.

Glenn, Donald. "Ecclesiastes," in Bible Knowledge Commentary, ed. John F. Walvoord and Roy B. Zuck. Volume I. Wheaton: Victor Books, 1983.

A skilled Old Testament faculty member at Dallas Theological Seminary contributed this good brief study, giving frequent help on exegesis, connections of verses, and theology.

Goldberg, Louis. Ecclesiastes (Bible Study Commentary). Grand Rapids: Zondervan, 1983.

A conservative survey, well-organized, doing a lot to clarify meaning especially for laypeople and pastors needing a quick overview of the book or sections.

Gordis, R. Koheleth: The Man and His World. NY: Schocken Books, 1968rp of 1951 ed. 396 pp.

Here is a detailed, critical work by a liberal Jewish scholar, discussing textual and linguistic matters. Gordis uses the Hebrew substantially. He has delved into detailed research on such areas as background, style and content, and gives conclusions in concise, popular presentation.

Hengstenberg, E. W. A Commentary on Ecclesiastes. Edinburgh: T. & T. Clark, 1860.

This is one of the finest, most scholarly works on Ecclesiastes.

Jones, Edgar. Proverbs, Ecclesiastes (cf. on Proverbs).

Kaiser, Walter C., Jr. Ecclesiastes: Total Life. Chicago: Moody Press, 1979.

An evangelical book in the Everyman's Bible Commentary series written in a very interesting fashion on the central concern Kaiser sees in Ecclesiastes: ". . . that basic hunger of men to see if the totality of life fits into a meaningful pattern" (p. 8). The theme is not "All is vanity" but an optimistic "Fear God and keep His commandments." The author's "words of delight" (12:10) estimating his own work focus not on thinking like a natural man entrapped in "pessimism, skepticism, materialism, fatalism, and the like" (p. 15). The book, says Kaiser, is a divine revelation as surely as any Bible book. The real theme, as suggested in 3:11, is that "man can know how all things, men and ideas fit together . . ." when he "comes to know the One who built man in his own image with the capacity to understand who he is as a man, what he means, and what is the worth of things, even life itself" (17). Kaiser shows how Ecclesiastes is in tune with distinctive truths of earlier Scripture (33-38). This work is brief but outstanding in setting the message in its right perspective. It is footnoted throughout, and contains a small, select annotated bibliography. —Jan Sattem in part.

Kidner, Derek. A Time to Mourn, and a Time to Dance. Downers Grove: IVP, 1976.

In The Bible Speaks Today series, this is a lively, popular exposition of Ecclesiastes that relates the message, accurately given, to life today. Kidner feels the author is not Solomon but one very close to his spirit. For him 3:11 is a key to the book (God put eternity in man's heart), which moves toward the last two verses. All things will disappoint men; only God finally satisfies (cf. p. 98). Kidner's writing style communicates well; he (and Ecclesiastes) bring us to many fresh re-evaluations of what really counts in life, and he shows a fine grasp of the book from a scholar's perceptions and a simplicity at the same time. He even cites choice things from many sources. —Dan Phillips, in part.

Kidner, Derek. The Wisdom, etc. (Cf. on Proverbs).

Lange, J. P. "Ecclesiastes," in Commentary on the Holy Scriptures (Volume 7). Reprint, 25 volumes in 12. Grand Rapids: Zondervan, 1960.

Another of the very helpful older works, often rich in meaning on details, giving views, considering matters from different angles.

Leupold, H. C.   Exposition of Ecclesiastes.   Grand Rapids: Baker, 1987rp of work that first came out in 1952.   301 pp.

A thorough work, as Leupold's commentaries usually are, this is very helpful in a verse by verse study on a scholarly level.

Plumptre, E. H.   Ecclesiastes (Cambridge Bible for Schools and Colleges). Cambridge: University Press, 1888.

Though old, this still rates as one of the most helpful commentaries, brief and direct, for expositors.

Reichert, Victor E. and Cohen, A.   "Ecclesiastes," in The Five Megilloth.   London: Soncino Press, 1946.

A concise Jewish explanation, frequently giving good help that is right to the point, sometimes views.

Swindoll, Charles R.   Living on the Ragged Edge: Coming to Terms with Reality. Waco, TX: Word Books, 1985.

This is a series of messages preached by one of America's most sought after speakers, pastor of Evangelical Free Church, Fullerton, CA. Swindoll writes in a creative flow that captures the imagination, leading it through what he perceives the text means. He is perceptive on human problems and principles in passages relevant to these. Devotionally and as a general exposition pulling lay readers or pastors in by clear, interesting communication, the work helps expose how the message lives. Illustrations and applications help make the book a catalyst for seeing the relevance for preaching and living.

Whybray, R. N.   Ecclesiastes.   Grand Rapids: Eerdmans, 1989.   179 pp.

Adept in wisdom literature, the writer sees a positive outlook in the book. God bestows meaning to life, and a person's pursuits have fulfilling quality only from Him (cf. p. 27). He turns on light at many points exegetically, but conservative readers will not always think he does this in holding a third century B. C. writing. He also sees no unified flow through the book, but thirty-four unconnected subjects. At times his explanations leave matters not sufficiently clarified (cf. p. 127 on women in 7:28).

Wright, J. S.   "Ecclesiastes," in Expositor's Bible Commentary, Volume 5.   Ed. Frank Gaebelein and R. P. Polcyn.   Grand Rapids: Zondervan, 1991.

Arguing for a single writer, Qoheleth (except possibly 12:9-12), he does not certainly think it was Solomon but sees no passages that rule out that possibility (p. 1140). He is not certain of the date (1143). His statement of the book's purpose is very good (1144-46), he has a fine one-page outline and is judicious verse by verse, showing that pessimism can be overcome and life given meaning by relating it to God and His will, with the Christian revelation in other parts of the Scripture filling out the picture, as on 3:12-14 (p. 1162). In most cases this is a very good commentary of a conservative nature.

XVII. SONG OF SOLOMON

Burrowes, George. A Commentary on the Song of Solomon. **Swengel, PA: Sovereign Grace, 1958 reprint.**

A Princeton Theological Seminary graduate of 1835, the author has produced a work highly praised by Spurgeon and more recently by D. Martyn Lloyd-Jones. There are many good comments, but some fanciful typology. Burrowes sees the love relation here as an allegory of the union between God and man. Many, however, believe that the relationship of love is between a man and a woman as it seems to be, in the primary interpretation.

Carr, G. Lloyd. The Song of Solomon **(Tyndale Old Testament Commentary). Downers Grove: IVP, 1984. 175 pp.**

This commentary is well-respected. Carr, evangelical, is very learned, using scholarly sources, yet lucid in his lengthy introduction, statement of theme (two people celebrating a literal love relationship), and verse by verse commenting. He often has something quite helpful.

Deere, Jack S. "Song of Songs," in Bible Knowledge Commentary, **ed. John F. Walvoord and Roy B. Zuck. Volume I. Wheaton: Victor Books, 1983.**

A well-studied conservative treatment following the two character view, Solomon and a woman. He is clear, explains most matters that need explaining, and shows good expertise in the Hebrew word meaning and movement of the book. He develops the beauty of a love relationship as God intends it.

Dillow, Joseph C. (Jody). Solomon on Sex. **NY: Thomas Nelson, Inc., 1977.**

Dillow was a student at Dallas Seminary. He is already known for his work Speaking in Tongues, Seven Crucial Questions (Zondervan, 1975). He and his wife have ministered in a marriage seminar ministry, "Inherit a Blessing." He gives a verse by verse commentary. He believes that the Song was written by Solomon as a young man, with fifteen reflections on a beautiful love relationship between Solomon and Shulamith, a country girl. He rejects interpretations of the Song as allegory of Jahweh's love for Israel, and other allegorical explanations. The Song, he feels, is a portrait of idealized love in marriage according to God's design. Dillow uses many good sources (cf. footnotes) and has many helpful things to say about love in marriage. However, even on the assumption that his basic view of the Song is the right one, a reader can get the impression at some points that he has exercised a considerable imagination as to what the text says about married love so as to have it very interestingly applicable to countless matters today. His sections on applications are thought-provoking and speak to many needs in lovers today to help them enjoy a fulfilling marriage, whether these truly are what the Song itself means or not.

Fox, Michael V.   The Song of Songs and the Ancient Egyptian Love Songs.   Madison: University of Wisconsin, 1985.   454 pp.

Valuable, penetrating study of ancient love songs and certain similarities of the biblical Song to these. The work has three parts: translation and interpretation of late Egyptian songs; translation and commentary on Song of Solomon, and the literary method of discussing love in Egypt and Israel. He gives his own new translation of Song of Solomon, sensitive to meaning of idioms and usually natural in wording. He brings to the task good skill in grammar, syntax and word meanings from cognate languages. He holds to a post-exilic date. This late dating is not at all necessary to conservatives.

Gill, John.   An Exposition of the Song of Solomon.   London: Collingridge, 1854.

Many have regarded this as the most outstanding work from Gill's prolific and talented pen.

Ginsburg, C. D.   Cf. on Ecclesiastes.

Glickman, S. Craig.   A Song for Lovers.   Downers Grove: IVP, 1976.

After he wrote his Th. M. thesis at Dallas Seminary in 1974 on "The Unity of the Song of Solomon", he wrote this. He gives his own translation, paraphrase and practical comments on the love relationship within marriage. It is generally done well.

Gordis, Robert.   The Song of Songs.   NY: Bloch, 1962.

By a Jewish scholar, this book is good in Jewish culture and contemporary history of that day. He presents the leading theories of interpretation and has good materials, but his treatment is not an exposition.

Gordis, R.   The Song of Solomon and Lamentation. A Commentary and Translation.   NY: KTAV, 1974.   108 pp.

This highly regarded effort, though so brief, packs in much worthwhile content and shows some revision of his earlier book of 1962. Gordis will many times offer the expositor good textual data, word meanings and rabbinic help. He views the Song as celebrating human love. He is disappointing in devoting so little focus on theological emphases.

Henry, Carl F. H. (Ed.).   The Biblical Expositor.   3 volumes.   Philadelphia: Holman, 1960.

The discussion holds to the two-character view of the book, which says that the Song depicts the intimacies of love between Solomon and a Shulamite maiden.

Ironside, H. A.   Song of Solomon.   NY: Loizeaux, 1950.

Many have considered this book one of the most helpful for a practical exposition.

Kinlaw, Dennis. "Songs of Songs," in Expositor's Bible Commentary, Volume 5. Ed. Frank Gaebelein and R. P. Polcyn. Grand Rapids: Zondervan, 1991.

Kinlaw has a good statement of views in explaining the book (pp. 1202-06), and of purpose. The latter is to describe marriage with its physical intimacies as it ought to be, in God's will, a delight to both partners (1207). Yet he believes that proper marital love is also symbolical of God and His people (1209). He approves a tenth century date and thinks that Solomon may or may not be the writer. The commentary is in many parts rather good.

Lehrman, S. M. "The Song of Songs," in The Five Megilloth. London: Soncino Press, 1946.

As usual in the Soncino books, this is concise but reliable explanation by Jewish scholarship.

Mason, Clarence E. Love Song. The Song of Solomon Comes Alive for Today. Chicago: Moody, 1976.

Brief explanation, giving main views and taking the Song to be historical of Solomon and his Shulamite bride. The author taught for many years at Philadelphia College of Bible and was rather well-known as a Bible teacher.

Nee, Watchman. The Song of Songs. London: Christian Literature Crusade, 1965.

This 187-page work was originally a composition of notes from a Bible study. First published in Chinese in 1945, this 1965 English translation is consistent with much of Nee's prior work. The Song of Solomon is viewed as possessing both historical and spiritual content. Nee understands the Song as allegorical of the marital union between Christ and His church (the Shulamite bride is the individual believer as opposed to the corporate body). Nee outlines the volume as a developing love relationship from initial to mature love. —Jan Sattem

Newton, A. L. The Song of Solomon Compared With Other Parts of Scripture. London: James Nisbet, 1871.

This is a verse by verse study with a warm devotional element and frequent relating of aspects here to Christ and His church. It is arbitrary as to whether the Song should be applied to Christ as he does. It is an example of attaching the details to some corresponding truth about Christ and the Church. The present reviewer does not regard that as the point of the Song. It actually refers to a human love relationship.

Patterson, Paige. Song of Solomon (Everyman's Bible Commentary). Chicago: Moody, 1986. 124 pp.

In an Old Testament Survey course, this turned out to be very helpful, crammed as it is with statements showing awareness of problems, views, and sources, yet not going into great detail. Patterson thinks Solomon wrote the ideal of love in marriage early in his reign (p. 17), reflecting the companionship, loyalty, joy, peace, devotion, forgiveness, chastity, tenderness, and sexual union. The commentator discusses seven interpretations, preferring a literal human love but also an analogy of intimacy between the Lord and Israel, Christ and His church (22). Using a chapter to comment on each of the Song's chapters in English, Patterson is lucid and informed in verse by verse comment, perceptive about when to be literal and when to be figurative.

Pope, M. H.   The Song of Songs (Anchor Bible).   NY: Doubleday, 1977.   743 pp.

This is liberal and highly commended by many. A very full bibliography appears, and Pope has a masterful survey of the history of interpretations. To the diligent he offers the profit of much help in textual, lexical, exegetical matters more often than in his own interpretation of the meaning. He ties the marriage relationship with rites of cults in the ancient Near East, wandering afield from a view conservatives will accept as natural. One will need to exercise much discernment, finding much help at times, much that is not helpful at others, despite the high regard in which liberals hold the work.

Rowley, H. H.   The Servant of the Lord and Other Essays.   London: Blackwell, 1965.

Cf. the essay on the different approaches to the interpretation of the love relationship in the Song. Rowley, a liberal scholar, had much to offer from his vast reading in Old Testament studies. As to orientation, this work can be helpful for trained students.

Stuart, Moody.   The Song of Songs: An Exposition of the Song of Solomon.   London: James Nisbet, 1857.

He regards the book as a spiritual allegory on the Christian's wealth in and relation to Christ which gives one a rare sense of privilege. Spurgeon said of Stuart, "He has poetry in his soul, and beyond that a heart like that of Rutherford, food with love to the altogether Lovely One" (Commenting and Commentaries). But the devotional direction misleads, as Burrough's, Nee's and Newton's above.

Taylor, Hudson.   Union and Communion.   China Inland Mission, now Overseas Missionary Fellowship, c. 1910.

Taylor, like some writers above, saw the relationship allegorically in terms of the union between God and man, and gets away from the real point.

Tournay, Raymond J.   Word of God, Song of Love.   NY: Paulist Press, 1988. 194 pp.

He has the Song written in the Persian era but is weak on evidence. He combines two themes, levels of meaning, one about Solomon and his Egyptian wife in lovers' intimacy and the second an allegorical idea—Messiah and the daughter of Zion with her city where she dwells. The second is a Messianic yearning to encourage Jews in the Persian era to believe in the Messianic Kingdom to come. It is as if the Messiah is asleep, delaying that new era. Here, Tournay labors at the notion that the person sleeping in the Song is the many, not the woman.

Tournay has steeped himself in rabbinics and the Hebrew language as well as scholarly literature on the Song.

XVIII. ISAIAH

Alexander, Joseph A. Isaiah, Translated and Explained. 2 volumes. Philadelphia: Presbyterian Board of Publication, 1851.

This is one of the best older expositions of the book from a Hebrew scholar. There are frequent word studies; he deals with syntax; he has an original translation; his commentary is more detailed than most and is usually helpful verse by verse.

Allis, O. T. The Unity of Isaiah: A Study in Prophecy. Philadelphia: Presbyterian and Reformed Publishing Co., 1950.

A noted conservative Old Testament scholar of a few decades back builds a carefully reasoned case for one author and unity of the book. This is his aim, and not the task of writing a commentary.

Archer, Gleason L., Jr. "Isaiah." The Wycliffe Bible Commentary. Chicago: Moody, 1961.

Archer has packed a lot of good material into this commentary and is very helpful in historical and cultural details as well as the interpretation of difficult phrases. He takes a premillennial covenant viewpoint, so it is nothing unusual for him to refer prophecies concerning Israel to the church.

Baron, David. The Servant of Jehovah. Grand Rapids: Zondervan (n. d.).

Covering chapter 53 only, this is a masterful work by a careful scholar. See also E. J. Young, The Suffering Servant, on chapter 53.

Blocher, Henry. Songs of the Servant. London: IVP, 1975. 79 pp.

This paperback by an evangelical helps the reader see the way in which the New Testament is sprinkled with references to the Servant Songs of Isaiah, and how Jesus viewed the expectations of the Messiah, Son of Man, and the Servant as realized in Himself.

Bullock, C. Hassell. An Introduction to the Old Testament Prophetic Books. Chicago: Moody, 1986. 391 pp.

A well-ordered study of introductory aspects on each prophet, showing much use of modern literature on issues. It is a conservative approach, and quite valuable.

Bultema, Harry. <u>Commentary on Isaiah</u>. Translated from Dutch by Cornelius Lambregtse. Grand Rapids: Kregel, 1981, original publication in Dutch, 1923. 630 pp.

Bultema (1884-1952), greatly nurtured for Christ by a Christian mother in the Netherlands, studied at Calvin College and Seminary and pastored Christian Reformed churches. He became persuaded of premillennial dispensationalism and left the Christian Reformed movement to found the Muskegon Berean Church. He writes a respectable commentary verse by verse, sometimes going into detail on arguments to distinguish Israel with its past and future from the church of the present (cf. pp. 51-53 and often in Chapters 40-66). He prefers the Messianic view of 7:14 but is brief and weak in discussion of such a debated verse. He argues on 11:9 that there will be literal animals in the glorified state of the new earth, that 14:12 refers not merely to the king of Babylon but to Satan, and that 26:19f refers to resurrection of believers. In introducing Chapters 40-66, he offers ten arguments that the same writer who penned 1-39 also wrote these. This is a fairly good commentary.

Calvin, John. <u>Isaiah</u> (4 volumes). Grand Rapids: Eerdmans.

A lucid amillennial commentary, in this reviewer's judgment good but not as directly to the point and certainly not as recent as amillennial works by Leupold, Young, etc.

Culver, Robert. <u>The Sufferings and the Glory of the Lord's Righteous Servant</u>. Moline, IL: Christian Service Foundation, 1958.

A rich, competent evangelical study of Isaiah 52:13—53:12 helpful in preaching and teaching. Culver is perhaps better known for his <u>Daniel and the Latter Days</u>. He graduated from Grace Theological Seminary and taught for many years at Trinity Evangelical Divinity School, but has pastored for a number of years. His writings reflect sound research and mature scholarly judgment.

Delitzsch, Franz. <u>Isaiah</u>. 3rd edition. 2 volumes in Keil and Delitzsch <u>Commentaries of the Old Testament</u>. Grand Rapids: Eerdmans, 1964.

Among technical works for trained students who are able to grapple with and appreciate the Hebrew, this is one of the outstanding linguistic commentaries on Isaiah. Delitzsch put great exegetical, historical and theological learning into the work, which is highly respected. In prophecy it is amillennial.

Ellison, H. L. <u>Men Spake From God</u>. Grand Rapids: Eerdmans, 1958.

An evangelical work giving a summary to acclimate a reader to each of the prophets. The book serves as an older, helpful introduction to the subject, but see such newer works as C. H. Bullock, R. Chisholm, and Leon Wood.

Engnell, I. <u>The Call of Isaiah</u>. Uppsala Universitets arsskrift, 1959.

Those who plan a technical study of Isaiah 6 may wish to include this probing investigation into the text.

Garland, David. Isaiah, A Study Guide. **Grand Rapids: Zondervan, 1968.**

A handy premillennial survey of Isaiah, holding to the book's unity, using a good outline, giving a competent overall view of the book and comments on some key passages.

Gray, G. B. A Critical and Exegetical Commentary on the Book of Isaiah **(ICC). Edinburgh: T. & T. Clark, 1912.**

A liberally-oriented work that is an aid on many of the textual/linguistic details, which a more technical study is concerned to note.

Grogan, G. W. "Isaiah," in the Expositor's Bible Commentary, **Volume 6, editors Frank Gaebelein and R. P. Polcyn. Grand Rapids: Zondervan, 1986.**

Grogan is Principal of the Bible Training Institute, Glasgow, Scotland. He argues for the unity of the book, Isaiah as author and a premillennial view. He has a good bibliography of books up to 1981 but lists only six journal articles (p. 23). He sees some prophecies fulfilled to Israel as distinct from the church in the land of Palestine during a future millennial era after the Second Advent. He regards Revelation 20:4-6 as referring to an earthly kingdom after the Second Advent (14) and thinks Isaiah 7:14 has a double fulfillment. The discussion throughout seems to be quite able.

Hercus, John. More Pages from God's Casebook. **Downers Grove: IVP, 1965.**

As he has done with characters in Genesis and David, Hercus sketches Isaiah, Jeremiah and Ezekiel in a fashion that makes their lives relevant today as they ought to be. Hercus is vivid.

Jennings, F. C. Studies in Isaiah. **NY: Loizeaux (n. d.).**

Premillennial in approach, this work by a well-known Plymouth Brethren writer relates the argument of the book and the political and religious background. It is old, but helpful.

Kaiser, Otto. Isaiah 1-12, A Commentary; **also** Isaiah 13-39, A Commentary. **2 volumes. Philadelphia: Westminster Press, 1972-74.**

An example of how a liberal scholar ascribes little of even "first Isaiah" (chapters 1-39) to Isaiah, son of Amoz. This is not to say that Kaiser has no helpful commentary on many of the details in the chapters.

Kelly, William. Lectures on the Book of Isaiah. **4th edition. London: Hammond, 1947.**

This is a very fine English exposition of the book, but offers no Hebrew help. It is quite thorough and premillennial and dispensational. Kelly usually tells the reader why he takes a certain view in the debated prophetical passages. A Plymouth Brethren author, he died in 1906.

Kidner, Derek. "Isaiah," in New Bible Commentary Revised, ed. D. Guthrie et al. Grand Rapids: Eerdmans, 1970, pp. 588-625.

Kidner usefully sums up critical arguments in his introduction, but defends unity and authorship by Isaiah with basic arguments. He believes that 11:6-9 refers to conditions in the ultimate state, the New Heavens and New Earth. On many prophetic texts he is vague (11:11ff.; 19:23ff.; ch. 35, etc.). He does not recognize a distinct future for Israel that premillennialists see, but expects fulfillment in the church (cf. on ch. 60, p. 621).

Kissane, Edward J. The Book of Isaiah. 2 volumes. Dublin: Browne and Nolan, Ltd., 1952-54.

An old, conservative commentary that offers much on the verse by verse line and takes views not in accord with modern critical theories. He is often fresh and original in comments, and is still of solid value.

Leupold, H. C. Exposition of Isaiah. 2 volumes. Grand Rapids: Baker, 1971.

Leupold, as usual, offers much detail in explaining verses from the standpoint of the background, Hebrew word meanings, customs, and the context. It is a fine commentary and is a good recent example of amillennial understanding of prophetical sections such as Isaiah 2, 4, 9, 11, 24-27, 35, 40-66 in relation to the fulfillment of messianic and kingdom hopes.

Lindblom, J. Prophecy in Ancient Israel. Philadelphia: Fortress Press, 1962.

A standard work on prophecy in Israel's history, which energetic students will want to consult. Yet Lindblom would be more valuable overall if he were more contributive on the doctrinal thrust of things.

Lindsey, F. Duane. The Servant Songs. A Study in Isaiah. Chicago: Moody, 1985. 170 pp.

A former professor from Dallas Theological Seminary deals in introductory fashion with special problems in the Songs, interacts with literature on them, and gives a commentary on them. He does well exegetically, and Kenneth Barker in the Foreword tabs it "one of the finest studies" on this subject. Lindsey argues for fulfillment of the Servant in Jesus Christ, taking a premillennial view. His lack of definitions for a number of terms may dishearten readers without a seminary background, i.e. "hapax legomenon," p. 84 and "hendiadys," p. 126. Lindsey often has good arguments to support his views; at times he waves aside other positions without looking at arguments for them. It is a valuable book.

MacRae, Allan A. The Gospel of Isaiah. Chicago: Moody Press, 1977.

The President and Professor of Old Testament at Biblical School of Theology in Hatfield, PA wrote this. He was one of Dr. Robert Dick Wilson's outstanding students. The work is not a commentary but a book elucidating themes in 40:1-56:8, showing the interrelation of thoughts and the development of themes, based on the original Hebrew. The section has more verses cited in the New Testament than any other Old Testament passage of its length. Several portions of Handel's Messiah came from here. The chapter on Cyrus as God's instrument has many good insights (cf. p. 29), as do the discussions on Isaiah 40 and the several chapters on the Servant of the Lord in Isaiah 41-53, and the thoughts on chapters 54-56.

Martin, John A. "Isaiah," in the Bible Knowledge Commentary, ed. John F. Walvoord and Roy B. Zuck. Volume I. Wheaton: Victor Books, 1983.

Martin briefly defends unity by Isaiah, then provides a succinct, carefully-studied and clear commentary following a good outline. On problem passages he often offers views and reasons, briefly due to his limitations of space. On the Servant Songs he provides logic for seeing fulfillment in Jesus Christ, and in many texts he argues for realization in a future earthly millennial era, after the Second Advent. He sees many passages fulfilled in Old Testament days and is quite specific about historical details that match these. Cf. also the related book he and his father wrote: Alfred Martin and John Martin, Isaiah: The Glory of the Messiah (Chicago: Moody, 1983).

Morgan, G. Campbell. The Prophecy of Isaiah. 2 volumes. London: Hodder and Stoughton, 1990.

A thorough analytical treatment of a premillennial nature which some have regarded as one of the finest broad studies on Isaiah.

North, C. R. The Suffering Servant in Deutero-Isaiah, An Historical and Critical Study. 2nd edition, revised and enlarged. Oxford, 1956.

A helpful work from the standpoint of gaining perspective on various views and scholarly work done on the identity of the suffering servant. The book shows a wide grasp of material on the subject, and acquaints a reader with what has been done.

Oswalt, John N. The Book of Isaiah: Chapters 1-39 (New International Commentary on the Old Testament). Grand Rapids: Eerdmans, 1986. 746 pp.

This first part of a 2-volume work replaces E. J. Young's 3-volume set, and ought to be highly regarded as a conservative work. Oswalt is Professor of Old Testament and Semitic Languages at Trinity Evangelical Divinity School, Deerfield, IL. He holds that Isaiah, son of Amoz, wrote the book, a unity. His introduction does much on the theology, taking the theme as servanthood (p. 54). He sees 7:14 having a double fulfillment, is often good on messianic texts (9:5, 6; 11:1-10), but often takes prophetic passages as figurative, not literal. He relates sub-sections to larger sections to show how things fit. Some wish the Hebrew words were in Hebrew letters, not in English transliterations.

Ridderbos, J.   Isaiah (Bible Students Commentary).   Grand Rapids: Zondervan, 1985.   580 pp.

This is evangelical, originally in a Dutch series in 1950-51 for lay readers without Hebrew. The NIV has been edited. The introduction is so taken up with authorship issues that it fails to deal with the aim, theology, unique characteristics and other matters that give perspective. Ridderbos sums up each section at the outset of it, and often has beneficial exegesis and theology on verses, with some freshly stimulating insights. He is amillennial on prophecy of Israel's future but gives reasons for Messianic fulfillment in such texts as the Servant Songs. It is a very good commentary on many passages, and in his amillennial stand shows how one of that persuasion reasons his view.

Scott, R. B. Y.   The Relevance of the Prophets.   NY: Macmillan, 1968.

This revised edition, like the first, assumes redaction criticism. In many respects this perspective does not seem to come into play, or appear persuasive. He does have much that helps the reader learn about prophecy as a channel of God's work with Israel, and how prophetic ministry had its effect among the people. One will receive profit here although may appreciate the overall conservative approach of Bullock, Chisholm, Wood etc. on the prophets.

Smith, W. Robertson.   The Prophets of Israel.   NY: Appleton, 1882.

A very respected work on the eighth century prophets, which still has much to offer.

Vine, William E.   Isaiah, Prophecies, Promises and Warnings.   London: Oliphants, 1953.

Though this excellent work of a premillennial nature is somewhat brief, it often refers to the original text and observes the syntax. It is helpful to the student who has other works which get into the details more at length.

Watts, John D. W.   Isaiah.   2 volumes (Word Biblical Commentary).   Waco, TX: Word Books, 1985-87.   450 + 386 pp.

Watts is quite liberal and given to late composition. After various writers had a hand in a long redaction history, a late author or group ca. 435 B. C. (the latest historical setting Watts sees in the book) molded traditions handed down and composed the parts into a thematic unity to speak to post-exilic needs. A conservative will gain some help from individual bibliographies of sections, comments on the Hebrew, and perception of how this liberal approach works. Watts thinks Isaiah should be divided up into twelve segments for twelve periods of time from the eighth century to Artaxerxes I's day ca. 460 B. C. His contrived scheme of connecting sections to particular generations will be an oddity to many, derived from his opinion and not from necessity in the text by convincing evidence. Sections are not seen addressing issues in Isaiah's day but rather post-exilic concerns. Watts argues against a messianic significance and supernatural fulfillment of such texts as 7:14; it was fulfilled only in the wife and son of Ahaz (p. 102). The new age is not messianic times but the fifth century B. C. Throughout, readers get more of Watts' theory imposed than an explanation of the text in a realistic historical setting that one more naturally gathers from the book. In 52:13-53:12 the servant is Darius and the sufferer is Zerubbabel, according to Watts, and so on.

Wood, Leon J.   The Prophets of Israel.   Grand Rapids: Baker, 1987rp.   405 pp.

A thoroughly conservative work, very clearly written, in two sections, prophetism and the prophets. Wood under the first division goes into the identity, meaning of "to prophesy," function, the Holy Spirit and prophecy and other aspects. In the second, he discusses in some detail prophets before Samuel, Samuel, monarchy prophets, and the writing prophets from the ninth century to post-exilic days. This is a fine book that gives the student or pastor a much better, integrated understanding of the prophets behind the prophetic books.

Young, Edward J.   Isaiah Fifty-Three.   Grand Rapids: Eerdmans, 1952.

Along with works by Baron and Culver, this is a solid evangelical study on Isaiah 52:13—53:12. Young was an outstandingly knowledgeable Old Testament scholar and deals with the text with a great amount of expertise, even making its message meaningful to readers who are not themselves Hebrew scholars.

Young, Edward J.   My Servants the Prophets.   Grand Rapids: Eerdmans, 1952.

Young, a strong conservative with the breadth of reading, interacts with critical views in ways that assist evangelicals. He also contended for the unity of Isaiah in Who Wrote Isaiah? (Grand Rapids: Eerdmans, 1958).

Young, Edward J.   The Book of Isaiah (NIC).   3 volumes.   Grand Rapids: Eerdmans, 1965-72.

This is the most detailed recent completed commentary from a conservative standpoint in giving an amillennial interpretation of the prophetical passages on Messiah and the kingdom over Israel and the world. It is usually exacting in its exegesis, as are other exegetical works by Young, a member of the faculty at Westminster Theological Seminary in Philadelphia until his death in 1970. It has value as an aid in historical and cultural matters, and grapples at length with important problems like 7:14.

XIX. JEREMIAH

Brueggemann, Walter.   To Pluck Up, To Tear Down: A Commentary on The Book of Jeremiah 1-25 (New ICC).   Grand Rapids: Eerdmans, 1988.   222 pp.

Much good detail will help students on the text and principles for today. But the commentary is not especially good in comparison with other works, and redactional ideas show up often. Often passages are said to have been written at a later date and redacted in, as 3:15-18 and 24:1-10. Sources in his bibliography provide help for one who wishes to do research on facets of Jeremiah, though heavily from liberal circles.

Bright, John. **Jeremiah. Introduction, Translation and Notes** **(Anchor Bible). 2nd edition. NY: Doubleday, 1978. 372 pp.**

Bright covers many key matters informatively in his introduction, but his liberal thinking rearranges the text by his arbitrary opinion. He does not offer the really good commentary on verses that can be found in such sources as Feinberg, Dyer, Thompson, or Keil or Streane.

Calvin, John. **Commentaries of Jeremiah and Lamentations** **(5 volumes). Grand Rapids: Eerdmans, 1950.**

Calvin is always worth reading, and one will find much insight on verses as well as the character of Jeremiah. The sheer length will keep many away, and several other works get to the point more directly. Calvin is amillennial on passages about Israel's long-range future.

Carroll, Robert P. **Jeremiah, A Commentary** **(Old Testament Library). Philadelphia: Westminster, 1986. 874 pp.**

In 1986 alone three massive works were published on Jeremiah (cf. Holladay and McKane as well). In Carroll's subjectivism, a Jeremiah of factual history retreats into vagueness behind redactors and layers of tradition which made up speeches and events (p. 48). We are involved here at times more with Carroll's radical wanderings in assumptions than with the Book of Jeremiah many want help on. Still, on many matters of textual, lexical, exegetical nature where his theory does not so intrude, he can be very instructive. His bibliography and interaction with views is often quite valuable.

Clements, R. E. **Jeremiah (Interpretation). Atlanta: John Knox Press, 1988. 276 pp.**

This series is aimed at students, teachers and preachers, using the RSV. Clements is on the faculty at King's College, University of London. This is nowhere near the best commentary, but one can glean a wealth of information even if he is not ready to accept a lot that Clements says. He assumes that the book is by unknown scribes and compilers who preserved a record of Jeremiah's prophecies (p. 3). In chapters 1-25, prose discourses are not per se Jeremiah's words but those of composers "based on words, themes and situations authentic to the prophet" (p. 11). The commentary is broad, not always verse by verse, and since Clements does not use phrases from the RSV set off, a reader finds it hard to be aware of just what part of the text Clements is commenting on at times. He thinks editors may later have named the place "the Euphrates" where Jeremiah was to bury the cloth (ch. 13), rather than the words originally being in God's speech to Jeremiah (85). He sees it as unlikely that the New Covenant in

Jeremiah 31 in its words now could have come from the lips or pen of Jeremiah (190). To him it was only later at Qumran and in the Christian church that the idea evolved that God meant an entirely New Covenant (191). This will be difficult for many to agree with. The commentary is quite disappointing in many ways.

Driver, S. R.   The Book of the Prophet Jeremiah.   London: Hodder and Stoughton, 1906.

Though liberal in its approach, this work is helpful in its detailed notes on verses. Driver was a careful scholar and aids the expositor in understanding the meanings of difficult phrases.

Dyer, Charles.   "Jeremiah," in Bible Knowledge Commentary, ed. John F. Walvoord and Roy B. Zuck.   Volume I.   Wheaton: Victor Books, 1983.

A concise but carefully-researched conservative work that very often provides good help in explaining verses to preachers, students and lay people. Dyer gets to the flow of the message in Jeremiah, mingles summaries and sections on detail in a good balance, and usually has something worthwhile on key verses or problem passages.

Erdman, Charles R.   The Book of Jeremiah and Lamentations.   Westwood, NJ: Revell, 1955.

Here is a good overall synthesis for the student who is seeking to follow the thread of thought through Jeremiah in a broad fashion. Erdman's survey is good. He was a professor in the Princeton Theological Seminary.

Feinberg, Charles L.   Jeremiah, A Commentary.   Grand Rapids: Zondervan, 1982.

This well-done, 335-page work eventually came to be in Volume 6 of the Expositor's Bible Commentary. It joins Feinberg's other works on Ezekiel, Daniel, and the Minor Prophets. A good introduction on the most notable issues climaxes with a lengthy list of commentaries and a few journal articles, a six and a half page outline, then the text of the N. I. V. (North American, 1978), and the exposition. Comments clarifying Hebrew meanings appear both in the exposition and in special notes. Feinberg gives space to different views, as on the passage of the linen belt (13:1-7) and the Branch (23:5, 6), but clearly supports his preference. He favors a premillennial view on the fulfillment of prophecies about Israel's far future, and his work is the best by a premillennialist to date.

Guest, John.   "Jeremiah, Lamentations," in The Communicator's Commentary. Waco, TX: Word Books, 1988.   390 pp.

Guest stimulates preachers by his clarity, directness about the meaning, provocative titles, and relevant applications. In much of the book his work is a catalyst for a sermon series, though he slights passages about a future for Israel (chapters 30-33 etc.).

Habel, Norman C. Jeremiah, Lamentations (Concordia Commentary). Grand Rapids: Zondervan, 1981. 157 pp.

Using the RSV, Habel gives an 8-page outline at the outset and follows it throughout. However, he does not continue the enumeration, so that one can lose the relation of sections. The commentary is fairly solid in a concise, summary way in each pericope. There is discussion of some problems, others are ignored (as which river the cloth is buried in, Jeremiah 13). He cites but leaves unresolved the assumption of some scholars who say that points of comfort passages were by later editors (31:7-14; 32:17-23; 33:14-26, p. 227), texts which can reasonably be from Jeremiah. On the New Covenant, Habel discusses how New Testament texts relate. He sees restoration of Jerusalem in 31:38-40 fulfilled in the New Jerusalem, not in a millennial era after the Second Advent (251). Some restoration texts are not really explained but left vague, as 33:6-19, and fulfillment is placed in the church, the new Israel to Habel. How promises that sound like literal rebuilding are realized in this spiritual fashion realistically is left unexplained (265).

Harrison, R. K. Jeremiah & Lamentations (Tyndale Old Testament Commentary). Downers Grove: IVP, 1975. 240 pp.

This famous Old Testament scholar, conservative, concludes that we have here the basic teachings of Jeremiah under several kings. Lamentations is done by an eye-witness of Jerusalem's fall. In both books, Harrison offers a brief but well-informed commentary that is usually quite helpful in getting at what the text means and not substituting redactional theory from another era.

Holladay, W. L. Jeremiah I: A Commentary on the Book of the Prophet Jeremiah, Chapters 1-25 (Hermeneia). Philadelphia: Fortress Press, 1986. 682 pp. Jeremiah II, Chapters 26-52, 1989. 543 pp.

Like the works by Carroll and McKane this is highly-respected as a technical, critical commentary in the scholarly community. On text, grammar, structure, synthesis of sections and literature dealing with issues it offers much. A 95-page introduction begins Volume II, and a bibliography here updates the one in Volume I. This is the most massive of the recent detailed works, over 1,200 pages at more than 800 words a page. Holladay theorizes that 1:1 refers not to the year of Jeremiah's call but to his birth, 627 B. C., and uses this as a chronological starting point for the rest of the book. He often connects passages in Jeremiah with New Testament verses as to theme, and is skeptical about redaction that remodels the book in a Deuteronomistic pattern. Some criticize him for a highly individualistic translation in many passages, and his pleading that the original text was this way, the way of his emendations. In verse by verse commentary he explains more than Carroll or McKane, is masterful in grammar and syntax, and skillful in insights drawn from much study, so that he helps on many points, on views, etc. Still he retains a lucid flow. Many herald it as the definitive work on Jeremiah to date.

Huey, F. B., Jr. Jeremiah (Bible Study Commentary). Grand Rapids: Zondervan, 1981. 157 pp.

Conservative and concise, using a good outline and giving pastors, Sunday School teachers and lay people in general a quick look in a fairly able way. Dyer, Jensen, Kidner and Harrison do it better among the briefer works in overall helpfulness, though this is not to downgrade Huey.

Jensen, Irving L. Jeremiah and Lamentations (Everyman's Bible Commentary). Chicago: Moody, 1974. 153 pp.

A master at surveys does it again here for pastors, Sunday School teachers and lay persons needing a concise sketch. He has a clear outline, charts that put some material into helpful perspective (as oracles vs. the nations, chapters 46-51), and a map on Jeremiah's geography (p. 149). He sees a premillennial fulfillment of Israel's restoration as in Jeremiah 33 (p. 93 etc.), and offers brief comment on some problems, for example whether Jeremiah walked to a nearby creek or made a trek to the far off Euphrates River with the loin cloth of Chapter 13.

Jensen, Irving L. Jeremiah: Prophet of Judgment. Chicago: Moody, 1966.

Jensen has written a concise evangelical commentary for those who wish for a simple survey. The work is premillennial in its orientation, and is done by a man well-known for his helpful expositional works.

Kidner, Derek. The Message of Jeremiah (Bible Speaks Today). Downers Grove: IVP, 1987. 176 pp.

This is a broad exposition of the book something akin to those by Erdman and Huey, though more refreshing than either. Kidner as usual is very readable, conservative, concise and direct on many of the issues. However, he is amillennial on the main prophetical section (Chapters 30-33), expecting spiritual but not literal realization.

Laetsch, Theodore. Jeremiah. Saint Louis: Concordia, 1952. Also available in paperback.

This is, in the reviewer's opinion, still one of the best single conservative amillennial commentaries available at present on Jeremiah and Lamentations. It is detailed, helpful in Hebrew word studies and historical background, and has good insight into difficult verses. Laetsch is also a lucid writer.

Leslie, E. A. Jeremiah. New York: Abingdon, 1954.

A liberal work which at times is fairly good although brief in its commentary as far as explaining verses. Sometimes it is disappointing (to an evangelical) in its rearrangement of the material to construct what Leslie supposes is the right chronological sequence. However, there are problems in understanding Jeremiah's chronology, as even evangelical works acknowledge, so one needs to keep this in mind as he approaches the study. The work by Leslie, though helpful at times, is not as useful overall as Feinberg, R. K. Harrison, Laetsch, etc.

McKane, William. A Critical and Exegetical Commentary on Jeremiah, Volume I. Introduction and Commentary on Jeremiah I-XXV (ICC). Edinburgh: T. & T. Clark, 1986. 658 pp.

This provides meticulous detail in explaining verses—the text, word study, exegesis, customs, history etc.—and McKane is often helpful by giving views, though sometimes it is not easy or possible to decide what his preference is. As in much scholarship he theorizes a long history of different compositions in a haphazard, piecemeal growth that merged in what we have today. He offers copious use of words in Hebrew and Greek characters, and the Hebrew is unpointed, demanding that to follow it maximally readers need to know the languages. Overall it is so far an astute work on technical matters, views etc. What he will do with the great prophetical passages (Chapters 30-33) remains to be seen. It is liberal, and in much of the commentary attention is turned to source-critical issues his views exalt to importance, but which will not necessarily explain the text, at least for many. For some scholars it will offer help in its detail on versions, German sources and others, medieval Jewish comment, etc. For many it will be like a dry well of water but offering plenty of content in stones, some of which can be useful as one discerningly picks what he can accept.

Nicholson, E. W. Jeremiah (Cambridge Bible Commentary). 2 volumes. Cambridge: U.P., 1973. 221 + 247 pp.

These volumes on Chapters 1-25 and 26-52 use the NEB, aiming at teachers and young persons, assuming no specialized knowledge of Hebrew. The writer assumes that the prose sayings and sermons were composed by a group of Deuteronomic authors, mostly based on Jeremiah's original sayings but some not on anything he said (he cites 11:1-14; 17:19-27, p. 11) to meet needs of the exile. Also, many narratives in the book are from the later authors. Nicholson is assured, for he follows what is "now shared by most scholars" (p. 12). The commentary is brief, well-worded, explaining much but at times giving arbitrary opinions that are not necessary. For example, an editor expanded on Jeremiah's original account of his call (1:8, p. 25), and we do not have in Chapter 7 Jeremiah's original speech but an editor's version (p. 75). The visit to the potter is allegedly the work of a late editor, only based on a saying by Jeremiah (p. 155). The work leaves in the vagueness of non-explanation how the restoration of Jerusalem in 31:38-40 will be fulfilled; this also applies to 32:15; 33:6 etc. This liberal work has its times of helpfulness but is not worth the time too often.

Schaeffer, Francis. Death in the City. Downers Grove: IVP, 1969.

The famous speaker/writer shows how the message of Jeremiah and Lamentations applies to people of the modern era.

Sire, James W. Jeremiah, Meet the 20th Century. **Downers Grove: IVP 1975.**

Twelve topical studies do not give a commentary but show the relevance of Jeremiah's message to his own generation and to 20th century readers. The book is geared for personal profit and Bible study group use. Sire often points out parallels to today—moral decay, political ills, and spiritual deadness—and tries to elicit application consistent with the lessons. Sire offers "Notes for the Leader" with extra help on larger difficulties, and he is concise and sound. References to other sources which provide more detail can be valuable to readers. The book is brief (116 pp.).

Streane, A. W.   The Book of the Prophet Jeremiah, Together with the Lamentations (Cambridge Bible for Schools and Colleges).   Cambridge: U.P., 1885.

This is one of the most painstaking and contributing among older commentaries. It offers comments on verses some works skip over, material on many of the problems, and good synopses too. It does not have refinements in chronology and material from recent discoveries such as one will find in Bright, Feinberg, Harrison, Laetsch, Holladay, Carroll, McKane, Thompson, etc. but certainly explains much of what a teacher or pastor needs.

Thompson, J. A.   The Book of Jeremiah (New International Commentary on the Old Testament).   Grand Rapids: Eerdmans, 1980.   819 pp.

This is the most detailed evangelical commentary of recent vintage, competent in its lengthy introduction (pp. 1-136) on scholarly issues and views, details of text, exegesis, history and theology. Much of the commentary is lucidly helpful for the general reader as well as teachers and church workers. It does not take up a number of questions some scholars would like or give a bibliography of the length Thompson might offer. But he is helpful on archeology and the Near Eastern treaty concept.

von Orelli, Hans C.   The Prophecies of Jeremiah.   Minneapolis: Klock & Klock, 1977rp.   384 pp.

This work was originally from T. & T. Clark in Edinburgh in 1889. Cf. also his works on Isaiah and the minor prophets. He is one of the able earlier exegetes upholding the integrity of the book from meticulous study. His introduction pays high tribute to Jeremiah's character and compares him with Jesus Christ. He defends several of the sections scholars have claimed did not belong to the book (cf. list, pp. 23-24, and the individual sections). Verse by verse, essential things receive good comment. Much is readily understandable, but Hebrew words and on occasion details in Hebrew grammar will be usable only to the trained. Orelli becomes general and vague as to when and in what connection God will fulfill forecasts of a future rebuilding of Israel's fortunes (Chapters 30-33). For the New Covenant passage in Chapter 31, he gives no discussion of New Testament texts. A compact version of his work on Jeremiah is found in "Jeremiah," the old

International Standard Bible Encyclopedia (Grand Rapids: Eerdmans, 1939, III, 1588-91).

Wood, Fred.   Fire in My Bones.   Nashville: Broadman Press, 1959.
Discussion here is topical, helping a student or any Christian get a taste of certain streams of thought vital in the message. Wood bases the title on Jeremiah 20. This is conservative and broad in its treatment.

XX. LAMENTATIONS

Albrektson, B.   Studies in the Text and Theology of the Book of Lamentations, with a Critical Edition of the Peshitta Text (Studia Theologica Lundensia).   Lund, 1963.
This liberal, highly-regarded monograph argues that the book presents a tension between the historical event of destruction on Jerusalem and some Jewish theological thinking that Jerusalem was to be inviolable. He feels that the message of the book aims at steering Israelites to trust in a Person, not a place. It has much that helps supplement the use of commentaries on the book.

Calvin, John.   Cf. on Jeremiah.

Dyer, Charles.   "Lamentations," in Bible Knowledge Commentary, ed. John F. Walvoord and Roy B. Zuck.   Volume I.   Wheaton: Victor Books, 1983.
This is a conservative, very able work that covers most bases quite well enough to be of real help to pastors, teachers and lay people. Dyer, in addition to good help verse by verse, has a whole page chart of "Parallels Between Lamentations and Deuteronomy," and a knowledgeable introduction arguing the reasonableness of seeing Jeremiah as author.

Ellison, H. L.   "Lamentations," in Expositor's Bible Commentary, Volume 6, ed. Frank Gaebelein and R. P. Polcyn.   Grand Rapids: Zondervan, 1986.
Ellison provides a good, brief conservative introduction and terse commentary without an extensive bibliography (only ten sources, pp. 699-700). Still, he is quite capable and offers competent help on many of the most pertinent details so that the work is a worthy effort.

Erdman, Charles.   Cf. on Jeremiah.

Gordis, Robert.   Cf. on Song of Solomon.

Gottwald, N. K. <u>Studies in the Book of Lamentations</u> (Studies in Biblical Theology). Revised edition. London, 1962. 126 pp.

A very well-respected liberal monograph which reasons that the book relates to the problem Jews felt of suffering on a national basis. It gets at the tension between the historical sting of destruction and the Deuteronomistic concept about retribution and reward. Gottwald feels that the book shows that sin is the answer to the question some asked, why supposedly godly Israel should receive punishment after reforming in Josiah's reign (2 Kings 22-23). He shows that even though the calamity occurred the book reveals hope for the future, but thinks much of the explanation is left as a mystery of God's ways. Some have faulted Gottwald for not putting enough emphasis on Israel's sin as really taking the mystery out of the matter.

Guest, John. Cf. on Jeremiah.

Habel, Norman. Cf. on Jeremiah.

Harrison, R. K. Cf. on Jeremiah.

Hillers, D. R. <u>Lamentations: Introduction, Translation and Notes</u> (Anchor Bible). Garden City, NY: Doubleday, 1972.   116 pp.

Hillers furnishes a lot of able assistance on details of the Hebrew text, word meaning, syntax, history, etc. He says he writes for the general reader and does not include much technical detail. He actually has much of this. He devotes pages xv-xlvii to introduction. His discussion of reasons for and against authorship by Jeremiah (xxi-xxii) is somewhat helpful but can leave some readers with the impression of subjectivity. His bibliography is made up of non-conservative sources and heavy on German writings. His only outline is a title to each chapter of Lamentations, though he also gives certain suggestions in his "comment" sections. The patient, advanced student, especially, can work with the Hebrew and sift out much from the "notes" methodically. "Comment" sections open things up to see a greater flow and connection; they point out form, analyze shifts in thought, and often look at views as on the issue of who the sufferer is in Chapter 3. It is, overall, a valuable work for serious students wishing such detail as the above.

Jensen, Irving. Cf. on Jeremiah.

Kaiser, Walter C. Jr. <u>A Biblical Approach to Personal Suffering</u> [Lamentations]. Chicago: Moody, 1982.

This is a very good and helpful examination of the lessons learned from the text of Lamentations. Should be useful to a wide audience, in that Kaiser provides an introduction which analyzes the structure of the Hebrew text and finds a personal application from Jeremiah's handling of his grief over the fate of Jerusalem. Kaiser's chief goal in this study is the determination of a Biblical guide for managing grief. He interacts with a broad array of literature and reflects a study of the Hebrew text, dealing with translation difficulties when relevant. Recommended. —Dan Phillips

Kent, Dan G. Lamentations **(Bible Study Commentary). Grand Rapids: Zondervan, 1983. 64 pp.**

Kent thinks someone during the time of Jeremiah wrote the book, but gives arguments for and against Jeremiah (pp. 14-15). His commentary is a good, brief survey, well-informed and organized. It ought to help pastors and lay readers who need a quick, dependable short commentary that handles some of the problems in a sketchy way and keeps to the flow as well.

Provan, Iain. Lamentations **(New Century Bible Commentary). Grand Rapids: Eerdmans, 1991. 142 pp.**

Provan is a lecturer in Hebrew and Old Testament studies at the University of Edinburgh. He appears to be liberal. His introduction is informative and up to date on views of authorship, date and place, but he himself is unable to arrive at a view except that the book was written between the sixth and second centuries B. C. (p. 19). He has much assisting information, yet does not believe a commentary should give the text's meaning. Rather it should be "a catalyst for the reader's own imaginative interaction with it" (29). So usually he does not state his own view, and seems unsure the book refers to the fall of Jerusalem or what is the setting (11, 29). Still, one can find much information on verses as to the text, meaning of words, etc. He is of the opinion that Lamentations 3:21-27 focuses on humble repentance and trust in God's love, yet that Chapter 5 swings to an attitude opposed to this, reproaching God for unfairness (23). So, he feels that the theology of the book is left "ending in a question mark" (24). Many disagree with him here.

Streane, A. W. Cf. on Jeremiah.

von Orelli, Hans C. Cf. on Jeremiah.

XXI. EZEKIEL

Alexander, Ralph. Ezekiel. **Chicago: Moody Press, 1976.**

In the Everyman's Bible Commentary series, this work by the former Associate Professor of Old Testament Languages and Exegesis at Western Conservative Baptist Seminary is a very well-studied, helpful survey. Alexander is keenly aware of interpretive problems and engages them discerningly even if briefly due to his limited space. His outlook is premillennial and dispensational. The discussion of views in Ezekiel 38-39 is one of the especially helpful sections.

Blackwood, Andrew. Ezekiel: Prophecy of Hope. **Grand Rapids, MI: Baker, 1965.**

This is a good broad sweep of the message and is well written. But it does not involve itself enough with contextual problems to satisfy serious students. Chapters 40-48 are interpreted in a general, even vague fashion involving spiritualization, rather than in a literal way including an earthly temple in the future Messianic Kingdom.

Brownlee, W. H. and Leslie C. Allen. Ezekiel. **2 volumes (Word Biblical Commentary). Dallas, TX: Word Books, 1986-90. 301 pp.**

Brownlee prepared notes on Chapters 1-19, then died. Allen and Gerald Keown took the material, finished it, and Allen did the second volume covering the rest of the book. One will, in Chapters 1-19, find strange opinions in place of a sane explanation of the text (cf. on 1:3; 2:9—3:2; 4:4, etc.). Generally he does not manipulate texts but sometimes he does. More often he is careful and reliable on detail of the text, philology, etc. But he strains to contend for his idea that Ezekiel is in Gilgal, Jordan Valley, not in Babylonia. Seeing Ezekiel 26 fulfilled by Alexander the Great, Brownlee construes matters to have references to Alexander taken as glosses, redacted later, so the passage is not miraculous prophecy (p. xxxvii). The introduction overall reveals a scholar given to radical critical theory. Allen seeks a line between older, higher critical treatment and a newer literary method. He sees most of the book as from Ezekiel but feels that others redacted the text later. At many points he shows a good amount of light on passages. He sees the King of Tyre and not Satan in 28:11-19. The dispensational approach to prophecies is untenable to him. The two sticks passage is realized in the church, he says, and he is vague about Chapters 40-48, not helpful, viewing a dispensational, futurist explanation as "desperate." The work is, overall, a disappointment.

Carley, Keith W. The Book of the Prophet Ezekiel **(Cambridge B. C.). New York: Cambridge U. P., 1974.**

Carley, lecturer in Old Testament at Rarongo Theological College, Papua, New Guinea, says some material is from followers or editors, not Ezekiel. His argumentation for this is subjectively weak. The battle of Ezekiel 38, 39 is not to be at the end of the present age but Gog and Magog are only representative of nations in chapters 34-37. Discussion of the temple (40-48) is very vague and generalized, with no effort to consider if it can be a material temple to be realized in a future day. Ezekiel, in Carley's mind, is only stressing the urgency to be vigilant against corrupting holy things (p. 321). The commentary is of small help to those looking for an awareness of issues in dealing with interpretive problems and taking a perspective that explains prophecies according to their natural, meaningful import.

Cooke, George A.   A Critical and Exegetical Commentary on the Book of Ezekiel (ICC).
2 volumes.   London: T. & T. Clark, 1936.

A helpful work in philological detail and some problem verses because it presents material on possible interpretations.

Criswell, W. A.   Expository Sermons on the Book of Ezekiel.   Grand Rapids:
Zondervan, 1987.   269 pp.

This comes from a great man and preacher but is not good on Ezekiel in too many places. It is warm, compassionate, and has much practical comment for lay people and pastors on spiritual lessons of the book. That part is worthwhile. He is helpful, for example, on "Why Study Prophecy?," "The Preaching of Ezekiel," etc. And he is good on his appeal to readers to lay hold of hope in God, casting away transgressions, "for why will ye die?" (18:31, p. 22). He takes a stand for a premillennial view, but does not defend it well here. He sees the origin of Satan in Chapter 28 and Isaiah 14, with more light assertion than evidence. He assumes that Chapter 37 teaches bodily resurrection as well as restoration to Palestine, the northern invader of Chapter 38 is Russia (215), etc. One is disturbed by his strange mixture of convictions on the temple in Chapters 40ff. It is a literal one with a literal river in Palestine, yet blessings flow out of the church, and the river somehow flows throughout the world today, "blessing the deserts of the nations of the world" (227-58). The book is a disappointment.

Davidson, A. B.   The Book of the Prophet Ezekiel, With Notes and Introduction.
Cambridge: The University Press, 1892.   Revised edition, 1916.

Excellent verse by verse detail on word meanings and background. At the start of each chapter, Davidson gives a good, concise synthesis of the argument in that chapter, which is helpful. This is a valuable book to have.

Dyer, Charles.   "Ezekiel," in Bible Knowledge Commentary, ed. John F. Walvoord and
Roy B. Zuck.   Volume I.   Wheaton: Victor Books, 1983.

Dyer surveys well, mixing synopsis with detail, hitting problem areas competently and offering much help on much in the book from a conservative, dispensational stance. He is often quite worthwhile in passages about a future for Israel, on history, background, and theology. Even some dispensationalists will disagree with his case for the northern invader of Ezekiel 38 coming within the tribulation period, and his reasoning which is not always well-informed about other views and how they can answer him (cf. Alexander on Ezekiel, for example). Much in Chapters 40ff. is helpful, and he has some well-done charts of the temple, altar, division of the land to portions of Israel, etc.

Eichrodt, Walther.   Ezekiel, A Commentary.   Philadelphia: Westminster Press,
1970.

Mildly liberal, this recent work has the results of a lifetime of study finished in Eichrodt's old age. In many places his discussions are very full and helpful, as in the lengthy introduction and on a verse by verse basis involving background, word meanings, and the like. Though it does not have a system of understanding prophecy consistently with the premillennial view, it does have an excellent diagram sketch visualizing the lay-out of the temple the Lord shows Ezekiel (chapters 40-46).

Ellison, H. L.   Ezekiel: The Man and His Message.   Grand Rapids: Eerdmans, 1956.

This is a brief work of only 144 pages, but it is thought provoking. Ellison views 28:11-19 (and Isaiah 14:4-23) as not speaking of the fall of Satan, as many believe. He interprets the revolt of Gog in chapters 38-39 as occurring at the end of the millennium in Revelation 20:7-11, as does Erich Sauer in From Eternity to Eternity (p. 134). He also takes chapters 40-48 as allegory and rejects the view of a re-establishing of a literal temple and sacrifices during the millennium. Yet he devotes only eight pages to these nine chapters. Ellison is also contributor of I and II Kings and I and II Chronicles in the New Bible Commentary.

Enns, Paul.   Ezekiel (Bible Study Commentary).   Grand Rapids: Zondervan, 1986. 199 pp.

As in his books in this series on Joshua, Judges and Ruth, Enns provides an excellent survey as a conservative, here developing a dispensational stance for a future for Israel in the land of Palestine. He explains many details well, provides good synopses of sections, often supplies reasons for his views. He believes the invader in Ezekiel 38 comes in the middle of the tribulation period, as J. Dwight Pentecost argues in Things to Come. Good argumentation is used for seeing the temple in Ezekiel 40ff. as literal in Palestine after the Second Advent. He handles verses in an attempt to answer criticism on a dispensational view, gives good charts on temple, altar, land area, etc. and distinguishes the river in Chapter 47 from that in the New Jerusalem (p. 194).

Fairbairn, Patrick, 1838-1912.   An Exposition of Ezekiel.   Grand Rapids: Zondervan, 1960.

This amillennial work is quite old but shows the student how a man of that persuasion dealt with the great prophetical portions like chaps. 34-48.

Feinberg, Charles L.   The Prophecy of Ezekiel.   Chicago: Moody Press, 1969.

This treatment of the book is very helpful from the premillennial dispensational viewpoint. The author grapples with most of the problems and is lucid in his development of the argument. The fact that he has a consistent system of prophecy relating to the Messiah and his kingdom, whereas many commentators do not, really shows up in his insistence on a literal understanding of chaps. 40-48. In addition to this commentary, one should also read his paper delivered at the Jerusalem Conference on Biblical Prophecy, 1971, "The Rebuilding of the Temple", printed in Prophecy in the Making, Editor Carl F. H. Henry, published by Creation House, Carol Stream, Illinois.

Fisch, S. Ezekiel (Soncino Books of the Bible). Bournemouth: Soncino, 1950.

This is a verse by verse study based on the Hebrew which is printed at the top of each page. It shows how a Jewish scholar handles the text, and is one of the better volumes in this series.

Gaebelein, Arno C. The Prophet Ezekiel, An Analytic Exposition. New York: Our Hope Magazine, 1918.

Good book to get a dispensational interpretation, though it unfortunately does not grapple with the details as do Davidson, Cooke and others.

Greenberg, Moshé. Ezekiel 1-20: A New Translation with Introduction and Commentary (Anchor Bible). Garden City, NY: Doubleday, 1983. 388 pp.

A Jewish scholar's translation and detailed exegesis done in the belief that we have Ezekiel's material. Greenberg has invested much labor to explain the text, not frequently offer his own arbitrary and unconvincing speculations of what is in view in place of the text, as Brownlee does (cf. above). The work is not far enough along to evaluate much more. Readers can wonder how Greenberg will deal with the great prophetic passages on Israel's future.

Keil, C. F. The Prophecies of Ezekiel. 2 volumes. Grand Rapids: Eerdmans, 1950.

Valuable from the standpoint of the Hebrew text. Deals with problems verse-by-verse. Usually very helpful. Amillennial.

Taylor, John B. Ezekiel, An Introduction and Commentary. Downers Grove, IL: Intervarsity Press, 1969.

This evangelical, amillennial viewpoint is quite excellent in most places in explaining verses. Especially helpful are the introduction, comments on some problem verses, and sketches such as those of the altar of burnt offering and the temple lay-out (chapters 40-46).

Tatford, Frederick. Dead Bones Live: An Exposition of the Prophecy of Ezekiel. Eastbourne, Sussex: Prophetic Witness Publishing House, 1977.

A prolific writer (ca. 50 titles) on a lay-person's level, who has specialized in prophetic books, authored this premillennial study. He argues for connecting the Palestinian invader of chapters 38, 39 with the Gog-Magog battle (Revelation 20) at the climax of the millennium, a thousand years after the Second Advent. He sees a physical return of Jews to Palestine, and sees Ezekiel 37 as predicting both this and a spiritual revitalizing of the nation. The temple of chapters 40-46 is, to him, a literal structure of the future millennium with animal sacrifices literally offered as "visible reminders" of Christ's death for atonement (p. 258). The work is 275 pp.

Wevers, John W.   Ezekiel (New Century B. C.).   Grand Rapids: Eerdmans, 1969.

A liberal lecturer on Old Testament and Near Eastern studies at Princeton and the University of Toronto looks at Ezekiel from the perspective of Form Criticism and Tradition-History analysis. The English text is the RSV. Works listed at the outset are by liberal writers and rather heavy on the German side. Wevers accepts a 593-71 or final dating for the prophecies and the traditional belief that originally Ezekiel wrote near Babylon, despite much attack on this. To him, however, Pelatiah's death (11:13) is not a historical occurrence but only part of a vision (p. 25). Wevers very frequently picks and chooses what in his opinion are additions to the book by later readers on subjective, arbitrary reasoning that these are somehow at variance with some statement in the original book (cf. pp. 27, 37). The smaller type in the commentary is not easy on the eyes. His continual theorizing about different layers of tradition at different dates is a feature of the work, and the subjectivism is strong, giving more his opinion than commentary on the prophetic message. The lack of clarity in many places as well as the high degree of subjectivism work against the usefulness of this book.

Zimmerli, Walther.   A Commentary on the Book of the Prophet Ezekiel, 2 vols. (Hermeneia).   Translated by Ronald E. Clements.   Philadelphia: Fortress Press, 1979.

A monumental critical study of Ezekiel showing a very broad acquaintance with scholarly works ancient and modern along critical lines. The work appeared in the German in 1969. The bibliography is 27 pp. He offers many good insights into the Hebrew, and cites other scholars in support of his own convictions or for other views. Penetrating evangelical students, though perceptive of Zimmerli's naturalistic bent which shows up at many a point, can glean much that is of profit in explaining the book with precision more attuned to the Hebrew. Volume I on Chapters 1-24 (1979) was followed by Volume II completing the book (1983) in the Hermeneia series. The two total to 1,115 pp. Zimmerli's is a form-critical work that takes the place of G. A. Cooke's ICC book in exhaustive probing of facets thought to be of critical and textual relevance. The student dealing with the Hebrew in detail will not want to bypass such a work on the text, exegesis, philology, problems of a technical nature and views on them. On many matters he can expect to meet with liberal thinking, but he will mine out much that is of high value if he is patient and discerning.

XXI. DANIEL

Anderson, Sir Robert.   The Coming Prince.   London: Hodder and Stoughton, 1909.

The premillennial author presents a detailed work on the 70 weeks of Daniel 9. In this popular treatment he reckons the chronology of the first sixty-nine weeks from the decree of Artaxerxes (Nehemiah 2) to rebuild Jerusalem to the triumphal entry of Christ (Luke 19). He figures the exact number of days involved in 483 prophetic years which he believes would contain 360 days each, not 365 as Julian years. In his reckoning, the sixty-nine weeks end in A. D. 32 which poses a problem in light of more accepted views today that Christ died in A. D. 30 or 33.

Baldwin, Joyce. **Daniel, An Introduction and Commentary** (Tyndale Old Testament Commentary). **Downers Grove: IVP, 1978.**

The main contribution of this brief work is in the many references to literature in Baldwin's sometimes broad reading and awareness. Baldwin is also helpful in referring at times back and forth from liberal to conservative views (cf. on resurrection, 12:2), so that the reader sees the difference in interpretative systems. One is disappointed in what she does (or fails to do) with some texts, such as 7:12, "the rest of the beasts." Cf. by comparison Leon Wood. Baldwin's work seems to lack a grasp of eschatological details whereas Walvoord, Wood etc. are more clear-cut in a consistent system they can verify in a meaningful way from Scripture.

Boutflower, Charles. **In and Around the Book of Daniel.** **London: S. P. C. K., 1923.**

The author, a postmillennialist, presents more historical background and deals adequately with more critical problems than most writers on Daniel. He defends the book against many attacks. This book is valuable, though it is not a commentary per se.

Calvin, John. **Daniel** (Geneva Series). **Carlisle, PA: Banner of Truth Trust, 1986rp. 409 pp.**

This work appeared first in Latin in 1561. The reader will find much judicious comment with spiritual perception on the character of Daniel. The prophetical view Calvin advocates is amillennial, so one will see how he explains and defends that perspective on such passages as Daniel 2, 7, 9, 11, and 12.

Campbell, Donald. **Daniel, Decoder of Dreams.** **Wheaton: Victor Books, 1977.**

A popular, brief premillennial exposition of Daniel by an expositor who is a master of synthesis. Campbell has taught Bible exposition at Dallas Seminary for many years. He illustrates vividly and gears the work for lay people.

Criswell, W. A. **Expository Sermons on the Book of Daniel.** 4 volumes. **Grand Rapids: Zondervan, 1972.**

The volumes in this series involve Criswell's preaching through Daniel at the First Baptist Church, Dallas, Texas. The first volume is particularly helpful on introductory issues and provides a popular yet competent answer to critics who have dated Daniel late, denied certain statements of the book, etc. Unlike many Southern Baptists, he firmly teaches a premillennial, dispensational view (cf. also his works on Matthew and Revelation). Criswell has fairly normative dispensational views on most passages but leaves the impression that "Ancient of Days" and "Son of Man" in Chapter 7 are both the preincarnate Christ, rather than God the Father and Christ the Son as evangelicals typically hold. The volumes have many practically stimulating statements, but the exposition is sweeping, not detailed.

Culver, Robert. <u>Daniel and the Latter Days</u>. **Westwood, NJ: Revell, 1954.**

In a very systematic and thorough way, the author delves into Daniel to compare the amillennial, premillennial and postmillennial interpretations. He defends the premillennial view and presents several arguments to show that it is superior. It is a penetrating work and very valuable to have. In an appendix, he gives seven arguments in support of his view that the new heavens and new earth will come at the beginning of the millennium and not at the end.

Davies, P. R. <u>Daniel</u> **(Old Testament Guides). Sheffield, England: JS Old Testament Press, 1985. 133 pp.**

Here is typical liberal late-dating in the time of Antiochus Epiphanes. Davies does not believe the book deals with visions of Daniel in the sixth century B. C. He surveys works he esteems on important critical aspects (these are late-daters too) and makes no serious effort to discuss conservative arguments. Rather, he sees it as "trivial to deal with such protests on their logic, here."

Dougherty, R. P. <u>Nabonidus and Belshazzar: A Study of the Closing Events of the Neo-Babylonian Empire</u>. **New Haven, CT: Yale, 1929.**

This work is very helpful in relation to the problem about the reference to Belshazzar as king of Babylon in Daniel 4-5. Scholars had long denied that there was a Belshazzar and had claimed that the Bible was in error until fairly recent times when evidence was found to support the reign of a Belshazzar. Dougherty cites evidence including ancient inscriptions which have come to light, showing that there was a co-regency of Nabonidus and Belshazzar and that Nabonidus entrusted the throne at Babylon to his son Belshazzar during part of the time.

Feinberg, Charles L. <u>Daniel, The Man and His Visions</u>. **Chappaqua, NY: Christian Herald Books, 1981.**

A quick-moving, simple dispensational work aimed at laymen by an astute Hebrew Christian scholar who has taught more than forty years, been Dean of Talbot Seminary, and authored many books. Usually the work does not take up problem areas in verses (except some aspects of more obvious ones, at times, as "Son of Man" in 7:13, 14, = Jesus Christ, using mostly New Testament evidence, and the first sixty-nine "weeks" in 9:25, 26 come to A. D. 32, he says).

Ford, Desmond. <u>Daniel</u>. **Nashville: Southern Publishing Assocation, 1978. Foreword by F. F. Bruce.**

A leading man in new emphases within the Seventh Day Adventist circles shows how a SDA scholar who gained his Ph. D. under Bruce deals with eschatological details here. He tries to combine what he feels are the best elements in

Preterism, idealism, historicalism and futurism but regards much of the prophecy as related to the ultimate consummation (69-70). He shows awareness of some problems and solutions (as 1:1, 2) but is very brief on some verses (1:17-20; 2:4; 2:36-45 verse by verse; ch. 6; 7:13, 14, sparse on proof for identity of the Son of Man as Messiah, and of the kingdom; 7:7, vague on the ten horns, etc.). On p. 151 he finds the "little horn" of ch. 7 in the system of church and state in medieval times, and relates "a time, times, and half a time" to 3 1/2 prophetic years (1260 actual years) from A. D. 537 to 1798, a year-day view, citing H. G. Guinness, Romanism and the Reformation, pp. 41-43. His "proof" for his little horn theory is unfortunate. The text of Daniel 7 itself puts the horn and the ten horns in the final phase of the fourth empire, that is, in the time that flows right into the future judgment (7:9-14). And Revelation 19 has the Beast of Revelation 13:1-10 on earth at the Second Coming of Christ, who is the Son of Man receiving the kingdom in Daniel 7:13-14. Ford wants the little horn to mean the Antichrist of the centuries and the end-time too, as if it did not refer to one specific person at one particular time. His identification of the "little horn" in chapter 8 as Antichrist also raises questions. Ford feels the 2,300 days of 8:14 represent years from 457 B. C. to A. D. 1844. "In 1844 began the cleansing of the sanctuary . . . " (p. 189). He regards 9:24-27 as speaking of 490 years from 457 to A. D. 33, and believes this is the first segment of 2,300 years which he sees in 8:14 (p. 207). He cites SDA writers such as Wm. Miller and Ellen White (p. 243). He has some good material on Antiochus in 11:21-35, and believes Antichrist is in view in 11:36-45. His is a good effort to look at Daniel from a SDA perspective and a year-day system.

Gaebelein, Arno C. The Prophet Daniel. **NY:** Our Hope Magazine, 1911.

Dividing the book of Daniel according to the languages in the original text, the writer gives a brief yet helpful survey of a dispensational interpretation.

Goldingay, John E. Daniel (Word Biblical Commentary). **Dallas:** Word Books, 1989. 351 pp.

Immense research in books and journals has gone into this. It has excellent footnote details, many word studies, and a long, learned discussion on introductory matters that is quite informative for many. It summarizes the history of interpreting Daniel from the LXX to Goldingay's work. Goldingay favors a second century date and sees much fulfillment of prophecy in Maccabean times; it is history written after things happen. He feels the author stretches history at times, and favors saying that the fourth empire in Daniel 7 is an elephant. Often numbers are symbolical. The work has much to offer on literature and views in many cases but is not of the same value in handling prophecy, in the minds of premillennialists.

Goss, Glenn. "The Chronological Problems of the Seventy Weeks of Daniel." Unpublished doctoral dissertation, Dallas Theological Seminary, Dallas, Texas, 1966.

The student who can obtain this work on an inter-library loan will find it valuable in presenting a somewhat different dispensational view of the chronology in Daniel 9:24-27 than that given by Anderson's popular book. Goss defends the position that the sixty-nine weeks date from 457 B. C. and end at the baptism of Christ (A. D. 26). Thus, in the view of Goss, the 483 years are regular Julian years and not prophetical years of 360 days each. Goss thus avoids the two-year discrepancy if the A. D. 30 date for Christ's death is correct.

Hartman, L. F. and A. A. Di Lella. The Book of Daniel. A New Translation with Notes and Commentary (Anchor Bible). Garden City, NY: Doubleday, 1978. 360 pp.

A liberal effort that sets the book in the Maccabean era and often takes a low view of prophecy as foretelling as he favors a forthtelling idea. One can derive some profit from textual and exegetical comments on part of it, but it is not of high value to many conservatives. Hartman did Daniel 1-9, Di Lella 10-12.

Jerome. Jerome's Commentary on Daniel. Translated by Gleason L. Archer, Jr. Grand Rapids: Baker, 1977, rp of 1958 translation.

This publisher reproduces what Wilbur Smith called in its introduction "The most important single work produced by the Church Fathers on any of the prophetic writings of the Old Testament . . . ." Jerome wrote in Latin, and Archer's English translation is done well. One value of the work is Jerome's citation of and answer to Porphyry's famous argument against the date and authorship by Daniel.

Leupold, H. C. Exposition of Daniel. Columbus: Wartburg, 1949.

This amillennial work is quite detailed and helpful in showing the amillennial type of approach to the crucial prophecies. The work by Young, however, is better.

MacArthur, John F., Jr. The Future of Israel (Daniel 9:20-12:13). Chicago: Moody, 1991.

A brief premillenial dispensational series on the verses by one of America's most able expository pastors.

McClain, Alva J. Daniel's Prophecy of the Seventy Weeks. Grand Rapids: Zondervan, 1940.

This booklet is a concise presentation of the view taken by Sir Robert Anderson. McClain systematizes the view so that it is easy to follow the line of thought.

Montgomery, James A.   A Critical and Exegetical Commentary on the Book of Daniel (ICC).   Edinburgh: T. & T. Clark, 1964.

This is a detailed study of the text from a critical standpoint, and is, in this regard, very helpful to the serious student who is dealing with problems.

Newell, Philip.   Daniel, The Man Greatly Beloved and His Prophecies.   Chicago: Moody, 1962.

A dispensational exposition based upon an expanded Bible correspondence course. It is one of the better-known dispensational works.

Phillips, John and Jerry Vines.   Exploring the Book of Daniel.   Neptune, NJ: Loizeaux Brothers, 1990.   279 pp.

Dispensational exposition with clarity of interpretation and practical application to stimulate thought about relevance today. It is not deep in wrestling with issues.

Porteous, Norman.   Daniel, A Commentary.   Philadelphia: Westminster, 1965.

This is a liberally-oriented work as is plain when Porteous places all the details of Daniel 2, 7 in Maccabean times. He assumes rather than proves a second-century date. His commentary is a brief example of one liberal scholar's thinking.

Pusey, Edward B.   Daniel the Prophet.   NY: Funk & Wagnalls, 1885.

The author was the Regius Professor of Hebrew at Oxford who, though trained under German critics, became a solid conservative. He was amillennial in prophecy. His greatest contribution is in historical backgrounds, and in the key prophetical portions he often allegorizes.

Russell, D. S.   Daniel (The Daily Bible Study Series).   Philadelphia.   Westminster, 1981.

This is by the famous author of The Method and Message of Jewish Apocalyptic (1964), later General Secretary of the Baptist Union of Great Britain. The series purports to have experts in their field write in a form that will appeal to the general public. Russell dates Daniel ca. 165 B. C., using arguments such as vocabulary and style. These have been answered well in favor of a 6th century date by such men as Edwin Yamauchi, Greece and Babylon. Yet there is much elucidation from careful scholarship even for evangelicals whose studies lead them to different conclusions. Russell in typical liberal fashion sees the parts of the image as depicting Neo-Babylon, Media, Persia and Greece. The fulfillment of God's Kingdom is not in a far off kingdom (that, says Russell, is strained and fanciful exegesis), but in the writer's own time. His hopes were not realized, for the kingdom did not come literally in the way he expected in his day (p. 54). Yet Russell does believe in the New Testament hope of the kingdom at the end of history. On 12:2, he says that the earlier Hebrews had no belief in individual life beyond the grave (p. 218). While the work often does not offer reliable help that understands the writer's expectation in the futuristic way the writer most naturally seems to mean it, there is much to open up vividly many of the verses on other details. The work is helpful if one wants to see how a liberal mind deals with what is said.

Seiss, Joseph.   Voices From Babylon or, The Records of Daniel the Prophet. Philadelphia: The Castle Press, 1879.

A premillennial work well-known for its breadth of knowledge, it consists of lectures and not a verse by verse study.

Stevens, W. C.   The Book of Daniel.   NY: Revell, 1918.

There is a good tracing of the thematic development here as Stevens covers the entire book chapter by chapter and lays out his material systematically. He points out many spiritual truths in Daniel's prayer life and non-compromise. It is a refreshing commentary. Most of what he says is good material.

Talbot, Louis T.   The Prophecies of Daniel.   Wheaton: Van Kampen, 1954.

This book gives a very clear and lucid development of the theme in Daniel. It is an interestingly written work and handles the prophecies in a careful way, though it is homiletical and not critical in its comments. Many of the statements are gripping in their warmth. The author has combined detail with popular appeal. From the dispensational viewpoint, this is a very fine treatment of the book on a popular level and is good to put into the hands of a layman.

Tatford, Frederick A.   The Climax of the Ages.   London: Marshall, Morgan & Scott, 1953.

As a premillennial and dispensational book, this gives a somewhat helpful discussion of several problems and goes into more detail on key passages than most dispensational works. It can take the place of several of the other dispensational works combined because it is fuller in its discussion. The higher critics, in their reviews, regard the book as "imperfectly acquainted with scholarly work" (See H. H. Rowley, Eleven Years of Bible Bibliography, p. 677). Tatford makes several statements in which he dismisses the beliefs of S. R. Driver and other critics as without substance, and this naturally is not popular with their group. Walvoord and Wood are both better.

Terry, Milton S.   The Prophecies of Daniel Expounded.   NY: Hunt & Eaton, 1893.

Terry believed that the four kingdoms were Babylon, Media, Persia and Greece and said that the seventy weeks were an indefinite period from the end of the exile until the final disruption of national Judaism at the destruction of Jerusalem and the temple in A. D. 70. He suggests that from 10:1 to the end of chapter 11 is an interpolation.

Tregelles, Samuel P.   Remarks on the Prophetic Visions in the Book of Daniel. London: The Sovereign Grace Advent Testimony, 1965.   Reprint or work which originally appeared in 1845.

The author deals with several critical problems well and devotes fine treatment to the key chapters. He takes the view that the "little horn" of chapter 7 is the same as the "little horn" of chapter 8. He explains that while in a general way this horn can be represented as arising out of the fourth kingdom (Rome) in chapter 7, it can also be said to come more particularly out of the Grecian area in chapter 8 which was amalgamated into the fourth kingdom and became a part of it. For the view that the "little horns" must be distinguished, see E. J. Young, Appendix V.

Walvoord, John F.   Daniel, The Key to Prophetic Revelation.   Chicago: Moody, 1971.

In the opinion of the reviewer, this and Wood's 1972 work are the finest overall commentaries of a popular nature on Daniel by premillennial dispensational scholars to date. Walvoord weaves into the work an up-to-date understanding of archaeological and historical confirmations of Daniel that offset the critics with a solid reasoning for a premillennial perspective of Messianic prophecy. He very capably answers the late-daters of Daniel, argues that the four kingdoms of Daniel 2 and 7 are Babylon, Media-Persia, Greece, and Rome, and deals with most problem areas in adequate detail. Still he manages to keep the great theme of the work before the reader.

Whitcomb, John C.   Daniel (Everyman's Bible Commentary).   Chicago: Moody, 1985.   176 pp.

A dispensational survey, documenting his use of scholarly literature and mingling exegesis and devotional elements. His dispensational interpretations are fairly standard.

Whitcomb, John C.   Darius the Mede: A Study in Historical Identification.   Grand Rapids: Eerdmans, 1959.

In this specialized work, which is not a commentary, a professor formerly from Grace Theological Seminary explores the problem of the identity of the Darius in Daniel 5. It is a penetrating study and is a refreshing contrast to remarks like those of H. H. Rowley in his work Darius the Mede. Rowley takes an extreme position, calling the Daniel 5 statement a confusion of confused traditions. Whitcomb argues that Darius was a subordinate official placed over Babylon by Cyrus. His name was Gubaru. Whitcomb gives positive arguments for this view and answers crucial objections to it (cf. review by F. F. Bruce in The Evangelical Quarterly, July-Sept., 1959, pp. 176-77).

Wilson, Robert Dick. <u>Studies In the Book of Daniel: A Discussion of the Historical Questions.</u> NY: Putnam's, 1917.

This is one of the outstanding conservative defenses of historical matters in Daniel.

Wood, Leon J. <u>A Commentary on Daniel.</u> Grand Rapids: Zondervan, 1972.

Wood has produced after several years a detailed verse-by-verse commentary patterned much like Keil-Delitzsch, though he argues for a premillennial dispensational viewpoint. His constant reference to Hebrew and Aramaic words and sometimes a critical discussion of them will give the work appeal to some. Yet his explanations are such that less skillfully trained students may profit from using the commentary. The introduction, word studies, references to modern-day validations of Daniel, and correlation with other Scriptures building a prophetical picture make it a very worthwhile contribution done in a competent, scholarly way.

Wood, Leon J. <u>Daniel, A Study Guide.</u> Grand Rapids: Zondervan, 1975.

A 160-pp. survey in the "Study Guide" series, much briefer than his <u>A Commentary on Daniel</u>, with a list of suggestions for further study at the end of each chapter, various charts and maps, and a brief bibliography mostly by evangelical authors. This is a knowledgeably helpful brief treatment for laymen along premillennial dispensational lines of chronology on the visions.

Young, Edward J. "Daniel," in <u>New Bible Commentary Revised,</u> edited by D. Guthrie et al. Grand Rapids: Eerdmans, 1970.

The amillennial work is quite brief (pp. 688-702), a nutshell of his regular commentary. He defends Daniel as author and answers several main problems raised against historical accuracy. He also answers late-dating critical views at key points, for example against Media, Persia and Greece as the last three empires in Daniel 2 and 7. He shows briefly how an amillennialist deals with prophecies of future tribulation and kingdom.

Young, Edward J. <u>Daniel's Vision of the Son of Man.</u> London: Tyndale, 1958.

A brief but very fine study of 7:13, 14. Young defends in detail his view that the "one like a son of man" is an <u>individual</u> (not corporate = the people of Israel later in 7:18, 22 etc.), specifically the Messiah who turns out to be Jesus Christ in the Gospels. He offers persuasive evidence even in the context and in Old Testament usage of phrases here such as coming on the clouds of heaven.

Young, Edward J. <u>The Messianic Prophecies of Daniel.</u> Grand Rapids: Eerdmans, 1954.

This is a solid work showing how an outstanding fairly recent amillennial scholar deals with so crucial a book on eschatology. It reveals the vital points at which he attacks dispensationalism. The commentary is very good in its verse by verse exegesis but is weak in eschatology, as shown by his treatment of Daniel 9:24-27 and the "stone" in chapter 2. He fastens upon the dispensational teaching that the kingdom of the future will be a thousand years, then argues from chapter 2 that the kingdom has to be eternal. Actually, dispensationalists are misrepresented here, for they believe in both.

XXII. MINOR PROPHETS

GENERAL WORKS

Boice, James M. The Minor Prophets. An Expositional Commentary. **Grand Rapids: Zondervan, 1983-86. 542 pp.**

Boice has a catchy title for each chapter or section of the prophets. Pages are large with two columns and he provides much good material on the relevance then and now, lessons such as God's love, repentance, sincerity (Hosea 6), etc. If a Christian took time to read these pages and dwelt on the principles over a span of weeks or months, he could grow much by applying them. Boice at times could be more definite in specifying in what framework God will bless Israel in the future, as in Hosea 14. He can be vague, as in Joel 2:1-11 where he says the invader is neither locusts nor a human army (I, 107). He can be very wordy and wander on, too, as in using Joel 2:28 as a take-off into a long discussion of clericalism. He sees Joel 2:28 fulfilled at Pentecost, yet it would help if he showed some aspects were not yet fulfilled. He is more to the point on Zechariah 14.

Bullock, C. Hassell. An Introduction to the Old Testament Prophetic Books. **Chicago: Moody Press, 1986. 391 pp.**

The author of An Introduction to the Old Testament Poetic Books (Moody, 1979) and An Introduction to the Old Testament Pentateuch (Moody, 1991) covers major and minor prophets here. He places them where he judges they fit historically, not in the canonical sequence, using three periods, Neo-Assyrian, Neo-Babylonian and Persian. An introduction discusses such topics as the roots of prophecy, terms for this ministry, non-literary prophets, culture, relation of prophets to kings, and priests, ministry in social oppression, devices used (oracles, visions etc.), and others. Bullock thinks Jonah is introductory to the prophets and takes up among other aspects the views on the book (parable, history etc.), structure, message etc. His vagueness on Amos 9:13-15 does not clarify when such a future boon will occur (75-76, p. 82). He is more helpful on Amos the man and the structure. His discussion of views about Gomer in Hosea 1-3 offer good help. In Isaiah, H. Freeman's ordering of material seems to get at issues more forthrightly and to the point, though Bullock is very aware of views and issues in a drawn out way. A fog descends on some aspects, as Zephaniah's long-range reach of the Day of the Lord, so that the best readers can glean of when that will occur is "the gospel era" (172). Even amillennialists can concur with that generality. The same hazy non-commitment about when, specifically, the long-range realization of the kingdom will come occurs on Jeremiah 30-33 (199, 201, 211) and Ezekiel 34-48 (247). To Bullock Ezekiel's temple of chapters 40-46 is fulfilled in part in temple rebuilding of 520-516 B. C., but more fully in eschatological times; he leaves this in a misty non-commitment of just what he means (249). In Daniel he deals fairly well with key matters (281-88). He is a bit more specific in Daniel 7, saying that the little horn "may represent the Antichrist" before the Second Advent (296). The final "seven" of Daniel 9 is fulfilled at the time of Christ's Death and the temple destruction in A. D. 70, but Bullock lets the seventieth go on open-ended and commits himself to a view like that of E. J. Young (297-98). He is extremely fuzzy on convictions about Daniel 11:36-45 and 12:1-3 where he is quite general.

Calkins, Raymond. <u>Modern Messages of the Minor Prophets</u>. **NY: Harper, 1947.**

This recent book is helpful and stimulating in regard to the overall pertinent applications of the messages of the individual Minor Prophets. It is very suggestive for the preacher or teacher and is lucid in its style.

Calvin, John. <u>The Minor Prophets</u>. **5 volumes (Geneva series). Carlisle, PA: Banner of Truth Trust, 1986rp. 2,699 pp.**

This work, published first in 1563 in the French, was also published by Eerdmans as part of <u>Calvin's Commentaries</u>. Calvin wrote the works in the 1540's. He usually devotes 1-5 pages to a verse, giving much rich, lucid explanation. He gives his judgment on problems, sometimes at length, as on God's command to Hosea to marry a wife of whoredoms (he says Hosea did this not in a literal sense but in an imaginary way, a figurative sense, a parabolic representation (I, 45). The future for Israel in Hosea 1:11 is realized in the church, amillennial fashion, under Christ the one head. In Hosea 2:18-27 fulfillment is in Christians who, when they obey God, find that brute animals are at peace with them (I, 111). Israel's return in Hosea 3:5 is fulfilled today in uniting with others who worship the one head, the greater king, Jesus Christ (I, 134). Joel 3:16ff. refers to blessing on the church, the true Israelites (II, 136). Return to the land in Amos 9:11-15 is fulfilled not literally but when people come to Christ and reign spiritually with Him, finding abundant blessings (II, 413). Calvin assigns figurative meanings in Zechariah 14. Attack on Jerusalem is attack on the church (V, 409). Christ standing on the Mount of Olives means that in trials we are to set God before our eyes and He will command deliverance from the top of the mountain (V, 411-12).

Chisholm, Robert B., Jr. <u>Interpreting the Minor Prophets</u>. **Grand Rapids: Zondervan, 1990. 317 pp.**

This well-informed survey is by a professor of Old Testament studies, Dallas Seminary, who wrote on Hosea and Joel in the <u>Bible Knowledge Commentary</u>. Chisholm looks broadly at each prophet's structure, message, doctrinal themes, literary and rhetorical features. After a brief survey of overall themes—sin, judgment, salvation—he takes up each prophet from Hosea to Malachi successively.

On long-range prophecy he is presumably premillennial, but in several texts where one would expect a commitment, he keeps things so vague that one finds no distinct word as to when the fulfillment will come (Hosea 3, 14; Joel 3:9ff.; Zechariah 14, etc.). He surveys each book section by section with much that helps, dealing briefly with main problems. At the end of each survey of a book he sums up points of theology. He views Joel 2:1-11 as meaning a human army but is not distinct on what army and when. The work is good but general. The reader who has the BKC from Dallas Seminary would already have the books covered in greater premillennial specificity in many cases.

Cohen, A., ed. **The Twelve Prophets (Soncino Bible).** **Bournemouth, Hants: Soncino, 1948. 368 pp.**

Jewish scholars give the Hebrew text and the Jewish Publication Society English translation, then a commentary. Different books are treated in different depth, usually concise, general, and minimal in remarks. Many details are passed over. Occasionally one finds real help on Hebrew idioms, word meanings, and views from rabbis. In certain prophetical texts the commentators take passages as teaching a glorious future for Israel (Joel 3:16ff.; Zechariah 14:9ff.).

Feinberg, Charles L. **The Minor Prophets.** **Chicago: Moody Press, 1976.**

A Jewish Christian scholar in Hebrew who taught in Old Testament at Dallas Seminary and later at Talbot Seminary, where he also was Academic Dean, did this exposition of all the minor prophets. Feinberg has made biblical prophecy one of his specializations and does a good survey, being aware of interpretive problems, main views, contextual factors and correlation with other Old Testament and New Testament prophetic passages in a premillennial dispensational understanding. This is a 1-volume edition of what originally was issued as 5 small volumes.

Fink, Paul. **"Minor Prophets," in Liberty Bible Commentary, ed. Jerry Falwell et al. Nashville: Thomas Nelson, 1983.**

On pages 1661-1864, Fink gives what is usually a quite helpful, concise premillennial, dispensational commentary, gives good attention to expositional problems and often mentions views and arguments. His premillennnial stance is clear on such texts as Hosea 1:10, 11; 2:18-27; 3:5; Joel 3:9ff.; Amos 9:11-15; Zechariah 14.

Freeman, Hobart. **An Introduction to the Old Testament Prophets.** **Chicago: Moody Press, 1968. 384 pp.**

This was in many aspects very helpful, probably the best contribution by Freeman, a premillennialist. Later he went into a healing movement that to many brought discredit on his ministry (cf. Bruce Barron's survey in The Health and Wealth Gospel, Tyndale). Here, in a book now hard to obtain, Freeman has solid material in introduction (origin and development of Old Testament prophecy, function, true and false prophets, language of prophecy, Messianic prophecy, etc.). He also deals with each book by a prophet—nature, date, the prophet, background, main problems, outline. On Joel he looks in some detail at views and reasons for whether 2:1-11 describes literal locusts or a human army, and also at views and reasons in 2:28-32. He treats several key issues in Jonah and main ones about Gomer in Hosea. In Isaiah, Freeman probes into problems of unity and date, views on 7:14, and identity of the servant. In Daniel he takes up such matters as date, chronology, Belshazzar, Darius, time of the ten kings, seventy "weeks," etc. The work has been reprinted in fairly recent years after Moody dropped it.

Hailey, Homer. <u>A Commentary on the Minor Prophets</u>. **Grand Rapids: Baker, 1972.**

A non-technical work of 428 pp. for lay people, taking an amillennial stance on the kingdom issue: in his opinion there will not be a future kingdom for Israel after the Second Advent of Christ (cf. in this work pp. 126, 200, etc.; cf. also his commentary on the Book of Revelation).

Henderson, Ebenezer. <u>The Book of the Twelve Minor Prophets</u> **(Thornapple Commentaries). Grand Rapids: Baker, 1980.**

This 1858 work supplies much help on matters of the text, word meaning, resolving some problems, etc. Some have found it one of the most contributive sources in getting at what a text means.

Ironside, H. A. <u>Notes on the Minor Prophets</u>. **NY: Loizeaux (n. d.).**

Expository addresses with practical value to the pastor-teacher along dispensational lines.

Kaiser, Walter C., Jr. <u>Micah - Malachi</u> **(The Communicator's Commentary). Dallas, TX: Word Books, 1992. 494 pp.**

A careful evangelical gives contemporary outlines usable to pastors. He has occasional illustrations and serious explanation of the text. He is premillennial, as on Zechariah 14, and packs in much expositional help, relating it strategically to life. In this series Lloyd Ogilvie wrote the <u>Hosea - Jonah</u> section, with good practical application but not as much expertise on the text as Kaiser.

Keil, C. F. and Franz Delitzsch. <u>The Twelve Minor Prophets</u>. **2 volumes. Grand Rapids: Eerdmans, 1961.**

The Hebrew exegesis is helpful verse-by-verse. See earlier comments under Old Testament sets.

Laetsch, Theodore. <u>The Minor Prophets</u>. **Saint Louis: Concordia, 1956.**

This is the outstanding amillennial commentary on the minor prophets as a whole. Laetsch deals with the text verse-by-verse, grapples with difficult phrases and explains them, uses the Hebrew extensively, and presents illuminating word studies. The lucid presentation helps make it a very interesting commentary to read. In crucial prophetical sections, his strong amillennialism appears. His weakness here is offset by his helpfulness in exegesis generally plus his good background material.

Morgan, G. Campbell. The Minor Prophets: The Men and Their Messages. **Old Tappan, NJ: Revell, 1960. 157 pp.**

Morgan wrote another book on the Minor Prophets, Voices of the Twelve Hebrew Prophets, published in England and Scotland, examining one key verse from each prophet. In the present work he goes into some detail at times. He assigns a title to each prophet, such as "Jonah—Condemnation of Exclusiveness." Unfortunately, a complete English translation of each book is given, taking up much space. Morgan offers an outline with points that express ideas of verses, but beyond this has space only to say something of an explanatory nature now and then. He leaps over problem verses, such as Hosea 1:2, "wife of whoredoms." He does have a brief synopsis on the message in the prophet's time and in Morgan's around 1900 A. D. Overall this is far down the line in helpfulness, despite the once great name of Morgan.

Pusey, Edward B. The Minor Prophets. **2 volumes. Grand Rapids: Baker, 1953.**

This work originally appeared in 1860. The present publication is set up in two columns to the page with the text of the Authorized Version reproduced at the top. Scripture references, Hebrew words, and other citations are relegated to the bottom of the page. The work is detailed and analytical in nature. Introduction, background and explanation of the Hebrew are quite helpful. Pusey holds to the grammatical-historical type of interpretation until he gets into sections dealing with the future of Israel, and here Israel becomes the church in the amillennial vein.

Robinson, George L. The Twelve Minor Prophets. **Grand Rapids: Baker, 1976. 203 pp.**

This is a reprint of the 1926 edition (New York: Harper and Brothers). He devotes a chapter to each prophet, "Hosea the Prophet of Love," etc. The studies are terse summaries. On Hosea he lists and comments on steps in Israel's downfall and has five points on the message to men today. He packs a lot of information in and organizes it well. His word portrait of Jonah is choice (pp. 74-75), and he has interesting accounts of great fish swallowing men. Though brief, the book has frequent material a preacher can use.

Smith, George A. "The Book of the Twelve Prophets," in The Expositor's Bible, **Volume 4. Grand Rapids: Eerdmans, 1956rp.**

Though old this is well-written and often cited, with many good statements on spiritual truths. Users will find much that is worthwhile, and sometimes may disagree, as when he sees the Jonah account as allegorical.

Taylor, John B.   The Minor Prophets (Scripture Union Bible Study Books).   Grand Rapids: Eerdmans, 1970.   94 pp.

This succinct effort gets directly at issues, as in giving three views on what Gomer was when Hosea married her, and views on the woman Hosea took in 3:1. He is fuzzy on what the future of Israel will be (1:10; 2:16-23 etc.) but a bit clearer on 3:5 (p. 7; cf. p. 20). Sometimes he is clear, sometimes vaguely general, as on the heavenly signs in Joel 2. He sees Amos 9:11-15 as not fulfilled literally in such aspects as agricultural prosperity, but figuratively, as if 9:13b proves his view. Reference, he feels, is to the New Jerusalem. Strangely, he also sees Zechariah 14:20-21 as in the New Jerusalem, after describing the verses before where imperfection is evident. Often, though, his work gives the lay reader a good survey without getting bogged down.

von Orelli, Hans C.   The Twelve Minor Prophets.   Edinburgh: T. & T. Clark, 1897.   405 pp.   Reprint by Klock & Klock (Minneapolis, 1977).

This widely-read Jewish scholar of Germany defended the integrity of the Old Testament in days of Wellhausen higher critical theory. He is exegetically skilled but has a heavy technical style that makes study slow and often not easy to follow. Still, he has much good material. Gomer, he says, was a harlot before marriage. He is vague as to when blessings for Israel in Hosea will be fulfilled. Often he deals with details but provides no synthesis to allow perspective. To a large degree it is not worth the time as there are so many better works now available.

Wood, Leon J.   The Prophets of Israel.   Grand Rapids: Baker, 1979.   405 pp.

This quite readable work by a premillennialist covers the overall range of Old Testament prophets, various key subjects under "Prophetism" such as what "to prophesy" means, the prophets' function, early prophets, Samuel, monarchy prophets, and writing prophets both major and minor. Wood has solid sections on Elijah and Elisha (their spiritual features, episodes, miracles). The Elisha part surveys each miracle. Some sections, as on Hosea, even discuss in some detail leading problems such as whether Gomer was tainted before marriage or became unfaithful later. But sections on the books do not delve into nearly the detail Chisholm gives. Wood does sum up the message well, has an outline on each book, and organizes much on background, character qualities and work of each prophet. He deals with each prophet in relation to the reign he fitted into. Chisholm and Freeman deal more with various problems.

INDIVIDUAL WORKS

B. Hosea

Andersen, F. I. and D. N. Freedman.   Hosea: A New Translation with Introduction and Commentary (Anchor Bible).   New York: Doubleday, 1980.   701 pp.

The student, teacher or preacher finds a lengthy introduction reviewing issues important to the book, some good exegesis, copious bibliography (pp. 82-111), and some help on doctrinal aspects. One introductory section discusses the text of Hosea competing with Job for having more unintelligible passages than any other book of the Hebrew Bible (p. 66). The authors argue that Gomer's unfaithfulness came after marriage to Hosea (69, 116 etc.), and they present data from the language to support this. They also believe that the woman in 3:1 is Gomer later on. The discussion verse by verse is ponderous and at times so detailed that only the more serious, motivated student will take the time. Most verses are made clear, but not all. Hosea 3:5 is dealt with at length, yet never with a clear view really explaining a future for Israel in any definite framework. One is lost in a haze of words, and feels the authors have no theological system on eschatology. The size and price will make this formidable to some, but it is a wealth of information in many respects. The introductory section on how Hosea has been interpreted (68-76) is a good review, for example.

Beeby, H. D.   Hosea: Grace Abounding (International Theological Commentary).   F. C. Holgren and G. A. F. Knight, editors.   Grand Rapids: Eerdmans, 1989.   189 pp.

Rich in helpful analysis of the text, this work also has a good bit to offer on word study, exegesis, historical background, theological comment and devotional principles. It must, however, be read with alertness to Beeby's assumptions from critical theories that lead at times to excising verses as a redactor's additions where it is subjective opinion and not based on what many will consider convincing evidence. The work is not bad in many respects but also not truly great.

Chisholm, Robert, Jr.   "Hosea" and "Joel," in Bible Knowledge Commentary, ed. John F. Walvoord and Roy B. Zuck.   Volume I.   Wheaton: Victor Books, 1983.

Premillennial dispensational commentary based on careful study, use of sources, etc. Though concise, he shows good expertise in mingling synopsis with detailed comment and dealing with problems. His discussion of views on Hosea 1:2, for example, is compact but helpful; he favors saying Gomer became unfaithful after marriage. Passages on Israel's future are usually handled without the vagueness that abounds in many commentaries, for Chisholm is definite. On Joel 2:1-11, he has four arguments for literal locusts and four for a human army, a view he favors (pp. 1410-11). Overall the work is of a high calibre.

Cohen, Gary G. and H. R. Vandermey. <u>Hosea and Amos</u> **(Everyman's Bible Commentary). Chicago: Moody, 1981. 172 pp.**

Vandermey does Hosea and Cohen Amos. Both conservatives use detailed outlines and a brief introduction. The comment on Hosea 1:2 is unclear. The writers are premillennial on Israel's future (Hosea 3:5; 14:4-9; Amos 9:11-15). Both survey fairly well. The bibliography on Amos is very general, listing only two commentaries, both very old.

Feinberg, Charles L. <u>Hosea: God's Love for Israel</u>**. NY: American Board of Missions to the Jews (n. d.).**

Premillennial and dispensational in its interpretation, this work is not a verse-by-verse study but deals with the text in a survey fashion. It does grapple with most of the problems, however, and seeks to explain Jewish culture and background. See also other books in the same series: <u>Joel, Amos and Obadiah</u> (1948); <u>Jonah, Micah and Nahum</u> (1951); <u>Habakkuk, Zephaniah, Haggai and Malachi</u> (1951); and <u>Zechariah: Israel's Comfort and Glory</u> (1952). All of these are very helpful to the expositor.

Garland, David. <u>Hosea</u> **(Bible Study Commentary). Grand Rapids: Zondervan, 1975. 81 pp.**

A conservative, he keeps a reader guessing as to what his view really is on Israel's future. He is vague in the latter half of Hosea 2, and not clear on whether the bliss is in a future millennium after the Second Advent or in the ultimate state. On 3:5 he sounds as if he sees the ideal, ultimate future (p. 35). However, much of the book is fairly well-done. On many of the problems he at least has a brief survey. One may not be persuaded by his judgments on 1:2. The first child is Hosea's, the next two are not.

Harper, W. R. <u>Amos and Hosea</u> **(International Critical Commentary). Edinburgh: T. & T. Clark, 1905.**

An old liberal work with much contribution on technical aspects of text, word meaning, syntax, helpful to the trained student.

Hubbard, David A. <u>Hosea: An Introduction and Commentary</u> **(Tyndale Old Testament Commentary). Downers Grove: IVP, 1989. 245 pp.**

A highly readable conservative effort, often refreshing in its discussion of passages. It has sections on the broad perspective and some good verse by verse comment. The introduction, among other things, is orientating on the message of Hosea. But on prophecies, he is not clear-cut as to a long-reaching millennial fulfillment where many premillennialists will feel he could be definite.

Hubbard, David A. <u>With Bands of Love</u>**. Grand Rapids: Eerdmans, 1967.**

A very readable and clear study of Hosea by an evangelical scholar bringing the message home to people today. A good thought-provoker for one planning a series on Hosea.

Kidner, Derek. <u>Love to the Loveless</u>. Downers Grove: IVP, 1981.

In the Bible Speaks Today series, this work on Hosea is scholarly in a readable, practical thrust. Kidner gives "A bird's-eye view of the book" in 5 1/2 pages (137-42) that helps the reader see main thoughts quickly. Though without a numbered outline, the exposition is set off under catchy headings. Kidner favors seeing Hosea 3:5 ultimately fulfilled in what Paul predicts for literal Israel at the end of the present age in Romans 11:12, 15, 25ff. (p. 44). This is a brief but very competent work presented in a refreshing style by an evangelical of international repute.

Knight, G. A. F. <u>Hosea, God's Love</u> (Torch Bible Commentary). London: SCM, 1960. 127 pp.

Knight has a so-so work. He has a Deuteronomistic view of Old Testament books. Strangely, he asserts that Hosea 3:1 is the first time in history, chronologically, where we hear of the love of God (p. 62). He does not put everything together on Hosea 1:2 when he lists views, leaving out the view that Hosea married a woman who later proved unfaithful, the children in Chapter 1 were literally hers and Hosea's, but they were part of a spiritually unfaithful people. Knight discerns no messianic figure in 3:5, and discusses a future for Israel (2:16ff.) without clarifying in what framework or sense it will occur, rather all is fuzzy.

Mays, J. L. <u>Hosea: A Commentary</u> (Old Testament Library). Philadelphia: Westminster, 1969. 190 pp.

This liberal work is highly-regarded by many. Mays has detailed exegesis and comments of a theological nature for pastors and students. He holds that 1:2 means God commanded Hosea to marry a woman who already was a prostitute, but does not deal with how God could command this morally. He gives much good explanation on verses, but subjectively judges that "David their King" and "at the end of days" in 3:5 are later additions that do not fit the context (p. 60).

McComiskey, Thomas, Raymond Dillard and Jeffrey Niehaus. <u>Hosea, Joel, Amos</u> (An Exegetical and Expository Commentary). Grand Rapids: Baker, 1992. 509 pp.

This launched a new series of volumes on the Minor Prophets, with McComiskey editing. It is evangelical and shows expertise in exegesis, background, and sensitivity to hermeneutics, plus having a good use of recent scholarship and a fine bibliography. Its format has a textual section, then an expository part.

Morgan, G. Campbell. <u>Hosea: The Heart and Holiness of God</u>. London: Marshall, Morgan and Scott, 1935.

This is a series of 12 meditations of the book. It is good broad expository material but not too helpful for a deep study.

Riggs, Jack R. Hosea's Heartbreak. Neptune, NJ: Loizeaux, 1983. 171 pp.

A Cedarville College (Ohio) faculty member wrote this worthy survey, using a clear outline, discussing views and reasons on problem texts such as marrying a wife of harlotries (1:2), and helping readers see the relation of truths to life now. Riggs favors the view that Gomer did not fall into the impure physical relations until after Hosea married her and the three children were born to their union. He takes "that day" in 2:14ff. to be the future period of judgment and then the Messianic Kingdom after the Second Advent as he also believes on 3:5 (pp. 62, 67, 82). The woman in 3:1 is Gomer, after the events of Hosea 1. Riggs gives practical applications at the end of each chapter, many of which are quite arresting.

Rowley, H. H. The Marriage of Hosea. Manchester, England: University Press, 1956.

This is only a 34-page discussion, but it is good. It will be helpful to the student who seeks to plunge deeply into the problem of whether Hosea married a harlot or whether Gomer became unfaithful after the marriage (cf. Hosea 1:2).

Stuart, Douglas. Hosea-Micah (Word Biblical Commentaries). Waco, TX: Word Books, 1987. 537 pp.

This is by the Professor of Old Testament at Gordon-Conwell Theological Seminary. Conservative, he believes that Hosea wrote the book and favors chronology that E. Thiele has set forth. He has impressive bibliographies on all the books, some good notes on details in the Hebrew text, summaries to give perspectives in pericopes, and full comments with much light. In Hosea 1:2 he sees a woman tainted by spiritual unfaithfulness of Israelites, who is physically legitimate at marriage to Hosea and has three children with him. He sees Israel's blessing of 2:18-27 and 3:5 fulfilled in the church today, in amillennial fashion (pp. 61, 69, 218), for the church "has inherited the restoration promises of Hosea and the rest of the Old Testament (Galatians 3:29)" (218).

Ward, J. W. Hosea: A Theological Commentary. New York: Harper & Row, 1966.

This is one of the better theological studies on Hosea. Yet an evangelical will want to exercise discernment in the use of a liberal work, reacting with his own perspectives at some points.

Wolff, Hans Walter. Hosea: A Commentary on the Prophet Hosea (Hermeneia). Translated by Gary Stansell. Philadelphia: Fortress Press, 1974.

Wolff is an Old Testament scholar at the University of Heidelberg. His well-informed exegetical comments provide considerable help usually, as do the sometimes substantial footnotes and excursuses such as on the Valley of Achor (pp. 42, 43). A bibliography appears for each section. The work, technically critical in its purpose, is for the more seriously equipped student.

C. Joel

Allen, Leslie C. <u>The Books of Joel, Obadiah, Jonah and Micah</u> (NICOT). Grand Rapids: Eerdmans, 1976.

The author holds that Joel is late pre-exilic or early post exilic. Obadiah is from the early postexilic times. Jonah is a tale perhaps devised by wisdom teachers of the fifth or fourth century B. C. and not by Jonah. Micah is from ca. 701 B. C. The author was lecturer in Old Testament language and exegesis at London Bible College and now is at Fuller Theological Seminary. He has rather thorough word studies and a discussion of many issues, e. g. the relationship of Joel 2:28ff. with Acts 2 and with final times, and Joel 2:32a with Romans 10:13 (pp. 97-105). He shows good awareness of recent scholarly literature on his subjects, but many will not agree with some of his views, such as his suggestion that Jonah is simply a tale made by wisdom writers to convey a message (see p. 191).

Allen, Ronald B. <u>Joel</u> (Bible Study Commentary). Grand Rapids: Zondervan, 1988. 120 pp.

Allen is skilled in Hebrew and interpretation and writes attractively. He is conservative and premillennial. In his view the locusts are literal in both Chapters 1 and 2, yet supernatural in the latter case. He never seems to clear up what the supernatural locusts are in the future Armageddon time but stays general and vague. They sound like angelic hosts when Allen links them with Revelation 9:11-16. Allen has good emphases about God's grace, compassion, anger and love in 2:12-17. Apparently he sees the "northern army" of 2:20 as a human one, not identified with the locusts of 2:1-11. He has a long, helpful discussion on whether Acts 2 fulfills the outpouring of the Spirit, and sees a partial fulfillment (p. 95). In 3:9ff., he believes the blessing is in the millennium after the Second Advent, yet he identifies the fountain of verse 18 as the river in the ultimate state, the New Jerusalem (116), and is not clear on why or how he leaps from the millennium to the ultimate bliss.

Cripps, Richard S. <u>A Critical and Exegetical Commentary on the Book of Amos.</u> NY: Macmillan, 1929.

Though this work is in the higher critical vein and, for example, argues against the unity of Amos 9:11-15 with the rest of the book (see his introduction), it is helpful on details of exegesis. One can find much aid though he does not agree with many of the conclusions of Cripps.

Eaton, J. H. <u>Obadiah, Nahum, Habakkuk and Zephaniah</u> (Torch Bible Commentary). London: SCM Press, 1961.

This is a good exegesis of these books, with much help.

Finley, Thomas J. <u>Joel, Amos, Obadiah</u> (Wycliffe Exegetical Commentary). Chicago: Moody, 1990. 417 pp.

A conservative, premillennial work by the Professor of Old Testament at Talbot School of Theology. He has a good bibliography of 5 pages and a very full discussion of many issues, a rich use of other studies, help in Hebrew exegesis, and a good effort on word meaning. Hebrew words are transliterated into English. Finley sees literal locusts in chapters 1 and 2 of Joel. One wishes that he had listed and given arguments, yet he does give some when he arrives at individual verses. It sounds like he believes rich blessing will come to Israel (not the church in this case) in 2:18-27, but it also sounds like he sees it realized in past history; it is not wholly clear. He sees a partial fulfillment of Joel 2:28-32 in Acts 2ff., and details of 3:9ff. fulfilled in the future tribulation period and Messianic Kingdom after the Second Advent, not in the church or ultimate state. The treatment on Amos 9:11-15 could be stronger on reasons for a premillennial view, and the reader can feel discussion is vague about when the fulfillment will come to Israel.

Gaebelein, Arno C. <u>The Prophet Joel: An Exposition.</u> NY: Our Hope Press, 1909.

A dispensational exposition and translation. It is quite thorough.

Gaebelein, Frank E. <u>The Servant and the Dove.</u> NY: Our Hope Press, 1946.

An exposition of Obadiah and Jonah, with their practical relevance today.

Gaebelein, Frank. <u>Four Minor Prophets: Obadiah, Jonah, Habakkuk, and Haggai.</u> Chicago: Moody, 1970.

The stress in this evangelical work is on the practical aspects of the prophets, though he does give some attention to the prophetical facets. Fairly good surveys for lighter use.

Marsh, J. <u>Commentary on Amos and Micah</u> (Torch Bible Commentary). London: SCM Press, 1959.

A fairly good work on Micah, where Marsh's treatment is more of a contribution than his discussion on Amos.

McComiskey, Thomas. Cf. on Hosea.

Patterson, Richard. "Joel," in <u>Expositor's Bible Commentary</u>, Volume 7, editor Frank Gaebelein. Grand Rapids: Zondervan, 1985. 725 pp.

A skilled Old Testament scholar who is premillennial handles the text and exegesis adeptly and shows good awareness of literature and views and reasons. He takes the locust plague in Joel 1 as literal and in 2 as the human (Assyrian) army, not a far-off end-time invasion. Outpouring of the Spirit begins fulfillment in Acts 2, and the last part of Joel 3 is treated as giving events of the future tribulation period and kingdom after the Second Advent. This is a very capable work.
Cf. comments on Patterson on I Kings.

Price, Walter K. <u>The Prophet Joel and the Day of the Lord</u>. Chicago: Moody Press, 1976.

An amillennialist turned dispensational wrote this work with a foreword by John F. Walvoord, Dallas Seminary. Price writes in a readable, inviting style. He expounds Joel section by section, seeing the "Day" as taking in not only the millennial reign after the Second Coming but the Great Tribulation up to the Coming. He believes in a pretribulation rapture of the church as he ties in the Thessalonian letters. The outpouring of the Spirit begins to be fulfilled at Pentecost, continues through the present age, and will have its ultimate fulfillment at the Second Advent. Price makes some good applications of the message to today that can help preaching and teaching.

Stuart, Douglas. Cf. on Hosea.

Thompson, J. A. and Norman F. Langford. "The Book of Joel," in the <u>Interpreter's Bible</u>, Volume 6. New York: Abingdon, 1956.

Thompson did the introduction and exegesis, and Langford the exposition sections. The work favors a post-exilic date based partly on 3:1-2 (seeing Israel in captivity). It is even after the return to rebuild, based on Chapter 2. Locusts are seen as literal in both chapters. Apparently the blessings for Israel in 3:16ff. are placed in the New Jerusalem, not a millennium after the Second Advent (p. 735). How they see 2:18-27 fulfilled in past history is not explained convincingly. The work is unclear on when aspects of 2:28-32 are fulfilled, as it just meshes them all in one complex. Overall this is not an outstanding commentary even if one can discern his way between the liberal parts and grasp what is being done to passages about a future Israel.

Veldkamp, Herman. <u>The Farmer from Tekoa</u> (Amos). St. Catherine's, Ontario: Paideia Press, 1977.

A 276-pp. work done in a fresh, readable style with 33 short chapters pulling in lay persons with intriguing captions and applications sensitive to 20th century life. Veldkamp is a minister in the Reformed Church of the Netherlands. The book makes the main aspects of Amos' prophecies come alive for the lay audience as well as pastors and teachers.

Watts, John D. W. <u>The Books of Joel, Obadiah, Jonah, Nahum, Habakkuk and Zephaniah</u> (Cambridge Bible Commentary). New York: Cambridge University Press, 1975. 190 pp.

Watts uses the NEB and gives brief introductions (1-3 pp.) and expositions. He late dates Joel. On problem verses he is usually succinct. Locusts are literal in both chapters, but in the latter case Watts sees them as symbolic of the Lord's "true <u>Mighty army</u>" (p. 26), whatever that means. He sees a future for Israel (Joel 2:18-27) but leaves vaguely obscure what this means. He refers to use of Joel 2 in Acts 2 but does not discuss the problem of some details not seeming to have been realistically fulfilled in Acts 2. He discusses Joel 3:9ff. in a general haze, and is mediocre among commentaries on these books.

Watts, J. D. W. Vision and Prophecy in Amos. **Grand Rapids: Eerdmans, 1958.**

There are four chapters, dealing with the kind of prophet Amos was, the structure of the book, the hymn it preserves, and the eschatology of the book. Overall it is a stimulating study.

Wolff, Hans W. Joel and Amos: A Commentary (Hermeneia). **Philadelphia: Fortress Press, 1977. 392 pp.**

A highly-regarded and much-cited work by a liberal using form critical methodology. He often helps on technical details and use of literature on the books. He has a detailed bibliography on Joel and Amos and copious footnote references. He uses inconclusive arguments to date Joel late. Joel 2 describes locust-like apocalyptic creatures, not ordinary locusts and not humans (p. 42), yet carried out by the nations and later identified as humans, as Jeremiah 4:6 predicted (62). Wolff's apparent contradiction makes his position unclear. He sees Amos as finalized in post-exilic days after a long literary process (107). He discusses what he regards as six literary strata in highly speculative theorizing (107-13); 9:11-15, for example, with its comfort, could not have been in unity with the harsh judgment sections, so it must have been added by another writer (113). Even 9:11-15 is segmented into different layers of tradition (352). The eschatology of 9:11-15 is not set in a specific future, distinct situation, but generalized and fuzzed in relation to the people of God. Wolff likewise seems to see the latter part of Joel 3 as fulfilled in the church (15). The commentary evidences great learning and in this is often helpful, but it also has frequent lack of clarity. One is often unsure of where the fulfillment of things is placed.

D. Amos

Andersen, Francis I. and David N. Freedman. Amos: A New Translation with Introduction and Commentary (Anchor Bible). **Garden City, NY: Doubleday & Company, 1989. 979 pp.**

The work of these two scholars is ponderous here as it is on Hosea. They uphold the book's unity, often dealing rather conservatively with the text. The length allows careful explanation, sometimes overly so. However, there ought to be, but does not appear to be, a lengthy discussion on such a vital concept as the day of the Lord. The writers regard 9:11-15 as in unity with the judgmental focus in the rest of the book. However, in considerable searching this reviewer found no clear statement telling the reader when or in what framework of eschatology the blessing for Israel will be fulfilled, despite the lengthy section. On many of the verses in Amos the student will find clearer help than this in the work.

Cohen, Gary. Cf. on Hosea.

Finley, Thomas J.   Cf. on Joel.

Garland, David.   Amos (Bible Study Commentary).   Grand Rapids: Zondervan, 1966.   96 pp.

This is handled much as he did Hosea in this series. He is conservative, usually clear, succinct, and aware. The outline is good. In 9:11-15, he continues to be vague on the nature of the future of Israel. But some of his wording about the future messianic age gives the impression by its detail that he means the millennium after the Second Advent, though he has no mention of Revelation 20. He does not clarify this.

Hasel, Gerhard F.   Understanding the Book of Amos.   Grand Rapids: Baker, 1991. 171 pp.

This is not a commentary per se but a lucid and excellent survey drawing into a rich tapestry some of the helpful lines of thought in research opinions on the book. He sees Amos as the first of the writing prophets, ca. 780-760 B. C., and as a "microcosm for the study of all prophetical writings of the Old Testament" (p. 11), so a key to all. He articulates issues in such a way as to point to the unity of the book.

Mays, J. L.   Amos: A Commentary (Old Testament Library).   Philadelphia: Westminster Press, 1969.   176 pp.

A well-respected liberal work with much good information on many parts of the book. Mays, as many, lets his theories limit Amos and lead him to deny things conservatives believe can be defended reasonably. For example, Mays follows the frequent liberal line of denying that 9:11-15, with its bright hope for Israel's future, could be by the writer who spoke of harsh judgment earlier. Amos, he feels, did not speak of anything besides judgment (p. 9, 165), and 9:12 belongs after the fall of Jerusalem (165), a contention that is not necessary. Still, Mays has a lot of help in verse by verse study, and keen users can glean this out.

McComiskey, Thomas E.   "Amos, Micah," in Expositor's Bible Commentary, Volume 6, ed. Frank Gaebelein and R. P. Polcyn.   Grand Rapids: Zondervan, 1986.

A competent conservative introduction and commentary. It surveys sections well, explains things solidly verse by verse, and offers special notes on more technical aspects. He uses other Scripture cogently. He seems to hold a premillennial view on Amos 9:11-15. His bibliography work, though, is quite brief.

Motyer, J. A.   The Day of the Lion: The Message of Amos (The Bible Speaks Today). Downers Grove: IVP, 1975.   208 pp.

A brief, competent, evangelical effort that succeeds in making the message articulate, often bringing out stimulating and refreshing lessons and applying them to people today. Expositors will find it helpful. As in many books, the description about Israel's future blessing in 9:11-15 is left in glowing language but in dim light as to the framework in which fulfillment in the land will come, millennially or in the ultimate bliss.

Paul, Shalom M. Amos **(Hermeneia). Minneapolis: Augsburg Fortress, 1991. 409 pp.**

A magisterial work which seems on top of everything, impressively thorough, well-written, showing awareness of many issues, possibilities, and literature. Cf. the lists of sources (xix-xxvi, 299-367, nearly 80 pp.). This is a second commentary in the Hermeneia series since Hans Wolff's work was already out. Paul has a very full discussion on the situation in which Amos ministered, his kind of ministry, features of it, views about when oracles occur here, literary traits of the oracles, etc. Paul defends the authenticity of the oracles against arguments of interpolation. The commentary verse by verse is on large double-column pages. It is quite full of details of text, word meaning, geography, customs, relation to other Scripture, views on problems, etc. Footnotes steeped in further help are abundant and often long. Summary remarks at the outset of pericopes help readers see connections, overall ideas, and movement of the book. Paul defends 9:11-15 against arguments from the majority who see it as unauthentic, from an exilic or post-exilic theologian-redactor. He shows how it fits well with the book. He also does much to recognize the prophecy of a future glorious state for Israel and ties it with other passages. But he does not go on to relate 9:11-15 to James's use of it in Acts 15:13-18. His bibliography does list two works on this under "Early Christian Interpretation" (pp. 316-17). In his section on Indices (364-406) where he lists literature consulted, the "New Testament" entry includes only seven passages and in Acts only 7:43 (394).

Sunukian, Donald. "Amos," in Bible Knowledge Commentary**, ed. John F. Walvoord and Roy B. Zuck, Volume I. Wheaton: Victor Books, 1983.**

A fairly clear, diligent conservative work that concisely deals with many of the expositional issues so that a reader has something solid to explain verses. The outline is well-done. Unlike many commentaries, Sunukian's work on 9:11-15 is clear-cut, and he even has a good discussion of how James uses part of the passage in Acts 15. He is premillennial.

Smith, Gary V. Amos, A Commentary **(Library of Biblical Interpretation). Grand Rapids: Zondervan, 1989. 307 pp.**

A good, thorough conservative commentary leaving few key stones unturned in exposition based on the Hebrew exegesis. He is helpful on the book's unity, interpretation verse by verse, and theological relevance then and now. The work is of substantial helpfulness to expositors and lay readers.

Stuart, Douglas. Cf. on Hosea.

de Waard, J. and W. A. Smalley. A Translator's Handbook on the Book of Amos (United Bible Societies' Translator's Handbooks). United Bible Societies, 1979. 274 pp.

This offers considerable basic assistance on the text, philology, geography etc. in its detailed exegesis.

Wolff, Hans W. Cf. on Joel.

E. Obadiah

Allen, Leslie C. Cf. on Joel.

Baker, D. W., Desmond Alexander and Bruce K. Waltke. Obadiah, Jonah and Micah (Tyndale Old Testament Commentary). Downers Grove: IVP, 1988. 207 pp.

A good, concise conservative commentary, with Baker on Obadiah, Alexander on Jonah and Waltke on Micah. Overall it is quite competent and carefully thought through. Baker sees Obadiah 21 fulfilled in a king on earth after the Second Advent (p. 43) and defends the unity of verses 17-21 with the earlier part of the book. Alexander defends an early date of the Book of Jonah (8th century) against several arguments (51-63), and authorship by one writer (63-69), apparently Jonah of 2 Kings 14:25. He favors actual, historical events, not a parable or any fiction form, and sums up answers to problems he does well, but appears thin on how to explain a great fish taking in Jonah, though he believes it was a miracle (110-11). Waltke provides a good verse by verse study, enriched by expertise in exegesis, history, customs, etc.

Beyer, Bryan and Walton, John H. Obadiah/Jonah (Bible Study Commentary). Grand Rapids: Zondervan, 1988. 122 pp.

Beyer teaches Bible at Columbia Bible College, and Walton at Moody Bible Institute. Beyer dates Obadiah after 586 B. C. (Fall of Jerusalem), since verses 10-14 describe Edom's gloating at that fall. He appears to hold a premillennial view with a future millennial kingdom after the Second Advent in verses 17-21. However, he never says it is millennial, only that it is God's kingdom. But he does see a resettling of Israel in its land. Walton has packed in much good information, as on lots in Jonah 1. But since God's preparation of the great sea creature was a miracle, he sees no need to cite accounts of marine creatures taking in men (p. 29). He apparently does not view Nineveh's repentance as being a conversion to the Lord, Judaism or even monotheism (51). It was not to salvation spiritually (53). Some will not regard his explanation for why Jonah was angry (Ch. 4) as very persuasive or helpful.

Coggins, Richard J. and Re'emi, S. Paul.   Israel Among the Nations: Nahum, Obadiah, Esther (International Theological Commentary).   Grand Rapids: Eerdmans, 1985.   140 pp.

Coggins does Nahum and Obadiah. He feels it is impossible to outline Nahum, yet sees a structure (p. 7), which he does not use in the commentary later. His introduction to Nahum is not very helpful, and his commentary lays out material without synthesis to pull things into perspective. A reader can laboriously sift out some things, but only the very patient will probably plod through. The theological help for the church promised in the series is not easy to find here. No outline of Obadiah appears anywhere, and no framework is given as to when verses 17-21 will be fulfilled. The work on Esther at least follows an outline and is more lively. Re'emi proposes a set of details known under Artaxerxes II that might fit the book's claims (106-07), but feels "legendary and pictorial elements" have been added (109). He gives much good comment, shows seeming contradictions between the book and history, but also details that fit history. While Coggins' work is far down the line, Re'emi's has much that is helpful.

Eaton, J. H.   Obadiah, Nahum, Habakkuk and Zephaniah (Torch Bible Commentary).   London: SCM Press, 1961.

This is a good exegesis of these books, with much help.

Finley, Thomas J.   Cf. on Joel.

Stuart, Douglas.   Cf. on Hosea.

Watts, John D. W.   Cf. on Joel.

Watts, J. D. W.   Obadiah: A Critical and Exegetical Commentary.   Grand Rapids: Eerdmans, 1967.

A worthwhile work to use in getting at the meaning of the text verse by verse, and in gaining an appreciation for its theological message.

Wolff, Hans W.   Obadiah and Jonah. A Commentary.   Minneapolis: Augsburg Publishing House, 1986.   191 pp.

A liberal redaction-critical effort that one will need to sift discerningly as regards composition, integrity of the book, theology etc. However, a great scholar offers some help in basic, thorough comments on the text, lexical details, exegesis, and bibliography. Among critical scholars Wolff is highly regarded, and his works much cited.

F. Jonah

Aalders, G. C.   The Problem of the Book of Jonah.   London: Tyndale, 1948.

The student will find a stimulating discussion of the problem of Jonah in this booklet.

Alexander, Desmond. Cf. Baker on Obadiah.

Beyer, Bryan and John H. Walton. Cf. Beyer on Obadiah.

Elluk, J. The Judgment of Jonah. Grand Rapids: Eerdmans, 1971.

Elluk, known for his perceptive writings which speak to men today, moves in the reformed tradition. Like many but unlike many others, he considers Jonah a type of Christ.

Epp, Theodore. Jonah the Prophet. Lincoln, NE: Back to the Bible Broadcast, 1960.

Solidly evangelical, dispensational, and popular in its treatment, helpful primarily for laymen desiring simplicity and brevity with a mingling of practical comment.

Hannah, John. "Jonah," in Bible Knowledge Commentary, ed. John F. Walvoord and Roy B. Zuck, Volume I. Wheaton: Victor Books, 1983.

A careful conservative study that is clear, concise, and helpful on the main issues. His introduction answers several main objections to the authenticity of the book, and the commentary offers information to explain very well verse by verse. Much good material is packed in. Curiously, he says that Jonah's prayer has no petitions in it (p. 1467), then later says "his petitions rose to heaven . . ." (1468). Overall, however, this is a very fine concise commentary from one well-versed on the issues and the literature.

Kennedy, James Hardee. Studies in the Book of Jonah. Nashville, TN: Broadman Press.

When authoring this book, Kennedy was serving as Professor of Old Testament and Hebrew at New Orleans Baptist Theological Seminary. He presents the basic teachings of the book and shows their relevance for Christian living. The exposition is careful, even introducing elements of exegesis from the Hebrew text. Though not every preacher will be able to follow him in the fine points of Hebrew grammar, he will appreciate the help he receives from the details on Jonah.

Kohlenberger, J. R. III. Jonah and Nahum (Everyman's Bible Commentary). Chicago: Moody, 1984. 127 pp.

This is a conservative exposition based on analysis of the Hebrew, using the NIV, following a good outline. The writer is lucidly helpful on the meanings of details, connections, and doctrinal significance. He does seem beside the point in faulting conservatives for attempting to suggest possibilities of the kind of sea creature that could swallow a man, as if such attempts slight the power of God, which they do not (cf. p. 43). God can work a miracle and use a sea creature He has made in doing it. The writer argues that the repentance of the Ninevites was done in genuine faith and was unto spiritual salvation as well as physical (61).

Martin, Hugh. <u>The Prophet Jonah.</u> **London: Banner of Truth Trust, 1958, reprint.**
This work was out in Spurgeon's day, and he exulted in it. The student will find here a provoking exposition that is one of the best.

Stuart, Douglas.   Cf. on Hosea.

Walton, John H. <u>Jonah.</u> **Grand Rapids, MI: Zondervan Publishing House, 1982.**
Dr. John Walton (b. 1952) has written this 82-pp. paperback for the Bible Study Commentary series to which Leon J. Wood and John F. Walvoord are notable contributors. Walton has chosen not to write a detailed verse by verse analysis, but to deal with many problem areas of Jonah. He puts background and introductory remarks at the end and begins instead with the body of the Biblical book. He addresses such issues as casting lots in 1; the great fish in 1:17; the three-day journey of 3:3 and Ninevite beliefs of 3:4ff. With respect to the three-day journey, Dr. Walton points out that the term for journey can also be understood as "project". This rendering is necessitated because of the 500-600 mile journey between Joppa and Nineveh even though other scholars have located "Nineveh" significantly closer to Joppa than Walton allows. Walton places the author (not necessarily a man named Jonah) in the reign of Jeroboam II of Israel (II Kings 14:25) and defends a date of writing somewhere within the first half of the eighth century B. C. Jonah is understood as a pre-classical prophet and thus, his mode of prophecy disclosure is a strong factor in Walton's dating schema. Conclusion: This book is helpful to those acquainted with the problems of the book of Jonah. —Jan Sattem

Watts, John D. W.   Cf. on Joel.

Wolff, Hans W.   Cf. on Obadiah.

G. Micah

Allen, Leslie C.   Cf. on Joel.

Copass, B. A. and E. L. Carlson. <u>A Study of the Prophet Micah.</u> **Grand Rapids: Baker, 1950.**
An evangelical study that may help on a book that has received less special attention.

Hillers, D. R. <u>Micah: A Commentary on the Book of the Prophet Micah</u> **(Hermeneia). Philadelphia: Fortress Press, 1984.   116 pp.**
Steeped in scholarly literature of a critical type, Hillers provides a rather copious work on technical aspects of the text, syntax, exegesis, and views on problems, then goes on to exposition in a cursory way which is not outstanding. In his introduction, he is unconvinced by redactional schemes on Micah such as Wolff's, and often just seeks to interpret the text as from one situation, in unity.

At times, however, he too speculates subjectively on a text he sees as having the marks of editing or modification.

Martin, John A. "Micah," in Bible Knowledge Commentary, editors John F. Walvoord and Roy B. Zuck, Volume I. Wheaton: Victor Books, 1983.

A conservative work which handles many of the problems knowledgeably and takes a premillennial view of the kingdom in Chapter 4.

Mays, James L. Micah: A Commentary. Philadelphia: Westminster, 1976.

Using his own rendering from the Hebrew, Mays comments under creative captions such as "Capital Punishment for the Capital Cities" (1:2-16). The 169-pp. work is a fairly good commentary, with arresting comments in places (cf. 6:6-8, p. 142). Mays, however, believes only chapters 1-3 give us what Micah wrote ca. 701 B. C. The rest comes from prophets in late exilic and post-exilic days.

McComiskey, Thomas. Cf. on Amos.

Riggs, Jack R. Micah (Bible Study Commentary). Grand Rapids: Zondervan, 1987. 92 pp.

A Dallas Seminary graduate and professor at Cedarville College in Ohio uses a clear, simple, overall outline—Judgment (1:2—2:13), Messiah (Chapters 3-5), and pardon (6-7). He fills in sub-points helpfully, commenting competently on main details. His view of the kingdom is premillennial (p. 49). His work is helpful for pastors, Sunday School or Bible class teachers and lay people in general.

Smith, Ralph L. Micah-Malachi (Word Biblical Commentary). Waco: Word Books, 1984. 358 pp.

Smith is Professor of Old Testament, Southwestern Baptist Seminary, Fort Worth, TX. While he lets critical assumptions often sway him against conservative perspectives, he has much that helps in clear exposition of these seven books in some parts. He has good bibliographies, discusses views, gives a wealth of information on text, exegesis, background, etc., and often is clear. He is vague on when blessing will be fulfilled for Israel as in Micah 4. He has much good comment on Habakkuk 2:4, but inadequate discussion of the New Testament use of the passage, leaving the impression that the New Testament has misused it, being misled by the LXX (p. 107). He leaves some key verses poorly explained (Habakkuk 3:19) and deals with many in a skimpy way in general with other verses, as the whole of Habakkuk 3. Sometimes he is not easy to follow, as when Zechariah 14:6-11 depicts to him the New Jerusalem, yet 14:16-21 are handled as if they are in an imperfect situation.

Waltke, Bruce K. Cf. on Obadiah, under Baker.

Wolff, Hans W. <u>Micah, A Commentary.</u> Minneapolis: Augsburg Fortress, 1990. 258 pp.

A work exalted in critical circles, given to the idea that the book is written in post-exilic times, the product of centuries of composition, with only some passages stemming originally from Micah (cf. list on his pp. 8-9). His redaction segments are subjective and lacking hard evidence that they are necessary. One can glean much that does help on Micah, but he is often meeting up with Wolff's theories about composition, which are obtrusive and interruptive to the person looking at the text as a unity by one writer.

H. Nahum

Baker, D. W. <u>Nahum, Habakkuk and Zephaniah</u> (Tyndale Old Testament Commentary). Downers Grove: IVP, 1988. 121 pp.

As Baker did in Obadiah in this series, he again presents a brief introduction and a well-studied survey of each book with a good outline, handling most things rather carefully, in a conservative stance. He sees the "Day" of Zephaniah 3 as one of wrath and also hope and help (p. 116), but is very general and vague about when and where and in what form the blessed state will be realized. He is typical of many who do not nail down things in any framework so as to clarify just where he stands.

Coggins, Richard J. Cf. on Obadiah.

Davidson, A. B. <u>Nahum, Habakkuk, Zephaniah</u> (Cambridge Bible for Schools and Colleges). Cambridge: University Press, 1896.

A fairly helpful brief commentary to use only along with fuller studies that explain more.

Freeman, Hobart E. <u>Nahum, Zephaniah, Habakkuk, Minor Prophets of the Seventh Century</u> (Everyman's Bible Commentary). Chicago: Moody Press, 1973.

A helpful survey by the author of the very fine <u>Introduction to the Old Testament Prophets</u>.

Heflin, J. N. Boo. <u>Nahum, Habakkuk, Zephaniah, Haggai</u> (Bible Study Commentary). Grand Rapids: Zondervan, 1984. 190 pp.

Heflin is quite capable and well-informed in his introductions and commentaries, obviously having given matters adequate study. He defends Nahum against critical attacks, points out three theological themes (God is sovereign Lord, righteous judge, merciful Savior (pp. 29-31)), and helps on doctrinal themes of the other books too. He explains main details. Judicious comments appear on how Habakkuk 2:4 and Paul's concept in citing it can be correlated in the final analysis (92-93). He is quite clear on the picture from the gazelle in Habakkuk 3:19 (109). The day of the Lord in Zephaniah 3:9ff. entails both judgment and blessing (150). Heflin usually helps on ways a problem may be solved, as the meaning of purified lip in Zephaniah 3:9. He fails to specify the state in which restoration occurs in 3:9ff.; he tabs it "the new Jerusalem" (which could be identified with Revelation 21-22, the ultimate state), yet describes it in details that could be seen as millennial, before the ultimate state.

Johnson, Elliott. "Nahum," in Bible Knowledge Commentary, editors John F. Walvoord and Roy B. Zuck. Volume I. Wheaton: Victor Books, 1983.

Here is a concise conservative commentary that looks carefully at verses, gives views on problems and makes good decisions often. Much of the book is explained very well even with space limitations. A chart on page 1495 lists fulfillments for twelve prophecies of Nahum, using ancient sources. Johnson is better known for his Expository Hermeneutics (Zondervan, 1990).

Kohlenberger, J. R. III. Cf. on Jonah.

Maier, Walter. The Book of Nahum. Saint Louis: Concordia, 1959.

The author, who was heard for years on the "Lutheran Hour," has contributed a book very rich in exegetical detail and effective in answering higher critical views. This is the finest detailed work by a conservative and is highly desirable for the serious student. It is also lucid. The author received his Ph. D. degree in Semitics at Harvard in 1929 and served as Professor of Hebrew and Old Testament at Concordia Seminary in Saint Louis. Edward J. Young of Westminster Theological Seminary said in Christianity Today (May 25, 1959, p. 38): "This book comes to serious grips with questions of introduction and exegesis. It is solid treatment of the Hebrew text, a real commentary, the kind of work that will prove of inestimable benefit to any student who truly desires to understand the message of the prophet Nahum."

Patterson, Richard. Nahum, Habakkuk and Zephaniah (Wycliffe Exegetical Commentary). Chicago: Moody, 1991. 416 pp.

This is an outstanding conservative, detailed work backed by scholarly awareness and expertise. Comments reflect fine-tuned ability in the Hebrew text, philology, exegesis, history, and literature. Patterson has premillennial convictions in the final verses of Zephaniah. He shows the shaky reasoning of critical arguments against the unity of Nahum, and defends unity of Nahum and Habakkuk. In a long Excursus he defends New Testament uses of Habakkuk 2:4 (pp. 21-23). But some will doubt that he captures the significance of the picture of a hind in Habakkuk 3:19 when he sees only swiftness ascending and gracefully gliding (262-63). But in most details he is excellent, and the work is well worth the cost and time.

Robertson, O. Palmer.   The Books of Nahum, Habakkuk and Zephaniah (New International Commentary on the Old Testament).   Grand Rapids: Eerdmans, 1990.   357 pp.

This is a very good conservative work, both perceptive on issues and in lucid style. The writer provides a good translation and commentary, often graphic. He looks at Habakkuk 2:4 from many angles (pp. 173-83), and also clearly catches the picture of living by faith in 3:19 that ties in with 2:4b. To a large extent the explanations of verses are full enough and satisfying. At times, however, questions in serious minds are not dealt with. For example, why make a sweeping statement in Zephaniah 3:12 about no deceit in the future remnant if this is in a state of imperfection and believers still have some deceit when less than absolutely perfect?

Smith, Ralph L.   Cf. on Micah.

I. Habakkuk

Baker, D. W.   Cf. on Nahum.

Barber, Cyril J.   Habakkuk and Zephaniah (Everyman's Bible Commentary).   Chicago: Moody, 1985.   127 pp.

Barber, perhaps best known for his The Minister's Library, gives a knowledgeable introduction of Habakkuk with a clear outline of the book. Synopses at the outset of sections offer perspective, he deals with verses well and has some help on problems. He sees the gazelle in 3:19 as picturing the sure-footedness and freedom in a life of faith. He is helpful on the Day of the Lord, seeing it as both near and far and involving both judgment and blessing (pp. 79-81). He is premillennial on Zephaniah 3:9-20.

Blue, J. Ronald.   "Habukkuk," in Bible Knowledge Commentary, editors John F. Walvoord and Roy B. Zuck, Volume I.   Wheaton: Victor Books, 1983.

A conservative look informed by careful study and done in a clear, concise style. Blue offers some help on most issues of the book.

Gowan, Donald E.   The Triumph of Faith in Habakkuk.   Atlanta: John Knox, 1976.

This 94-pp. book is by the then Associate Professor of Old Testament at Pittsburgh Theological Seminary. He focuses on Habakkuk's theological thrust as it addresses deep needs of people oppressed by baffling problems such as "Why does evil prosper in a world over which a good God rules?" Gowan does not feel that Habakkuk supplies an answer to the problem of evil, but he does believe the book tells those who are just how to live by faith in God even without all the answers. And the truly just will show they are by continuing in faith even when the just do not always receive rewards now for godliness.

Heflin, J. N. Boo.   Cf. on Nahum.

Lloyd-Jones, D. M.   Faith Tried and Triumphant.   Downers Grove: IVP, 1987.

This is a reprinting of a very good work on Habakkuk called From Fear to Faith (IVF, 1953). Expositors will find help on how the great English preacher brought out principles that have living force today.

Patterson, Richard.   Cf. on Nahum.

Robertson, O. Palmer.   Cf. on Nahum.

Smith, Ralph.   Cf. on Micah.

Szeles, Maria Eszenyei.   Wrath and Mercy: A Commentary on the Books of Habakkuk and Zephaniah (International Theological Commentary).   Grand Rapids: Eerdmans, 1987.   118 pp.

This is by Professor of Old Testament, United Protestant Theological Seminary, in Cluj-Napoca, Romania. The work has many thorough and good exegetical comments on the Hebrew drawn from much study, yet some thin and cursory statements. Often the book furnishes help on theological meaning. But the authoress at times reflects higher critical loyalties as in claiming arbitrarily that certain statements must be a redactor's later insertion if the writer does not grasp them. She is flimsy or non-existent in convincing proof (cf. on Habakkuk. 2:6-20 at p. 36; also cf. p. 41, etc.). A pastor or student using the work with good discernment can profit from it by exercising his own judgment.

J. Zephaniah

Allen, Ronald B.   A Shelter in the Fury. A Prophet's Stunning Picture of God.   Portland, OR: Multnomah Press, 1984.   129 pp.

Allen is Professor of Hebrew Scripture at Western Conservative Baptist Seminary, Portland, OR. This is a very popularly-written work that shows attractively the secret in Zephaniah of finding a hiding place and a song in God to avert God's wrath and relate to His love. Allen uses several illustrations and creative writing to pull readers in, but at times drags out getting to aspects of the message. If one stays with the book patiently he eventually gets a lot of good lessons amidst all the dressing as Allen works his way through Zephaniah. The book is suggestive for teachers and preachers, and refreshing for any Christian who uses it in devotional times.

Baker, D. W.   Cf. on Nahum.

Barber, Cyril J.   Cf. on Habakkuk.

Hannah, John D.   "Zephaniah," in <u>Bible Knowledge Commentary</u>, editors John F. Walvoord and Roy B. Zuck, Volume I.   Wheaton: Victor Books, 1983.

A good conservative, premillennial short study of Zephaniah by a good scholar. The work is well-informed in history, and explains verses competently within a good outline.

Heflin, J. N. Boo.   Cf. on Nahum.

Patterson, Richard.   Cf. on Nahum.

Robertson, O. Palmer.   Cf. on Nahum.

Smith, Ralph.   Cf. on Micah.

Szeles, Maria.   Cf. on Habakkuk.

K. Haggai

Baldwin, J. G.   <u>Haggai, Zechariah, Malachi</u> (Tyndale Old Testament Commentary). Grand Rapids: Eerdmans, 1972.

The work furnishes a detailed exegesis and rather thorough use of other writers, giving evidence of wide study.

Coggins, Richard J.   <u>Haggai, Zechariah, Malachi</u> (Old Testament Guides).   Sheffield, England: JSOT Press, 1987.   90 pp.

This work, available via Eisenbrauns, Winona Lake, Indiana, offers brief assistance on critical issues, historical matters and exegesis. Coggins is not a particularly interesting writer, but he offers quite a bit of expertise that can be of help as one reads and discerns carefully, choosing what is usable and bypassing other material.

Heflin, J. N. Boo.   Cf. on Nahum.

Lindsey, F. Duane.   "Haggai," in <u>Bible Knowledge Commentary</u>, editors John F. Walvoord and Roy B. Zuck, Volume I.   Wheaton: Victor Books, 1983.

A Dallas Seminary faculty member has done this very able, brief work covering most of the vital bases for an expositor. He is helpful on historical background, flow of the context, meanings of verses, etc. The section on the future millennial temple in 2:6-9 and the reference to Zerubbabel in 2:20 are well done.

Mason, Rex.   <u>The Books of Haggai, Zechariah and Malachi</u> (Cambridge Bible Commentary).   New York: Cambridge University Press, 1977.

Using the NEB text, this series aims to bring the learning of modern scholarship to general readers, assuming no theological knowledge or grasp of Hebrew or Greek. The work is fair at times as a general, concise survey often swayed by redaction criticism. Sometimes the possible long-range Messianic reach of a prophecy is not even referred to (cf. Haggai 2:6-9) or mentioned only barely or incidentally (2:23). Some of Mason's suggestions of a redactor will be subjectively arbitrary to some who use the work. Certain details are left vague, as for example no effort to suggest who the four "smiths" may possibly represent (Zechariah 1:20, 21). Some will not be convinced that chapters 9-14 are from later hands than 1-8, in a "continuing tradition" but "farther down-stream" (p. 79 with 80-82). The author engages in a lot of shuffling of the order of the text, a disconcerting feature to many of his "general" audience. Mason discusses 12:10 without seeing a reference to a Messiah's suffering (p. 119).

Moore, T. V.   Haggai, Zechariah and Malachi.   Carlisle, PA: Banner of Truth Trust, 1979rp.   426 pp.

This work came out in 1856. It is competent in exegetical detail of a reformed nature, explaining much in the books, but disappointing to premillennialists in passages on the future kingdom. Being so old, the work will not acquaint the reader with literature of recent times.

Petersen, David L.   Haggai and Zechariah 1-8 (Old Testament Library). Philadelphia: Westminster Press, 1984.   320 pp.

A liberal work detailed in verse by verse comment, form structure, word meanings, and the like. He uses his own translation and sometimes quotations from the RSV. At times he defends verses as fitting meaningfully, not agreeing with scholars who judge them as secondary and superfluous (as Haggai 1:13, p. 57; some aspects in 2:3-9, pp. 65-66). Some verses though dealt with in detail do not seem to be explained well, as when he does not make clear when the shaking in 2:6 will occur. The glory of the future temple appears to be put in the near historical future and a future millennial temple is not even mentioned as a possibility in 2:7-9. On 2:23 he has much discussion but little light, no messianic import, and vagueness. Patience is often needed in searching for some crystallization of his interpretation in the midst of ponderous wording, for he is not soon to the point and can be nebulous about when things will be fulfilled. An example is the fuzziness about the removal of evil to Babylon in Zechariah 5:5-11.

Smith, Ralph.   Cf. on Micah.

Verhoef, Pieter A.   The Books of Haggai and Malachi (New International Commentary on the Old Testament).   Grand Rapids: Eerdmans, 1987.   364 pp.

This is by the Professor of Old Testament, Emeritus, University of Stellenbosch, South Africa. It is conservative and offers much on current literature, introductory matters, and verse by verse content, adeptly explaining the text and flow of thought. He takes issue with W. Rudolph who says in his commentary on Haggai that the book has no relevance at all for the Christian faith (Verhoef, p. vii), and strives to show the significance of both Haggai and Malachi to today. He has interacted with much scholarship within the text and in footnotes. He believes that someone close to Haggai in his day wrote the book with authentic material from Haggai. He upholds the unity of the book, and traces the movement through the verses carefully in relation to its background. He seems to be premillennial, seeing the fulfillment of prophetical aspects about the temple beyond the Second Advent. He deals at length with many of the problems, giving different views and factors to weigh, as on God's love and hate (Malachi 1:2-3), "one" in 2:15, the messenger concepts of 3:1, and "Elijah" in 4:4-6.

Wolf, Herbert M. **Haggai and Malachi** (Everyman's Bible Commentary). Chicago: Moody, 1976. 128 pp.

This is clear exposition based on skill in Hebrew. On many verses he is helpful, and traces the thought through in a well-organized way. He seems vague on when the glorious temple of Haggai 2:6-9 will be realized; he says at the Second Advent in a kingdom of Christ, a generality that could fit different views, but hints at a premillennial view. In Malachi 4 he sees a fulfillment in John the Baptist as "Elijah" and a possible further fulfillment in the tribulation period before the Second Advent.

Wolff, Hans W. **Haggai, A Commentary.** Minneapolis: Augsburg, 1988. 128 pp.

This work by an expert in exegesis, history and critical study is a translation from the German Biblischer Kommentar series. Wolff sees three layers of composition from Haggai to the final writer. The chronicler, he feels, added interpolations at 2:5, 9, 14, 17-19, 21-22. The good of the large amount of information and expertise on exegesis is disturbed by what some will consider arbitrary opinions about composition and rearrangement.

Wolff, Richard. **The Book of Haggai: A Study Manual.** Grand Rapids: Baker, 1967.

A soundly evangelical and careful 84-page exegetical work reflecting broad study and attention to problems historically, exegetically and theologically in careful exposition. Wolff handles difficulties well in most cases and writes clearly. He is premillennial. This is one of the better commentaries on Haggai.

L. Zechariah

Baldwin, Joyce. Cf. on Haggai.

Barker, Kenneth. "Zechariah," in **Expositor's Bible Commentary**, Volume 7, editors Frank Gaebelein and R. P. Polcyn. Grand Rapids: Zondervan, 1985.

Conservative, premillennial expertise on the text, exegesis, scholarly literature etc. The careful writer, who correlates many things in a mature study, articulates a future for ethnic Israel in such texts as 13:1 and 14:1ff. It is the best recent premillennial work.

Baron, David. **Commentary on Zechariah.** Grand Rapids: Kregel, 1988. 555 pp.

A converted Jew gives a deep understanding from the Hebrew text.

Coggins, Richard J.   Cf. on Haggai.

Heater, Homer, Jr.   Zechariah (Bible Study Commentary).   Grand Rapids: Zondervan, 1987.   122 pp.

Here is a good survey by a premillennialist, well-organized, aware of main issues, contributive on most. He takes the four horns of 1:18-19 to be not the four empires of Daniel 2 and 7 or any other specific four but coming from the four quarters of the earth, a world-wide context (p. 21). The four craftsmen are likewise. He sees the future for Jerusalem in Chapter 2 as millennial, after the Second Advent. He appears to be vague on God taking evil from Israel and "setting it up among those who reject Him . . ." in Shinar (Zechariah 5, p. 43). The explanation of details in Chapter 14 as fitting in a premillennial view is helpful but brief.

Feinberg, Charles L.   God Remembers: A Study of Zechariah.   4th edition. Portland: Multnomah Press, 1979.

This is a reprint of one of the best premillennial expositions by an established Old Testament scholar. Feinberg taught Zechariah for many years at Dallas Seminary and Talbot Seminary in Hebrew exegesis classes. He, Barker and Unger have the best premillennial commentaries of a verse by verse nature on the book.

Feinberg, Charles L.   Zechariah: Israel's Comfort and Glory.   NY: American Board of Missions to the Jews, 1952.

Also note his commentary on Zechariah in the one-volume Wycliffe Bible Commentary as well as a larger volume God Remembers, which was first issued as a series in Bibliotheca Sacra.

Laney, J. Carl.   Zechariah (Everyman's Bible Commentary).   Chicago: Moody, 1984.   143 pp.

A lucid, well-paced premillennial exposition showing an evident keenness about explaining main issues. See, for example, pp. 24-25 as well as all his comments on Zechariah 14. He is Associate Professor of Biblical Literature at Western Conservative Baptist Seminary, Portland, OR.

Leupold, H. C.   Exposition of Zechariah.   Columbus: Wartburg, 1956.

In this commentary the student will find a good example of how an amillennial scholar of top rank deals with the crucial prophecies relating to Israel's future. As usual, Leupold is detailed and seeks to grapple with the problems.

Lindsey, F. Duane.   "Zechariah," in Bible Knowledge Commentary, editors John F. Walvoord and Roy B. Zuck, Volume I.   Wheaton: Victor Books, 1983.

Lindsey covers many of the interpretive issues fairly well, often mentioning views and sometimes bringing good reasoning to bear. He sees the eight night visions in 1:7—6:8 as God's work which "bridges the centuries from the rebuilding of the

Individual Commentaries on Old Testament Books ❖ 179

temple in Zechariah's day to the restoration of the kingdom to Israel under the Messiah . . . to be fulfilled at Christ's Second Advent . . ." (p. 1549). He deals with Chapters 12-14, particularly, in a premillennial framework, and makes things clear.

Moore, T. V.   Cf. on Haggai.

Petersen, David L.   Cf. on Haggai.

Smith, Ralph.   Cf. on Micah.

Unger, Merrill F.   Commentary on Zechariah.   Grand Rapids: Zondervan, 1963.
Based on the Hebrew text, this detailed work is the result of more than 15 years of lectures on Zechariah. The author was Chairman of the Department of Old Testament and Professor of Hebrew Exegesis at Dallas Seminary. He writes with lucid literary style. His interpretations are premillennial and dispensational in orientation. He uses a large variety of words, and meets the amillennial system of interpretation squarely in the key passages. An outline is given, a translation of the text is printed at the top of the page, and the commentary is set up in two columns on each page. The student will find help also in the extensive bibliography given at the end of the commentary though lacking studies of more recent years. This work and the commentaries by Barker and Feinberg are the most valuable longer premillennial studies of Zechariah.

M. Malachi

Baldwin, Joyce.   Cf. on Haggai.

Blaising, Craig.   "Malachi," in Bible Knowledge Commentary, editors John F. Walvoord and Roy B. Zuck, Volume I.   Wheaton: Victor Books, 1983.
A capable conservative, premillennial study that provides considerable help, even if concise, to expositors. Blaising takes Malachi as a personal name (p. 1573), defending this against four arguments. He has good discussions of some problematic verses, as the "one" in 2:15, and details in 3:1, and 4:5-6. In the latter, he does not believe that John the Baptist fulfilled the "Elijah" expectation (1588), but Elijah is yet to come.

Coggins, Richard J.   Cf. on Haggai.

Glazier-McDonald, Beth.   Malachi, The Divine Messenger.   Atlanta, GA: Scholars Press, 1987.   288 pp.
This 1983 dissertation at the University of Chicago does several things. It stands against the tide holding that the book is prose and contends for the poetic character of the larger part. It explains the text, often in as much detail as many verse by verse commentaries, and is against emendations. It argues for every verse fit-

ting the flow of the context and being cogent to the situation of Malachi's day ca. 450 B. C. The writer shows wide knowledge of scholarly literature, but often reasons against commonly accepted critical theory. For example, the "messenger of the covenant" in 3:1 is to her the Lord, not an addition to the text. Conservatives appreciate much of the work, but textual and redaction-critical scholars frown on her upholding the text as it is, though she has done her homework.

Isbell, Charles D. Malachi **(Bible Study Commentary). Grand Rapids: Zondervan, 1980. 80 pp.**

Isbell decides Malachi is not the prophet's name but descriptive of his role, "my messenger." His explanation of God's love and hate (1:2-3) does not relate this to Romans 9 in the larger picture and show how the explanation is consistent (if so) with it. His comments on 4:4-6 do not explain much on Elijah; there is no relationship made to New Testament passages and possibilities. But earlier on 3:1 (p. 59) he offers a little on this, although it is a bigger problem than he offers help on. Overall this is a fair commentary but not high on the list.

Kaiser, Walter C., Jr. Malachi: God's Unchanging Love. **Grand Rapids: Baker, 1984. 172 pp.**

A fine work on exegesis of the text and practical import for life today. It is conservative and premillennial, and will make some contribution in an expositor's preparation to speak on the book.

Logsdon, S. Franklin. Malachi, or Will A Man Rob God? **Chicago: Moody, 1961.**

Available as a paperback of only 128 pages, this book is helpful to the pastor but not a thorough work involved with the details of exegesis.

Moore, T. T. **Cf. on Haggai.**

Morgan, G. Campbell. Malachi's Message for Today. **Grand Rapids: Baker, 1972.**

Even though Morgan's ministry was completed in the early part of this century, his exposition still has emphases relevant and timely today. He makes Malachi's comments live. The book is provocative for a preaching series and for leading Bible studies. He excels at times in rich, provocative word studies (cf. on 3:16, "they feared the Lord and thought on his name," showing a tie-in with other Scripture, with profound help for the spiritual life).

Smith, Ralph. **Cf. on Micah.**

Verhoef, Pieter A. **Cf. on Haggai.**

Wolf, Herbert M. **Cf. on Haggai.**

GENERAL COMMENTARIES
ON THE NEW TESTAMENT

I. GREEK

Alford, Henry. The Greek New Testament. 4 vols. Chicago: Moody, 1958, Revision by Everett Harrison.

This was the great work in the life of the versatile Dean of Canterbury. An outcome of this production was the New Testament for English Readers (4 vols.). Alford was a Calvinist, conservative and premillennial, though not dispensational. He takes a literal interpretation of the thousand years in Rev. 20 and has a famous quote there, is strong on sovereign election as in Rom 8:29-30 and I Pet. 1:2, but, unfortunately, holds to baptismal regeneration in such texts as Titus 3:5 and John 3:5. He shows a great knowledge of the Greek text and faces problems of both a doctrinal and textual nature.

Bengel, J. A. Bengel's New Testament Commentary. 2 volumes. New translation C. T. Lewis and M. R. Vincent. Grand Rapids: Kregel, 1981rp.

This work, originally issued in 1742, has considerable comment on the Greek, flavoring the effort with judicious details about the spiritual life. It has much that helps, but has been surpassed by many other commentaries since its day.

Ellicott, Charles J. A New Testament Commentary for English Readers. 3 vols. New York: E. P. Dutton & Co. (n. d.).

Though concise in its statements, this commentary reveals a thorough knowledge of the Greek and is very helpful in matters of grammar and word meanings.

Lenski, R. C. H. Commentary on the New Testament. 12 vols. Columbus: Wartburg, 1937-46.

This Lutheran scholar is careful and thorough, giving the reader much material which seriously grapples with the meaning of the text. He is evangelical and amillennial.

Marshall, I. Howard, and W. W. Gasque, eds. **New International Greek Testament Commentary.** **Grand Rapids:** **Eerdmans, 1978ff.**

This rather thorough evangelical exegetical work reveals scholarly study steeped in the literature pertinent to passages. New volumes continue to appear. Advanced students find it very helpful, and other serious readers can glean much. It interacts with modern critical discussion in books and journals. Marshall's 928-page commentary on Luke started it off (first at Exeter, England: Paternoster Press). Other authors chosen are usually well-established in New Testament scholarship. So far volumes published are by Paul Ellingworth (Hebrews), George W. Knight (Pastorals), F. F. Bruce (Galatians), Peter O'Brien (Philippians). C. A. Wanamaker (Thessalonians, Epistles), and Peter Davids (James).

Meyer, H. A. W., ed. **A Critical and Exegetical Commentary on the New Testament.** **11 volumes.** **Translated from 6th edition of German of 1884.** **Winona Lake, IN:** **Alpha Publications, 1979rp.**

One of the finest old works on meticulous exegesis of the Greek verse by verse, informed by much expertise and study. It provides very well-respected discussion on all but the Book of Revelation. Meyer, J. E. Huther and G. Lunemann did different parts. It is conservative in places but not in others, and helpful to trained users who know how to follow the intricacies of grammar.

Moule, C. F. D. (Ed.). **Cambridge Greek Testament Commentary.** **Cambridge:** **University Press, 1957.**

Appearance of this Cambridge University Press production began in 1955. The aim was to present a work replacing the former Cambridge Bible for Schools and Colleges and the Cambridge Greek Testament for Schools and Colleges. It is an attempt to give a theological commentary founded upon careful linguistic and historical study.

New International Biblical Commentary. **Peabody, MA:** **Hendrickson, 1989ff.**

An evangelical series by scholars who for the most part are well-known, such as Robert Mounce (Matthew), F. F. Bruce (Philippians), Gordon Fee (Pastorals), and Peter Davids (James). In cases just named they rank high, offering well-studied detail arising out of sound hermeneutics in many cases. The series began as the Good News Commentary in the early 1980's using the Good News translation (Harper and Row), but switched in the late 80's to Hendrickson and NIV.

Nicoll, W. Robertson (Ed.). **The Expositors' Greek Testament.** **5 vols.** **Grand Rapids:** **Eerdmans, 1951.** **Reprint.**

This is a thorough exegesis of the Greek text. It is considered to be one of the standard tools for exegetical study.

Pillars Commentary Series. Grand Rapids: Eerdmans, 1988ff.

This is an ongoing evangelical product with solid efforts so far by Leon Morris (Romans, 1988), D. A. Carson (John, 1991) and P. E. Hughes (Revelation, 1990). The works by Morris and Carson are very helpful to expositors, elucidating most of the main passages in fairly adequate detail and readable fashion, backed by perceptive awareness of literature. Hughes takes an amillennial approach. "Pillars" is a name some use since the dust jacket cover had broad line like pillars at the far left.

Robertson, Archibald T. Word Pictures in the New Testament. 6 vols. Nashville: Broadman, 1931.

Authored by one of the foremost Greek scholars in the 20th century, this work is very helpful in matters of grammar and word meanings throughout the New Testament. Robertson, a Southern Baptist, was the author of a monumental grammar of the New Testament.

Vincent, M. R. Word Studies in the New Testament. 4 vols. N. Y.: Scribners, 1887-1900.

Often helpful in discerning meanings of words in a passage and thus cited frequently by some writers. It is in many places good, but not as valuable as A. T. Robertson's Word Pictures.

II. ENGLISH

A New Testament Commentary. Eds. G. C. D. Howley, F. F. Bruce, and H. L. Ellisen. Grand Rapids: Zondervan, 1969. 1 vol.

Twenty-five evangelical scholars (though most names are not well known in America) contributed. The work begins with a section of general articles on areas such as authority of the N. T., the text and canon, the language of the N. T., archaeological discoveries, environmental background, historical and political background, chronology, pagan and Jewish background, N. T. use of the O. T., etc. Bruce does the commentary on the Book of Revelation. Comments throughout are terse; there is no room for discussing issues at length. As a one-volume work it should be helpful in a limited way.

Alford, Henry. The New Testament for English Readers. 4 vols. Chicago: Moody, 1955.

This contains much that is valuable in the Greek New Testament authored by Alford, though all of the Greek New Testament words have been changed to English throughout.

Barclay, William. <u>Commentary on the New Testament.</u> **Philadelphia: Westminster, 1957-63.**

Now also available in paperback which is much more economical, this set is very rich in background, word studies and illuminating material on manners and customs. It is a good commentary to have. However, the student should realize that it sometimes is weak theologically, showing liberal bias at some points.

Erdman, Charles R. <u>Commentary on the New Testament.</u> **17 vols. Philadelphia: Westminster, 1916-36.**

Concise treatments are given to each of the N. T. books. The main value of the set lies in its clear synthesis which helps the student grasp the flow of thought as he moves through a book. Erdman possessed a lucid writing style. He was amillennial.

Gaebelein, Arno C. <u>Gaebelein's Concise Commentary on the New Testament.</u> **Chicago: Moody, 1991.**

This is a revision, in one volume, of the New Testament part of the multi-volume <u>Annotated Bible</u> by one of America's popular Bible teachers in the first half of the twentieth century. It includes diligent explanation that helps pastors and lay readers and also frequent application, somewhat akin to the broad H. A. Ironside expositions.

Jensen, Irving L. <u>Jensen's Survey of the New Testament.</u> **Chicago: Moody, 1981.**

A firmly evangelical work of 535 pages written on a Bible college text-book level with broad surveys of N. T. books, many charts and maps, lists of applications, study questions, selected reading lists, good organization in chapters. He takes an early date for Mt. (late 50's), says very little of substance at times in a section (cf. Mt. 13:1-53, p. 125), tends frequently to leave out some of the top-notch commentaries in reading lists (cf. Mt., Mk., Lk., Rom., etc.). But considering his objective, to furnish a book that aims to get a student into the Bible text itself, he may well go with a light survey and not give so much on key details. Outlines tend to be brief and simple. Surveys at times are mere outlines (1 Cor. 1-6), at times a long discussion (7 & 8) etc. All things considered, the survey is bound to be a great help to those who need a light, yet well-organized overview which puts in certain key information to orientate them.

Ironside, H. A. **(addresses on individual New Testament books). N. Y.: Loizeaux, Inc. Various Dates.**

He has authored works on all 27 New Testament books. These are premillennial and dispensational but of a popular strain, having grown out of messages delivered from his pulpit, the Moody Memorial Church in Chicago.

<u>New American Commentary.</u> **Nashville, TN: Broadman Press, 1990ff.**

This new series takes the place of the old American Commentary on the New Testament, in which John Broadus on Matthew was a standout. All NAC authors "affirm the divine inspiration, inerrancy, complete truthfulness, and full authority of the Bible" (Editor's Preface). Craig Blomberg's entry on Matthew is a very good survey, marked by careful study, wide acquaintance with the literature, and perceptive handling of many problems. John Polhill's on Acts is also quite good. Some volumes, as the one on the Pastorals, are surveys that make good contributions at times but do not come up to the standard of the efforts on Matthew and Acts.

Ogilvie, Lloyd J. (Gen. Ed.) The Communicator's Commentary (N. T.). Waco, Texas: Word Books, 1982—1991.

A 12-vol. set done by 12 men selected for unusual ability to make the Bible come alive in biblical exposition, with spiritual refreshment and insight. These are Myron S. Augsburger (Mt.), David McKenna (Mk.), Bruce Larson (Lk.), Roger Fredrikson (Jn.), Lloyd Ogilvie (Acts), D. Stuart Briscoe (Rom.), Kenneth Chafin (1, 2 Cor.), Maxie Dunham (Gal., Eph., Phil., Col., Phile.), Gary Demarest (Thess., Pastorals), Louis Evans, Jr. (Heb.), Paul Cedar (James, 1, 2 Pet., Jude), Earl Palmer (1, 2, 3 Jn., Rev.) The authors seek to combine scholarship on biblical meaning, illustrations to spark applications, and outlines based on the new KJV. Frequent bold-faced headings appear over smaller sections throughout a biblical book. On many passages the sweeping comments on the main emphases are quite good and at times well-illustrated. That does not mean that readers will be able to agree on every point. See, for example, on Mt. 19:9 (Mt. 19, p. 76) where porneia is said to mean what Schweizer thought, "continual infidelity rather than a single act of adultery." The commentary does not always explain (but which commentary does?) how a point is consistent with some other main truth many in the audience will probably wonder about. For example, many will wonder how a person paying all to secure the pearl (Mt. 13:46) to gain the goal is consistent with God giving eternal blessing as an outright gift. Granted there is a good explanation; it would be helpful to comment on such a vital point, even if briefly. Briscoe's treatment of Romans is very well-written in the literary sense and illustrated in a very choice way. It is refreshing to see him explain such a passage as 2:7 as Cranfield and Käsemann, not as hypothetical but as actual, lived by grace consistent with justification by grace and not merit in 3:28. However, the comments on 2:11-15 do not explain much that will answer key questions people have put to me on the implications. The same is true of 3:27-31, where arousing illustration is good but basic explanation is thin (how do "we establish the law", for example?). What does 4:15 mean? (The comment on 5:13, 14 on p. 123 may help a little.) He does a fairly good job on 5:12ff., 6:6, 7:14ff., etc. The work on the Epistles of John and the Book of Revelation is too often so generalized that one can come away with little that really helps (cf. I Jn. 5:16; Rev. 2:10, 11; 7:1-8; 9:1-11 etc). The bibliography at the end is rather thin on better helps that make a solid attempt at interpreting the Revelation. In looking through several vols. of this commentary, the feature that has struck me as helpful is the aspect of illustrations which are often superbly refreshing and suggestive as preaching helps.

The actual verse by verse explanation as to reflecting a perceptive grasp of what really is vital to be explained and then nailing down the explanation solidly is quite good in some places but weak or non-existent on key details in others.

Ritchie New Testament Commentary Series. 10 volumes. **Kilmarnock, Scotland: John Ritchie, Ltd., 1988ff., or Neptune, NJ: Loizeaux, 1988ff.**

Simple laypersons' commentaries done in a firm evangelical conviction of inerrancy and even according to a dispensational view but sometimes without a very broad effort to look at other literature that can help. For further comment, cf. John Heading, "Gospel of John," in this list.

Wesley, John. Explanatory Notes Upon the New Testament. 2 vols. **Grand Rapids: Baker, 1981.**

Here is one good source in which to find Wesley's view of a given text most readily, even if he is brief.

Wiersbe, Warren. The Bible Exposition Commentary. 2 volumes. **Wheaton: Victor Books, 1990.**

One of America's most appreciated staunchly evangelical Bible conference teachers gives diligent, refreshing expositions. These are all of his 23 separate, earlier books in the "Be" series on the New Testament. He strikes a particular appeal with lay people as he crystallizes sections, deals with some of the verses, handles certain problems and backgrounds and applies principles. He is premillennial.

BACKGROUND WORKS AND
SPECIAL STUDIES IN THE GOSPELS

Andrews, Samuel J. **The Life of Our Lord Upon the Earth.** Grand Rapids: Zondervan, 1954.

One of the top older works on the life of Christ, this book originally appeared in 1862. It is primarily for the advanced students, though it is helpful also to the general reader. Chronological and geographical factors are discussed carefully. However, he does not deal adequately with critical and philosophical attacks on the reliability of the gospel records.

Bruce, A. B. **The Training of the Twelve.** N. Y.: Hodder and Stoughton (n. d.).

Dr. W. H. Griffith-Thomas held this work in such regard that he rated it "one of the greatest books of the nineteenth century." It is a standard treatment of Christ's association with His disciples.

Culver, Robert D. **The Life of Christ.** Grand Rapids: Baker, 1976.

A widely-known former professor at Trinity Evangelical Divinity School and in recent years a pastor gives us a sweeping survey with photographs, diagrams and maps. Certain of the eleven special "excursus" sections on problems are helpful summaries on such matters as the length of Jesus' ministry, Jewish national responsibility for Jesus' ministry, Jesus' use of parables, some apparent discrepancies, etc. It is a fine brief work from the man who wrote Daniel and the Latter Days defending a premillennial perspective in Daniel's prophecies.

Edersheim, Alfred. **The Life and Times of Jesus the Messiah.** 2 vols. Grand Rapids: Eerdmans, 1953.

New Testament scholars generally regard this as the top work on the life of Christ. It is extremely valuable in its information about Jewish and Hellenistic background, with many citations from primary sources in ancient literature. The author's flare for vivid description enhances the work. A recent one-volume abridged work is available, but the two-volume set is recommended. Eternity Magazine in 1958 wrote to several N. T. scholars to get their opinions on the best works on the life of Christ, and this work was rated best.

Enns, Paul, ed., Moody Gospel Commentary. Chicago: Moody Press, 1992ff.

Edited by Paul Enns who has written several books. This very readable evangelical series is designed to cover the gospels for expositors and lay readers. J. Carl Laney's 407-page volume on John began it, and other volumes are to follow. Enns and Laney are premillennial and dispensational. Cf. Laney on The Gospel of John.

Fairweather, W. The Background of the Gospels. Edinburgh: T. & T. Clark, 1920.

The significance of Gospel events is illumined by this book which presents many helpful facets of history.

Farrar, F. W. The Life of Christ. N. Y.: Dutton (n. d.).

This is one of the most famous and most readable older works on this greatest of all subjects.

_____. The Life of Lives.

This is a sequel to The Life of Christ, dealing with the Acts and Epistles.

Foster, R. C. Studies in the Life of Christ. 2 vols. Grand Rapids: Baker Book House, 1962.

A Church of Christ scholar, Prof. of N. T. at that time in the Cincinnati Bible Seminary, presents a life of Jesus with several special studies in which he interacts with liberal scholars and takes a conservative approach.

Guthrie, Donald. Jesus the Messiah. Grand Rapids: Zondervan, 1972.

A widely-recognized evangelical scholar presents a competent survey of the life of Christ. It is 386 pages with rather frequent pictures, a good index of subjects and Scriptures, a devotional flavor and yet a work careful about theological and historical aspects. He takes sayings and incidents in the ministry of Jesus and gives a comprehensive survey of salient points he feels most important to treat. Cf. also Guthrie's A Shorter Life of Christ (Gd. Rapids: Zondervan, 1970), which concisely surveys the area and deals with problems about the historicity of Jesus.

Hastings, James. Dictionary of Christ and the Gospels. 2 vols. N. Y.: Scribner's, 1906-08.

Excellent for detail on various facets of a study of the life of Christ. The student should find it helpful in good background information.

Hoehner, Harold. Herod Antipas. Cambridge, Eng.: Cambridge University, 1972.

Written by the Professor of New Testament Literature and Exegesis at Dallas Theological Seminary, this conservative work is the most thorough and up to date (to 1972) in its field. The author, who received both the Th. M. and Th. D. degrees at Dallas Seminary before writing this as a dissertation at Cambridge, seems to have dealt with all the facets and N. T. verses relating to the Herod who beheaded John and tried Jesus Christ. The bibliography shows great breadth in research.

Morgan, G. Campbell. The Crises of the Christ. **N. Y.:** **Revell, 1903.**

Dr. Wilbur Smith has said: "I think this is the most important single volume that Dr. Morgan ever wrote. It is a masterpiece. It is a study of the Incarnation, the Baptism, the Temptation, the Transfiguration, the Crucifixion, the Resurrection and the Ascension" (His, April, 1951). Morgan's insight into these events is penetrating, stimulating, and suggestive for teaching or sermonic material as well as devotionally enriching.

Pentecost, J. Dwight. The Words and Works of Jesus Christ. **Grand Rapids: Zondervan, 1981.**

The 629-pp. work represents the results of many years expounding his "Life of Christ" course in English Bible at Dallas Seminary, a very popular class. Pentecost's great theme is Christ presenting Himself as King, offering the Messianic Kingdom, with some receiving and some rejecting and His program with Israel as a nation postponed until the Second Advent. He handles much of the text of the gospels in a popular, expository way, explaining portions such as parables in some relation to the kingdom theme and seeking to give information on many aspects of customs, background, and dispensational place in the flow of thought. He has appendices on geography, historical setting, religious setting, social environment and chronology, and lists such as on parables and miracles, a bibliography, and documentation along the way. The intent of the work is to trace a theme expositionally, which Pentecost adheres to well. Some have faulted the work for its lack of involvement with critical issues and failure to comment on many areas debated in scholarly N. T. circles today. The flavor of the book is strongly conservative, with much to aid the pastor or teacher moving in a series through the life of Christ. Also available is a companion volume, A Harmony of the Words and Works of Jesus Christ (Zondervan, 1981, 272-pp.).

Scroggie, W. Graham. Guide to the Gospels. **London:** **Pickering & Inglis, Limited, 1952.**

This is a gold mine of carefully systematized information on many aspects in a thorough study of each Gospel. No serious student should be without it.

Shepard, J. W. The Christ of the Gospels, An Exegetical Study. **Grand Rapids: Eerdmans, 1939.**

This amillennial work is profitable for an exegetical study of the Gospels step by step through the life of Christ. Though it takes the Two-Document theory of Synoptic origins, it is generally solid in doctrine and helpful in shades of Greek word meanings.

Stier, Rudolph.   The Words of the Lord Jesus.   4 vols.   London: T. & T. Clark 1869.

This is a detailed, helpful commentary on just the words spoken by Jesus. It is heavy but thorough.

Whyte, Alexander.   The Walk, Conversation, and Character of Jesus Christ Our Lord. N. Y.:   Revell, 1905.

The author, famed for his brilliant works on Bible characters and his great oratorical skill, has given in this work an exposition of selected texts in the Gospels. These are among the best highlight chapters ever written on certain moments in the life of our Lord on earth.

COMMENTARIES ON INDIVIDUAL NEW TESTAMENT BOOKS

I. MATTHEW

Armerding, Carl. <u>The Olivet Discourse of Matthew 24-25 and other Studies.</u> Findlay, Ohio: Dunham Publishing Co., 1955.

A noted Bible teacher (Wheaton College and Bible conferences) of a past era wrote this dispensational work. He contends that "Thy coming" (24:3) is the Second Advent at the end of the future tribulation period, not Christ's coming at the rapture of the Church, which he exempts from the days to which he believes the parables of 24-25 point. An earthly regathering of Israel fulfilling Old Testament promises of a regathering is in view in 24:31, not the Church's rapture when Christ meets His own "in the air" (I Thessalonians 4:16). In 24:40, 41 those "taken" are taken off the earth to judgment. Those "left" are left on earth to enter the kingdom begun on earth. Unlike Gaebelein, Armerding says 24:45ff., 25:1-13 and 25:14-30 refer to the separation at the end of the age, at the Second Advent, not the separation of the church from the unsaved by the rapture.

Barbieri, Louis. "Matthew," in <u>Bible Knowledge Commentary</u>, ed. John F. Walvoord and Roy B. Zuck, Volume II. Wheaton: Victor Books, 1985.

A fairly good dispensational survey, helpful to pastors as well as lay readers.

Beare, Francis W. <u>The Gospel According to Matthew.</u> Peabody, MA: Hendrickson Publishers, 1981. 550 pp.

A liberal work arguing for Markan priority (p. vii). Matthew is almost totally taken over from Mark. Conservatives will sift much that is good, but disagree with many of the statements, such as "Matthew has given us a grim book, singularly lacking in those notes of joy that sound through . . . Luke," etc. (viii). He dates Matthew in the late first or early second century (7-8). He denies that the sermon on the mount was given at one time and place and says the "mountain" was not a particular geographical location (13). Questions the disciples ask Jesus may or may not grow out of a tradition of questions really put to Jesus; they are used to call forth answers for Christians of the later writer's day (14). Some of the scenes are "artificially constructed settings for sayings of Jesus" (14-15). We see things that happened mixed with fiction that is added, and imagination is given a large place (15). Matthew has done violence to his sources in his artificial genealogy (63). Beare seems to take Mary's conception as supernatural (66-67, 70), but denies that Isaiah 7:14 in its own right predicted a miraculous birth from a virgin centuries later (71). In gospel stories the point to Beare is not whether they have any "possible kernel of historical fact" (72), but the purpose the writer intends them to serve. Sometimes Beare has much learning on a verse and is helpful, at other times he provides little real help, as on the use of Old Testament "prophets" in 2:23. The bibliography is years out of date.

Blomberg, Craig L.   Matthew (New American Commentary).   Nashville, TN: Broadman Press, 1992.   464 pp.

This work using the NIV is a major contribution in the 40 volume re-doing of an old evangelical series in which John Broadus was notable on Matthew. The NAC claims inerrancy. Blomberg, Associate Professor of New Testament, Denver Seminary, has such standout works as Interpreting the Parables (Downers Grove: IVP, 1990). Here he has a brief, well-packed, knowledgeable introduction (21-49), favoring a date between ca. A. D. 58-69 and authorship by Matthew. He sees this gospel as historically reliable (47) as he argues in his The Historical Reliability of the Gospels (IVP, 1987). He sums up sections awarely, handles problems usually in a concise but informed and pertinent way, and often offers relevant footnote material to add help from much reading. Examples are his handling of the Isaiah 7:14 problem in 1:22, 23, the Hosea 11:1 citation in 2:14, 15 and the Sermon on the Mount (eight views). He deems adultery a valid ground for divorce and remarriage in 19:9, but is sensitive to different sides of the issue. He views "great distress" in 24:21 as the period from A. D. 70 to the Second Advent (359-60), a whole era of tribulation for the saved. He sees 24:40, 41 as meaning that the unsaved are the ones "taken" from earth in judgment and the saved as "left" on earth with the coming of Christ, who will reign during the millennium (366). He appears to hold a post-tribulation rapture of the church (370), but with some lack of clarity.

Boice, James.   The Sermon on the Mount.   Grand Rapids: Zondervan, 1972.

This is a noted preacher and evangelical leader expounding the sermon in a practical style relevant to people today. It is one of the better, more detailed expositions of recent years especially useful for the preacher, Sunday School teacher or lay person in general.

Broadus, John A.   Commentary on Matthew.   Grand Rapids: Kregel, 1990 rp. 610 pp.

In many ways it is the finest and most satisfying overall commentary on Matthew, though it is old. It helps the student on almost every verse. Broadus deals frontally with problems and gives much rich material that throws light on the text. His citations from other sources are often very helpful. From the stand-point of the Greek text, he is also sound. This 1886 work, long a part of the American Commentary on the New Testament series, is still one of the best in detailed explanation of the text where it counts.

Bruce, F. F. Matthew. **Grand Rapids: Eerdmans, 1970. In the Scripture Union Bible Study Books series.**

This concise paperback enables the reader to see the various parts of Matthew quickly as explained by an outstanding expository scholar.

Bruner, Frederick D. The Christbook: Matthew. **2 volumes in 1. Waco: Word Books, 1987-90. 1,127 pp.**

This is a too wordy effort to teach Matthew doctrinally. Bruner feels that Matthew emphasizes particular doctrines chapter by chapter: chapter 1, God with us; chapter 2, man (magi, human nature under the power of sin); chapter 3, repentance; etc. He assumes Markan priority (xvii), and has artificial distinctions such as Mark being the gospel for evangelists, Matthew for teachers, Luke for deacons or social workers, John for elders or spiritual leaders (xvii). He says that theologically Mark is Luther, Matthew is Calvin or Thomas, Luke is Wesley or Xavier or Chrysostom, and John is Augustine or Barth (xvii). Many have difficulty seeing validity here. Often he is very instructive in detail and is steeped in the lit-erature. Apparently liberal, he believes that Matthew erred in having only 13 names in his third series in Matthew 1 (p. 15). He feels that Jesus as a child made mistakes (15). Sometimes the detail goes rather afield from the point, and one gets more of Bruner than Matthew. But he can offer help at times. An example is 16:18 where he has sections on "the Roman Catholic position on Peter" and "The Reformation Position on Peter." He sees the church's rapture in 24:40, 41, taken away to salvation, post-tribulationally (882). He sees sexual infidelity as a ground for divorce in 19:9 and a second ground, willful desertion, in I Corinthians 7:15. He says that in 25:1 Jesus originally taught the coming bridegroom as God, but the church substituted the coming Christ for the coming God (895), yet the church is Spirit-led and we must follow this. Do we know more than Jesus?

Carson, Donald A. "Matthew," in Expositor's Bible Commentary, **Volume 8, ed. Frank Gaebelein and R. P. Polcyn. Grand Rapids: Zondervan 1984. 596 pp.**

A conservative, 350,000-word commentary, longer than most in the EBC, up to date in sources, with a good blend of perceptive commentary that explains most verses well and has material to help readers spiritually. Many regard it as one of the top two or three by evangelicals. Its frequent helpfulness on passages seems to justify that. Some will not agree with the favoring of Markan priority.

Carson, Donald A. The Sermon on the Mount: An Evangelical Exposition of Matthew 5-7. **Grand Rapids: Baker, 1978.**

A fine verse by verse work that illumines things well for the teacher or preacher and relates to devotional life well enough to have great appeal to most readers. Quite good, it ranks close to the works of D. M. Lloyd-Jones and John R. W. Stott, although it does not contribute as much as they do and is more on a level with James Boice's work.

Carson, Donald A. When Jesus Confronts the World: An Exposition of Matthew 8-10. **Grand Rapids: Baker, 1987. 154 pp.**

Six chapters here are drawn from sermons at Eden Baptist Church, Cambridge, on Jesus' authority, authenticity, mission, trustworthiness, compassion and decisiveness. Carson has much that opens up the text for expositors, and also makes some good applications of principles for life today.

Davies, W. D. and D. C. Allison. A Critical and Exegetical Commentary on the Gospel According to Saint Matthew. **2 of 3 proposed vols. have appeared to date (International Critical Commentary). Edinburgh: T. & T. Clark, 1988—.**

This critical work, going through Matthew 18 with a third volume to come, replaces W. C. Allen's effort in the ICC (1912). The amount of information on issues of verses makes it outstanding, though very expensive. Despite being liberal if offers much good material even to evangelicals, giving views, arguments and sources. The 26-pp. general bibliography lists mostly liberal works, ignoring W. Hendriksen but including another evangelical, R. H. Mounce. The discussion of introductory matters runs 148-pp. The authors conclude that the Jewish favor and use of the Old Testament point to a Jewish author (33, 58). They see a "massive unity" overall in the structure, but a "structurally mixed" situation that yields no good outline (72). They hold the priority of Mark (73) and simply sum up Allen's most vital conclusions (73, etc.). They are helpful on features such as semitisms, numbers such as triads, repetition, headings, and conclusions. Various tables appear. They conclude that many statements are redactional. Their dating for Matthew is between 80-95 A. D. (138). They lean toward the gospel being put together for the church at Antioch (146-47). Among technical works this is the best, with much exegetical detail. They are immense in assembling views and documentation, as eight views on the structure of 1:2-17 and eight views on the Son of Man coming in 16:28. Nine reasons are given on why Mary's pregnancy can be thought due to the Holy Spirit (201-02). The authors do a lot to be fair with the book's use of Old Testament verses, such as the citation of Hosea 11:1 in Matthew 2:15 (263).

English, E. Schuyler. <u>Studies in the Gospel According to Matthew</u>. NY: Our Hope Publications, 1935.

Though a survey-type work, this book deals with dispensational problems in a helpful way in some cases. It does not grapple with the exegesis of the text, however.

Filson, Floyd. <u>The Gospel According to St. Matthew</u> (Black's New Testament Commentaries). London: Adam & Charles Black, 1975 reprint.

A professor at McCormick Theological Seminary in Chicago did this knowledgeable yet brief and to the point work. He is abreast of much scholarship on Matthew. He believes in Marcan priority and an author who was not Matthew. On 1:23 with Isaiah 7:14 he says Isaiah 7:14 meant a supernatural but not a virgin birth. He is disconcertingly brief on some key problems where many desire much more, as in writing little more than an inch of copy on who the "rock" is in 16:18. In 27:51-53, the account of saints coming out of their tombs could at first have been a figurative teaching, but the writer of this gospel takes it as a real event. There are these and many other comments where many will not agree with Filson. But he is briefly helpful at times on passages.

France, R. T. <u>The Gospel According to Matthew: An Introduction and Commentary</u> (Tyndale New Testament Commentary). Downers Grove: IVP, 1985. 416 pp.

This was done to replace R. V. G. Tasker's work. It handles many matters well, concisely, and usually hits the crux of interpretation, showing awareness of considerable scholarly literature and main views. France uses the NIV text. He draws up summaries of sections and shows the meaning and connection in context.

Gaebelein, A. C. <u>The Olivet Discourse</u>. NY: Gospel Publishing House [n.d.].

An influential Bible teacher, as in his work on Matthew 13, argues for a premillennial dispensational exposition. He rejects the view that most of the verses were fulfilled in the first century, also the view that the church will go through the tribulation period leading up to the Second Advent. He contends that Israel, not the church, is in view. He argues that the gospel of grace is relevant for the church to preach today but that the gospel of the kingdom is special before the cross and again just before the Second Coming. The unsaved are the ones "taken" in 24:40, 41, the saved are "left" on earth to enter into the kingdom, the opposite of "taken" and "left" when the church's rapture occurs. Yet Gaebelein suddenly switches and says that 24:45ff. and 25:1-13 refer to the separation between the true church and the unsaved at the church's rapture. Many even among present dispensationalists consider his view arbitrary and inconsistent here. The parable of the talents is related to the Israel/church issue in Gaebelein's treatment; he definitely does associate it with the church (p. 113).

Gaebelein, A. C.   The Seven Parables, Matthew XIII.   20th edition.   NY: Our Hope, [n.d.]

A 56-pp. dispensational work of a simple, popular nature contending that the kingdom, rejected by Israel, will be set up by Christ at His Second Advent and that in this age "mysteries" of the Kingdom outlined here are developing in Christendom, not the church. But the church is in the larger sphere, the kingdom of the heavens, he says. He contends for a pretribulation rapture of the church but believes the developments here go to the end of the future tribulation. The mustard tree with its birds, as well as the leaven, are interpreted to refer to evil vs. the almost universal explanation of these outside dispensationalism. The treasure and pearl, likewise, are explained differently than in the common view, viz. both refer to Christ having a value in men He saves, not men seeing Christ, or the kingdom, or salvation as the value above all else. Many modern dispensational thinkers disagree with Gaebelein and do not see inconsistencies between the common views and other Scripture where Gaebelein insists on irreconcilables.

Gaebelein, Arno C.   The Gospel of Matthew.   NY: Loizeaux, 1961.

Here is another dispensational work which is helpful on some problems but which does not get down into the exegesis of the text in a serious way. Some of the conclusions on dispensational issues are not accepted by leading dispensationalists today.

Green, H. Benedict.   The Gospel According to Matthew in the Revised Standard Version (New Clarendon Bible).   Oxford: University Press, 1975.

This work based on Marcan priority is in the series of updating the scholarship of the Old Clarendon Bible first published in 1936. Green takes a date of A. D. 90-100 (p. 33). Much of the commentary text is printed in small type that soon tires the eyes. While showing a fair grasp of pertinent aspects and often adequate though terse, it sometimes falls short of explaining enough to resolve why a statement is necessary (cf. on 3:15, p. 65). Some important details are passed over without even a comment, e. g. the promised reward in 5:12. Green at the time of writing was principal and associate lecturer in theology at the College of the Resurrection, Mirfield, at the University of Leeds.

Griffith-Thomas, W. H.   Outline Studies in the Gospel of Matthew.   Grand Rapids: Eerdmans, 1961.

This 476-pp. volume of 60 studies was put together from his writings as an evangelical devotional commentary by his daughter Winifred Gillespie after his death. It is a very well-outlined, concise work by the author who was a key figure in English Keswick circles and in the founding of Dallas Theological Seminary in 1924. The crisp, quick-moving lay-out of points makes this a good survey and a catalyst for a teacher of a Bible class of laymen. The work is dispensational in its perspective, e.g. Matthew 5-7, 13:31-33 and even pretribulational as to the rapture (p. 347). The author was unusually well-organized and knowledgeable as to pertinent biblical details and their correlation which in many places makes this a profitable synopsis of strategic points pulled into a unit.

Guelich, Robert A.   The Sermon on the Mount: A Foundation for Understanding. Waco, Texas: Word Books, 1982.

Though this has elements of a critical literary nature that will please some and displease others, it is highly regarded in acquainting readers with issues and recent studies. Along the line of general works on the SOM, one also will still want to consult W. D. Davies, The Setting of the Sermon on the Mount (Cambridge: U.P., 1964) and Warren S. Kissinger, The Sermon on the Mount: A History of Interpretation and Bibliography (Scarecrow Press, 1976). Davies is often helpful in showing ties with Jewish literature and Pauline thought.

Gundry, Robert.   Matthew: A Commentary on his Literary and Theological Art. Grand Rapids: Eerdmans, 1982.   652 pp.

A thorough-going redaction-criticism approach by a conservative, with much that distresses many other conservatives. According to Gundry, Matthew embellishes things for Jews after the pattern of Jewish Midrash. Some of the accounts are made up, and did not happen historically. Gundry sees some texts as irreconcilable, and does not accept harmonizations some have proposed even where many believe that they are quite possible. Cf. much of an entire Journal of the Evangelical Theological Society issue taken up with scholars' arguments against Gundry and Gundry's rejoinders (26:1, March, 1983).

Hendriksen, William.   The Gospel of Matthew, in New Testament Commentary. Grand Rapids: Baker, 1973.

This 1,015-page work is one of the best recent works of solid evangelical scholarship for teachers, preachers, and serious lay readers who desire to see views, detailed arguments at times, and explanations at length on problem passages. Yet Hendriksen as always maintains a warmth that speaks to the heart. He has many good footnotes of length documenting sources and providing further help. He is amillennial on chapters 24-25.

Hill, David.   The Gospel of Matthew (New Century Bible).   London: Marshall Morgan Scott, 1975 reprint.

A lucid commentary by the Senior Lecturer, Professor of Biblical Studies, University of Sheffield, England. He shows a lot of reading breadth in recent scholarship at times and gives views that sometimes expand the American reader's awareness on interpretations, but shows a lack of awareness of views they are already aware of at times. He often reflects concessions to higher critical ideas that evangelicals in the more fundamental group would reject in favor of what they regard as more defensible views. All in all, it is helpful at many points but not as often helpful to expositors as Hendriksen and Broadus.

Hoehner, Harold W.   Chronological Aspects of the Life of Christ.   Grand Rapids: Zondervan, 1977.

This is a fine, careful study of such aspects as the date of Jesus' birth, commencement of His ministry, duration of His ministry, day and year of His crucifixion, and the chronology of the Seventy Weeks in Daniel 9 in relation to the gospels. Hoehner holds to an A. D. 33 crucifixion and Friday as the day, presenting the different views in some detail and arguing at length for his own views.

Hunter, A. M.   A Pattern For Life. An Exposition of the Sermon on the Mount. Philadelphia: Westminster Press, 1965, revised edition (original in 1953).

This little 127-pp. book takes the sermon as Christ's "moral ideal for committed Christians" (p. 6). The former New Testament scholar of King's College, University of Aberdeen has brief chapters on "The Making of the Sermon," "The Manner of the Sermon," and "The Matter of the Sermon," then 67 pp. on the exegesis and finally 23 pp. on "The Meaning of the Sermon." He has brief but choice words about "The Doctrine of Reward" on 5:12 (pp. 41-44). This is an excellent, concise survey of the sermon verse by verse, with timely illustrations and provocative quotations usable for life and for speaking.

Jeremias, Joachim.   The Sermon on the Mount.   Translated Norman Perrin. Philadelphia: Fortress Press, 1963.

The 36-pp. work first appeared in German as Die Bergpredigt in 1959. Jeremias was a long time Professor of New Testament Studies at Gottingen University. He reacts against Hans Windisch's charge (The Meaning of the Sermon on the Mount) that Matthew 5-7 gives complete heresy, law righteousness by works and not gospel. He shows four great differences between Jesus' demands and the ethic of late Judaism in the Talmud (pp. 5, 6). He also finally turns away from the view that the sermon is an impossible ideal to drive men to God's mercy, and the view that the sermon gives an interim ethic (Albert Schweitzer, etc.). For the view Jeremias favors, he thanks literary and form criticism: the sermon, he concludes, is not a continuous sermon Jesus delivered but a collection of His sayings. The key verse is 5:20, speaking of a righteousness of theologians (scribes), another of pious laymen (Pharisees), and that of the disciples of Jesus. The instructions strung together in one place originally functioned as catechetical helps for candidates for baptism or as discipleship instruction for the newly baptized. If so, it was preceded by preaching the gospel, conversion, and empowering (p. 23). This, Jeremias argues, makes understandable Jesus' heavy demands. Lives rooted in the kingdom show the victory of that kingdom. So we have not law but gospel.

Johnson, S. Lewis. Series on highlights in the life of Christ appearing in <u>Bibliotheca Sacra</u>: baptism, Volume 123 (July, 1966), 220-29; temptation (Oct., 1966), 342-52; transfiguration, 124 (1967), 133-43; triumphal entry, 124 (July, 1967), 218-29; agony, 124 (1967), 303-13; death, 125 (1968), 10-19.

Here is excellent, stimulating exposition based on careful exegesis and profound insight, given with warmth. The teacher or preacher who reads a Johnson article before he ministers is bound to come away feeling he has been treated to a thought-provoking and competent study by a very competent scholar of New Testament and theology. Johnson has served on the faculties at Dallas Theological Seminary and Trinity Evangelical Divinity School.

Kent, Homer A., Jr. "Matthew," in <u>Wycliffe Bible Commentary</u>, ed. C. F. Pfeiffer and E. F. Harrison. Chicago: Moody, 1962. 1,525 pp.

Kent, who served several years as president of Grace Theological Seminary, Winona Lake, IN, did this dispensational study. He brought a lot of understanding to the task, and provides a reliable commentary on many matters, often giving good reasoning for views.

King, Guy H. <u>New Order. An Expositional Study of the Sermon on the Mount</u>. London. Marshall, Morgan & Scott, Ltd., 1943.

King was minister at Christ Church, Beckenham and a speaker at Keswick. As in his other books he writes in a freshly devotional, creative strain. He ties the truth of the sermon in with biblical truth elsewhere. He is persuaded that while Christ will set up His kingdom at His Second Coming and the principles will apply then, the truth is His mind and will for His people also apply now, just as principles in the epistles (pp. 11, 12). The life-style here is lived in dependence on the Holy Spirit through grace by those who first have been born again (12). Many apt side captions appear over sections, and the outline of the sermon runs throughout in larger headings. The print of the commentary is small. King's work is a devotionally edifying treat, served in an appetizing manner with many things suggestive for a closer walk with God, leading Bible studies, or preparing sermons.

Kingsbury, J. D. <u>The Parables of Jesus in Matthew 13, A Study in Redaction-Criticism</u>. Richmond, VA: John Knox Press, 1969.

This 180-page book views chapter 13 as being in a pivotal place in Matthew and a good test case for redaction-critical procedure. The detailed verse-by-verse discussion, growing out of a doctoral dissertation at Basel (1966), takes the view that this gospel presents parables here to allow Jesus as Lord to speak to circumstances in the church later but Jesus may not have said them in His day (not a position this reviewer holds).

Kissinger, W. S.   The Sermon on the Mount: A History of Interpretation and Bibliography.   American Theological Library Association, Bibliography Series, Number 3.   Metuchen, NJ: Scarecrow Press and the American Theological Library Association, 1975.

Kissinger, a cataloguer of religion at the Library of Congress in Washington, D. C., surveys the history of the interpretation from the early fathers to the present, then gives a lengthy bibliography (148 pp.) of literature on the sermon and issues in Matthew 5-7.

Lloyd-Jones, D. Martyn.   Studies in the Sermon on the Mount.   2 volumes.   Grand Rapids: Eerdmans, 1962.

This is one of the very finest expositions of the sermon by an evangelical preacher of the modern era, a deeply perceptive man relevant to his age and a man of scholarly awareness. He is stimulating, practical, wise in his interpretations of problem verses. It is well worth the money.

MacArthur, John, Jr.   Kingdom Living Here and Now.   Chicago: Moody Press, 1980.

Exposition of the Beatitudes (Matthew 5:1-12). A good evangelical study in detail that shows the relevance today. MacArthur believes that the beatitudes give features in the life-style of the truly saved person, all in some measure present in his composite experience as fruit of the Spirit, wrought through grace. He cannot tolerate "easy-believism" that allows the gift nature of salvation but does not balance this with a call to manifest the fruit of authentic life.

MacArthur, John, Jr.   Matthew.   4 volumes (The MacArthur New Testament Commentary).   Chicago: Moody, 1985-90.

Conservative, premillennial exposition which often deals in some detail with problem verses and shows the vital lessons of Jesus' teachings in a very readable manner. The author often explains customs, gives views and reasons. In Matthew 13, he sees the fourth soil only as representing a genuinely saved person, and the leaven in a good sense. In Matthew 24, he views verses 15ff. as related to tribulation and Second Advent, not A. D. 70, the one taken as removed in judgment and the one left as preserved on earth safely to enter the earthly kingdom promised in Old Testament prophecy.

McNeile, Alan H.   The Gospel According to Matthew.   Grand Rapids: Baker, 1980rp,   formerly NY: St. Martin's Press, 1915.

The work is still respected in exegesis but is far out of date as to interaction with literature. Liberal in its approach, this book is still helpful in tracing the argument. It is helpful on many details and thus one of the better serious commentaries, though it often leaves the student wishing it would say more about a problem.

Mounce, Robert H. Matthew (New International Bible Commentary). Peabody, MA: Hendrickson, 1991. 228 pp.

This was formerly the Good News Commentary (San Francisco: Harper and Row, 1985). It switched from the Good News translation to the NIV. Mounce is President of Whitworth College, Spokane, WA, and author of several New Testament commentaries (cf. on Book of Revelation, etc.). He gives a mere 5-page introduction and a fairly conservative, amillennial study of Matthew.

Plummer, Alfred. An Exegetical Commentary on the Gospel According to Matthew (Thornapple Commentaries). Grand Rapids: Baker, 1982. 451 pp. Formerly Grand Rapids: Eerdmans, 1953, from 1915 ed.

Any work by Plummer is helpful, for he possessed a keen ability to speak with clarity and deep scholarship. He is good in the Greek and historical background, and does not dodge problems, though he at times takes a liberal view. He was amillennial in eschatology. He held a position which the liberals of his day considered too conservative and which the conservatives reckoned too liberal. This commentary is valuable. He holds to a non-Matthean authorship of the book.

Ridderbos, Herman N. Matthew (Bible Students Commentary). Grand Rapids: Zondervan, 1987. 556 pp.

This is from the famous Dutch series (cf. Aalders on Genesis, etc.), originally from 1950-51. It offers expositors quite a lot of help in explaining verses, looking at views, giving reasons etc. in a competent fashion, etc. In prophecy Ridderbos is amillennial, and he does not concern himself much with critical issues that some scholars want. Due to the dating, it cannot show awareness of work done in Matthew since the 1940's.

Robertson, Arthur. Matthew (Everyman's Bible Commentary). Chicago: Moody, 1983. 168 pp.

An evangelical work of a concise nature with a brief introduction looking at the importance, uniqueness, theme (King), purpose, relationship to the other gospels, author, date (A.D. 50-60), Jesus's teaching methods, relevance to today, etc. The commentary follows a clear outline, has apt comments usually, and is right to the point on problem verses. Robertson is only rarely unclear, as on mystery (ch. 13), third soil (13), etc. He interprets 24:40-41 to mean taken in deliverance and left to face judgment, yet sees chapters 24-25 overall in a premillennial, dispensational way.

Robinson, Haddon W. What Jesus Said About Successful Living. Principles from the Sermon on the Mount for Today. Grand Rapids: Discovery House, 1989. 298 pp.

An outstanding preacher, former Dallas Theological Seminary faculty member and President of Denver Theological Seminary and now teacher at Gordon-Conwell Theological Seminary has done this conservative book. The reader will soon see the popularly written, devotionally enriched nature of the work and will be able to draw out material for life or sermons. Like Don Carson, D. M. Lloyd-Jones and John R. W. Stott, Robinson exposes the meaning for today in graphic style.

Shepard, Thomas. **The Ten Virgins.** **Macdill AFB, Florida:** **Tyndale Bible Society [n.d.].**

This recent paperback is a reprint of the Boston printing of 1852, dating back to the first published work in 1659. Shepard, a Puritan, preached the messages between 1636-40. Here we have 243 pp., whereas the 1842 ed. had 630! There is very detailed explanation and a thorough application of each point to believers. Shepard develops two great lessons for the religious community: (1) he shows the relation between assurance of salvation and the growth of fruit in the life-style, which are evidences of God's gracious salvation; (2) he holds that the inward response of the "hypocrite" is distinct from that of a truly saved person. He expounds these in the contrast between the wise and foolish virgins. About ten percent of the book expounds the parable. Shepard correlates with this such subjects as: the true nature of a saving response; the character of mere profession; the power in expecting Christ's future coming to arouse devotion in believers and disturb the false security of the mere professor; the nature of repentance, etc. Shepard tries to deal with every excuse a lost person might make to Christ's appeal, so as to awaken him to his need. Yet he seeks to buttress and encourage real Christians.

Stott, John R. W. **Christian Counter-Culture. Studies in the Sermon on the Mount.** **Downers Grove:** **IVP, 1978.**

This is a flowing, articulate exposition by one of the world's masters. Stott as usual is well-organized, sharply perceptive of the points that need to be expounded, and sensitively relevant in practical principles. This is one of the very best, most helpful books on the sermon in capturing cogently what Jesus said and meant.

Walvoord, John F. **Matthew: Thy Kingdom Come.** **Chicago:** **Moody Press, 1974.**

A recent effort by a leading dispensational scholar to trace the theme of the Messianic Kingdom step by step through the first gospel. The work is written clearly and seeks to survey the main ideas of each section without becoming involved in minute detail or a verse-by-verse study. It is often quite brief and general.

Watson, Thomas. **The Beatitudes. An Exposition of Matthew 5:1-12.** **London: Banner of Truth Trust, 1971.**

This is a reprint of a Puritan study. Watson explains the text well, with much food for thought for those preparing Bible studies or sermons.

Zodhiates, Spiros. The Pursuit of Happiness. Grand Rapids: Eerdmans, 1966.
The author, a faithful witness for Christ among the Greek speaking world and writer of several other fine books, discusses in rich detail the meaning of the beatitudes. His thorough treatments on word meanings, backgrounds, and spiritual truths flowing from them are very refreshing and rewarding.

II. MARK

Alexander, Joseph A. Commentary on the Gospel of Mark. Grand Rapids: Zondervan [n.d.], reprint of 1864 edition.
The Presbyterian author graduated from Princeton and later served on the faculty, where he was Professor of New Testament Literature at the time of his death, working with other fine scholars such as Charles Hodge and William Henry Green. His father, Archibald, was an organizer of Princeton Theological Seminary and the first professor. He usually explains verses rather fully in the English, based on the Greek, providing one of the better detailed older works. He seems to favor a move from A. D. 70 to the remote future in 13:24, but he is not distinct (cf. on 13:26, 27). The abomination in 13:14 is only related to the A. D. 70 scene. The lack of a good introduction, failure to discuss the disputed ending (16:9ff.), and its dating before discussions of the past 120 years are problems of an otherwise fairly good commentary.

Anderson, Hugh. The Gospel of Mark. (New Century Bible Commentary). Grand Rapids: Eerdmans, 1981. 366 pp.
The Professor of New Testament and Theology at the University of Edinburgh has done a thorough-going redaction criticism of Mark. He favors Marcan priority and a date shortly after A. D. 65 by a writer other than John Mark. He brings vast awareness of literature to his work, and helpfully discusses possibilities on many problems: John's baptism had its closest similarities to Qumran ceremonials yet is in contrast to them (70-71); "The Kingdom of God is at hand" means just that, not "has come (arrived)," and Anderson sees both present and future aspects; as a prelude to the Sower and the Seed (4:1-9), he gives two pages of general survey on the history of interpreting the parables; later he thinks he has strong reasons for saying the explanation of this parable comes not from Jesus but from the church (132), and feels there are inconsistencies in the details (133). He is not sure to what extent sayings in Mark 13 go back to Jesus himself or to redaction (290). Sometimes he makes no effort to explain how a view may be compatible with theological factors, e.g. on 13:13, how enduring to the end and being saved may integrate with the gift aspect of salvation (295). On the whole, this is a work of high quality that usually helps if one is discerning where the writer's assumptions on redaction are subjective and arbitrary.

Beasley-Murray, G. R.   A Commentary on Mark Thirteen.   NY: Macmillan & Co. Ltd., 1957.

The reader can also consult the author's work on criticism and theology of Mark 13, Jesus and the Future, an Examination of the Criticism of the Eschatological Discourse, Mark 13, with Special Reference to the Little Apocalypse Theory (London: Macmillan, 1954). Beasley-Murray does an exposition based on his earlier work, and also summarizes critical issues in Mark 13 as he sees them. Still, Jesus and the Future discusses these more in detail than this 124-pp. book. He believes that details of Mark 13 have a high claim to authenticity as representing the words Jesus Himself spoke to His disciples. He inclines to the opinion that "the abomination that causes horror" (13:14) is purely historical, not a reference to the Antichrist, not to be elucidated by II Thessalonians 2:4 (pp. 682-690). Greater clarity on what happened in A. D. 70 and what was yet future to that would serve many of the readers better. Yet the work has a wealth of competent material that serious students will find valuable.

Brooks, James A.   Mark (New American Commentary), Volume 23, ed. David Dockery.   Nashville: Broadman Press, 1991.   288 pp.

The NAC is an evangelical Southern Baptist effort of 40 volumes based on the NIV, new in distinction to the American commentary edited by Alvah Hovey, in which John Broadus on Matthew was one of the standouts. Brooks' commentary is fair but not high on a list of fine works. He is readable and upholds full trustworthiness (inerrancy), shows how the text applies to life, stresses the unity, but fails at a number of points to be convincing. He assumes Marcan priority, and fails to explain what "baptized with the Holy Spirit" means in 1:7-8, sees the Kingdom in Mark as God's kingly rule in hearts (p. 47) with the possible exception of 14:25 and 15:43, sometimes is extremely brief, and almost skips over some verses, as 4:13-20, making but the barest comment. Sometimes he deals with a verse in more adequate detail, as "abomination of desolation" (13:14) and the Son not knowing.

Burdict, Donald W.   "Mark," in Wycliffe Bible Commentary, ed. C. F. Pfeiffer and E. F. Harrison.   Chicago: Moody, 1962.   1,525 pp.

A careful New Testament scholar from Conservative Baptist Seminary, Denver, is the author. He has provided a solid, well-organized and knowledgeable study from a conservative, premillennial viewpoint. Though brief it is worth the time.

Cole, R. Alan.   The Gospel According to St. Mark. An Introduction and Commentary (Tyndale New Testament).   Grand Rapids.   Eerdmans, 1961.

A minister in the Church of Southeast Asia wrote this evangelical study, concluding for Marcan priority (p. 47) yet not for any direct literary dependence but Matthean, Marcan and Lucan "use of the same, or similar tradition blocks" (p. 48). The commentary itself is provided with a 4-pp. outline set down at the outset and is terse but knowledgeable. Cole sees the Olivet Discourse as referring directly to the destruction of Jerusalem in A. D. 70, though he acknowledges that the meaning reaches on to later fulfillment also (p. 203), a double fulfillment of the same words.

Cranfield, C. E. B.   The Gospel According to St. Mark **(Cambridge Greek Testament Commentary). New York: Cambridge University Press, 1966.   496 pp.**

One of the finer commentaries on Mark by the famous exegetical scholar from The University of Durham in Scotland. Cranfield is quite helpful on the Greek text, word meanings, customs etc., and is clear, insightful, and refreshing to those who believe in the historical veracity of words and events in Jesus's ministry.

Earle, Ralph.   Mark, The Gospel of Action **(Everyman's Bible Commentary). Chicago: Moody, 1970.   127 pp.**

Here is a brief conservative survey by a professor (then) at the Nazarene Theological Seminary, Kansas City, MO. Earle is usually helpful. At times he is overly general, not nailing things down as on the identity of the second and third soils in Mark 4; at other times he commits himself, as in expecting a yet future, final fulfillment of the "abomination of desolation" in Mark 13.

English, E. Schuyler.   Studies in the Gospel According to Mark.   **NY: Our Hope Publications, 1943.**

A layman who was converted under the ministry of Dr. Donald G. Barnhouse, English has demonstrated what can be done by a serious-minded Christian though he may not have had the benefits of special seminary training. His work shows diligence. This is one of the best older, dispensational commentaries on the English text.

Grassmick, John D.   "Mark," in the Bible Knowledge Commentary**, ed. John F. Walvoord and Roy B. Zuck, Volume II.   Wheaton: Victor Books, 1985.**

A rather careful, diligent contribution from a conservative and premillennialist. He holds Markan priority (p. 98) after giving arguments for views. One will find the priority of Matthew favored in the Matthew introduction of the same commentary. Grassmick seems informed by good use of the Greek and scholarly literature, and sometimes goes into some detail summing up arguments for views, as on the disputed ending in 16:9ff.

Guelich, R. A.   Mark 1:1-8:26 **(Word Biblical Commentary).   1st of 2 Volumes. Dallas: Word Books, 1989.**

A much-praised moderately conservative work (some will not feel it is conservative) showing a lot of expertise in linguistic details, giving of views and arguments, and listing or citing many more modern scholarly sources. It will be quite helpful to scholars, including pastors who grapple with interpretive issues.

Hendriksen, William. <u>The Gospel of Mark</u>. **Grand Rapids: Baker, 1975.**

All of Hendriksen's commentaries offer very helpful material that shows aware-ness of issues in the interpretation and deals well with most of the problems. This is no exception and is one of the better works of a less technical nature. Hendriksen seriously attempts to resolve problems and sometimes has good footnotes. He has, however, been faulted on some counts, as when his 858 foot-notes have only 17 references to books and articles from the previous 15 years of scholarship (Peter R. Jones, review, <u>WTJ</u> 39 (Fall, 1976), p. 140).

Hiebert, D. Edmond. <u>Mark: A Portrait of the Servant</u>. **Chicago: Moody Press, 1974.**

A detailed and competent work by a soundly evangelical scholar of the Mennonite Seminary in Fresno. It usually offers good help on a passage because Hiebert shows awareness and discussion of problems. Readers will face some difficulty at times finding a verse or section quickly because the Table of Contents does not identify which part of Mark is being treated. However, there is a very detailed outline at the outset and then sections are marked off by headings throughout the commentary. It will be particularly helpful to pulpiteers, serious lay students, and Bible College students, among others.

Hughes, R. Kent. <u>Mark: Jesus, Servant and Savior</u>. **2 volumes (Preaching the Word Commentary). Westchester, IL: Crossway Books, Good News Publishers, 1989.**

A good expositor who pastors Wheaton College Church and has done several commentaries in this series (cf. Joshua, etc.) gives broad, flowing studies that can be provocative for sermons and a spiritual enrichment in day by day lay reading. He is conservative, premillennial, and draws material from many sources to illustrate the passages.

Hurtado, L. W. <u>Mark</u> **(New International Bible Commentary). 2nd ed. Peabody, MA: Hendrickson, 1989. 306 pp.**

This was originally in the Good News Commentary (1983), and has changed to the NIV. It is a mild redactio-critical work by the Professor of Religion at the University of Manitoba. Discerning evangelicals will, if well-trained, sift much that is good here as they use this with other works that see some things quite dif-ferently. It is at times fairly good but not among the better commentaries.

Lane, William L. <u>The Gospel According to Mark</u> **(NIC). Grand Rapids: Eerdmans, 1974.**

The author writes from the standpoint that "redaction criticism is a valid hermeneutical approach to understanding the text of Mark and the intention of the evangelist", though he does not believe this necessarily "should lead to the dehistoricizing of the New Testament Gospel" (p. 7). His commentary and copi-ous notes reflect a good awareness of scholarly sources and acquaint one quickly with problem areas, views, and recent literature on various issues. Lane often defends the text against criticism that impugns its authenticity.

Mann, C. S. Mark **(Anchor Bible). Garden City, NY: Doubleday, 1986. 716 pp.**
Basically a liberal work but often profitable in technical aspects and thoroughness. He surveys scholarly thinking on Mark and reviews approaches of recent years. His bibliographies are valuable, and he frequently has good input on Greek grammar, words, customs in Jesus's day, etc. In his mind, Mark is the third gospel to be written, and all three synoptics date before A. D. 70.

Martin, Ralph P. Where The Action Is**. Glendale, CA: Gospel Light Publications, 1977.**
This paperback provides a very concise and an easier commentary for laymen. One will not necessarily always agree with Martin's concepts, as when he argues that Jesus did not in His triumphal entry ride in as king (Mark 11:1-19, pp. 98-99).

Plummer, Alfred. The Gospel According to St. Mark**. In the Cambridge Greek Testament. Cambridge: University Press, 1938.**
This is an excellent liberal study of the book from the standpoint of the Greek. There are excellent cross-references on key words, and usually serious efforts to explain the meaning.

Scroggie, W. Graham. The Gospel of Mark**. Grand Rapids: Zondervan, 1976 edition.**
The author (1877-1958) first published this through Marshall, Morgan & Scott in London as part of "The Study Hour Series". Scroggie was perhaps best known for his Guide to the Gospels. He ultimately succeeded Charles Haddon Spurgeon as pastor of the Metropolitan Tabernacle in London. This volume is a 285-page verse by verse exposition with its main attention paid to the English text. Scroggie assumes Marcan priority, as did many of his day, and concurs with A. T. Robertson on an A. D. 50 date. Scroggie's writing style is well-organized and clear, and the work is peppered with valuable illustrations for the Bible student and Sunday School teacher. —Jan Sattem

Swete, Henry B. Commentary on Mark**. Grand Rapids: Kregel, 1977. Reprint of 1913 work.**
Swete's work is one of the best older conservative commentaries on the Greek text. Swete was an Anglican minister and a scholar in Latin, Greek, and theology, and taught at Cambridge. He does a fairly good job on the Messianic character of the suffering Servant.

Taylor, Vincent. The Gospel according to St. Mark. Grand Rapids: Baker, 1966. 696 pp. 2d rev. ed.

Though liberal in viewpoint, this is a work very helpful in the Greek grammar. The introduction is valuable and the commentary is rated by some as the best on Mark up to its time.

Wolff, Richard. The Gospel of Mark. Wheaton: Tyndale House, 1971.

Though brief, this commentary helps the reader to see the movement and meaning in Mark quite well. Wolff became known a few years ago for his competent writings that have a lot to offer (See The General Epistles of James and Jude, etc.).

Wuest, Kenneth S. Mark in the Greek New Testament. Grand Rapids: Eerdmans, 1957.

This is a verse-by-verse evangelical, expository work which deals with the Greek text but does so in a way which the English reader can follow though he does not know Greek. It is a good book to give to a layman who is serious about studying Mark, and also helpful to the pastor or teacher.

III. LUKE

Arndt, William. The Gospel According to Luke. St. Louis: Concordia, 1956.

This conservative commentary is a detailed work in the Greek and is well-written. The author did the famous Greek-English lexicon and two books on alleged contradictions.

Bailey, Kenneth E. Poet and Peasant. Grand Rapids: Eerdmans, 1960. Also Through Peasant Eyes: More Lucan Parables, Their Culture and State. Eerdmans, 1981.

Bailey discusses four Lucan parables at length in the first book, making a great contribution as to cultural data that opens up the parables. His data is based on studies while teaching for many years in the mid-East, also on extensive travels, correspondence, and scholarly probing into the literature. Particularly insightful are his remarks on Luke 15 (the triad of parables) and Luke 11 (Friend at Midnight). The second book continues to be rich in peasant cultural background, with data not available to many who study the parables. But the second book treats ten further parables (7:36-50 and others in 9:51—19:48, Luke's travel narrative). These are well-done but not treated as much in detail. Both books are excellent in making parables "come alive" and making readers think. In more recent years both volumes have been put into one book.

Benware, Paul N. Luke (Everyman's Bible Commentary). Chicago: Moody, 147 pp.

A conservative, premillennial survey by a diligent young scholar. Often the book is helpful on problem areas, though brief. At other points the brevity of the series and length of Luke are among the reasons for over-generality that adds nothing to the understanding.

Creed, J. M. The Gospel According to St. Luke. London, 1965.

A detailed, technical work on the Greek text. It is, with the commentary by Plummer and the works by Fitzmyer and Marshall, among the best along these lines.

Ellis, E. Earle. The Gospel of Luke (New Century Bible). London: Oliphants, 1966.

One of the better commentaries of more recent years from the standpoint of explaining the text even where there are problems, though briefly. The author is an evangelical and well-versed in critical scholarship today.

Evans, Craig A. Luke (New International Bible Commentary). Peabody, MA: Hendrickson, 1991. 416 pp.

A lucid study, often of help on problem texts but cursory at times.

Fitzmyer, Joseph A. The Gospel According to Luke (Anchor Bible). 2 volumes. Garden City, NY: Doubleday, 1981-85. 1,642 pp.

An internationally known Catholic scholar presents an excellent appraisal of "The Current State of Lukan Studies" (3-34) and has "A Sketch of Lukan Theology" (143-270). In explaining the gospel text, Fitzmyer has often helpful sources on various points. This will rank as one of the best-regarded commentaries from the standpoint of awareness of critical literature and comments reflecting current learning. He gives his own translation and a fairly lucid, detailed exposition that is abreast of language, background, and views. It is a mixed bag with Fitzmyer, though. He often takes views that evangelicals appreciate, such as Jesus's resurrection body being able to eat food. At other times he stumbles where there are possible solutions, as when he feels that there is no way to harmonize the accounts of Jesus's resurrection. Indices to both volumes help find material.

Geldenhuys, T. N. Commentary on the Gospel of Luke (NIC). Grand Rapids: Eerdmans, 1952.

Amillennial in its interpretation of the kingdom program, this work is solid and explains many verses rather well but is not the best.

Godet, Franz L. A Commentary on the Gospel of St. Luke. 2 volumes. Edinburgh: T. & T. Clark, 1982; available from Philadelphia: Fortress Press; also 1-volume ed. available from Grand Rapids: Kregel. Originally issued in 1870.

Though old, this work is almost exhaustive in dealing with interpretive problems and shows a wide acquaintance with commentators of all ages up to his day. He is regarded by Greek authorities as weak on textual criticism but strong on exegesis. Zondervan in 1959 also issued a reprint of the 1881 edition.

Griffith-Thomas, W. H. Outline Studies in Luke. A Devotional Commentary. Grand Rapids: Kregel, 1984. 410 pp.

This outlines sections, arranges ideas homiletically, gives practical insights, and crisp simplicity in wording. The author (1861-1924), Welch by birth, was a professor of Systematic Theology at Wycliffe College, Toronto, also a pastor, world-conference speaker, writer of many books and a co-founder of Dallas Seminary. He died before he was to become the first professor of Systematic Theology, Dallas Seminary. Here as in Matthew, Romans and Hebrews he offers considerable help for pastors and the gist of things pulled together devotionally for lay people. He is well-known for his devotional work on Genesis.

Kistemaker, Simon. The Parables of Jesus. Grand Rapids: Baker, 1980.

A past national secretary-treasurer of Evangelical Theological Society deals with all of Jesus's parables and shows a lucid style, warmth, and broad acquaintance with scholarly writings on his material which is obvious in footnotes. He uses the NIV text. The contribution is very good on background, the main thrust of parables, key expository details, and the practical contribution for life. This is the best recent evangelical survey of the parables in general.

Liefeld, Walter L. "Luke" in Expositor's Bible Commentary, Volume 8, ed. Frank Gaebelein and J. D. Douglas. Grand Rapids: Zondervan, 1984. pp. 797-1,059.

Liefeld has a generally good introduction with a fine discussion of themes and theology (13 points). He is disappointing in his discussion of distinctive features (p. 798). He can be vague and not nail things down as on baptism with fire (857) and what 16:8b-9, 17:7-10 and 19:11-27 are getting at. Still, in many passages he is helpful on main aspects and clear, giving the expositor aid, mingling informative comment with practical material. He is conservative and premillennial.

Marshall, I. Howard. The Gospel of Luke. London: Paternoster, 1977.

One of the leading evangelicals of the British Isles has written this. It was my privilege to read a section before Dr. Marshall sent it to Paternoster. It is a serious attempt to explain verses in detail, with a keen perception of problems and different recent views, and an attempt to take a stand on most issues. The form is somewhat like the ICC, and the author has sought to provide for serious evangelical scholars a technically and exegetically-based answer to Bultmannian-type theories that are destructive to the Gospel's real authority.

Martin, John A. "Luke," in Bible Knowledge Commentary, ed. John F. Walvoord and Roy B. Zuck, Volume II. Wheaton: Victor Books, 1985.

Conservative, premillennial work of a concise yet clear and well-informed nature. Despite the brevity to which he is held, Martin frequently gives views and an assessment, as in mentioning two views on the parables of Luke 15: restoration of a saved person to fellowship and bringing of unsaved people to salvation, the latter of which he favors (p. 244). Usually he has something helpful to say on problem verses.

Morgan, G. Campbell. The Gospel According to Luke. NY: Revell, 1931.

This is a valuable commentary to have on the English text. It is one of Morgan's better works in detailed exposition.

Morris, Leon. Luke. Grand Rapids: Eerdmans, 1974.

Morris has written a good conservative commentary of some detail. It is lucid and not technical in nature.

Plummer, Alfred. A Critical and Exegetical Commentary on the Gospel According to St. Luke (ICC). NY: Scribners, 1910.

This used to be often considered the best older commentary on the Greek.

Spencer, W. D. and Spencer, A. B. The Prayer Life of Jesus: Shout of Agony, Revelation of Love, a Commentary. NY: University Press of America, 1990. 296 pp.

A comprehensive work dealing with Matthew 6:9-13; Luke 11:2-4 as well as with parables on prayer, Jesus's emphasis on prayer in His busy life, New Testament words for prayer, Jesus's positions while in prayer, John 17, Gethsemane, and the cross. It has a lot of good comment and ought to be refreshment amidst other studies. The authors teach at Gordon-Conwell Theological Seminary, South Hampton, MA.

Tenney, Merrill C. "Luke," in Wycliffe Bible Commentary, ed. C. F. Pfeiffer and E. F. Harrison. Chicago: Moody, 1962.

Tenney is limited in his space, but usually makes good use of it to explain verses so as to provide help. He is conservative and premillennial. Sometimes he is quite clear, other times one can only guess what he means when he is vague, as when he says that "the kingdom of God is nigh at hand" (21:29) are words complementary to 17:21, "The kingdom of God is within you" (p. 1063). Overall he offers a fairly good commentary for those wanting a brief study with considerable competence behind it.

Wilcock, Michael.   Saviour of the World: The Message of Luke's Gospel.   Downers
Grove, IL: IVP, 1979.

In the Bible Speaks Today series. It is a clear, homiletically well-organized
215-pp. exposition of the main thrust in passages, not an attempt at a phrase by
phrase commentary. He often shows a refreshingly high view of the gospels; as
when he takes the talents (Matthew 25:14-30) and pounds (Luke 19:11-27) to be
different, though similar parables with complimentary emphases.

IV. JOHN

Barrett, C. K.   The Gospel According to John.   NY: Macmillan, 1955.

Though liberal, this is probably the best critical commentary on the Greek text,
especially on the grammar, where he is superior to Westcott, Godet and others.

Beasley-Murray, G. R.   John (Word Biblical Commentary).   Waco, TX: Word Books,
1987.   441 pp.

An evangelical of a somewhat critical leaning has done this competent, usually
detailed work on text, grammar, movement of passages, and bibliography. He
provides a fairly good survey on the relationship between the fourth gospel and
the synoptics (xxxv-xxxvii). He argues for leaving the text in its present order
rather than rearranging it a la Bultmann and others (xliii). Still, he sometimes
allows his eye for critical theories to see this as more important than explaining
the text. He remains subjective at times as when citing with seeming acceptance
the idea that John the Baptist said "Look, the Lamb of God" (1:36) and verse 29
gives the evangelist's addition, "who takes away the sin of the world" (lii). Yet he
states his conviction for a high view of the reliability of the material as of God
(liii). The fourth gospel was written, he supposes, by one of a circle associated
with the beloved disciple whom he feels was not one of the twelve (lxxiv); in that
circle John the Apostle is a possibility. On some problems he helps in a cursory
manner, as on "born of water and of the Spirit" (3:5), on others he is thinner, as
on 3:14-15. More should be done with the relation between verses, as the
description in 10:27 of the people God keeps safe in 10:28-29. His explanation of
15:2 pitifully leaps over details without meaningful comments; he generalizes
what "abide" means in a rather meaningless way. On 20:22 he is confusing. The
work is good at times, fair at others and weak in some.

Bernard, J. A.   Gospel According to St. John (International Critical Commentary).
Edinburgh: T. & T. Clark, 1928.

A liberal work, now outdated as to literature but long held in high esteem on critical and exegetical matters.

Blum, Edwin. "John," in Bible Knowledge Commentary**, ed. John F. Walvoord and Roy B. Zuck, Volume II. Wheaton: Victor Books, 1985.**

Though limited to conciseness, Blum poured much expertise into this, so it is a good survey, often helpful on problems, connections, and exegetical points. Blum on such texts as 15:2a takes what has come to be called a lordship salvation perspective.

Boice, James M. The Gospel of John: An Evangelical Commentary**. 5 Volumes. Grand Rapids: Zondervan, 1975-79.**

A keen scholar and good evangelical Bible pastor-teacher contributed this work based on his thorough messages. Boice often presents various possible interpretations and shows his reasons for the view he prefers. His good illustrations and frequent outstanding evangelistic content add value to the work. At times he becomes more topical than expositional in the sense of following the text verse by verse as he seeks to draw in so many truths in relation to John's Gospel. Boice is not afraid to disagree with the majority of commentators. For example, on 15:2 most say that "takes away" (airo) refers to the Father's removal of unfruitful people. Boice takes the view that airo here means God "lifts up" the unfruitful among the saved so that they may begin to bear fruit.

Bonar, Horatius. Studies in the Gospel of John**. Grand Rapids: Zondervan, 1921.**

This 110-pp. paperback is a revised reprint of a work in the past century. Bonar deals with selected texts, not all the gospel, and has 31 brief chapters with good outlines and thoughts for messages which edify the heart.

Bowman, Robert M., Jr. Jehovah's Witnesses, Jesus Christ and the Gospel of John**. Grand Rapids: Baker, 1989. 171 pp.**

He puts his focus on John 1:1, answering Jehovah's Witnesses who have changed their line of argument from a few years ago. Bowman also deals with 8:58 and 20:28. For years Bowman has shown skill in refuting cultic error as associate editor of Christian Research Journal and in other capacities.

Brown, R. E. The Gospel According to John **(Anchor Bible). 2 volumes. Garden City, NY: Doubleday, 1966, 1970.**

A Catholic work of much learning, which rates among the top recent studies especially for serious students or for teaching the book in-depth and being made aware of scholarly study done on this Gospel. Brown brings immense learning to the task, and leaves few stones unturned. At 1,208 pages this is one of the most detailed fairly recent works in English on the Gospel of John. He analyzes views and issues, reasons, the current status of studies, etc. Notes and comments explain verses very fully as he uses the translation of the New American Bible (Patterson, NJ: St. Anthony Guild Press, 1970). Many regard as arbitrary his five-stage theory of composition. He also has a shorter work, The Gospel and Epistles of John: A Concise Commentary.

Bruce, F. F. <u>The Gospel of John: Introduction, Exposition and Notes</u>. Grand Rapids: Eerdmans, 1983. 425 pp.

Bruce gives a fresh translation of the Greek, much good commentary, a copious use of current literature, and application. Clarity prevails as he offers help for pastors, seminarians and lay people. At times, however, his vocabulary will mystify some, e. g. "sotto voce," p. 174; "ingressive sense of the aorist," p. 246, etc. Overall it is a very fine commentary by one of the leading evangelicals of recent decades.

Bultmann, Rudolf. <u>The Gospel of John, A Commentary</u>. Translated G. R. Beasley-Murray. Philadelphia: Westminster, 1971. Translated from <u>Das Evangelium des Johannes</u>. Göttingen: Vandenhoeck and Ruprecht, 1964.

A 744-pp. work late in Bultmann's life. Walter Schmithals wrote the introduction for this English edition, since Bultmann had not done an introduction. Form-critical and redaction-critical theories stand behind introduction and commentary. Schmithals says the author of the gospel is unknown but that the composition and redaction lay in the period A. D. 80-120. There is much of value for mature, discerning evangelicals, but they must always be able to sift the worthwhile from among many liberal conclusions.

Burge, Gary. "John," in <u>Evangelical Commentary on the Bible</u>, ed. Walter A. Elwell. Grand Rapids: Baker, 1989.

Although brief, Burge shows awareness of issues and often uses his space well to provide help.

Carson, Donald A. <u>The Gospel According to John</u>. Grand Rapids: Eerdmans, 1991. 715 pp.

An excellent commentary out of an evangelical's breadth of scholarly study and keen awareness of recent literature. He aims the work for teachers and preachers but it is readable for lay-people too. The introduction is 84 pages, giving characteristics of this gospel, how it has been interpreted, its genuineness, purpose, doctrinal distinctives and other matters. He has technical notes and comments, but his focus is more on seeing the flow of the text and drawing out doctrinal principles. Some will be rating it at the top of evangelical works, or a close run with the work by Leon Morris.

Carson, Donald A. <u>The Farewell Discourse and Final Prayer of Jesus</u> [John 14-17]. Grand Rapids: Baker, 1980.

One of the better expositions of John 14-17 in some detail with frequent meaningful articulation of principles for daily life. This study is meant to distill the fruits of scholarly labors and research for the church at large, and it succeeds at that. Carson's style is fairly vivid, and easily grasped, with an excellent forward dramatically setting the stage for the discourse. Many of the problems are faced rather squarely and are fairly satisfactory. The book's appeal as one of the better evangelical expositions in recent years is expanded by the presence of several personal illustrations (e. g. p. 109ff.) and a frank style. —Dan Phillips.

Godet, F. Commentary on the Gospel of John. 2 volumes. Grand Rapids: Zondervan (n. d.). Reprint of 3rd edition of 1893.

A good scholar is at his best here. He is exhaustive and excellent, though this work is old.

Harrison, Everett F. John, The Gospel of Faith. Chicago: Moody, 1962.

This work is contained in The Everyman's Bible Commentary series and is concise as it provides a well-written, easy-to-read survey and overview. Along this line it is helpful. See also Harrison's work on John in Wycliffe Bible Commentary, ed. Pfeiffer and Harrison.

Haenchen, Ernst. A Commentary on the Gospel of John (Hermeneia). 2 Volumes. Philadelphia: Fortress Press, 1984-86. 674 pp.

This is a translation from a German work of 1980, Das Johannes Evangelium: Ein Kommentar (Tübingen: J. C. B. Mohr). Liberal in orientation, he holds to three authors, one for the gospel of miracles, one an evangelist, and one an ecclesiastical supplementer. So, some of the account was added from church tradition by a redactor (3:20-21; 6:51-58, etc.). Much critical theory appears, picking and choosing on subjective bases. Since Haenchen worked on the manuscript from 1954 until around 1975, the year he died, his use of other scholarly literature often does not bring things up to date to 1975. However, lengthy bibliographies added after his death draw things into the 1980's and have value for earnest researchers as they read with due awareness of the liberal slants. Haenchen's work on Acts also is respected.

Heading, John. What the Bible Teaches: John (Ritchie New Testament Commentaries), Volume 6. Kilmarnock, Scotland: John Ritchie Ltd., 1988. 349 pp.

This work and others in the Ritchie series is distributed in the States by Loizeaux Brothers, Neptune, NJ. The series is ten volumes, taking a stand on inerrancy and premillennial dispensational interpretation, even a pre-tribulational rapture. It is very simple, geared for some lay readers, and does not reflect a breadth of study though it has many helpful comments. The bibliography (pp. 15-16) is heavily evangelical and quite turned to older works—David Brown, E. W. Bullinger, J. N. Darby, F. Godet, Matthew Henry, William Kelly, F. B. Meyer, J. C. Ryle, etc. It overlooks some key details, such as "born of water and of the Spirit" (3:5), and emphasizes some things that are not the point, as having the lifted brazen serpent "retaining the purity and metallic perfection of brass that remained uncontaminated," so that it might speak of Jesus's "infinite divine perfection" (p. 62). It neglects aspects that are important, as in being silent about looking to be healed in Numbers 21, and believing in John 3. In 15:2, the branch not bearing fruit represents a saved person who needs to be "lifted up by exhortation . . . to rise to spiritual heights (Colossians 3:1-4) . . ." (254). Yet 15:6 refers to a mere professor (255).

Hendriksen, William. Exposition of the Gospel According to John. **2 Volumes in one. Grand Rapids: Baker, 1961.**

Trained in the Christian Reformed tradition, Hendriksen is thoroughly conservative and believes in plenary verbal inspiration. He served for ten years as Professor of New Testament Literature in Calvin Seminary. His introductions are quite extended and carefully written. In his commentary, which is very usable, he first presents a brief synthetic outline of a section, follows up with a detailed discussion verse-by-verse, then gives a survey of the argument in that section. His footnote discussions show a wide breadth of reading. He is usually quite helpful on problems, Greek word meanings, and matters of history, culture or geography. There are many stimulating sermon hints and devotional thoughts. He is good in presenting several different views to a question and documenting them thoroughly. He is amillennial in matters pertaining to the kingdom (cf. his comment on 10:16 as well as his book More Than Conquerors, pp. 222ff). Though the author is very helpful in the Greek, the manner of discussion can be extremely valuable to the layman.

Hengstenberg, E. W. Commentary on the Gospel of St. John. **2 Volumes. Edinburgh: T. & T. Clark, 1865.**

This work, recently reprinted, has much judicious material tying the thought to Old Testament background theology. At times it is very provocative (cf. on Jn. 1:15, 30, "He is *preferred* before me," italics mine). Hengstenberg is one of the towering older names, well-known for Christology of the Old Testament, for example.

Kent, Homer A., Jr. Light in the Darkness, Studies in the Gospel of John. **Grand Rapids: Baker, 1974.**

Kent's paragraph-by-paragraph survey of John's Gospel deals with some of the main problem areas in exposition. It is geared to be a guide for personal or group study. Kent utilizes photographs, maps, and diagrams. It is a good expositional survey by an evangelical (former President, Grace Theological Seminary, Winona Lake, IN).

Laney, J. Carl. John **(Moody Gospel Commentary). Chicago: Moody, 1992. 407 pp.**

This initiated a new, conservative paperback series under general editor Paul Enns, who has written in the Bible Study Commentary (Joshua, Judges, Ruth, Ezekiel). Laney, Professor of Biblical Literature at Western Conservative Baptist Seminary, Portland, OR, shows keen awareness of textual and critical matters, also historical and cultural aspects, and theme (belief and unbelief, with 20:30-31 on the purpose). He writes clearly, verse by verse, explaining the main issues and applying lessons in well-organized homiletical sections, aiming primarily to help teachers and preachers. He meets many of the problems head on and discusses them clearly. He sees 15:2a as referring to a nominal, so-called Christian who is not saved and is cut off, and 15:6 to this kind of person also. Jesus breathing on the disciples in 20:22 is a temporary giving of the Spirit to enable until Pentecost. Overall this is a good survey, competently done.

Lindars, Barnabas. The Gospel of John (New Century Commentary). Greenwood, SC: Attic Press, 1981. 648 pp.

Lindars posits that John has material irreconcilable with the Synoptics, for "both cannot be right" (p. 26). He rejects an eye-witness, hence authorship by the Apostle John, concluding that he does not know who wrote it but calling him "John" for convenience (34). He believes he sees fictional descriptions of character (34) and some distortion (55). The date is ca. A. D. 85-95. "John's" having Jesus attend feasts in Jerusalem is "a literary device rather than historical . . ." (55). Often the verse by verse explanation is very well-done in relation to the Greek, Old Testament background, and discussion of different interpretations (cf. on 1:18; "the only-begotten one, God"; 3:5, 36; 7:37-39; etc.. Sometimes he slides over verses without really commenting in any important detail (10:27) or makes claims that can easily be challenged from evidence to which he does not give proper weight or in which he fails to discern the full implications (15:2, 6), or imagines unnecessary disharmony with other passages (20:22 with Synoptics and Acts 1:8). The work is large (648 pp.) and all in all a fine recent commentary written in the trend of assuming much redaction.

Lloyd-Jones, D. M. John 17. 4 volumes: Saved in Eternity (17:1-5); Safe in the World (17:6-19); Sanctified Through the Truth (17:17-19); and Growing in the Spirit (17:17-24). Westchester, IL: Crossway Books, 1988-89.

These expositions, which overlap on verses, are from 1952-53 messages. Lloyd-Jones, Westminster Chapel's minister for around thirty years in London, helps other pastors and lay readers find much devotional stimulation for spiritual triumph by dwelling on their position in God's grace. Cf. other works on John 17 under Rainsford in this section. Lloyd-Jones is best, Rainsford next, then Wiersbe and Brown.

Macaulay, J. C. Expository Commentary on John. Chicago: Moody, 1978.

An evangelical, devotional work which offers refreshing comments on parts of verses but often does not explain an entire verse. Previously it appeared under a more apt title, Devotional Studies in St. John's Gospel (Grand Rapids: Eerdmans, 1945), for it is more devotional than expository. Used with other sources, it can provide insights that can touch the life or be woven into sermons or Bible studies.

Macduff, J. R. **Noontide at Sychar. The Story of Jacob's Well.** London: James Nisbet & Co., 1877.

Detailed, stimulating facets for a preacher preparing a message on this area in John 4.

Meyer, F. B. **The Gospel of John, The Life and Light of Men.** London: Marshall, Morgan & Scott, 1950.

A well-organized, suggestively rich lighter, devotional commentary by the famous preacher and writer of a well-known series on Bible characters (Abraham, Moses, Elijah, etc.) and several insightful devotional books. Here is a commentary by a bright light that can refresh personally, stimulate messages and help illustrate them.

Michaels, J. R. **John** **(New International Biblical Commentary).** Peabody, MA: Hendrickson, 1989. 386 pp.

This was in the Good News Commentary (San Francisco: Harper & Row, 1984), but switched to the NIV. Michaels has also done I Peter (Word Biblical Commentary, 1988). The work on John is evangelical, shows marks of good scholarship, helps on many of the verses, and is fairly good overall though not outstanding.

Mitchell, John G. **An Everlasting Love. A Devotional Study of The Gospel of John.** Portland: Multnomah Press, 1982.

At the age of 90, the founder of Multnomah School of the Bible gives his readers some of the heart-warming fragrance of Christ he has long taught at Bible conferences, in the classroom, and as pastor of the Central Bible Church, Portland. The book is written as the man from England's Tyneside district spoke, simply and to the heart, moving verse by verse. There is much for the lay reader and refreshment from a lighter source for the pastor or teacher who also spends time in heavy, detailed analyses. Mitchell frequently makes pointed applications, offers illustrations, and ties things of Scripture together helpfully. He does not always nail down the meanings of verses specifically (cf. 17:15; 20:22 etc.).

Morgan, G. Campbell. **The Gospel According to John.** NY: Revell, 1933.

This is another of Morgan's better works and is good on the English text, though expositionally not as helpful as Hendriksen, Laney, Phillips and Pink.

Morris, Leon. **Commentary on the Gospel of John.** Grand Rapids: Eerdmans, 1971.

This very detailed work of 936 pages, abreast of modern scholarship on John, has much to offer in the introduction and in the verse by verse insights. It now ranks as one of the finest on this Gospel by an evangelical. It is based on the Greek.

Phillips, John. <u>Exploring the Gospel of John.</u> **Neptune, NJ: Loizeaux, 1988. 425 pp.**

An articulate exposition that relates well to life, done by one of the fine Bible conference leaders of today, a prolific writer. Phillips, an evangelical, is well-organized throughout as he follows his outline step by step. One can wonder why the 23-page outline is placed at the end rather than at the outset. Phillips helps the pastor or lay reader follow the flow of thought through John and touches lightly on some problems. It might serve best in a series of daily readings.

Pink, Arthur W. <u>The Gospel of John.</u> **3 volumes in 1. Grand Rapids: Zondervan, 1975rp. Formerly Swengel, PA: Bible Truth Depot, 1945.**

Before his death in 1952, Pink was a voluminous writer for the magazine, <u>Studies in the Scriptures</u>, which was published for 31 years. His expositions are non-technical and clearly intended for lay readers. Textual problems are for the most part untreated, but Pink does grapple seriously with doctrinal difficulties. He is conservative, Calvinistic, and switched from dispensationalism to amillennialism in his later years (compare his book <u>The Redeemer's Return</u> with his later <u>Exposition of Hebrews</u> and <u>Exposition of the Sermon on the Mount</u>). Ralph Keiper has written in <u>Eternity</u> (April, 1955, p. 32): "His works show hours of study; each line is filled with information and blessing. His books are not shallow. His studies fill the soul with 'strong meat' which needs to be well digested." His work on John has sometimes been called the best among older books on the English text.

Rainsford, Marcus. <u>Our Lord Prays for His Own.</u> **Chicago: Moody, 1950. 476 pp.**

This highly-esteemed older work of 1895 is by one of the finest expositors of the nineteenth century, sought after by men such as D. L. Moody. Rainsford, from Ireland, pastored St. John's Church (Belgrave Chapel) in London from 1886 to 1897 the year he died. Verse by verse he has a gold mine here, giving insight on most of the details of the great prayer. One pastor told this writer that Rainsford's book was the best on prayer he had read and that he made it a point to go through it afresh every year, finding himself often in tears as he identified with Jesus praying. Another fine work on John 17 is that of Lloyd-Jones (cf. above, this section). Still another is that of Warren Wiersbe (<u>Prayer: Basic Training.</u> Wheaton: Tyndale House, 1988. 144 pp.). Here are twelve chapters in which one of America's most beloved expositors digs out truths and lucidly articulates them in a way relevant for life today. Wiersbe's work was originally entitled <u>Listen! Our Lord is Praying.</u> Yet a further is by John Brown (<u>An Exposition of Our Lord's Intercessory Prayer.</u> Grand Rapids: Baker, 1980rp). Brown's work first came out in 1850 (Edinburgh: Oliphant & Sons. 255 pp.). He mentions several other expositions of John 17 before his book. He sets forth much of the basic meaning in the prayer in detail that will help a preacher and also edify any Christian who reads him.

Schnackenburg, R. Das Johnannes-evangelium. **3 volumes in Herders theologisch-er Kommentar zum Neuen Testament. Freiburg/Basel/Vienna: Herder, 1975.**

This Catholic scholar's work is widely regarded to be outstanding as a detailed critical, liberal study of John's Gospel in German circles. This work has also come out in English Translation in Herder's Theological Commentary on the New Testament. This is the new German ICC, in effect, and was published in 1980-1982.

Scroggie, W. G. The Gospel of John. **Grand Rapids: Zondervan, 1976, reprint, paperback.**

A concise, well-organized tracing of the exposition by an evangelical master of synthesis, primarily helpful to pastors and laymen seriously inclined to study but not ready for something technical or detailed.

Stott, John R. W. Christ the Liberator. **Downers Grove, IL: InterVarsity, 1971.**

This book has other messages at Urbana, 1970, but Stott's expositions on John 13-17 fill the first 89 pages. In the opinion of the reviewer, they are some of the best ever published with respect to coming right to grips with the message for Christians in a concise focus. Stott is well-organized in elucidating the passage, and he brings key issues out clearly in their application to spiritual living and representing Christ in the world now.

Swete, Henry B. The Last Discourse and Prayer of Our Lord. A Study of John XIV-XVII. **London: Macmillan and Co., 1913.**

Swete has much good content, but usually only his own view (e.g. 14:6, "truth" and "life" are but other aspects of "the way" to bring out its meaning more clearly; 15:2, the unfruitful branch is in Christ "by the communion of the Sacraments" and can lose his part in Christ, with no elucidation on what that means exactly, how it comports with 6:37-41, 10:28, 29 etc.). Swete, known for fine older commentaries on Mark and Revelation, was Regius Professor of Divinity in the University of Cambridge and Honorable Chaplain to the King.

Tenney, Merrill C. John, The Gospel of Belief. **Grand Rapids: Eerdmans, 1976rp, originally in 1948.**

This is an analytic survey of John which traces the flow of argument with an allit-erated outline. It is very good in helping the student to see the movement in the book though it should not be expected to get down into exegetical detail as the verse-by-verse studies can. Cf. also Tenney's "John," in the Expositor's Bible Commentary, Volume 9, ed. Frank Gaebelein and J. D. Douglas (Grand Rapids: Zondervan, 1981). This is a verse by verse commentary by the noted New Testament scholar, and it offers considerable help on the flow of thought as well as some of the problems, though he is vague on some as well (as 15:2a, 6).

Wenham, John. Easter Enigma: Are the Resurrection Accounts in Conflict? **Grand Rapids: Zondervan, 1984.**

An evangelical seeks to fit the gospel accounts of the resurrection together, whereas some have seen them as contradictory.

Westcott, B. F. The Gospel According to St. John. **Grand Rapids: Eerdmans, 1973.**

This is a reprint of a 1908 work which used to be generally regarded as the classic commentary on John. Westcott, born in England in 1825, studied at Dublin and was called "in learning a second Origen, in piety a second Augustine." He teamed with F. J. A. Hort to labor 28 years in producing the famous Greek New Testament. He was conservative and Calvinistic. His knowledge of Greek was extensive, and he uses Greek and Latin in his comments. This plus his involved thinking at times makes it rather difficult for many to follow him. This is a good work to consult in any thorough study of John, and the student who wants to build his library with the best will not pass it by.

V. ACTS

Alexander, J. A. Acts. **Carlisle, PA: Banner of Truth Trust, 1991rp.**

This work, originally out in 1857, has proved helpful to many, though it is now far out of date as to literature commenting on Acts. For many basic details verse by verse, it still is of good value and often will help on word meaning and special problems. The fact that it was reprinted is indicative of its respected place in Acts studies.

Arnot, Wm. Studies in Acts. **Grand Rapids: Kregel, 1978, reprint of 1883 work.**

The original title was The Church in the House: The Book of Acts. It is conservative and devotional with some thoughts for messages, but not of great help for solid explanation of the text interpretively.

Arrington, F. L. The Acts of the Apostles. An Introduction and Commentary. **Peabody, MA: Hendrickson, 1988. 298 pp.**

This is a fairly good work done by Professor of New Testament Greek and Exegesis, Church of God School of Theology, Cleveland, TN. It helps on many of the basic points in passages in an evangelical vein, though it does not rank high.

Blaiklock, E. M. Acts, The Birth of the Church. **Old Tappan, NJ: Fleming H. Revell, 1980.**

This is done by an Emeritus Professor of Classics at the University of Auckland, New Zealand. It is a cursory, light treatment that discusses sections of verses with a fleeting glimpse that is written well but says little that solidly explains problem areas beyond generalizations. Most of the help is also given in other commentaries that offer a lot more besides on a more consistent basis.

Bruce, F. F. The Acts of the Apostles. The Greek Text with Introduction and Commentary. **3rd ed., revised and enlarged. Grand Rapids: Eerdmans, 1990. 569 pp.**

This is an effort to be a bit more technical, using Greek grammar more than in his work on Acts in the NICNT. It is briefer, but good. The larger work explains more. The author, one of the foremost New Testament scholars of recent years, has been editor of The Evangelical Quarterly. All of his works are exacting in their scholarship. This is a revision and enlargement since the 1951 first edition and the 1952 second edition. Bruce weaves into it comments in light of scholarly study since those years. The 96-page introduction has a new section on the theology of Acts.

Bruce, F. F. The Book of the Acts **(New International Commentary on the New Testament). Grand Rapids: Eerdmans, 1988. 541 pp.**

This work, first issued in 1954, is now revised not long before Bruce's death, with a new translation of the Greek text in place of the ASV. The bibliographical lists are extensively updated in footnotes, Bruce has interacted with later studies, arranged comments on fewer verses, and achieved a more lucid style in places. However, the basic verse by verse commentary remains substantially the same. It remains the finest commentary on Acts as to exposition in detail. Bruce points to I. H. Marshall's commentary for detail on Luke's theology. He shows a fine grasp of pertinent history, a sound explanation of most passages, and insights on many of the problems.

Bruce, F. F. "The Acts of the Apostles," **in** New Bible Commentary Revised, **ed. J. D. Douglas. Grand Rapids: Eerdmans, 1970.**

A boiled down version of Bruce's expertise, quite helpful in itself.

Carter, C. W. and Ralph Earle. The Acts of the Apostles. **Grand Rapids: Zondervan, 1973.**

The introduction and exegesis are by Earle, and the outlines, expositions, and special notes are by Carter. It is a fairly good commentary by these Nazarene scholars and will be of help more especially for preparing church sermons, Sunday School lessons, and Bible studies.

Conzelmann, Hans. Acts of the Apostles **(Hermeneia). Philadelphia: Fortress Press, 1987. 287 pp.**

Using the RSV, the author furnishes frequent help on texts, commenting on syntax, background, customs, etc. He is liberal and features copious use of redaction criticism for suppositions on parts of Acts. He considers many things, such as miracles, as untrustworthy. As a much-studied scholar immersed in the book and the literature, he does have much to assist the pastor or student who knows how to draw out what is worthwhile and leave what is not, as in any commentary.

Gaebelein, Arno C. The Acts of the Apostles. NY: Loizeaux, 1961.

This is one of the best older dispensational works on Acts and is at times helpful in studying the transitional problems. It does not involve itself with exegetical details as do the works of Bruce.

Gasque, W. W. A History of the Interpretation of the Acts of the Apostles. Peabody, MA: Hendrickson, 1989. 359 pp.

Gasque's work was originally a doctoral dissertation at Manchester under F. F. Bruce (1969). He has taught at Regent College. He surveys 19th and 20th century work in Acts, and reveals the methodology of scholarship with its conclusions and biases about critical problems. Gasque is evangelical. Fourteen years after his first edition in 1975 (A History of the Criticism of the Acts of the Apostles. Grand Rapids: Eerdmans), Gasque has a paperback edition that adds a 15-page supplement on work in Acts since his doctoral studies.

Griffith-Thomas, W. H. Outline Studies in the Acts of the Apostles. Grand Rapids: Eerdmans, 1956.

An extremely carefully-outlined study of the key facets chapter by chapter. It is helpful for quick overviews where many of the most pertinent aspects are pulled together, as also in his volume on Matthew (cf. on Matthew).

Haenchen, Ernest. The Acts of the Apostles: A Commentary, Translated by B. Noble et al. Philadelphia: Westminster Press, 1971.

This is a standard work of well-read scholarship on Acts in detail, but is quite liberal. It does offer much help on many of the passages, and can be of service for more serious study if balanced with Bruce's evangelical commentary, which is better. Haenchen's work is from the Meyer Kommentar in German (14th ed.). The lengthy introduction has, among other things, a helpful survey on scholarly work done on Acts. The commentary is accompanied by bibliographies on each area of Acts.

Harrison, Everett F. Interpreting Acts: The Expanding Church. Grand Rapids: Zondervan, 1986. Originally in 1975 (Chicago: Moody).

A well-organized and non-technical commentary by a fine evangelical scholar with a clear outline and a brief but broad, discerning discussion of vital issues in some problem passages (e.g., 1:23-26; 9:7 with 22:9; 15:15-18; 21:10-11; 23:5 etc.). Some classic problems receive too little comment. The commentary reads easily and comes directly to the point.

Hemer, Colin J.   The Book of Acts in the Setting of Hellenistic History.   Tübingen: Mohr-Siebeck, 1989.   482 pp.

A noted author seeks to establish a case for the historical accuracy of Acts on the ground of Luke's correctness in aspects of detail not essential to the spiritual message, as supported by external historical data (p. 104). In his method he will be viewed as supporting himself well in places and building on suppositions in others. Cf. also his work The Letters to the Seven Churches of Asia (Section on Revelation). One will also find much help on the kinds of matters Hemer takes up in such works as those by Sir William Ramsay, Merrill F. Unger (The Archaeology of the New Testament), commentaries on Acts by F. F. Bruce, R. L. Longnecker, etc.

Ironside, H. A.   Lectures on the Book of Acts.   NY: Loizeaux, 1943.

Good expository messages with a practical vein and illustrations. The interpretation is dispensational. Trained as well as lay readers find Ironside's books helpful for edification and for preparing Bible class lessons.

Kent, Homer A.   Jerusalem to Rome, Studies in Acts.   Grand Rapids: Baker, 1977.

This paperback is a good brief survey of Acts by the former president at Grace Theological Seminary in Winona Lake, Indiana. He is helpful on the general progression of thought and on selected problem areas.

Kistemaker, Simon J.   Exposition of the Acts of the Apostles.   Grand Rapids: Baker, 1990.   1,010 pp.

A 40-page introduction is followed by a detailed commentary on each pericope, giving notes on the Greek text, exposition, and doctrinal and practical remarks. Kistemaker has much that contributes as an evangelical as he elucidates the flow of the book, gets underneath problems, and shows the relevance. It is one of the better conservative works, and is in the Hendriksen NT Commentary series.

Knowling, R. J.   "The Acts of the Apostles" (Expositor's Greek Testament, Volume 2).   Grand Rapids: Eerdmans, 1970rp.   Pp. 3-554.

A work nearly a century old arguing for authorship by Luke, this is one of the fine older exegetical efforts on Acts. It is not done in an easily readable flow and it follows no outline, but it brings together much that is solid. For the most part only those very familiar with the Greek will appreciate and follow in the slow plodding.

Krodel, G. A.   Acts (Augsburg Commentary on the New Testament).   Minneapolis: Augsburg, 1986.   527 pp.

This is by the Dean and Professor of New Testament, Gettysburg Seminary, Gettysburg, PA. He has also written Acts (Proclamation Series: The New Testament Witnesses for Preaching), Philadelphia, Fortress Press, 1981. 118 pp. The present commentary is fair, showing investment of considerable research.

Though it does not rank near the top in overall contribution, it will help as one uses it along with other works.

Ladd, George E.   "Acts" in Wycliffe Bible Commentary, ed. E. F. Harrison and Charles Pfeiffer.   Chicago: Moody, 1962.

This is a good, brief commentary by a knowledgeable scholar. The work handles many of the problems well, even if briefly.

Longenecker, Richard N.   "The Acts of the Apostles," in Expositor's Bible Commentary, Volume 9, ed. Frank Gaebelein and J. D. Douglas.   Grand Rapids: Zondervan, 1981.

Allowed pages 207-573 for a substantial commentary, Longenecker provides a high-ranking evangelical work. He views Luke as the author and has good sections on criticism of Acts by scholars, Luke's purposes, the narrative of Acts (taking up criticisms versus the historical accuracy), speeches (taking up criticisms versus them), a lengthy bibliography, and a commentary that does not evade problems (cf. on 1:26; 2:4; 7:2-8; 15:13-18; 19:11-12 etc.) and is only at times vague (2:38, eis in relation to baptism and forgiveness, etc.). The work rates well with Bruce, Marshall, Polhill etc.

Marshall, I. Howard.   The Acts of the Apostles (Tyndale NTC).   Grand Rapids: Eerdmans, 1980.

Marshall has written a good commentary to replace E. M. Blaiklock's work. He reflects a wide awareness of current viewpoints on introductory matters and takes the stance that Luke completed the composition toward A. D. 70, leaving the place open. He provides a three-page outline right before the commentary and it appears throughout as well. Marshall usually offers reasonable evidence for views on problem verses, even if at times briefly, as in the selection of Matthias in 1:23-26. In 2:2, 3 some will feel that he confuses the Spirit's filling of believers with baptism in the Spirit. Sometimes he puts forth views but takes no clear stand, e. g. whether tongues in Acts and I Corinthians were always human languages or sometimes non-human or some other view (cf. 2:4). Sometimes, as in 7:4, he does not refer to a view often held that might resolve an apparent tension with another biblical text, e. g. the possibility that Abram is mentioned first in Genesis 11:26 not because he was born when Terah was 70 but because he was the most prominent of the three sons in regard to God's purposes. All in all, the handling of problems and the verse by verse comments are well-done. This, with Bruce's NIC work, is one of the finer, more often helpful evangelical commentaries on Acts in recent times.

Morgan, G. Campbell.   The Acts of the Apostles.   London: Pickering and Inglis, 1947.

This is another good English exposition but it sometimes is not helpful on real problems (cf. 2:38; 15:14-17, etc.), though it is one of Morgan's better commentaries and one which the student can profitably consult.

Morgan, G. Campbell. The Birth of the Church. Old Tappan, NJ: Revell, 1968.

Here are detailed expositions treating various aspects of Acts 2. Morgan originally delivered them as Bible studies moving through the narrative of the Day of
Pentecost.

Phillips, John. Exploring Acts. Neptune, NJ: Loizeaux, 1986. 528 pp.

An evangelical Bible teacher's articulate, flowing exposition that is helpful as a
survey for students, preachers and Sunday School teachers, who ought to use
some of the more masterful works as well (Bruce, Harrison, Longenecker,
Marshall, Polhill, etc.).

Polhill, John B. Acts (New American Commentary), Volume 26. Nashville:
Broadman Press, 1992. 574 pp.

This is a very good, well-studied work by a Southern Baptist scholar who shows
keen awareness of a wide range of literature and does the new series proud. The
series is new in distinction to the old American Commentary works such as that
of John Broadus on Matthew. It is evangelical, upholds inerrancy, and Polhill is
amillennial. Polhill argues for historical reliability of details in the book, usually
has perceptive comments, is helpful on problem verses, cites good sources, and
uses the Greek competently. He believes Christians are "the true or 'restored'
Israel" (p. 67; cf. for this view also Jervell, Luke and the people of God.
Minneapolis: Augsburg, 1972; and H. C. Kee, Good News to the Ends of the Earth:
The Theology of Acts. Philadelphia: Trinity, 1990). He is almost always clear on a
difficult text. One exception is on 8:14-17 where he seems weak on why the Spirit
was delayed after baptism. Another is 15:13-18, where he sees Amos 9:11-15 as
fulfilled in the church (p. 330) in amillennial fashion but does not say a word
about the land aspects for Israel in Amos 9:13-15. He is not distinct on 19:1-7 on
whether the twelve "disciples" were saved already in the Old Testament sense or
unsaved until they responded to Paul's more complete message.

Rackham, Richard B. The Acts of the Apostles. Grand Rapids: Baker, 1978, rp of
1964 rp of work dating back to 1901.

This is a very good though at times terse commentary from the standpoint of
Greek and historical background. Rackham was conservative but amillennial.
Verse by verse he often offers good help, and he has addenda on topics such as
breaking of bread, Sadducees and Pharisees, etc.

Ryrie, Charles C. The Acts of the Apostles. Chicago: Moody, 1960.

Though brief, this paperback is often clear from the dispensational viewpoint
and handles transitional problem passages in a helpful way (cf. 8:14-17; 19:1-6,
etc.). The author used to be Dean of the Graduate School and Chairman of the
Department of Systematic Theology, Dallas Theological Seminary, and is also
author of Dispensationalism Today (Moody Press, 1965), a definitive work on
older dispensationalism which also helps in understanding Acts.

Scroggie, W. G. The Acts of the Apostles. Grand Rapids: Zondervan, 1976 reprint, paperback.

A homiletically suggestive organization and exposition by an evangelical who knew how to articulate the main points that are pertinent.

Stott, John R. W. The Message of Acts: The Spirit, The Church and the World (Bible Speaks Today series). Downers Grove: IVP, 1990. 405 pp.

This evangelical exposition is verse by verse, and it also takes up key questions such as charismatic gifts, signs and wonders, baptism in the spirit, etc. After his introduction, Stott has four divisions: Jews (1:6-6:7); foundations for world mission (6:8-12:24); the apostle to the Gentiles (12:25-21:17); and on the way to Rome (21:18-28:31). As he usually is, Stott is very articulate in capturing the message, showing the flow, and letting the text come alive. This and the work by Phillips are both lucid for lay people and also helpful at times for pastors.

Walker, Thomas. The Acts of the Apostles. Chicago: Moody, 1965.

This work, originally in the Indian Commentary series (1910), was written for missionary workers. It is excellent on problems and detailed in general (586 pages). Wilbur Smith, who searched for years to obtain a second-hand copy while it was long out of print, describes the work as "without question the greatest commentary on the Book of Acts from a missionary standpoint that has been written in our language" (cf. preface written by Smith). It is a very helpful commentary.

Williams, D. J. Acts (Good News Commentary). San Francisco: Harper and Row, 1985. 478 pp.

For the most part this is a good commentary in its exegesis and information on historical setting. Williams is thorough, immersed in literature on Acts but often using information well. In some things he sounds evangelical, in others he will astound many evangelicals by his rationalizing. For example in the reference to angels in 1:11 when Jesus ascended, Williams offers, "perhaps all he wanted to say was that there was an overwhelming sense of the divine in what happened" (p. 9).

VI. ROMANS

Anderson, Norman. Freedom Under Law. Eastbourne: Kingsway, 1988.

A professor emeritus of legal studies and biblical scholar shows how law relates to true freedom. Various types of freedoms flourish under protection by laws. Later, Anderson takes up law in the spiritual life according to the Scripture. He argues in Matthew 5:17-20 for fulfillment of the law in an appropriate sense that

God has designed for it to have (p. 121). God purposed that Mosaic rules and regulations on ceremonial cleanness have their place in Old Testament times but also look forward to moral cleanness such as was realized in Jesus's spiritual life teaching and spiritual power. The Mosaic law was not aimed to be a way to merit salvation by obeying, but revealed ways God willed for saved people to live for their well-being (p. 155). The law could inform of the need for life, but could not impart life; God gives the life in grace through Christ in the gospel. And in the gospel way God gives power to obey God's will shown in moral principles of the law, etc.

Barnhouse, Donald Grey. <u>Expositions of Bible Doctrines</u>. **12 volumes. Grand Rapids: Eerdmans, 1952-64.**

The late editor of <u>Eternity Magazine</u> authored this excellent set which uses Romans as a point of departure for thorough studies on crucial themes and whole Bible orientation. He handles Romans in an expository manner which is very rich. His many striking illustrations help make the series especially valuable to the pastor as well as the teacher.

Barrett, C. K. <u>A Commentary on the Epistle to the Romans</u> **(Harper's NTC). San Francisco: Harper and Row, 1991. 2nd ed., revised from 1st ed. of 1957, reprinted in 1971.**

Barrett deals briefly but perceptively with much of the book, but many including this reviewer cannot take seriously certain statements such as his belief, however popular in liberal circles, that Paul in Romans 5:12 did not necessarily view Genesis 1-3 as "a straightforward narrative of events that really happened" (p. 111). Yet on many parts of Romans Barrett does grapple helpfully with interpretive issues.

Black, Matthew. <u>Romans</u> **(New Century B. C.). Grand Rapids: Eerdmans, 1973.**

This work by a scholar at the University of St. Andrews was done before the commentaries by Cranfield, Käsemann, etc. and so does not list them as bibliography. And many older works certain U. S. readers might miss are Godet, Hodge, Shedd, etc. However, Black is a widely-read scholar using good footnotes showing conversance with much modern literature and frequently furnishing lists of sources on key points along the way. He argues for the integrity of Chapter 16 as originally a part of the epistle. This is at the most a good brief commentary. Now and then Black makes odd statements — e.g. on 1:3 Jesus seems to have "found difficulty with this popular belief" of his being of Davidic descent and "to have taken exception to it" in Mark 12:35ff. (p. 35), even in a context where Black apparently accepts his Davidic descent. His treatment of "from faith to faith" (1:17) is not compelling (p. 46), or his assumption that only Gentiles are indicated in 1:19-32 and Jews in 2:1-29, though he has a brief footnote acknowledging recent challenges to this sharp categorizing (p. 54). One wonders why he handles 2:13 in less than a full line on the page or why he does not do more with 3:31, or why he does not explain how the physical body is annulled in 6:6, or why he flies through 6:22, 7:9 and 8:13 so quickly and does not grapple more with views on 7:14-25 (cf. p. 101). Still, he is very helpful in many places, such as on robbing temples (pp. 59-60), Christ as a propitiatory sacrifice in 3:25 (p. 69). Many on 5:12 will be more satisfied reading Murray or S. L. Johnson, Jr. ("Romans 5:12—an Exercise in Exegesis and Theology," New Dimensions in New Testament Study, ed. R. N. Longenecker and M. C. Tenney. Grand Rapids: Zondervan, pp. 298-316).

Blaiklock, E. M.   The Way of Excellence.   Grand Rapids: Zondervan, 1968.

This 78-pp. book does an exposition of I Corinthians 13, then of Romans 12 as examples of vital chapters illustrating Paul's view of ethics, their standards and power. The title is derived from the last verse of I Corinthians 12. Blaiklock has been a long-time Professor of Classics, University of Auckland. He writes simply, introducing interesting quotes, bits of relevant history, and other thought-provoking material that is devotionally easy and refreshing to read as he explains verse by verse. Captivating captions stand over the verses, but a meaningful expository outline would pull the good thoughts into greater cohesiveness. Much here is provocative to flavor sermons.

Boice, James M.   Romans, An Expositional Commentary, Volume I, Justification by Faith, Romans 1-4.   Grand Rapids: Baker, 1991.

The Philadelphia preacher gives expositions highlighting doctrinal points and their application to human life. It looks like another commentary of several volumes. It has a lot to teach and build up a believer. A briefer work that brings the doctrinal truth home to believers in general is that by R. Kent Hughes.

Bruce, F. F.   The Letter of Paul to the Romans: An Introduction and Commentary (Tyndale NTC).   2nd ed.   Grand Rapids: Eerdmans, 1985.   274 pp.

This is a very solid exegetical work abreast of good scholarship in the Greek and in the backgrounds of the New Testament epistles. But it is brief in spots. It was revised before Bruce's death so the research is updated in a few footnotes. It also now uses the RSV instead of the AV.

Calvin, Jean.   The Epistles of Paul the Apostle to the Romans and to the Thessalonians (Calvin's Commentaries).   Translated by Ross Mackenzie, edited by David W. and Thomas F. Torrance.   Grand Rapids: Eerdmans, 1961.

Calvin sees the theme of Romans as righteousness for men by God's mercy in Christ, offered in the gospel and received by faith (p. 5). He takes six pages to survey the epistle chapter by chapter, then begins verse by verse comments, without giving an outline. He has many perceptive discussions that are deeply enriching. He takes 2:7 as the life pattern of the truly saved through grace; 3:28 as meaning justification by faith without any merit by works but James 2 as speaking of works out of faith that prove the reality of justification practically; 7:14ff. as depicting a regenerate person, etc. As a clear, engrossing commentary that explains most points with a keen grasp of how things relate, this is one of the finer, old evangelical works from a theological standpoint.

Cranfield, C. E. B. __A Critical and Exegetical Commentary on the Epistle to the Romans__ (New ICC). 2 volumes. Edinburgh: T. & T. Clark, 1975-79.

An exceptionally good commentary in meeting the exegetical issues in a perceptive and well-organized way. Cranfield often presents various views from very wide reading, and gives specific reasons for his own as well as reasons why the others are not as good. (cf. on 2:6ff.; 7:14ff., etc.). I personally regard this as the best work on Romans so far to help the scholar who is knowledgeable in the Greek. Even others who are willing and able to study where technical matters are discussed can find much that they can follow in getting at the basic thrust of things on a passage.

Cranfield, C. E. B. __Romans, A Shorter Commentary.__ Grand Rapids: Eerdmans, 1985.

This is a single volume that condenses the two volumes but retains lists of arguments on crucial matters, also lists of main views, etc. It gets to the point faster, and saves those who want the shorter version a lot of money. The person with the longer work need not buy the shorter.

Dunn, James D. G. __Romans.__ 2 volumes (Word Biblical Commentaries). Dallas, TX: Word Books, 1988. 976 pp.

This is the Professor of Divinity, University of Durham, Scotland. He has bought into critical theories more than will please some conservatives, but certainly brings massive study to the task and will contribute much on views, reasons, word meaning, grammar, and bibliography on each pericope. In interaction with other scholarship this is one of the best on Romans.

Gifford, E. H. __The Epistle to the Romans.__ London: John Murray, 1886.

A careful work which traces the argument closely and states it well, this commentary is also helpful in most of the details of exegesis. It does lack in word studies in depth and does not comment upon the text as much as some would prefer at times. But it is one of the top commentaries.

Godet, F. __Commentary on St. Paul's Epistle to the Romans.__ Grand Rapids: Kregel, 1977rp. 542 pp.

This famous work was translated from the French in 1864, and has gone through several printings in English. Godet, also known for other fine commentaries as on Luke (2 volumes), gives good detail on what verses mean, providing much that evangelicals easily identify with. Of course such an older work cannot be up on current studies as newer works can be.

Govett, Robert. <u>Govett on Romans</u>. Miami Springs, FL: Conley & Schoettle Publishing Co., 1981, rp. of <u>The Righteousness of God, The Salvation of the Believer</u>. London, 1891.

This 556-pp. evangelical work treats some aspects in detail but it is not always easy to find Govett's comments on a given verse quickly since not all verses are marked off. Govett brings other passages to bear on a verse (cf. 2:7). He does not always explain how his view is in harmony with other statements in Romans (cf. 2:7, which poses tensions for some with 3:28; 4:4,5 etc.). He is sweepingly brief or almost nil on some long sections (cf. 2:17ff., pp. 34-35; 3:10-18, pp. 43-44, etc.). But Govett is helpful in some ways (3:31; 4:4; he even writes many pages, 94-124, on Genesis 15 and 17 in relation to Romans 4). Some of Govett's ideas are not easy to harmonize with Scripture, e. g. his statement that "if you have accepted by faith the eternal righteousness of God, yours is eternal life. If you are beside that a worker of righteousness through faith, a walker in newness of life, you are on the way to the first resurrection of blessedness" (p. 143). He distinguishes eternal life from "the reign in life" for the worthy. To him, the "mercy justified" will not necessarily obey Christ's commands, do His will, and enter the kingdom of heaven, which he apparently equates with the millennial era after the Second Advent. Eternal life is by faith without works, but special reward—the millennial kingdom blessings, to him—is obtained according to works. So, men may be eternally saved, yet shut out of the millennial kingdom but participate in the eternal blessings after that. Along the same lines Govett distinguishes between the "gift" (eternal life) and the "prize" or "crown" of I Corinthians 9:24-27, Philippians 3:14 etc., the crown referring to the special reward in the millennium before the eternal state, special reward only for the so-called obedient among the justified (cf. pp. 153-154, 158-178; cf. also his remarks on 6:22, 23 at pp. 229-235; and on 8:13-14, pp. 301-313, etc.). As we might expect from this line of things, we are told on 8:16 that "not all children are sons" (p. 317), for we become "children" by His grace, "sons" by obedience (318). And he sees two inheritances in 8:17: All the saved are "heirs indeed of God," but only some of the saved suffer with Christ and are "joint-heirs with Christ" (pp. 319-321).

Haldane, Robert. <u>Exposition of the Epistle to the Romans, with Remarks on the Commentaries of Dr. MacKnight, Professor Moses Stuart, and Professor Tholuck</u>. NY: Robert Carter, 1847.

This is a much-respected 746-pp. work (668 pp. through Romans 16:27, then several appendices on subjects relating to Romans. Though hampered by lack of any outline to relate things, the work has much gold if one has time and is willing to read voluminously to dig out the many nuggets. Whether or not one agrees with Haldane on a verse, his awareness of (or reviews of) many aspects of truth brought together is bound to prosper. Unlike most English expositors of which he is aware, Haldane sees 2:7 as hypothetical, law and not gospel. We may sample other verses: 5:14, "even over them," infants who did not actually sin but sinned in Adam's act as the representative head of the race; 7:14ff. refers to Paul even as a mature believer representative of all Christians (cf. p. 297); 8:5, 13 contrast the unsaved and the saved; God finally works all things absolutely to the good of His children, 8:28; the section in 8:28-39 has much to help a believer grow in assurance of God's preserving grace; in 9:22, vessels of wrath are "fitted for destruction" by their sins, whereas vessels of glory are fitted by God; 11:26 speaks of literal and spiritually saved Israel, as distinct from Gentiles, being joined to Christ, along with saved Gentiles. Israel will be restored to its own land (p. 556). This is one of the greatest of the older commentaries, almost always offering solid help and much to stimulate the heart.

Hamilton, Floyd E. <u>The Epistle to the Romans. An Exegetical and Devotional Commentary.</u> Grand Rapids: Baker, 1958.

Hamilton has a brief introduction affirming conservative views, even the belief that the original autograph manuscripts of the Bible were without error. He provides a clear outline of Romans sprinkled throughout. The commentary is competent in explaining the sense, though does not always give the reader the precise sense of a Greek phrase (cf. "obedience of faith," 1:5) as one finds Cranfield attempting to do. He often gives different main views (cf. on 2:7), but does not necessarily resolve a problem due to the brevity of attempted proof (again 2:7). He favors the representative, federal view in 5:12. Hamilton often seeks helpfully to explain for general readers various aspects theologically, so answering some lead questions (5:12; 7:14-25 in general). In 8:5 he basically sees the patterns of unsaved and saved. Each chapter closes with a list of questions on the chapter. This is a fairly good commentary for the general reader who seeks things explained briefly and with some correlation of theological aspects.

Harrison, Everett F. "Romans," in <u>Expositor's Bible Commentary</u>, Volume 10, ed. Frank Gaebelein. Grand Rapids: Zondervan, 1976.

This substantial work (pp. 1-171) is in many places one of the more excellent commentaries. Harrison was a skilled, meticulous exegete (cf. on 5:12ff). But on 7:14ff. he presents arguments well for two main views, then is disappointing to this reviewer when he selects another view that does not seem to be defended well and is only hypothetical. Still, by and large Harrison's work makes a solid contribution.

Hodge, Charles. <u>A Commentary on Romans</u> (The Geneva Series of Commentaries). London: Banner of Truth Trust, 1972.

This is a reprint of an 1864 work by Hodge, who lectured at Princeton Theological Seminary for many years. He deals with the epistle verse-by-verse with good theological perspective and use of the Greek. It is a good, solid evangelical commentary helpful to a teacher, preacher, or layman on the problems because it delves into them with a zest.

Hughes, R. Kent. Righteousness from Heaven (Preaching the Word). Westchester, IL: Crossway Books/Good News Publishers, 1991. 339 pp.

Very readable expositions that explain sections of Romans and bring in frequent items from broad reading to stimulate the user. Hughes, a diligent student, works hard at communicating winsomely with punch and representing what the text says, then making applications to show how the truth can be real in daily life. His studies are broad, and will be of more use to lay-people wanting a quick, interestingly-related escort through Romans.

Johnson, Alan F. The Freedom Letter (Romans). Chicago: Moody Press, 1974.

One of the finer, more readable recent surveys which explains the passages carefully and competently based on much study and grasp of things. Johnson even comments briefly on many of the expositional problems and stays in touch with the reader by way of illustrations and practical comments. For the general reader, who desires to follow the main flow and see how to deal with some of the main problems in interpretation without descending into the depths of complications, this is a fine work. The author is a professor at Wheaton College and a recent past national president of the Evangelical Theological Society. He earned his Th. D. from Dallas Seminary.

Käsemann, Ernst. Commentary on Romans. Translated from the 4th ed. of An Die Romer. J. C. Mohr (Paul Siebeck): Tübingen, 1980. Grand Rapids: Eerdmans, 1980.

A thorough, 428-pp. work of big pages without an introduction but with the attempt to interpret verse by verse. Käsemann's discussions are carried on within an orbit of higher critical scholars for the most part. He shows very wide awareness of literature within this range, his students supplying detailed bibliographies loaded with German studies for each set of verses. Many of the discussions are ponderous, introducing at times so many big points and side points that it is a problem seeing the forest for the trees, keeping to the thread of thought in Romans, and seeing an explanation of exegetical phrases converging with clarity as so often in Cranfield. Certainly Käsemann tries not to leave many stones unturned. More paragraphs summarizing synthesis would pull his heavy details into greater effectiveness, as would having interpretations of verses within a section marked off distinctly. The reference in 7:14-25 is to the results of sins in the pre-Christian experience. All in all, this is one of the more contributing recent works of technical theology and word usage by a liberal scholar of international stature. There is much of value for those willing and able to do very patient, probing study and to come to deeply thought out convictions, whether or not they finally agree at every point with Käsemann. Käsemann does not always make clear what he means by a point. Sometimes familiarity with terminology and ideas in Bultmann and after him helps to follow Käsemann's lines of thought.

Kaye, Bruce N.   The Thought Structure of Romans with Special Reference to Chapter 6.   Austin, TX: Schola Press, 1979.

This 202-page work was originally presented to the theology faculty of the University of Basel in Switzerland as a dissertation. Written under the tutelage of Dr. Bo Reicke, it should prove invaluable to the seminarian and pastor who desire precise knowledge of Romans 6. Dr. Kaye deals in the five basic areas of sin, relationship with Christ, law and grace, baptism, and slavery and freedom as they grow out of the text. Heavy reference is made to the original Greek when deciphering Pauline writing style and logic. The volume is thorough in its approach and quite conservative. The footnotes and bibliography alone are worth the price of the book. —Jan Sattem

King, John Phillip.   Death, Burial and Baptism in Romans 6:1-14.   Ph. D. dissertation, Emory University, 1977.

A detailed study (559 pp.) presenting baptism in Romans 6 as an initiatory rite of passage in the church. Looks at various views of baptism here, ancient attitudes toward the meaning and the significance of death, etc.

Leenhardt, Franz.   The Epistle to the Romans. A Commentary.   Translated by H. Knight.   Cleveland/New York: World Publishing Co., 1965.

This is a work widely held in good regard. It has insightful things to say on some of the key passages such as Romans 7:14ff. but sometimes lacks in comment one would appreciate on specific verses. It has a lot to contribute at some points if one uses it at various times in working on a series of studies, but I would not rate it at the very top as being as helpful as often as works by Cranfield, Hendriksen, Moo, Murray. And it is not one of the better general works that will most profit laymen, for it does not rate as well as Johnson, McClain, etc.

Liddon, H. P.   Explanatory Analysis of St. Paul's Epistle to the Romans.   Minneapolis: Klock & Klock, 1977, rp of 1899 work.

Though Liddon lays out immense detail, he does it in a point by point, systematic order that analyzes the text verse by verse as to grammar, logic, and doctrine. Serious readers can follow his clear outline and trace the argument of Paul's epistle. Liddon treats Greek words, views on problems, and pertinent details of syntax, history, and connection with other Scripture. This and Stifler's briefer work are models to help an expositor pursue the chain of argument.

Lightfoot, J. B.   Notes on Epistles of Paul: I-II Thessalonians, I Corinthians 1-7, Romans 1-7, Ephesians 1:1-14.   Grand Rapids: Baker, 1980.

A brilliant New Testament exegetical scholar well-known for masterful commentaries on such books as Galatians, Philippians, and Colossians makes comments here on each phrase of the verses he covers.

Lloyd-Jones, D. Martyn. <u>Romans</u>. **6 volumes. Grand Rapids: Zondervan, 1971-76.**

An outstanding preacher of Westminster Chapel, London, gave this series of sermons on Friday evenings. He covered 1:1—14:17 during the period October, 1955 to March, 1968. He begins here at 3:20 because he wants to start the published volumes at what he calls the "heart" of Romans. The content is very perceptive of how the great doctrines relate to life as he reasons things out in a readable way, talking directly to people (for these are edited sermons left pretty much as he delivered them). The material has much gold, but the detail will probably leave its impact primarily on preachers doing an extended series and scheduling the time to read the section on the verses they plan to cover in a given sermon. The studies are bound to leave their impact on the reader, broadening, deepening, enriching. Lloyd-Jones sometimes devotes entire sermons (chapters) to other passages related to a Romans text, e.g. on 8:17-39 he gives five chapters on problem passages such as II Peter 2:1, Matthew 25:1-13 (danger of false profession) and Hebrews 6:4-8; 10:26-29. He argues that 7:14-25 refers to pre-salvation experience.

Martin, Ralph P. **"Romans," in** <u>New Bible Commentary Revised</u>, **ed. D. Guthrie et al. Grand Rapids: Eerdmans, 1970.**

This survey by an outstanding New Testament scholar should not be overlooked due to the wealth of commentaries on Romans. Here and there he will make good contributions in a diligent study.

Mauro, Philip. **The "Wretched Man" and His Deliverance, Romans VII. Williamsport, PA: Bible Truth Depot [n.d.].**

Mauro argues that Romans 7 describes "a conscientious, unconverted Jew, fully instructed in the Law, and seeking zealously to accomplish a righteousness of his own by "works of law" (p. 22). In his mind he sees the spirituality of the law but is utterly unable to do it because of indwelling sin. The final two chapters deal with "Sickness among the children of God" and "The 'Cause' of Sickness among Saints" (emphasizing sin, as I Corinthians 11:27-32), but not contending that every illness in a saint is a chastening for some sin, p. 119; Mauro recognizes other purposes of illness). He argues for a view that the saved, when ill, should look to God only and use the means the Great Physician has prescribed, not resort to physicians. He and his family committed illness only to the Lord's hands, claiming Psalm 37:4 and being restored. This, he reasons, is God's way even in the face of problems such as people sometimes die who do not accept medical help, etc. (p. 123).

McClain, Alva J. <u>Romans, The Gospel of God's Grace</u>. **Chicago: Moody, 1973.**

A non-technical commentary but often perceptive in explaining what is crucial in a passage. McClain, better known for his premillennial work <u>The Greatness of the Kingdom</u>, is easy to read but has depth. In his thinking, 7:14ff. presents Paul as a saved man and 8:4-9 is a contrast not of two kinds of Christians but of Christians and non-Christians. The section in Chapters 9-11 is perceptive regarding Israel's role in God's plan for the future as distinguished from the church.

Mickelsen, A. B. "Romans" in Wycliffe Bible Commentary. ed. Charles Pfeiffer and E. F. Harrison. Chicago: Moody, 1962.

In the field of brief works this is one of the more contributing commentaries by an evangelical scholar of high competence. It is helpful to scholars, pastors and laymen alike, showing good awareness of issues and good hermeneutics.

Moo, Douglas. Romans 1-8 (Wycliffe Exegetical Commentary). Chicago: Moody, 1991. 591 pp.

Moo thoroughly analyses each passage, interacting with various views and arguments and sifting out, usually clearly, his own preferences with reasons. He has 21 pages of bibliography and copious citations throughout, using footnotes. He says that he particularly used twelve works: Barrett, Calvin, Cranfield, Dunn, Godet, Käsemann, Kuss, Michel, Murray, Nygren, Sanday and Headlam and Wilckens. He writes so cautiously at times that one has to search to decide his view. Whether one finally agrees with Moo, a careful reading will reward him with a broadening about different views. In comment on the Greek and discussion of theological ramifications, the work must now rank as one of the top evangelical discussions, along with Cranfield and Murray, and more involved with the Greek than Murray.

Morris, Leon. The Epistle to the Romans. Grand Rapids: Eerdmans, 578 pp.

The noted scholar completed this at 74 years of age in his retirement, providing a work that is quite thorough in many places. He is evangelical and on Romans 11 amillennial, and demonstrates a mature, profound grasp of issues that need to be explained and a broad knowledge of literature looking at Romans from various angles. He makes perceptive judgments on problems. Additional excursuses are included on God's righteousness, truth, the law, justification, judgment and sin. He is Reformed in his theology, and most of his statements are quite good or at least adequate. All in all, the commentary is worthy a place on the shelf alongside works by Cranfield, Hendriksen, Moo and Murray.

Murray, John. The Epistle to the Romans (NIC). 2 volumes. Grand Rapids: Eerdmans, 1959-65.

This is an outstanding work on Romans from the standpoint of exegesis and doctrinal discussion. Murray deals with problem verses with careful scholarship and good insight, leaving few stones unturned. It is one of the most helpful works on the epistle for the teacher or pastor who is serious about his Bible study.

Murray, John.   The Imputation of Adam's Sin.   Grand Rapids: Eerdmans, 1959.

An excellent little book surveying the main views on Romans 5:12ff. and looking at the chief arguments for them. Much of the essence is in his fine commentary on Romans. Murray's book is the best book by an evangelical on theological facets of the text, and grew out of a series in the Westminster Theological Journal.

Nee, Watchman.   The Normal Christian Life.   Fort Washington: Christian Literature Crusade, 1961.

Though not a commentary, this book is good as a more practical discussion of the Christian life according to the teaching of Romans 6-8. Nee deals with crucial concepts in these chapters, such as the "old man," "knowing," "reckoning," "yielding," and "walking by the Spirit." He illustrates his points well. This book has been a help to many and is suitable to give to laymen or youth.

Newell, William.   Romans Verse by Verse.   Chicago: Moody, 1948.

Dr. Chafer, president of Dallas Theological Seminary until 1952, used to say that Newell knew more about the book of Romans than any other man he knew. Newell has written here a detailed English commentary which is very helpful to laymen and easy to read.

Nygren, Anders.   Commentary on Romans.   Translated by Carl C. Rasmussen. London: SCM Press, 1958.

A very helpful treatment of Romans from the standpoint of its stimulating discussion of issues in Romans. It is not a verse-by-verse study, however.

Piper, John.   The Justification of God. An Exegetical and Theological Study of Romans 9:1-23.   Grand Rapids: Baker, 1983.

A competent, scholarly standard exegetical work of much research which reacts with major studies of today both in America and Europe. Piper seeks in this 316-page study to show how the passage reflects God acting in honor and in display of His glory even in unconditional election. Unlike many, he holds that election here reaches to individuals and pertains to eternal salvation. He sees double predestination in the chapter (cf. p. 194: Katertismena means that God fitted vessels of wrath for destruction). Piper has taught at Bethel College for several years and been pastor of Bethlehem Baptist Church, Minneapolis. He received his Doctor of Theology degree from the University of Munich.

Plumer, William W.   Commentary on Romans.   Grand Rapids: Kregel, 1971. Reprint of the 1870 work.

This is a verse-by-verse, practical, and rich exposition of the Greek text by a staunch 19th century Presbyterian.

Sanday, William and Arthur C. Headlam. <u>A Critical and Exegetical Commentary on</u> <u>the Epistle to the Romans</u> (ICC). Edinburgh: T. & T. Clark, 1950.

Because of its thoroughness in matters of the Greek text, some have regarded this as the best of the Greek works on Romans. It is good, but not as lucid and normally workable as commentaries by Bruce, Gifford, and Murray. These other works do not go into the minutia as Sanday and Headlam, but get to the point much better. However, the ICC work should be obtained by the serious student who can use his Greek. Cranfield's new ICC work on Romans is better overall.

Steele, David N. and Curtis C. Thomas. <u>Romans: An Interpretive Outline</u>. Nutley, NJ: Presbyterian and Reformed, 1963, reprint.

A survey designed to be an evangelical study manual, giving comments of interpretation and charts of major doctrines in the letter. The stance is Reformed, and the work considerably helpful for getting a brief, basic grasp.

Stier, Rudolf. <u>The Words of the Apostles</u>. Edinburgh: T. & T. Clark, 1869.

Stier wrote in great and helpful detail <u>The Words of the Lord Jesus</u> and also this volume on the apostles. Though old, the works are often quite insightful in solid commentary style that delves competently into meaning and implications.

Stifler, James M. <u>The Epistle to the Romans</u>. NY: Revell, 1897.

The author, who taught Romans from the Greek for many years, has produced this work which is accurate from the standpoint of the Greek, but geared for English readers. He traces the argument of the epistle very well so that the reader receives help in a nutshell form in thinking his way through Paul's profound reasoning. Stifler is dispensational (cf. 16:25ff).

Stott, John R. W. <u>Men Made New</u>. Chicago: IVP, 1966.

Excellent brief evangelical survey of Romans 5-8 with much articulate perception into the meaning and a very fine ability to marshal material in a well-organized and lucid way. Particularly helpful for laymen in general, teachers in church Bible classes, collegians, etc. Stott is always well-read, competent, and adept in clarifying.

Talbot, Louis T. <u>Addresses on Romans</u>. Los Angeles: Church of the Open Door [n. d.].

A popular series of radio expositions by a dynamic former pastor of The Church of the Open Door (Los Angeles) and key figure in the success of the Bible Institute of Los Angeles, now developed into Biola University, one of the leading Christian liberal arts institutions in the world. His wife, Carol Talbot, has written his colorful life in <u>For This I Was Born</u>. The work on Romans is basic exposition alive with frequent potent illustrations drawn mostly from Talbot's ministry. The material is an example of how one very effective channel of God's gospel communicated it, and has much that is helpful for personal reading by laymen and ministers alike. Many aspects will prime a preacher or Bible study leader. Many, however, will not agree with Talbot that 7:14-24 refers to the defeated Christian life, and hold that even the mature Christian life will experience in some degree daily the downpull of sin and yet the uplift of the Spirit described in chapter 8.

Thomas, W. H. Griffith. St. Paul's Epistle to the Romans. **Grand Rapids: Eerdmans, 1953.**

This is a devotional commentary based upon the English text and providing many homiletical suggestions which pastors will find helpful. It cannot rank with the detailed exegetical works on the Greek text, but in its class it is usable along with Barnhouse, Bruce, McClain, Morris, Murray, Newell, etc.

Watson, Thomas. A Divine Cordial: Exposition of Romans 8:28. **Wilmington, DE: Sov. Grace Publishers, 1972.**

This 94-pp. paperback is excellent in looking in tremendous detail at 8:28 to see if all things do work together for good to those who love God, who are called according to His purpose, and in what senses they do. There is much solid and rich food for thought and much to make one think through. If a preacher or teacher is preparing to speak on Romans 8:28 this is a good book to expand his thinking on various facets of the matter.

Wilson, Geoffrey B. Romans. A Digest of Reformed Comment. **London: Banner of Truth Trust, 1969.**

Wilson in many places in the 255-pp. verse by verse study attempts to provide a citation of what he regards as choice statements by reformed writers. So we often see names such as David Brown, R. Haldane, C. Hodge, J. Murray, and M. Poole. Disconcerting factors are the lack of an outline and absence of comprehensive surveys before plunging into a set of verses. There is much very fine explanation from a standpoint that many reformed writers favor (cf. 7:14-25), but sometimes vagueness as to what, exactly, is meant that relates to a larger picture (cf. 11:25, 26).

Witmer, John. "Romans," in Bible Knowledge Commentary, **ed. John F. Walvoord and Roy B. Zuck, Volume II. Wheaton: Victor Books, 1985.**

A careful theologian at Dallas Theological Seminary wrote this, a concise yet well-supported commentary. Expositors will find here pertinent, well-phrased comments on most verses and a capable handling of many of the problems. He sees 7:15ff. as Paul's experience as a believer. In 11:25-27, he is clearly premillennial and dispensational.

VII. FIRST CORINTHIANS

Barrett, C. K. **The First Epistle to the Corinthians.** London: Adam & Charles Black, 1971.

This is a fine recent scholarly explanation of First Corinthians. It is briefer on some problems than the serious student would like, but is nevertheless usually helpful. The work is in Harper's NTC in America.

Bartchy, S. S. Mallan Chresai. **First-Century Slavery and the Interpretation of I Corinthians 7:21.** Society of Biblical Literature Dissertation Series No. 11. Cambridge, MA: SBL, 1973.

This results from a 1971 doctoral work at Harvard University. It surveys the history of interpreting 7:21, also slavery in the first century A. D. The author discusses I Corinthians 7 as a whole, also verses 17-24, and v. 21 within its context. From the standpoint of increasing a reader's awareness of what Paul could mean, and insights on slavery, it is quite helpful.

Boyer, James L. **For A World Like Ours: Studies in I Corinthians.** Grand Rapids: Baker, 1971.

Boyer was Professor of New Testament and Greek at Grace Theological Seminary, Winona Lake, IN. This 153-pp. paperback is a study guide based on the Greek, giving maps, charts, pictures and comments of a brief nature plus a list of questions ending each chapter. It is geared for the popular audience as a thumbnail sketch.

Bruce, F. F. **1 and 2 Corinthians.** Grand Rapids: Eerdmans, 1980.

This is a knowledgeable, brief explanation of the books that is often helpful but at times too sparse. Bruce always, however, has a lot to offer on a number of areas and brings much expertise to his commentary from a grasp of the New Testament world. However, this does not rank with his outstanding works on Acts and Hebrews (NICNT).

Candlish, Robert S. **Life in a Risen Saviour.** Minneapolis: James and Klock, 1977 reprint of 1863 edition.

A minister in the Church of Scotland and later the Free Church of Scotland, Candlish is also known today for his works on Genesis and I John. In the present 398-pp. volume he expounds I Corinthians 15 verse by verse. He has much good content, but does not always clear up for readers what he means exactly. On 15:2, believing in vain, he apparently means in his generalizing comments that a saved person may lose salvation by a lack of obedience, but he is not really clear (pp. 11-12), and does not clear up how this fits with other Scriptures. He does not relate "believe in vain" to the vanity if the resurrection is not true (vv. 14, 17), as seems to be vital in the context. He sees 15:29 as referring to baptism in the sense of being baptized in a "vicarious occupancy" of the positions which believers filled before they physically died. Fresh recruits fill up the ranks (pp. 93-94). There is much in the book to edify although the author's style makes for slower reading.

Carson, Donald A. Showing the Spirit: A Theological Exposition of I Corinthians 12-14. **Grand Rapids: Baker, 1987. 229 pp.**

An evangelical exposition offering good insight at times on the ways issues can be treated through Chapters 12-14. Then Carson has a section discussing theology of spiritual gifts, drawing from the texts in Acts and I Corinthians. Chapter 5 evaluates charismatic claims and experience today. Carson concludes that charismatics should guard against pride in having gifts and saying that tongues are a sign of "the second blessing." Noncharismatics ought to guard against saying that the gifts ceased. Carson believes that "that which is perfect" (I Corinthians 13:10) relates to Christ's parousia. He feels that tongues can be valid privately and publicly today if proper conditions are met. He defends women's right to prophesy.

Clark, Gordon H. First Corinthians. A Contemporary Commentary. **Jefferson, MD: Trinity Foundation, 1991rp. 349 pp. Originally in 1975 (Nutley, NJ: Presbyterian and Reformed Publishing Co.)**

A worthy evangelical commentary of a Reformed nature that briefly discusses many of the main issues of interpretation and is aware of the Greek, yet readable and lucid.

Conzelmann, Hans. A Commentary on the First Epistle to the Corinthians (Hermeneia). **Philadelphia: Fortress Press, 1975.**

A lengthy bibliography, interaction with critical views, often long footnotes on additional help, and an awareness of relevant literature in New Testament times as well as recently unite in this technical, liberal work that is very well-respected. Subjective opinions that some sections show they do not fit their context and could not be of the same date as others are unconvincing (cf. 10:1-22, which Conzelmann thinks "fits badly into its context," p. 3). Read discerningly by evangelicals who are aware of basic exegetical issues, the subjectivism is immediately recognizable. Often the commentary shows good, discerning help on the meaning of a text and guards against misconceptions (cf. on 1:17, not depreciating baptism). But sometimes it is rather jumbled and muddies the waters in part (3:15, loss of salvation is a danger, he thinks) or very incomplete toward meeting the issues in very big problem verses or giving an adequate defense of his view or making a reasonably serious effort to explain or give other views (5:5; 7:15; 9:27; 13:8, 13; 15:2, 29, etc.). The commentary is primarily helpful to serious students, not so much for satisfying comments to resolve verses but for the occasional insights, references to early sources, and copious footnotes which can frequently contribute solidly.

Fee, Gordon H. <u>The First Epistle to the Corinthians</u> (New International Commentary on the NT). Grand Rapids: Eerdmans, 1987. 880 pp.

This is the all-around best evangelical commentary on the epistle at this time. Fee is well-organized, clear, and perceptive on issues. His work replaces the Grosheide commentary in this series in 1953. He is thorough verse by verse, skilled in Greek details, and keeps the argument of the epistle in view. His grasp of literature on I Corinthians is masterful, and he takes up more matters than other commentaries on the letter, looking at various views and reasons, supporting his views, applying truth to the church and the Christian life. He will meet with disagreement on some issues, of course. In a 10-page discussion he sees 14:34-35 as a textual gloss, thus having no bearing on women's role in the church. This is a curious conviction since such a gloss does not have a proper attestation. Fee devotes 40 pages just to 11:2-16, taking "head" to denote source, not authority. He is affiliated with the Assemblies of God and is sure all the gifts are for today, yet argues his position well, even if one disagrees with him.

Godet, Franz. <u>Commentary on the First Epistle to the Corinthians.</u> Grand Rapids: Kregel, 1977. Reprint of 1886 work.

Godet, a Swiss Protestant Reformed scholar, was Professor of New Testament in the Free Evangelical Theological School, Neuchatel. He deals seriously with the text in the Greek, usually giving solid comments in a serious effort to explain a passage and showing connections between sections. His is one of the finer works among the older commentaries, well-worth consulting for its scholarship and its warm strain. A 1957 printing was issued by Zondervan.

Gromacki, Robert G. <u>Called To Be Saints. An Exposition of I Corinthians.</u> Grand Rapids: Baker, 1977.

This Cedarville College (Ohio) New Testament professor has been prolific as a writer of commentaries. Skilled in the Greek, he does a survey that sums up sections, comments on many verses, and meets problem texts often with good insight. He has a high view of the text's integrity.

Grosheide, F. W. <u>Commentary on First Corinthians</u> (NIC). Grand Rapids: Eerdmans, 1954.

This is a lucid evangelical work of capable scholarship which ranks among the top commentaries from the standpoint of the Greek and dealing with problems.

Héring, Jean. <u>The First Epistle of Saint Paul to the Corinthians.</u> Translated by A. W. Heathcote and P. J. Allcock. London: Epworth, 1962.

Brief on many of the texts but often with fresh insights and a good grasp of issues. Evangelical and helpful quite often.

Hodge, Charles. <u>Corinthians 1 and 2.</u> Carlisle, PA: Banner of Truth Trust, 1978rp.

The famous theologian's work, originally in 1857, is very worthy of reprint and much used by pastors, students and lay people in general. As on Romans, he explains each verse in a careful manner, informed by much study, and is particularly adept and helpful in bringing out the doctrinal truth. Those who use his works find much assistance in thinking through issues consistently with Scripture, seen from a Reformed perspective.

Hughes, Robert B.   <u>First Corinthians</u>.   Chicago: Moody, 1985.   157 pp.

Clear, concise, conservative, competent survey. Those needing a simple discussion of some of the issues in a readable style will find this well-organized evangelical study suitable.

Ironside, H. A.   <u>Addresses on the First Epistle to the Corinthians</u>.   3rd edition.   NY: Loizeaux, 1952.

A popular work of a survey nature, this is helpful because of its insight into the problems of the Corinthians and the practical applications today. The illustrations are good.

Johnson, S. Lewis.   "First Corinthians."   <u>The Wycliffe Bible Commentary</u>.   Chicago: Moody, 1962.

This work in the English, based upon a careful study of the Greek text, is helpful because it gets right to the crux of problems. However, by necessity, it is brief.

Lowery, David.   "I and II Corinthians," in <u>Bible Knowledge Commentary</u>, ed. John F. Walvoord and Roy B. Zuck, Volume II.   Wheaton: Victor Books, 1985.

Lowery, teaching in the New Testament Department at Dallas Theological Seminary, did these surveys well, showing awareness of issues that need to be explained and getting to the point. In such a concise work he is sometimes quite helpful and sometimes general. His handling of problem verses often seems quite well-informed.

Luck, G. Coleman.   <u>First Corinthians</u>.   Chicago: Moody, 1958.

Like Ironside's work this is in a simple, evangelical popular style which gets right to the point in many of the problem passages. It is only for light reading, not for deeper study. It is in the Everyman's series.

MacArthur, John F., Jr.   <u>Spiritual Gifts</u> (I Corinthians 12).   Chicago: Moody, 1991.

An exposition on a key, much-discussed section and subject from a viewpoint that some gifts were intended to be permanent in the church age and some temporary, in the early church. Cf. also his <u>Charismatic Chaos</u> (1991).

Mare, W. Harold.   "I Corinthians," in <u>Expositor's Bible Commentary</u>, ed. Frank Gaebelein and J. D. Douglas.   Grand Rapids: Zondervan, 1976.

Another good survey invested with awareness of issues and literature, usually providing adequate reasoning. Evangelical. One will find considerable help here for preparing messages or Bible class sessions or Sunday School lessons, or just for informed Christian reading.

Martin, Ralph P. <u>The Spirit and the Congregation. Studies in I Corinthians 12-15.</u> **Grand Rapids: Eerdmans, 1984. 168 pp.**

This is a work helpful to those with a wide reading skill in Greek and seeking perception of different views Martin interacts with. It is a very contributing work on this part of Corinthians, whether one agrees with Martin or not. It is evangelical. Martin stimulates thinking on spiritual gifts, the nature of prophecy, and the nature of resurrection. He shows awareness of theological literature and aspects of history and Greek that may help in interpreting verses.

Morris, Leon. <u>The First Epistle of Paul to the Corinthians. An Introduction and Commentary</u> **(Tyndale NTC). Grand Rapids: Eerdmans, 1984, updated since 1958.**

Though the works in the Tyndale Series are concise, this is a good commentary and is recent. Morris is adequate in his comments on passages, but weak in detail on historical background, evidently because of the brevity to which he was held.

Orr, William F. and James A. Walther. <u>I Corinthians</u> **(Anchor Bible). New York: Doubleday, 1976.**

Orr was Professor of New Testament, Pittsburgh Theological Seminary. Walther was an Associate Professor in that department. They first give a study on the life of Paul (124 pp.), later the commentary. One sometimes can be disconcerted to have to keep switching from the brief sections verse by verse (finding some verses passed over) to the comments in the sweeping sections. Comments in both sections often tend to be sparse in explaining texts sufficiently, sometimes raising more questions than they answer (cf. 3:15; 7:15; 9:24-27) or not going on to tie things together. Sometimes comments focus on some odd view rather than on more likely views that might help the reader (5:5, p. 186). Still there are many helpful comments throughout based on study (6:4, etc.). This is a good work to consult in scholarly research, but not consistently as helpful in putting things together and in focus as some other works are, old and recent.

Prior, David. <u>The Message of I Corinthians: Life in the Local Church</u> **(Bible Speaks Today). Downers Grove: IVP, 1985. 285 pp.**

This expounds the broad message of paragraphs, and is not a verse by verse study. Footnotes cite reputed names (Barrett, Bruce, Conzelmann etc.), but there is a lack of reference to recent journal literature. Prior's exposition is practical, applied, often fresh with stimulating comment. Many will appreciate his insightful strokes that are relevant today on areas such as divorce, remarriage, and tongues. He has a fair discussion of tongues, yet some will not be convinced by his notion that tongues are ecstatic languages and will opt for earthly languages here and in Acts. Yet he has much to provoke thinking.

Robertson, A. T. and Alfred Plummer. A Critical and Exegetical Commentary on the First Epistle to the Corinthians (ICC). New York: Charles Scribner's Sons, 1911.

This, after Fee, is the most detailed and the best critical commentary on the epistle. Though not as readable as works by Godet, Grosheide, Johnson and Morris, it is far more detailed in discussing possibilities for a given passage.

Zodhiates, Spiros. A Richer Life For You in Christ. An Exposition of I Corinthians 1 Based on the Greek Text. Ridgefield, NJ: AMG Press, 1972.

Born on Cyprus of Greek parents, Zodhiates was president of American Mission to the Greeks, Inc., later headquartered in Chattanooga. His works on The Pursuit of Happiness (Beatitudes) and The Epistle of James and The Life of Faith (3 volumes) are known to many. In this paperback, as in his other works, he uses the Greek, and writes in great detail, with often choice illustrations as he expounds the passage in a simple, popular devotional way. Sometimes he has several chapters on a single verse as he does an evangelical study of different facets. The book is furnished with indices of subjects, English words, and Greek words.

Zodhiates, Spiros. A Revolutionary Mystery. An Exposition of I Corinthians 2:1-16. Ridgefield: AMG, 1974.

Zodhiates expounds and illustrates with interesting chapter titles, e.g. "God's Strength in Your Weakness," "Why So Many Mysteries in the Christian Faith?," "How to Enjoy God Without Fully Understanding Him," "How You Can Be Spiritual Yet Human," etc. For a devotional refresher, this in an interesting, often stimulating book for young believers, and has many good reminders or further lessons to edify the more mature as well. Zodhiates is a master of illustration, and in this respect provides help even in bringing together material to enhance a sermon or Bible study.

Zodhiates, Spiros. Getting the Most Out of Life. An Exposition of I Corinthians 3. Ridgefield: AMG, 1976.

I have seen few books written on I Corinthians 3 but enjoyed reading, from the archives of King's College, University of Aberdeen, Anthony Burgess's exposition of the entire chapter. It was The Scriptural Directory For Church Officers and Peoples, A Practical Commentary Upon the whole 3rd Chapter of the 1st Epistle of St. Paul to the Corinthians (London, 1659). Done in a reformed viewpoint with often choice statements to awaken believers to servanthood in church life and vital preparation for the judgment seat and reward, it gripped my heart at many a point. N. A. Woychuk wrote For All Eternity (NY: Books, Inc., 1955), a devotional on 3:10-15 with considerable arbitrary symbolism on "gold . . . straw" etc. Zodhiates, like Burgess, has done the entire chapter, using his customary explanations of Greek words, illustrating, exhorting along instructive but devotional lines. Again he has intriguing titles to sections, "Are You Still in the First Grade,

Spiritually Speaking?," "The Sin of Idolizing a Preacher," "The Only Thing You Can Do to Save Yourself," "What Kind of Reward Has God Promised to Believers?," etc. This paperback is 379 pages, with indices of English words, Greek words, and subjects. Zodhiates says that the reward is not so much what Christians will have as what they will be in enjoying God and other believers; the "crown" concept does not necessarily refer to a material reward but is symbolic of spiritual values (p. 215).

Zodhiates, Spiros. You and Public Opinion (I Corinthians 4:1-5); also Formula for Happiness (I Corinthians 4:6-21). **Chattanooga, TN:** **AMG, 1983.**

Note Zodhiates' change of address from Ridgefield, NJ to Chattanooga, TN. These 2 volumes are along the same lines as the other volumes on I Corinthians, very detailed and illustrated.

Zodhiates, Spiros. Tongues (I Corinthians 12-14). **Chattanooga, TN:** **AMGT 1981.**

An exposition of the 3 chapters with creative titles and illustrations and an effort to use the Greek as in the author's other books.

Zodhiates, Spiros. To Love is to Live. **Chattanooga, TN:** **AMG, 1983 reprint**

A detailed exposition of I Corinthians 13 with illustrations, done in the usual Zodhiates style which is very helpful, especially on 13:1-7. Preachers and Bible class teachers can find much usable material on a rich set of verses.

Zodhiates, Spiros. Conquering the Fear of Death. An Exposition of I Corinthians 15, Based Upon the Original Greek Text. **Grand Rapids:** **Eerdmans, 1970.**

An 869-pp. hardback for popular reading, with 164 studies expounding verse by verse and illustrating. Again the titles are often very inviting. This, as his other books, can be helpful not only for a general reader but for speakers looking for illustrations and refreshment amidst technical studies. It can be invigorating to read the book, or parts of it, over several weeks before Easter, and letting the truth of the resurrection get more into the spiritual bloodstream. He sees 15:29 as referring to believers being "baptized for the dead," i.e., undergoing baptism that "destined them for and allied them with the dead" (p. 502), in other words identified them with the saved who had died, many as martyrs (501). He frequently seeks to explain the rich meaning in a Greek word.

VIII. SECOND CORINTHIANS

Barnett, Paul. The Message of 2 Corinthians (Bible Speaks Today). **Downers Grove:** **IVP, 1988.** **188 pp.**

A flowing, competent, broad commentary on the message of sections and on Paul as a minister and human being with weaknesses facing problems and criticisms but experiencing God's power in his weakness. Barnett often has good application to concerns today. He devotes more detail to chapters 1-6 (100 pp.), and is cursory on such problems as "thorn" (Chapter 12). The book is a refreshment for a series of devotional times and often a catalyst for grasping and ministering the Word.

Barrett, C. K.   The Second Epistle to the Corinthians (Black's NTC).   London: Adam & Charles Black, 1973.

Along with works by Danker, Furnish, Harris, Hughes and Plummer this is one of the top commentaries in usually getting at key issues and bringing quality comments on these based on broad research and awareness. In America this is in Harper's NTC.

Bernard, J. H.   "The Second Epistle to the Corinthians," in The Expositor's Greek Testament, ed. W. R. Nicoll.   Grand Rapids: Eerdmans, 1970rp, originally 1903.

This study is in Volume 3, pp. 1-119. Bernard has been well respected for skillful comment on the Greek and insights on many of the verses. Though old and lacking in the literature the past 90 years, the work has much to say that is helpful in word study, grammar, customs, and handling of problem verses.

Bruce, F. F.   Cf. on I Corinthians.

Carson, Donald A.   From Triumphalism to Maturity. An Exposition of 2 Corinthians 10-13.   Grand Rapids: Baker, 1984.   186 pp.

False triumphalism is, to Carson, the selfish spirit of serving for what one can get out of it, whatever the form. Talk of success can be sinful; we need to be humble, not boastful in a wrong sense. The way to live is the way of self-sacrifice, depending on God's power to win over our weaknesses. Maturity flowing from Christ's death and resurrection exults in His power in servant living. Carson shows a competent awareness of the argument and issues in the passage and current scholarship, and applies principles to touch people now. Sometimes he is too quick and brief and general.

Danker, Frederick W.   II Corinthians (Augsburg Commentary on the New Testament).   Minneapolis: Augsburg, 1989.   223 pp.

An evangelical work that ranks high among commentaries conversant with much scholarly study into the setting of that day and offering a lot of information. It is by the author of Multipurpose Tools for Bible Study (Saint Louis: Concordia, 1970, 3rd ed., 295 pp.). Danker's background study of "Benefactor" helps him illumine chapters 8-9. See also his benefactor Epigraphic Study of a Graeco-Roman and New Testament Semantic Field (Saint Louis: Clayton, 1982). Benefactors might give out of wealth with a noble spirit of obligation, while also having a right to see those to whom they shared respond in a noble way according to their means. Danker is, overall, quite good in a number of ways, and will contribute to one's study in this book.

Denney, James. The Second Epistle to the Corinthians. London: Hodder and Stoughton, 1894.

A well-regarded older study filled with information explaining passages, well worth the time on much of the content.

Furnish, Victor Paul. II Corinthians. Translated, with Introduction, Notes and Commentary (Anchor Bible). Garden City, NY: Doubleday, 1984. 621 pp.

Some scholars regard this as the best on the epistle due to its copious comment, expertise and adeptness in current literature. It is by the Professor of New Testament, Perkins School of Theology, Dallas, and is liberal. Furnish has much to offer serious students. He writes clearly, discussing each section with its structure and themes, gives detail on text, word study, grammar, geography, history etc. He includes 38 pages of select bibliography, and interacts with primary and secondary sources. He thinks with certain others (Barrett, Bruce, etc.) that chapters 1-9 and 10-13 represent two separate letters originally, though they are coherent. He likewise does not grasp the meaningful way in which 6:14-7:1 fits in the epistle. But his richness in many aspects such as grammar provides much for mature users trained to discern, and for translators.

Gromacki, Robert G. Stand Firm in the Faith. An Exposition of 2 Corinthians. Grand Rapids: Baker, 1978.

This is a good evangelical commentary along the lines of his I Corinthians work, perceptive in Greek, upholding unity of the book, dealing well with problems in frequent cases, and showing connections in the flow as well as pointing out principles for life today.

Hafemann, Scott J. Suffering and Ministry in the Spirit. Paul's Defense of His Ministry in II Corinthians 2:14-3:3. Grand Rapids: Eerdmans.

This is an exhaustive effort to shed light on the text in an abridgement of a 1985 dissertation at Tübingen. The author argues that 3:6ff. is grasped only if we profoundly see the context in 2:14-3:3. In his argument we have here a brief on Paul's self-concept as an apostle and a potent apologetic on the authority and authenticity of his apostolic ministry (p. 1). On 2:14 he decides that thriambeuein ("to triumph") deals with the person conquered and led in procession, not the conqueror (33). Paul is a conquered slave of Christ being led to death so as to show forth the power of God, the conqueror. Paul fulfills his ministry through his weakness/death, through which the Spirit in power shows others the meaning of Christ's death. Hafemann also has much rich detail on the sacrificial language (2:14-16a) and Paul's suffering, as well as the significance of 3:1-3. On the idea of Paul's weakness and triumph, also cf. David A. Black, Paul, Apostle of Weakness (New York: Lang, 1984). Black is a graduate of Talbot School of Theology and has taught there as well as at Grace Theological Seminary, West.

Harris, Murray. "Second Corinthians," in Expositor's Bible Commentary, ed. Frank Gaebelein. Grand Rapids: Zondervan, 1981.

Harris, who wrote his Ph. D. dissertation at Manchester University on II Corinthians 5:1-10 and has taught at Trinity Evangelical Divinity School for many years, has contributed a fine commentary showing breadth of scholarly reading and often a good grasp of issues. One is bound to learn much and receive good help here on some passages.

Héring, Jean. The Second Epistle of Saint Paul to the Corinthians. Translated by A. W. Heathcote and P. J. Allcock. London: Epworth, 1967.

As his work on I Corinthians, this is concisely written with many good insights. It is helpful for those who desire a briefer study but it cannot measure up to the more thorough works such as those by Barrett, Furnish, Hughes and Plummer.

Hodge, Charles. An Exposition of the Second Epistle to the Corinthians. Grand Rapids: Eerdmans, 1953.

This is a solid work with good insight in following the reasoning of Paul, and helpful in most matters of exposition, including problems. Hodge, as usual, is helpful theologically.

Hughes, Philip E. Commentary on the Second Epistle to the Corinthians (NICNT). Grand Rapids: Eerdmans, 1962.

This is the best English evangelical commentary now available on the epistle. It is detailed (508 pages), uses the Greek carefully, discusses technical details in the footnotes, deals carefully and sometimes at length with problems, and shows acquaintance with a great number of other works. It is one of the finer contributions to the NIC series.

Kent, Homer A., Jr. A Heart Opened Wide: Studies in II Corinthians (NTS). Grand Rapids. Baker, 1982.

This book will be helpful for individual Bible study or preaching. The style is fairly popular, but most of the major phrases receive comment, even extending to some transliterated interaction with the Greek text (at times treating textual difficulties as well). Kent applies the text frequently to modern life and pastoral work. He includes questions for discussion purposes. Kent, well-known for other evangelical expositions on several New Testament books, outlines clearly and surveys well for those looking for a brief work on the progressing message of the epistle and the main expository problems.

Kruse, C. G. The Second Epistle of Paul to the Corinthians (Tyndale NTC). Grand Rapids: Eerdmans, 1987. 224 pp.

R. V. G. Tasker's work served well for years, but Kruse's replaces it with stronger exegesis. It is a fairly concise evangelical effort that brings together much that is of help in following the thought through and dealing with problems in a well-written flow, using the NIV.

Lewis, J. P., ed.   Interpreting 2 Corinthians 5:14-21. An Exercise in Hermeneutics (Studies in the Bible and Early Christianity, 17).   Lewiston, NY: Mellen, 1989.   194 pp.

This expensive book ($49.95 in 1989) is written by four writers and deals penetratingly with interpretive history, exegesis, problems and theology.

Lowery, David.   Cf. on I Corinthians.

Martin, Ralph P.   2 Corinthians (Word Biblical Commentary).   Waco, TX: Word Books, 1986.   527 pp.

A well-regarded evangelical scholar writes clearly, keeping account of the flow, connections and verse by verse detail, offering frequent help on the Greek, the setting, the doctrine, etc. By and large he makes a good contribution, weighing matters carefully in many cases but being questionable in others. He displays mastery of a great amount of current literature so as to cite views and reasons, and is sometimes lengthy on possibilities, as on Paul's thorn (pp. 411-16), though he concludes with uncertainty what the thorn was.

Plummer, Alfred.   A Critical and Exegetical Commentary on the Second Epistle to the Corinthians (ICC).   NY: Scribners, 1915.

This is one of the best older commentaries on the epistle from the standpoint of the Greek text and critical study.

Redpath, Alan.   Blessings Out of Buffetings: Studies in II Corinthians.   Westwood, NJ: Revell, 1965.

This is a series of sermons preached by the author as a former pastor of Moody Memorial Church in Chicago. It is practical, devotional, and challenging.

Robertson, A. T.   The Glory of the Ministry.   NY: Revell, 1911.

Over against an attitude of having wrong motives in the ministry and giving it up as too demanding, Robertson writes to expose from 2 Corinthians the glory of being in the ministry and living in the will of God. The book had a shaping effect on this writer's life when he was young and contemplating the rigors of public ministry. Robertson, a great Southern Baptist grammarian, is well-known for his large grammar, his Word Pictures in the New Testament (6 Volumes) commenting on most verses of the New Testament, etc.

Spencer, A. B. and W. D. Spencer.   2 Corinthians (Bible Study Commentary).   Grand Rapids: Zondervan, 1989.   144 pp.

The Spencers are faculty members at Gordon-Conwell Theological Seminary, South Hamilton, MA. They believe that Paul defends the leadership style that he and his associates model to help readers follow the right example, not be led astray. Their work is a survey but furnishes a clear flushing out of principles that can assist Christian workers.

Tasker, R. V. G. <u>Second Epistle to the Corinthians</u> **(Tyndale Series). London: Tyndale Press, 1978. Published in U. S. by Eerdmans.**

This is a good brief conservative work which, among other things, argues for the unity of the epistle. Kruse's study has replaced it.

IX. GALATIANS

Betz, Hans D. <u>A Commentary on Paul's Letter to the Churches of Galatia</u> **(Hermeneia). Philadelphia: Fortress Press, 1979.**

Betz has taught New Testament at the Claremont School of Theology and Claremont Graduate School, also the University of Chicago Divinity School. Serious students looking for vigorous critical comments on interpretation of the Greek with heavy awareness and use of critical studies will gain much help here. Betz favors the North Galatia theory (p. 5) and authorship by Paul within A. D. 50-55. He lays out a formal analysis (outline) of 8 pp., also develops a detailed 6 page conception of Paul's logic of theological argument to answer opponents. There is often much help on main possibilities in the grammar, problems and views critical scholars debate, and possible similarities with other ancient sources. The fact that the analysis (outline) printed in the introduction is not included throughout makes it very difficult to keep any overall threads of thought in mind as one gets enmeshed in ponderous verse by verse detail. Unless one can get inside the thinking of Betz, he will have frustrations trying to grasp how certain discussions really help him adequately resolve theological problems in some verses if they do (5:4, 21). On other verses clarity is more apparent (6:11). The copious, often lengthy footnotes are very instructive for examples of word usage, other textual readings, distinctions in interpretation, references to other literature, etc. Also, Betz' bibliography is very extensive at the end, and he provides excellent indices on references in the Old Testament and Apocrypha, Old Testament Pseudepigrapha, other Jewish literature, New Testament, early Christian writings, Greek and Latin authors, Greek words, subjects, and names of commentators and other authors of ancient and modern times.

Brown, John. <u>An Exposition of the Epistle of Paul the Apostle to the Galatians.</u> **Minneapolis: Klock and Klock, 1981rp of 1853 ed. 415 pp.**

Though old and lacking in current literature, Brown's work is worthy on many of the exegetical problems. One needs to be able to read Greek and Latin to follow the footnotes. It is evangelical.

Bruce, F. F.   The Epistle to the Galatians. A Commentary on the Greek Text (The New International Greek Testament Commentary).   Grand Rapids: Eerdmans, 1983.

The late Emeritus Professor of New Testament at the University of Manchester, whom some rated the foremost evangelical New Testament scholar of our day, has provided a work of first rank treating technical questions. He favors the South Galatian theory after a fair and lengthy review that shows a grasp of the breadth of literature, a grasp evident throughout the work. Bruce on a verse by verse progression shows good perception of which problems need comment and explains matters with a sharp insight usually (cf. 1:6, 7; 2:20; 3:16; 5:22, 23, 25, etc.). This takes its place as one of the truly great commentaries on Galatians on the technical, thorough side for students intense about their study.

Burton, Ernest D.   A Critical and Exegetical Commentary on St. Paul's Epistle to the Galatians (ICC).   London: T. & T. Clark, 1921.   Reprint 1962.

This is one of the most detailed critical works available and is very helpful in the Greek text, though liberal. Many regard it as the best technical commentary on the book, others say Betz.

Campbell, Donald.   "Galatians," in Bible Knowledge Commentary, ed. John F. Walvoord and Roy B. Zuck, Volume II.   Wheaton: Victor Books, 1985.

Campbell, third president at Dallas Theological Seminary and a long-time, excellent Bible teacher there, gives a very helpful brief survey, using his space well. He sometimes is contributive on problems, as on 3:17, the 430 years, and on 6:2, 5 on bearing one another's load and yet bearing one's own, etc. He concludes in 6:16 that the "the Israel of God" means believers who are Jewish, not the church.

Cole, R. A.   The Letter of Paul to the Galatians: An Introduction and Commentary (Tyndale NTC).   Grand Rapids: Eerdmans, 1989.   240 pp.

This is a revision of a work of twenty years before, interacting with scholarly studies since then. It is a good evangelical commentary, well-informed, solid, clear with good help at times on problem verses.

Cousar, Charles, B.   Galatians (Interpretation).   Atlanta: John Knox, 1982.

Not one recent evangelical commentary is cited in the bibliography, and the orientation seems to be approximately neo-orthodox. Little interaction with Greek is evident; the writer imagines that 3:26-29 is the climax of the entire epistle, of which the theme is unity (not justification?!). Very excited about 3:28, he uses this as a scalpel to relegate all passages on female subordination to non-Pauline or interpolative status. He cites Bultmann, Betz, Barth, Schweizer, Jewett, Ellul, and Käsemann. The work is not very useful to the conservative student. — Dan Phillips.

Eadie, John.   <u>Commentary on the Epistle of Paul to the Galatians</u>.   Grand Rapids: Zondervan (n.d.).   Reprint of 1894 edition published by T. & T. Clark.

Based on the Greek text, this commentary grapples with problems in an energetic fashion, presenting various views and coming to conclusions. It is voluminous (480 pages).

Fung, Ronald Y. K.   <u>The Epistle to the Galatians</u> (New International Commentary on the New Testament).   Grand Rapids: Eerdmans, 1988.   342 pp.

This takes the place of Hermann Ridderbos's work. It is thorough, usually with traditional conservative views and with many satisfactory explanations, some even excellent. On verses he is lucid, frequently with some detail, though he skips past some real problems such as having fallen from grace (5:4), not really explaining. The same thing happens on "crucified with Christ". He holds the South Galatia theory, takes an A. D. 48 date, has a fairly good introduction overall in which he updates scholarly discussion, and relates 2:1-10 to the famine visit in Acts 11:27-30.

Gromacki, Robert G.   <u>Stand Fast in Liberty: An Exposition of Galatians</u>.   Grand Rapids: Baker, 1979.

This is an evangelical work along the lines of his commentaries on both Corinthian letters, competent in Greek, keeping the flow of Galatians in view, getting to the point on most verses well but usually with brevity.

Guthrie, Donald.   <u>Galatians</u> (New Century Bible).   Greenwood, SC: Attic Press, Inc., 1974.

A brief evangelical commentary with a good consideration of arguments for the North and South Galatian views as to whom the letter was addressed (he favors South Galatian view). He is helpful on most matters but too scant on several problem verses, such as 5:4 and 6:16. Still, it is a good commentary for those wishing a brief treatment by a competent scholar.

Harrison, Everett F.   "Galatians," in <u>Wycliffe Bible Commentary</u>, ed. C. F. Pfeiffer and E. F. Harrison.   Chicago: Moody, 1962.

The author, a famous New Testament scholar at Fuller Theological Seminary for many years and a leading evangelical in his field, offers a concise, well-pondered work explaining many issues satisfactorily. His thoughts are carefully weighed, and he often provides good though brief reasons for views.

Hendriksen, William.   <u>New Testament Commentary: Galatians</u>.   Grand Rapids: Baker, 1968.   260 pp.

Staunch reformed commentary competent in the Greek and the background, offering rich detail on verses, documented views, reasons, and a warmth of practical comment, all of this helpful to expositors. Hendriksen's many New Testament commentaries are well-respected and widely-used by pastors, Bible class teachers and many lay people. Often his discussions are quite full and illuminating. Due to the date the work cannot be current in discussing scholarly contributions, but it does carry quite a weight of interaction up to its day.

Hubbard, David A. Galatians, Gospel of Freedom. **Waco: Word Books, Publisher, 1977.**

A 118-pp. paperback written by the President of Fuller Theological Seminary (Pasadena, California) along popular lines with intriguing chapter titles: "How Good is the Good News?", "Will My Faith Cost Me My Freedom?", etc. Hubbard delivered the messages orally at a Mt. Hermon (California) conference, to the Christian Endeavor of Australia, and to listeners of the radio program "The Joyful Sound." Vivid illustrations scattered throughout add to the enjoyment of reading devotionally. Chapter 8, "Will My Faith Cost Me My Freedom?" alone is worth the price of the book.

Kent, Homer A., Jr. The Freedom of God's Sons. Studies in Galatians. **Grand Rapids: Baker,**

This paperback is a well-outlined, brief evangelical exposition of competent quality, with a short introduction favoring Paul as author ca. A. D. 49 (linking 2:1-10 with Acts 11:27-30), a South Galatian view, etc. Kent shows good awareness of main possibilities in some problem areas (cf. on 1:6, 7; 6:11), treats others rather briefly where there are difficulties and widely varying views (5:4; 6:16).

Lightfoot, J. B. Commentaries on Galatians, Philippians, Colossians and Philemon. **3 volumes in 1. Peabody, MA: Hendrickson, 1981rp of 1890-97 works. 1,208 pp.**

Lightfoot is highly-regarded for his work on the Greek text, top notch exegesis verse by verse, special notes on key problems, giving of views and reasons, etc. He was rarely gifted, and his commentaries rich with assistance to pastors and students.

Longenecker, Richard N. Galatians **(Word Biblical Commentary). Dallas: Word Books, 1990. 323 pp.**

A noted evangelical scholar, who also wrote a fine commentary on Acts, has a long introduction that surveys scholarly issues and study, then a commentary verse by verse with each pericope carrying its own bibliography, translation, notes and literary analysis. Longenecker leaves few stones unturned, at least the more crucial ones, and is helpful on views, reasons, and summation as well as detail on individual issues. He is Professor of New Testament, Wycliffe College, University of Toronto. One of his early steps to fame was his good book Paul, Apostle of Liberty (NY: Harper and Row, 1964, 310 pp.).

Luther, Martin. Commentary on Galatians. **Translated by Erasmus Middleton, ed. John P. Fallowes. Grand Rapids: Kregel, 1979, rp of 1850 work.**

A fuller version of Luther on Galatians can be found in Luther's Works (volumes 26, 27) published by Concordia Publishing House. Varying sets of lecture notes by Luther on Galatians have led to more than 30 English editions. This Kregel edition abridges Luther. Much of the heart-pulse of Luther's stand for justification by faith appears here, as he distinguishes between the rigors of keeping the law to gain standing and the freedom God gives through grace, leading to a new life-style of fruit in grace.

MacArthur, John. <u>Galatians</u> **(MacArthur New Testament Commentary). Chicago: Moody, 1987. 221 pp.**

A fairly thorough evangelical work explaining in a lucid way the meaning of sections and verses, with sensitivity to grammar and word meaning. MacArthur places Galatians after Paul's first journey, before the Jerusalem Council in Acts 15 (p. xii). He sees "the Israel of God" in 6:16 as literal Jews who have become saved, not as people of the church per se including Gentiles. As in many commentaries, a discrepancy can occur, as when it is said that Paul finished a second journey to Galatia previous to writing Galatians (p. 118). In most respects the commentary is articulate in helping pastors and lay people grasp matters of the gospel of grace and freedom of the Christian life.

Machen, J. Gresham. <u>Machen's Notes on Galatians</u>**, ed. by J. H. Skilton, in An International Library of Philosophy and Theology, Biblical and Theological Studies. Philadelphia: Presbyterian and Reformed, 1972.**

Skilton combines Machen's comments on 1:1-3:14, added references to Galatians from Machen's other works, and gives a lengthy list of questions on the Greek, two synopses of Galatians, sections such as a discussion relating Galatians to Acts 15 and a discussion on faith and works.

Ramsay, William. <u>A Historical Commentary on Galatians</u>**. Grand Rapids: Baker, 1965.**

Here is a helpful commentary on the historical background of the epistle. Ramsay has been called an outstanding authority on the background of Paul's travels.

Perkins, William. <u>A Commentary on Galatians</u>**, ed. G. T. Sheppard (Pilgrim Classic Commentary). NY: Pilgrim, 1989. 615 pp.**

This is a reprint of the 1617 edition with some grammatical changes and modernizing of spelling. Perkins was a Puritan scholar (1558-1602) of the Reformed Church of England. This is his last work before death, a good verse by verse study that elucidates much of the epistle. Presaging it are introductory chapters by Sheppard, B. S. Childs and J. H. Augustine.

Ridderbos, H. N. <u>The Epistle of Paul to the Churches of Galatia</u> **(NIC). Grand Rapids: Eerdmans, 1953.**

This is a work more lucid than the more technical commentaries like Betz, Burton, Eadie and Lightfoot. It is good on the English text, with accurate knowledge of the Greek, but Betz, Burton, Eadie and Lightfoot are more valuable as are Bruce, Fung, Hendriksen, Longenecker, and MacArthur. Fung has replaced it.

Stott, John. **The Message of Galatians.** **London:** **InterVarsity, 1968.**

Here is a short but provocative expository treatment of the text. It is well-suited for the preacher/teacher or the interested layman and highly readable. It is now called Only One Way (IVP) and is in The Bible Speaks Today series.

Strauss, Lehman. **Galatians and Ephesians.** **NY:** **Loizeaux, 1957.**

The contribution of this work is mainly in its popular and simple expository method. Strauss, an outstanding Bible conference speaker, expounds the books somewhat like Ironside, but in more detail and with careful homiletical points.

Tenney, Merrill C. **Galatians: Charter of Christian Liberty.** **Grand Rapids: Eerdmans, 1950.**

The author presents a study of the epistle by using different methods of Bible study. It is difficult to find help on any given problem or passage.

X. EPHESIANS

Abbott, T. K. **A Critical and Exegetical Commentary on the Epistles to the Ephesians and to the Colossians (ICC).** **Edinburgh:** **T. & T. Clark, 1897.**

From the grammatical and philological standpoint, this is a desirable commentary. However, some of the material is not particularly helpful in unfolding meaning which the expositor can give in a normal presentation. On problems it is generally one of the most helpful for the careful and trained expositor who wants to view different sides to a question.

Barth, Marcus. **Ephesians.** **2 volumes (Anchor Bible).** **Garden City, NY: Doubleday, 1974.**

Ephesians is held to be by Paul, written from prison in Rome to Gentile Christians of the church at Ephesus. Barth, Professor of New Testament at Basel, has provided a detailed and very highly contributing commentary with footnotes and also bibliographies on each section of the epistle, acquainting the serious student with scholarly work up to 1974.

Bruce, F. F. **The Epistle to the Ephesians.** **Old Tappan, NJ:** **Fleming H. Revell, 1974rp.**

A frequently helpful brief commentary that touches on most main issues. One of the better brief works by an evangelical of scholarly stature.

Bruce, F. F. The Epistles to the Colossians, to Philemon and to the Ephesians (New International Commentary on the New Testament). Grand Rapids: Eerdmans, 1984. 442 pp.

This is a revision of his work on Colossians when he teamed in 1957 with E. K. Simpson (Ephesians) in the NICNT. It is also a replacement for J. Jac Muller's Philippians and Philemon in the NICNT, the Philemon part of it. Here, Bruce gives a longer introduction to Colossians and often more detail on views, along with footnote additions updating the work. Ephesians is given 170 pages and problems usually dealt with well, certainly with more help than Simpson's effort that was mostly eloquence and little solid content. The Ephesians part differs from Bruce's Revell publication of 1961, 1974. He feels that there is no solid proof that Onesimus was a runaway slave; he may have gone on business and not returned promptly enough (p. 197). Bruce is incisive and careful on many of the problems, furnishing a first-class commentary.

Criswell, W. A. Ephesians: An Exposition. Grand Rapids: Zondervan, 1974.

Criswell's 36 preached messages are printed, giving good detail on some matters, but passing over others, which can be frustrating. For the most part the doctrinal and exegetical basis underlying these studies is sound, and preachers will find some ideas for their own messages (cf. also his books on Genesis, Daniel, Matthew, and Revelation giving expository messages).

Eadie, John. Commentary on the Epistle to the Ephesians. Grand Rapids: Zondervan (n. d.). Reprint of 1883 edition by T. & T. Clark.

Eadie though outdated is good on the Greek text, often deals with problems quite extensively, and has a warm devotional spirit.

Foulkes, F. The Letter of Paul to the Ephesians: An Introduction and Commentary (Tyndale New Testament Commentary). 2nd ed. Grand Rapids: Eerdmans, 1989. 189 pp.

This revises his commentary of the 1960's, using the RSV and updating introductory matters. Foulkes' work is a good evangelical tracing of Paul's flow of thought, summing up sections, looking at views and arguments, dealing competently with words and exegesis, but sometimes being more brief than many readers would like.

Gnilka, J. Der Epheserbrief, in Herder's theologischer Kommentar zum Neuen Testament, Band (Vol.) X, No. 2. Freiburg/Vienna: Herder, 1971.

Gnilka, in this detailed commentary, views Ephesians as a pseudonymous epistle. His work is one example of higher critical handling of Ephesians. Gnilka's conclusion is by no means necessary. Cf. A. van Roon's The Authenticity of Ephesians (Leiden: E. J. Brill, 1974), translated from a theological dissertation at Leiden University under Dr. G. Sevenster in 1969. The conclusion of van Roon (p. 440), after considering various factors in great detail, is: "that it is not only plausible but even probable that Paul was the author of Ephesians."

Hendriksen, William. Epistle to the Ephesians. Grand Rapids: Baker, 1966.

The works of Hendriksen on Bible books are all worth having. Here, as always, he is scholarly, detailed, and warm in his comments.

Hoehner, Harold. "Ephesians," in Bible Knowledge Commentary, ed. John F. Walvoord and Roy B. Zuck, Volume II. Wheaton: Victor Books, 1985.

An outstanding New Testament scholar from Dallas Theological Seminary who gained his Ph. D. at Cambridge University has done this very fine, brief study, packing in much judicious explanation that helps the user. Hoehner is perceptive on problem phrases, as when he interprets "this" (touto) in 2:8 as referring back to the entire phrase involving salvation (p. 624), and when he discusses the "mystery" not being made known to men in Old Testament times "as" it has now been revealed, and gives five arguments for his view (629). He meets other problems head on (cf., for example, "one baptism," 4:5; "lower parts," 4:11; etc.). The section on the armor seems quite well-done. Overall, this is one of the more helpful commentaries despite its brevity (pp. 613-45 in double columns), tying together things that relate exegetically and doctrinally. Hoehner is well along on a detailed work on Ephesians for the Wycliffe Exegetical Commentary (now Baker Exegetical Commentary). It ought to be a standout.

Hughes, R. Kent. Ephesians: The Mystery of the Body of Christ (Preaching the Word). Westchester, IL: Crossway Books/Good News Publishers, 1990. 304 pp.

Cf. comment under Gospel of Mark. Hughes has a highly readable, practical exposition that is refreshing for any Christian's series of devotions. He not only explains Ephesians competently in a broad, sweeping fashion, but relates it winsomely and vitally to the Christian's life today. It is like an alpine breeze in its spiritually invigorating tone, while keeping true to the text.

Kent, Homer A., Jr. Ephesians, The Glory of the Church. Chicago: Moody, 1971.

A well-organized, evangelical survey that is good to have laymen read during a series on the book. Kent is aware of main views and issues in popular exposition of the meaning in an interesting fashion.

Lincoln, Andrew. Ephesians (Word Bible Commentary). Waco, TX: Word Books, 1990.

This detailed evangelical effort ranks at the top or near the best in overall exegetical explanation. Lincoln shows immense reading, views, reasons, turning of details, summary, and often judicious decisions.

Loane, Marcus L. Three Letters From Prison. Studies in Ephesians, Colossians and Philemon. Waco, TX: Word, 1972.

The archbishop of Sydney, known also for his work The Hope of Glory on Romans 8, comments only on a key passage from each chapter (but does all of Philemon): Ephesians 1:13-14; 2:4-9; 3:14-21; 4:29-32; 5:15-21; 6:10-18;

Colossians 1:9, 12-18; 2:8-15; 3:5-11; 4:1-6. What he says is suggestive for popular speaking but will not rank with the better commentaries on the passages.

Lloyd-Jones, D. Martyn.   Expositions on Ephesians.   **8 volumes under their various individual titles.   Grand Rapids: Baker, 1972-82.**

These are sermons by the reputed evangelical preacher of London's Westminster Chapel, who died in 1981. They are very choice/popular material, competent, perceptive, highly edifying and provocative on key points of faith, as well as helpful in planning sermons or Bible studies. Lloyd-Jones stood staunchly for fundamentals of the Christian faith, and also knew how to help people see the relation of verses to practical living. His volumes cover chapters 1, 2, 3, 4:1-16, 4:17-5:17, 5:18-6:9, 6:10-13, 6:10-20 (this volume goes back and covers vv. 10-13 again but the sermons are new). There are many rich, helpful comments on the husband-wife relationship in 5:21-33. The volume on 6:10-20 is quite instructive on being a good soldier and warring a good warfare.

MacArthur, John.   Ephesians (MacArthur New Testament Commentary).   Chicago: Moody, 1986.   402 pp.

The expository focus in the 29 sections is on laying hold of resources in Christ. MacArthur is at his best when explaining details of spiritual life, as he richly does here. Salvation is of grace, without merit of any kind (pp. 11, 23, 61-62). Redemption is seen more clearly in its aspects in 1:7. Comments on the Christian life (3:14-21; chapters 4-6) are instructive and refreshing. The author makes word meanings clear, as "worthy" (axios) in 4:1, prefers seeing "one baptism" as water baptism, has a good section on gifts and gifted people (4:7-11) and on each believer functioning in his or her role (4:12-16). He points out seven questions to ask in principle in deciding whether to drink wine (pp. 237-44). He develops the Spirit-filled life in much detail (5:18-21), as in a husband's love for his wife and her submission to him (5:21ff.). The section on the armor and prayer are edifying too. It is a lucid exposition, quite full at many points on essential matters, often helpful on problems, though not in great detail.

Martin, Alfred.   "Ephesians," in Wycliffe Bible Commentary, ed. C. F. Pfeiffer and E. F. Harrison.   Chicago: Moody, 1962.

The Dean of the Faculty and Professor of Old Testament Synthesis at Moody Bible Institute prepared this worthy commentary surveying Ephesians. While Martin has meaningful comments on verses usually, he is helpful on problem texts concisely (time of the Spirit sealing, 1:13; etc.). At points he states his view but leaves readers unclear as to his proof (2:8, "this"; 4:4, "one baptism," etc.). Hoehner's work is much better in giving substance to his views in a brief commentary.

Martin, Ralph P. "Ephesians," in <u>New Bible Commentary Revised</u>, ed. D. Guthrie et al. Grand Rapids: Eerdmans, 1970.

A concise evangelical summary showing awareness of issues and reasons but not as useful as often as Hoehner's similar brief work.

Patzia, A. G. <u>Ephesians, Colossians and Philemon</u> (New International Biblical Commentary). Peabody, MA: Hendrickson, 1991. 311 pp.

This work, based on the NIV, is too brief. Of course it provides some help, even rather frequently, but it is not right to the issues and reasons often enough to rank with the best of even brief works.

Paxson, Ruth. <u>Ephesians: The Wealth, Walk and Warfare of the Christian</u>. NY: Revell, 1939.

This is one of the richest devotional works on the English text. There is much spiritual insight, good outlines suggestive for preaching, and very colorful and refreshing phrases which leave the reader blessed with his unfathomable wealth in Christ. The comments are sprinkled with illustrations which are choice. For the most part it follows the epistle closely, but the author also uses Ephesians as a springboard into lengthy but rich discussions of vital subjects. For example, there is a systematic study of the different aspects of Satanic attack upon the believer in connection with 6.10ff. This work is edifying on the English text and is excellent for laymen.

Robinson, J. Armitage. <u>St. Paul's Epistle to the Ephesians: A Revised Text and Translation with Exposition and Notes</u>. 2nd ed. Grand Rapids: Kregel, 1979rp of 1904 revision. 314 pp.

Some rated this or Westcott as the best older commentary on the Greek text. It is valuable. It has been regarded well since 1904 for its sometimes valuable use of grammar and its exegesis. Other works have replaced its great usefulness by fuller discussions and awareness of later scholarly study on the issues.

Stedman, Ray. <u>Body Life</u>. Glendale: Gospel Light, 1972.

These chapters were originally clear, discerning messages taught by the late Pastor Stedman at the Peninsula Bible Church, Palo Alto, California. They explain Ephesians 4:1-16 competently and refreshingly, with many excellent indictments of failure to follow Paul's words in church-life today as well as many telling insights pointing the way Christ would have His people go. The book is one of the finest on this section of Ephesians and particularly contributes on 4:11-16.

Stoeckhardt, George. <u>Commentary on St. Paul's Letter to the Ephesians</u>. Translated Martin S. Sommer. St. Louis: Concordia, 1952.

The author lived in 1842-1913. The introduction of 32 pp. is soundly evangelical and shows a good awareness of critical views up to 1908, the arguments of which he discusses at some length and competently. He defends in detail the Ephesian destination (cf. p. 29). Constantly using Greek phrases, he explains in detail which helps general readers grasp much of the picture. However, some Greek grammar and Latin phrases are not explained for the uninitiated. The author often mentions differing views (cf. "in one body," 2:15, p. 149; "foundation of the apostles . . . ," 2:20, pp. 152-53 etc.) but supports his own from the context. Sometimes he does not give a second view (cf. "one baptism," 4:4-6, p. 180). But in most verses he offers rather detailed comments that cover the main points with competent awareness theologically and exegetically.

Stott, John R. W.   One People.   Downers Grove, IL: InterVarsity, 1968.

Discusses the clergy and the laity according to the New Testament metaphors for the church, the training and service of the laity, and fellowship in the church. It is helpful in relation to Ephesians 4:1-16.

Westcott, B. F.   The Epistle to the Ephesians.   Grand Rapids: Eerdmans, reprint, 1950.

Detailed and scholarly, this much respected old work is helpful in grammar and problems on the more technical side. Several commentaries now offer even more help.

XI. PHILIPPIANS

Abbott, T. K.   Cf. on Ephesians.

Beare, F. W.   A Commentary on the Epistle to the Philippians (Harper's New Testament Commentary).   NY: Harper & Row, 1959.

While this is a liberal work, it has much to offer on explanation of the text because the author wrestles with issues on hard verses.

Boice, James.   Exposition of Philippians.   Grand Rapids: Zondervan, 1971.

A lucid and very readable simple exposition that is helpful and competent on many of the issues. The work is geared more to simple study. The exposition is practical and sermonic, with sometimes good background and comparison with relevant passages from other Scripture. He illustrates heavily from literature, history, and contemporary life.

Bruce, F. F.   Philippians (New International Biblical Commentary).   Peabody, MA: Hendrickson, 1989.   208 pp.

This concise but direct and well-informed work by an evangelical giant among commentators was formerly in the Good News Commentary (San Francisco: Harper and Row, 1983). It has switched to the NIV, and Bruce before his death brought the citations of literature up to date. It has frequent comments that help, but the pastor or student will no doubt wish to use more detailed works too.

Collange, Jean-Francois. The Epistle of Saint Paul to the Philippians. London: Epworth Press, 1979.

A highly-praised French work seeing much use among scholars for its interaction with recent literature and views and often incisive comments on passages. Its liberal leanings at too many points limit its usefulness among staunch conservatives, yet employed by a mature and discerning student it yields substantial help at points.

Getz, Gene. A Profile of Christian Maturity. A Study of Philippians with 20th Century Lessons for Your Church. Grand Rapids: Zondervan, 1976.

A provocative catalyst for personal study, application and growth, or group or family use, this is a well-organized little book. Each chapter has several parts: Something to Think About, A Look at Paul's Letters, What Did Paul Say?, What Did Paul Mean?, Application, Life Response, and A Project. Each of the fourteen chapters takes a few verses, dealing briefly and simply with them.

Gnilka, J. Der Philipperbrief, in Herder's theologischer Kommentar zum Neuen Testament, Band X, Faszikel 3. Freiburg/Vienna: Herder, 1968.

If one wishes to see a thorough-going redaction-critical approach to Philippians, this 226-page study by a Catholic will be relevant. Gnilka believes that the epistle joins two original letters that were later redacted (1:1—3:1a, 4:2-7, 10-23, and 3:1b—4:1, 8-9, cf. his introduction). Gnilka thinks that the epistle originated in Ephesus while Paul was on his third journey. He also includes excursuses on episkopos and diakonos, "to be with Christ," the hymn in 2:6-11 which he believes to be pre-Pauline and the heresies related to the letter. The commentary is somewhat helpful in acquainting readers with discussions of research by those Gnilka regards as scholarly on various issues in Philippians, but one will not find an awareness of evangelical works here.

Gromacki, Robert G. Stand United in Joy. Grand Rapids, MI: Baker Book House, 1980.

Gromacki, Professor of Bible and Greek and Chairman of Biblical Education at Cedarville College in Ohio, has written this 197-pp. exposition for the New Testament Studies Commentary. The volume is divided into thirteen chapters and is an ideal tool for adult Bible study or Sunday School curricula. The author has included discussion questions of a relevant nature at the conclusion of each chapter. Gromacki's grasp of Philippians is evident from his thorough treatment of several difficult passages. He devotes an appropriate amount of space to the more difficult issues (e.g., Kenosis in 2:6-8) while not allowing less controversial areas to suffer. He is careful to include all lexical and syntactical information in a transliterated Greek form so that the layman can benefit. Gromacki places Philippians within Paul's first Roman imprisonment (59-61 A. D.). In his introduction, Gromacki also includes a helpful graphic relating Epaphroditus to Philippians and harmonizing other Biblical accounts. A brief work suitable for the layman, pastor or seminary student. — Jan Sattem

Gwyn-Thomas, John. <u>Rejoice . . . Always! Studies in Philippians 4.</u> **Carlisle, PA: Banner of Truth Trust, 1989. 159 pp.**

A pastor in Cambridge, England, gives messages on the one chapter, explaining verses perceptively and sensitively and relating how they apply today. J. I. Packer commends the book and the author in the introduction, saying that Gwyn-Thomas is a good spiritual shepherd.

Hawthorne, Gerald F. <u>Philippians</u> **(Word Biblical Commentary). Waco, TX: Word Books, 1983. 232 pp.**

Some rank this as the top commentary on Philippians due to the wide reading and masterfully good survey on introductory questions and its carefulness on grammar, philology, capture of the epistle's flow and handling of difficult passages such as 2:5-11, plus its frequent bibliographical lists that are so current. Cf. Hawthorne's shorter book of 1987 which sums up the detail here (<u>Philippians</u>, also Word Books, 118 pp.). In the summation work, he focuses on topics of theology, aiming to help pastors, Sunday school teachers and lay persons in general. Knowledge of Greek will help a reader follow quite a lot of the more thorough work. Hawthorne has indeed provided a wealth of help. He feels that Paul's opponents were Jewish missionaries rather than Judaizing "Christians" as Lightfoot held. He is evangelical, a faculty member at Wheaton College.

Hendriksen, William. <u>Exposition of Philippians.</u> **Grand Rapids: Baker, 1961.**

This work is based upon the Greek text but is not technical. It is rich devotionally and has a wealth of good commentary material. It is very helpful on problem passages (example, 3:1-2; 4:1-3), giving different views and coming to a conclusion, often with good reasoning.

Kent, Homer A. Jr. **"Philippians," in** <u>Expositor's Bible Commentary,</u> **Volume 11, ed. Frank Gaebelein and J. D. Douglas. Grand Rapids: Zondervan, 1978.**

A writer of many commentaries and a professor and past president at Grace Theological Seminary furnishes a substantial work that comes to grips with most of the issues in a clear evangelical competency. This one ranks high in its frequency of usefulness on views, reasons, etc.

King, Guy. <u>The Joy Way.</u> **London: Marshall, Morgan & Scott, 1952.**

This devotional commentary is rich in illustrations and sermonic material. Its style is vivid and interesting. It is a very good book to recommend to a layman and will do the preacher's heart much good! It may only be available at some school libraries.

Lightfoot, John B.   Commentary on the Epistle of St. Paul to the Philippians.   Grand Rapids: Zondervan, 1953.

This 1879 work is outstanding in Greek exegesis and thus is valuable to have. Other commentaries like Hendriksen, King, Robertson and Rees will have to supply the devotional aspect.

Lightner, Robert.   "Philippians," in Bible Knowledge Commentary, ed. John F. Walvoord and Roy B. Zuck, Volume II.   Wheaton: Victor Books, 1985.

An author of many books, this Professor of Systematic Theology at Dallas Theological Seminary contributes a worthy survey that touches contributively on many of the problem verses, taking a stand and giving reasons concisely.

Lloyd-Jones, D. Martyn.   The Life of Joy and The Life of Peace.   2 volumes on Philippians.   Grand Rapids: Baker, 1989.

Typical rich pastoral comments from a master preacher well-known for his Studies in the Sermon on the Mount and expositions such as on Romans, Ephesians and 2 Peter. This work has been republished from the Bristish edition of 1989, and gives messages preached at Westminster Chapel in 1947-48. Devotionally it ranks as one of the more capable and refreshing efforts to stimulate pastors and lay readers.

Martin, Ralph P.   Carmen Christi (Philippians 2:5-11).   Cambridge: University Press, 1967.

An exhaustive work on various views and thought on the verses based on immensely wide, thorough study. The work will acquaint the reader with various facets of this early Christian hymn and concepts of how it fits into its passage.

Martin, Ralph P.   The Epistle to the Philippians: An Introduction and Commentary (Tyndale New Testament Commentary).   Grand Rapids: Eerdmans, 1987.

This is a revision and updating after the 1959 edition by one of America's foremost evangelical New Testament scholars. It is usually insightful on meanings of verses in view of Greek grammar and exegesis and shows a fairly frequent use of other scholarly literature, critical positions, etc.

Martin, Ralph P.   Commentary on Philippians (New Century Bible Commentary).   Grand Rapids: Eerdmans, 1980.

Here Martin shows more use of critical sources and must be used with discernment since he has been inclined away from some of his older, some will feel more defensible positions. Conservatives will probably prefer his Tyndale effort for its theological convictions.

Meyer, F. B.   Devotional Commentary on Philippians.   Grand Rapids: Kregel, 1979.

One of the famous English devotional writers and spiritual life speakers during the late 19th century and early 20th authored this perceptive and easy-flowing book. Lay persons as well as pastors and Bible teachers looking for a work that speaks to the heart and offers many insights into a deeper maturity in commitments of faith will find this a fresh breath. Meyer is known well for his series on Bible characters — Abraham, Moses, Elijah, etc.

Motyer, J. Alec.   Philippian Studies: The Richness of Christ.   Chicago: InterVarsity, 1966.

A committed British evangelical Christian scholar has done this series of carefully-considered studies on the whole of the book. He deals with problems briefly, but with awareness (those who preach with envy, 1:15; 3:11, etc.), and also says many things that are enriching and highly readable for growing Christians and also stimulating for preachers, teachers, and anyone who speaks on the book.

Motyer, J. Alec.   The Message of Philippians (Bible Speaks Today).   Downers Grove: IVP, 1984.   234 pp.

This work, distinct from his 1966 Philippian Studies, is a lucid exposition of twenty- four sections, using the RSV text and a clear outline. Motyer (pronounced Mo-teer) gives good synopses of sections, keeps connections in the flow of thought in view, and deals with verses in an engaging style. He seems sound exegetically, theologically and applicationally. He defines many key Greek words such as those for "citizenship" (p. 93), "walk" (p. 181), etc. and offers an articulate discussion of many of the problems. Many references are footnoted, helping the readability. The work is stimulating for expositors but also for any lay person who wants to use a book with an attractive, simple flow without delving into technical points other works handle.

Moule, H. C. G.   The Epistle to the Philippians.   Grand Rapids: Baker, 1981rp.

Originally contributing to the Cambridge Greek Testament series in 1897, Moule still provides a very helpful treatment of the Greek text at an exegetical and devotional level. The author excels in blending the devotional and applicational with the analytical. — Dan Phillips

Muller, Jac. J.   The Epistles of Paul to the Philippians and to Philemon (NIC).   Grand Rapids: Eerdmans, 1955.

This is one of the more detailed commentaries that grapples with interpretations of problem verses. It ranks close to Bruce, Hendriksen, Lightfoot, Martin (Tyndale) and Robertson along this line but is not close to Hawthorne.

Mounce, Robert H.   "Philippians," in Wycliffe Bible Commentary, ed. C. F. Pfeiffer and E. H. Harrison.   Chicago: Moody, 1962.

Another competent, concise study by an evangelical, about as helpful as Lightner's entry, usually substantial on the issues verse by verse. He has had the space to write more at length in his works on Matthew and Revelation.

Pentecost, J. Dwight. <u>The Joy of Living</u>. **Grand Rapids: Zondervan, 1974.**

A simple and practical exposition by a fine Bible teacher on the Dallas Seminary faculty. Pentecost explains the book verse by verse and richly relates and illustrates how the truths can apply to daily Christian lives of joy.

Rees, Paul. <u>The Adequate Man: Studies in Philippians</u>. **London: Marshall, Morgan & Scott, 1958.**

A lucid devotional work, this book follows the thought of the epistle closely and deals with it in a rich sermonic way. There are many choice phrases and fitting illustrations which illumine the text, plus suggestive outlines. The author's central purpose is to show that the believer can live a wholly adequate life, like Paul, by divine resource. This is another recommended book which will be especially enjoyed by laymen in the church. It is usually sound from the standpoint of the Greek.

Rees, Paul S. <u>The Epistles to the Philippians, Colossians, and Philemon</u> **(Proclaiming the New Testament). Grand Rapids: Baker, 1964.**

A good attempt at bringing out homiletic points sometimes richly suggestive for preaching.

Robertson, Archibald T. <u>Paul's Joy in Christ</u>. **NY: Revell, 1917.**

Though he discusses Philippians in his Word Pictures, Robertson here devotes an entire detailed book on the epistle. He is rich in word studies and in the explanation of the text.

Silva, Moises. <u>Philippians</u> **(Wycliffe Exegetical Commentary). Chicago: Moody, 1988. 255 pp.**

A high-quality evangelical production, usually with good insights into the Greek and handling of different views in the current literature. Silva's is the first in this conservative, scholarly series. On many of the verses he is top-notch in perceiving and addressing issues in a clear wording. He sees two groups against Paul, true Jewish Christians holding that grace ideas led Paul too far in freedom from the law (Philippians 1) and Judaizers within the Christian circle (Philippians 3). The theme to Silva is not joy as many say but a steadfast continuance in sanctification, victorious over difficulties. Silva is saturated with a wide sweep of writings and carefully weighs interpretations.

Strauss, Lehman. <u>Studies in Philippians</u>. **NY: Loizeaux, 1959.**

A homiletical and lucid exposition with a wealth of helpful practical comments mingled into the explanation.

Walvoord, John F. <u>Philippians, Triumph in Christ</u>. **Chicago: Moody, 1971.**

A simple exposition of the book which is readable for the average lay person.

Wuest, Kenneth S.   Philippians in the Greek New Testament.   Grand Rapids: Eerdmans, 1942.

> This is one of Wuest's better expositions of a book. He is often sound in the Greek, explaining the text verse by verse and giving helpful word studies. Though he uses the Greek, he does not reproduce it in his book and so his commentary is very helpful even to the Christian who does not know Greek. Again, this is a good book to recommend to laymen as well as to use for preaching and teaching.

XII. COLOSSIANS

Abbott, T. K.   Cf. on Ephesians.

Bruce, F. F.   Cf. on Ephesians.

Ellis, E. Earl.   "Colossians," in Wycliffe Bible Commentary, ed. C. F. Pfeiffer and E. F. Harrison.   Chicago: Moody, 1962.

> A solid, concise survey by an evangelical, helping on verse by verse issues and on special problem texts.

Griffith-Thomas, W. H.   Christ Pre-eminent.   Chicago: Moody, 1923.

> A former noted Bible teacher, author of many books, did this refreshing focus on Christ in Colossians. He is articulate, sometimes provocative, and usually helpful for edification.

Gromacki, Robert G.   Stand Perfect in Wisdom: An Exposition of Colossians and Philemon.   Grand Rapids: Baker, 1981.

> A sound survey that keeps the flow of the books in mind, explains verses fairly well, and deals with some of the problems with insight. This work will be most helpful for lay reading and for Sunday School and Bible class teachers who need a simple, competent study to guide them.

Harris, Murray J.   Colossians and Philemon (Exegetical Guide to the Greek New Testament).   Grand Rapids: Eerdmans, 1991.

> This is the first of twenty commentaries planned in this new series. Harris, who has the fine commentary on the second letter to the Corinthians and teaches New Testament at Trinity Evangelical Divinity School, helps a person who is beginning to review his Greek to see, paragraph by paragraph, a structural analysis of every phrase and every word and virtually every feature of the message the Greek text conveys. One learns much in the Greek about the two epistles and also gets some homiletical suggestions from a meticulous scholar.

Hendriksen, Wm. Epistles to Colossians and Philemon. Grand Rapids: Baker, 1964.

See comments on John, Philippians. The same applies here.

Johnson, S. Lewis. "Studies in the Epistle to the Colossians," Bib. Sac. 118 (July—Sept., 1961) to 121 (Oct.—Dec., 1964).

One of the best discussions of Colossians verse by verse, with help on difficulties and evaluation of different interpretations, written by a former professor at Dallas Seminary who is outstanding as an exegete, expositor, and theologian. Johnson also has taught at Trinity Evangelical Divinity School.

Hughes R. Kent. Colossians and Philemon: The Supremacy of Christ (Preaching the Word). Westchester, IL: Crossway Books/Good News Publishers, 1989. 183 pp.

The evaluation here is much along the lines of his works on Mark and Ephesians. In vivid strokes he causes the vital message for Christians to be seen, and gives ideas to expositors as well as refreshing any Christians who read it in a devotional series.

Kent, Homer A., Jr. Treasures of Wisdom: Studies in Colossians & Philemon. Grand Rapids: Baker, 1978.

A clear, brief commentary that is very aware of problem verses such as 1:15 and even provides knowledge from Greek words, context, etc. to resolve them competently. Excellent footnotes from good sources help. The author served several years as President of Grace Theological Seminary and Professor of New Testament.

Lightfoot, John B. Commentary of the Epistles of St. Paul to the Colossians and Philemon. Grand Rapids: Zondervan, 1959.

Lightfoot is excellent in this 1865 work revised in 1879. His work on Colossians 1:15 ("first-born of every creature") is especially helpful on a problem text. Many regard the commentary as the best older work on the Greek text.

Lohse, Eduard. Colossians and Philemon (Hermeneia). Philadelphia: Fortress Press, 1971.

Though expensive, this is a very fine commentary for the teacher who wants an exacting inquiry into the text and possible background, and the benefit of Lohse's wide acquaintance with literature on or related to Colossians. Good use of Jewish and Hellenistic backgrounds, references to Qumran material that Lohse feels relates to thoughts in these epistles, and fine acquaintance with much scholarly work.

Lucas, R. C. <u>Fullness & Freedom: The Message of Colossians & Philemon</u> **(The Bible Speaks Today series). Downers Grove, IL: IVP, 1980.**

The rector of St. Helen's Church, Bishopsgate in London, wrote this work which is not a "commentary" but an accurate, readable exposition keyed to practical life. His fresh style is akin to John R. W. Stott's in the same series (<u>Only One Way</u>, on Galatians; <u>God's New Society</u>, on Ephesians, etc.). Lucas is aware of some problems and draws from Lightfoot, E. Lohse and others. While comments on many areas are good, brevity that the series necessitates makes some discussions disappointing, as on 1:15. The introduction to Philemon is good on slavery, yet one is astonished to find less that a page verse by verse. The main message of fullness and freedom beams brightly.

Martin, Ralph P. <u>Colossians and Philemon</u> **(New Century Bible). Revised ed. Greenwood, SC: Attic Press, 1978. 174 pp.**

A work of good competence by a recognized New Testament scholar, one of whose concentrations has been Colossians. He shows awareness of scholarly knowledge about backgrounds, views on problems and defense of his exegesis verse by verse.

Martin, Ralph P. <u>Colossians. The Church's Lord and the Christian's Liberty. An Expository Commentary with a Present-Day Application</u>. **Grand Rapids: Zondervan, 1973.**

Using the RSV text, Martin comments section by section in simple exposition backed by careful study on issues. This is a fine brief work.

O'Brien, Peter T. <u>Colossians, Philemon</u> **(Word Biblical Commentary). Waco: Word, 1982.**

A close and careful study of the Greek text, reflecting familiarity with journal articles, doctrinally satisfying from an evangelical perspective. O'Brien defends Pauline authorship for the letters, notes the existence of 44 different suggestions for the identity of the Colossian heresy before making a cautious and sound suggestion (which offers some help). Faces doctrinally difficult passages and phrases (1:15, 19; 2:llf.) squarely and with generally satisfying results (i.e affirming Paul's teaching on male headship in the home [3:18] as against modern predilections to the contrary). — Dan Phillips

Patzia, A. G. Cf. on Ephesians.

Peake, A. S. **"The Epistle to the Colossians," in** <u>The Expositor's Greek Testament</u>, **Volume 3. Grand Rapids: Eerdmans, 1951.**

One of the older, much-used commentaries, which offers considerable help on Greek words, grammar, background etc. and will prove rather contributive, consulted along with newer and longer studies.

Rees, Paul S. Cf. on Philippians.

Robertson, A. T.   Paul and the Intellectuals.   NY: Doubleday, 1928.

This exposition of the epistle comes from the Stone Lectures at Princeton Seminary in 1926. Robertson is helpful in the Greek and on the background.

Schweizer, E.   The Letter to the Colossians: A Commentary.   Minneapolis: Augsburg, 1982.   230 pp.

A highly-regarded work translated from the German. It is profitable often in exegesis, setting and discussion of many of the problems with awareness of views and reasons. It is liberal, technical to some degree, and will contribute well to serious students here and there.

Simpson, E. K. and F. F. Bruce.   Commentary on the Epistles to the Ephesians and the Colossians (NIC).   Grand Rapids: Eerdmans, 1957.

In the opinion of the reviewer, while the portion on Ephesians is not of great help, the work on Colossians by Bruce is excellent. It is worth the price of the book.

Vaughn, Curtis.   "Colossians," in Expositor's Bible Commentary, ed. Frank Gaebelein and J. D. Douglas.   Grand Rapids: Zondervan, 1978.

Author of several commentaries, Vaughn writes clearly but concisely, giving the reader help on most verses and sometimes good insights on problems. It often is substantial, but compared to longer evangelical works it is not as valuable.

Vaughn, Curtis.   Colossians and Philemon (Bible Study Commentary).   Grand Rapids: Zondervan, 1981.

A brief, well-ordered survey that sums up sections, keeps the flow of the books before the reader, and dips into some verses to make the meaning clear for lay people. At times it deals rather well with problems, but for the most part one will need to consult more detailed, scholarly works geared to that aim. Curtis is evangelical.

Wright, N. T.   The Epistles of Paul to the Colossians and to Philemon (Tyndale New Testament Commentary).   Grand Rapids: Eerdmans, 1988.

As is typical of this evangelical series, readers are given concise but well-thought-out comments on verses, some aid on difficult texts with reasons, and clarity.

XIII. FIRST AND SECOND THESSALONIANS

Best, Ernest.   The First and Second Epistles to the Thessalonians (Harper's New Testament Commentaries).   NY: Harper & Row, 1973.

A work with various liberal ideas, yet with much that a more serious and discerning student can find helpful on the detail of the Greek. Among more thorough technical studies this is widely acclaimed to be high on the list. Best acquaints readers with much in scholarly literature of recent years.

Bruce, F. F. <u>1 and 2 Thessalonians</u> **(Word Biblical Commentary). Waco, TX: Word Books, 1982. 228 pp.**

Exegesis of the Greek text. Disappointingly brief and vague in some respects for a series as ambitious as this one. Though taking <u>orgē</u> in 1 Thessalonians 1:10 and 5:9 to mean divine wrath at the end-time, Bruce does not seriously interact with any recent dispensational literature in examining 1 Thessaalonians 4 or 5. In analyzing II Thessalonians 2, the only dispensationalist cited is Kelly (1903), with an allusion to Darby and a dismissal of the school of thought; citation of Walvoord's <u>Blessed Hope and the Tribulation</u> in the bibliography, but no inter-action. Seems to see 1 Thessalonians 2:15-16 as a later insertion, presumably by a later anti-Semitic Gentile (pp. 48-51). Bruce is highly-regarded on exegesis and also on his skillful use of current literature. Those with training in Greek will be able to follow technical aspects in the notes and comments. He sees no distinction between "day of the Lord" and "day of Christ" etc., and disagrees with dispensational thinking that the rapture occurs before the "day of the Lord." This was the first work out in the 52-volume series. Also cf. Bruce, "1 and 2 Thessalonians," <u>New Bible Commentary Revised</u>, ed. D. Guthrie et al. Grand Rapids: Eerdmans, 1970.— Dan Phillips

Constable, Thomas. **"I and II Thessalonians," in** <u>Bible Knowledge Commentary</u>, **ed. John F. Walvoord and Roy B. Zuck, Volume II. Wheaton: Victor Books, 1985.**

A diligently prepared brief work by an evangelical, who explains well verse by verse and deals well with many of the difficult passages. He deals with passages about the rapture and "Day of the Lord" (I Thessalonians 4-5; II Thessalonians 2) in a premillennial, dispensational way. A similar but more detailed effort of this nature is in the commentary by Robert L. Thomas. Constable is quite helpful in giving views, for example in regard to problems in II Thessalonians 2:1-12. He takes the restrainer to be the Holy Spirit.

Frame, J. E. <u>A Critical and Exegetical Commentary on the Epistles of St. Paul to the Thessalonians</u> **(ICC). Edinburgh: T. & T. Clark, 1912.**

This is one of the works to consult on textual/linguistic issues, often at least. But it often does not actually explain the meaning of a passage as well as Best, Bruce, Hendriksen, Hiebert, Marshall, Morris, Thomas, Wanamaker, etc.

Hendriksen, William. <u>First and Second Thessalonians</u>. **Grand Rapids: Baker, 1953.**

As usual, the author is detailed, careful in word meanings and background, lucid and warm in application.

Hiebert, D. Edmond.   <u>The Thessalonian Epistles</u>.   Chicago: Moody, 1971.

This work by Dr. Hiebert, Professor of New Testament, Biblical Seminary, Fresno, California, takes its place among the best on Paul's two eschatological epistles. The author, taking the premillennial, pretribulational view, is not unaware of major interpretive problems, and he fairly presents different sides and then draws his conclusions. Many features make this volume valuable: background information, extensive bibliography, numerous footnotes, and a rich use of the original Greek.

Hogg, C. F. and W. E. Vine.   <u>The Epistles of Paul the Apostle to the Thessalonians</u>.   London: Alfred Holness, 1914.

A premillennial and dispensational work, this commentary is rich in word meanings and details in the Greek.

Lineberry, J.   <u>Vital Word Studies in I Thessalonians. A Sound Scriptural Presentation Based upon the Original Greek</u>.   Grand Rapids: Zondervan, 1960.

The author uses transliterations of Greek words into English to explain in considerable detail what I Thessalonians says in the Greek. He takes a very conservative view, and subscribes to a pretribulation rapture. The commentary is verse by verse and understandable to a serious student who does not know Greek.

Marshall, I. Howard.   <u>1 and 2 Thessalonians</u>.   Grand Rapids, MI: Eerdmans, 1983.

Marshall, Professor in New Testament Exegesis at the University of Aberdeen, Scotland wrote this 240-page volume to update the earlier commentary in this "New Century Bible" series by A. L. Moore. The author deals with much of the post-1972 critical literature bearing on these epistles. He builds upon E. Best's work in the Harper's New Testament Commentaries (1973). Marshall's introductory remarks reflect much awareness and are valuable. His conclusions for Pauline authorship and an early date for both epistles meet with the general consensus of conservative scholars. His verse by verse treatment is regrettably brief. References to the Greek abound, as do references to recent scholarly works. A tremendous help to the seminarian and pastor. —Jan Sattem

Milligan, George.   <u>The Epistles of Paul to the Thessalonians</u>.   NY: Macmillan, 1908.

Some regarded this as the best work on the Greek text. However, it is old, and the works by Best, Bruce, Hendriksen, Hiebert, Hogg and Vine, Marshall, Morris, Thomas and Wanamaker have been more helpful to some.

Morris, Leon.   <u>The Epistles of Paul to the Thessalonians</u> (Tyndale New Testament Commentary).   Grand Rapids: Eerdmans, 1984.   152 pp.   Revision of 1956 and 1959 edition.

This commentary is abreast of recent scholarship and grapples with most of the issues in a helpful way. It is on the English text but based on study of the Greek text, and is more complete than his shorter work done in the Tyndale Series. The revision is mainly along lines of updating with scholarly literature since the

1950's and a change to the NIV rather than the KJV. He argues for a post-tribula-tional rapture view in I Thessalonians 4-5, in distinction to Constable, Lineberry, Ryrie, Thomas and Walvoord. It is a good commentary in most respects, helpful to pastors, students and lay people.

Ryrie, Charles C. The Epistles to the Thessalonians. Chicago: Moody, 1959.

This paperback study is brief but expounds the epistles from the premillennial dispensational viewpoint in a helpful way. The brevity does not allow the author to grapple in a thorough way with the text so as to support his conclusions solid-ly on debated matters (examples: I Thessalonians 5:lff and 2 Thessalonians 1 and 2).

Stott, John R. W. The Gospel and the End of Time. The Message of 1 and 2 Thessalonians. Downers Grove: IVP, 1991. 220 pp.

Stott is evangelical and has unusual ability to write lucidly and sum up things, informed by good scholarly thinking. As in other expositions (Sermon on the Mount, Romans 5-8, Acts, Galatians, Ephesians, etc.) he has good comments. He is too brief on introductory matters (5 pp. on I Thessalonians and 3 on II Thessalonians), but his commentary is well-organized and articulate. He tends to be general quite often here, without detail on verses. One will be refreshed by the flow of the letters, at least. Stott stops at times to deal with problems, as how Satan hindered Paul's return (2:18), what "vessel" means in 4:4. He favors the state as God's agent for punishing evil (p. 170). This is not a top commentary, but will serve lay people in a series of readable devotional segments.

Thomas, Robert. "The Thessalonian Epistles," in Expositor's Bible Commentary, ed. Frank Gaebelein. Grand Rapids: Zondervan, 1976—1992.

Though held to brevity in this series, the Professor of New Testament Literature and Exegesis at The Master's Seminary offers a careful exegetical study rich in many aspects of the Greek and discussion of main views on problems. From the standpoint of a dispensational perspective on verses related to the Lord's com-ing this is the best exegetically-based work.

Walvoord, John F. The Thessalonian Epistles. Findlay, OH: Dunham, 1955.

Written by the former President of Dallas Theological Seminary, this expository work represents the premillennial dispensational approach in the crucial pas-sages on future things. It is along the popular line and is not exegetically detailed.

Wanamaker, Charles A. The Epistles to the Thessalonians (New Testament Greek Text Commentary). Grand Rapids: Eerdmans, 1991. 316 pp.

A new series offering considerable expertise on details of the Greek, views on interpretive issues, lines of argumentation, and interaction with other scholars. It is evangelical. Wanamaker's effort now has to rate among the top works.

Wolff, Richard.   General Epistles of First and Second Thessalonians.   Wheaton: Tyndale House, 1970.

For a study briefer than many, yet competent, this will be helpful.

XIV. PASTORAL EPISTLES

Barrett, C. K.   The Pastoral Epistles in the New English Bible (New Clarendon Bible). Oxford: The Clarendon Press, 1963.

A worthwhile scholarly study that deals well with many of the verses, although sometimes only briefly. Barrett shows, as usual, a good knowledge of scholarly work in recent years on different views.

Bernard, J. H.   The Pastoral Epistles.   Grand Rapids: Baker, 1980.

Earlier this was published in The Cambridge Greek Testament (Cambridge: University, 1922). It is one of the finest older works which grapples seriously with the Greek. Bernard was a fine scholar in his day.

Berry, Harold, J.   Studies in II Timothy. Gems from the Original.   2 volumes. Lincoln, NE: Back to the Bible Broadcast, 1975.

These are concise commentaries that seek to bring out the richness of the epistles for the edification of lay persons. The books are the result of thirty-nine installments originally in the Good News Broadcaster. The author is a graduate of Dallas Seminary.

Blaiklock, E. M.   The Pastoral Epistles: A Study Guide Commentary.   Grand Rapids: Zondervan, 1972.

Blaiklock believes in Pauline authorship (cf. also his entry on "Pastoral Epistles") (Zondervan Pictorial Bible Dictionary). This is a good brief discussion for a quick survey, by a good scholar. He handles some of the problem verses even if very concisely (I Timothy 2:15, etc.), and skips over others (Titus 3:5, etc.). Stimulating questions for discussion are given at the end of each chapter.

Dibelius, Martin, and Hans Conzelmann.   The Pastoral Epistles (Hermeneia). Translated by Philip Buttolph and Adela Yarbro.   Philadelphia: Fortress Press, 1972.

A technical, critical commentary referring the more advanced student to a plethora of scholarly literature and leading him through various form-critical positions. The writers say the Pastorals are not by Paul. Copious footnotes, as in other Hermeneia volumes, refer to recent literature, and the commentary frequently quotes ancient extra-biblical writings that might relate to the language and ideas in the epistles. For slow technical study the work offers some help, but very little along the line of spiritual stimulation from the emphases of the epistles.

Draper, James T., Jr. <u>Titus: Patterns for Church Living</u>. **Wheaton, IL: Tyndale, 1978.**

A 119-pp. evangelical work with popular expositions of a practical character. Draper was pastor of First Baptist, Euless, Texas at the time he wrote this.

Ellicott, Charles J. <u>A Critical and Grammatical Commentary on the Pastoral Epistles</u> **with a revised translation. Andover: Warren F. Draper, 1865.**

Though brief, Ellicott is outstanding in the Greek and very helpful.

Fee, Gordon D. <u>1 and 2 Timothy and Titus</u> **(New International Biblical Commentary). Peabody, MA: Hendrickson, 1988.**

This is a reworking of his 1984 work in the <u>Good News Commentary</u> (San Francisco: Harper and Row). As in his work on I Corinthians, Fee is clear in most cases (not easy to follow when he gets too terse), capable on Greek grammar and local setting, unity and integrity of the books. Each section has a summary. He aims to be of help to teachers, preachers and students. His contribution is that Paul authored the books and wrote to meet specific situations in the churches, not to give a manual for the church as some have held. The work has switched from the GNT to the NIV. Fee is evangelical, and Professor of New Testament at Regent College in Vancouver.

Getz, Gene A. <u>A Profile for a Christian Life-Style. A Study of Titus</u>. **Grand Rapids: Zondervan, 1978.**

Getz has authored several books on character studies and life-style principles in biblical books. Here again he has much practical helpfulness as he points out traits that believers today can emulate in the enabling of the Spirit. The book is simple, well-organized, and contributive for a leader or any Christian in a devotional series day by day.

Guthrie, Donald. <u>The Pastoral Epistles</u> **(Tyndale New Testament Commentary). Grand Rapids: Eerdmans, 1990. Revised edition.**

A recent work, this has a good introduction, but the commentary lacks the detail of Bernard and Huther. The author is better known for his three-volume work on New Testament introduction. This book is helpful, especially for an up-to-date conservative answer to critical views concerning introductory matters. The revisions are not extensive since the 1957 edition.

Hanson, A. T. <u>The Pastoral Epistles</u>. **Cambridge, 1967.**

A brief commentary, and not one of the better ones. His <u>Studies in the Pastoral Epistles</u> (London: SPCK, 1968) deals with difficult texts in the Pastorals and is often quite good.

Hendriksen, William. I and II Timothy and Titus. **Grand Rapids: Baker, 1957.**

As usual, Hendriksen is detailed and offers much aid in word meanings, possible views which he documents, and full discussion of the passages. His commentary is one of the finer works for serious students.

Hiebert, D. Edmond. First Timothy, Second Timothy, Titus and Philemon. **Chicago: Moody Press, 1957, 1958, 1957 respectively.**

These three works in the Everyman's Bible Commentary series are fine brief commentaries by a careful conservative scholar. They are helpful on most verses and on certain problems.

Huther, J. E. Critical and Exegetical Commentary on the Pastoral Epistles. **H. A. W. Meyer's Commentary on the New Testament. Edinburgh: T. & T. Clark, 1873-85.**

This work, with that of Bernard among older efforts, deals with the Greek text in a thorough manner and offers the student much help. It is one of the more valuable commentaries on the Greek.

Kelly, J. N. D. A Commentary on the Pastoral Epistles **(Harper's New Testament Commentary). Grand Rapids: Baker, 1981rp. 264 pp.**

A thorough explanation which usually deals with problems perceptively and mentions differing views. This is one of the better commentaries of recent years. Held in high respect by scholars, the effort concludes for authenticity of the epistles and carries on a judicious exegesis often quite instructive in reasoning.

Kent, Homer A., Jr. The Pastoral Epistles. **Revised edition. Chicago: Moody Press, 1982.**

This is a fairly detailed exposition that usually gives various views on many of the larger interpretive problems and provides reasons for the view favored. Kent uses his own translation. The outline is very clear, and the evangelical exposition is geared for Bible college students, pastors desiring a brief, knowledgeable survey that comes right to the point without being technical, and laymen wanting a commentary that will satisfy them without losing them.

King, Guy. A Leader Led. **London: Marshall, Morgan & Scott, 1953.**

_____. To My Son. **Fort Washington, PA: Christian Literature Crusade, 1944. 1958 reprint.**

The two books above are expositional studies of I and II Timothy respectively. They are based on the English text and are outstanding popular treatments with many thoughts provocative for the preacher and the teacher. The very interesting writing style makes them ideal to recommend to laymen. King, a noted spiritual life speaker in his day, has given much rich food for thought here.

Lea, Thomas and Griffin, Hayne Jr.   I, II Timothy, Titus (New American Commentary).   Nashville: Broadman, 1992.   352 pp.

Lea who does I, II Timothy is Professor of New Testament, Southwestern Baptist Seminary, Fort Worth. Griffin, writing on Titus, has a Ph. D. in New Testament from King's College, University of Aberdeen, Scotland. The authors give seven arguments for Paul as author of the epistles (23-49). They have good discussions on doctrinal themes, significance of the Pastorals and surveys of each. They follow clear outlines, devote good space to verses, deal with problems in a survey fashion without depth, etc. Sometimes explanations do not go very far to satisfy, as on the law not being made for the righteous in I Timothy 1:9, and on the spiritual status of the two in 1:20. "Husband of one wife" is resolved to mean a one-woman man, free of sexual promiscuity and laxity (110), but discussion covers only about two-thirds of a page. The work has a fairly adept survey of views and some of the vital arguments on some texts, such as women being saved through child bearing (2:15), and is disappointingly vague and brief on some, such as Timothy saving himself and others (4:16), the status of the unfaithful in 2 Timothy 2:20, etc. Sometimes it states bare views but does not give arguments to grapple with matters, such as on what "crown of righteousness" means in 2 Timothy 4:8. Excursuses appear at times, as on biblical evidence and Baptist practice on ordination (141-44). Some good explanations and sources in footnotes add to the value.

Litfin, A. Duane.   "I and II Timothy and Titus," in Bible Knowledge Commentary, ed. John F. Walvoord and Roy B. Zuck.   Volume II.   Wheaton: Victor Books, 1985.

An evangelical survey championing authorship by Paul and dealing with much of the material in a concisely helpful fashion, assisting at times on problem texts, following a good outline, etc.

Lock, W.   A Critical and Exegetical Commentary on the Pastoral Epistles (ICC).   Edinburgh: T. & T. Clark, 1924.   163 pp.

An introduction of 44 pages is followed by 159 pages of commentary. Lock overall has his contributions but falls short of giving one of the better commentaries. He is unable to decide whether Paul or one later, influenced by Paul, wrote the books (p. xxx etc.). Much of his material, as for example vocabulary statistics, is now superseded, and works he used are now 70 to 150 years old. He does hold that there is nothing in the letters that Paul could not have written, and that the epistles are written as if by Paul. His exegesis is at times rather helpful. Explanation of phrases varies between good-fair or too brief really to satisfy (as on I Timothy 2:11-15). His discussion on 3:2, "husband of one wife," is fair but could go on to be more helpful. He has no comment on 4:16, "you shall both save yourself and those who hear you." In what sense is this meant?

Plummer, Alfred.   The Pastoral Epistles in the Greek New Testament.   Grand Rapids: Eerdmans, 1964.

The author is lucid in his statements and has written a fair commentary based upon the Greek. Among older works it is not as helpful as Bernard and Huther, however.

Stott, John R. W.   Guard the Gospel.   Downers Grove: IVP, 1973.

An articulate and well-organized exposition of Second Timothy that is very suggestive for messages in the epistle. Though brief, Stott has quite good insight into the meaning of verses and has a rare ability to state truth succinctly.

Wuest, Kenneth S.   The Pastoral Epistles in the Greek New Testament.   Grand Rapids: Eerdmans, 1964.

This work is helpful to the serious student because of its Greek word studies and verse by verse clarity in exposition and frequent application.

XV. PHILEMON

Bruce, F. F.   Cf. on Ephesians.

Ellis, E. Earle.   Cf. on Colossians.

Gaebelein, Frank.   Philemon: The Gospel of Emancipation.   NY: Loizeaux, 1960.

This is an expository work on Philemon and is good on the English text.

Hendriksen, William.   Epistles to Colossians and Philemon.   Grand Rapids: Baker, 1964.

See comments on John, Philippians, etc., on Hendriksen.

Gromacki, Robert G.   Cf. on Colossians.

Ironside, H. A.   Charge That to My Account.   Chicago: Moody, 1931.

A good practical discussion of the book, with Ironside's usual illustrative richness.

Kent, Homer A., Jr.   Cf. on Colossians.

Lightfoot, John B.   St. Paul's Epistles to the Colossians and Philemon.   Grand Rapids: Zondervan, 1965.   Reprint of 1879 work.

As earlier stated, this work is excellent on Colossians and is also helpful on Philemon in the Greek text.

Lohse, E.   Cf. on Colossians.

Lucas, R. C.   Cf. on Colossians.

Martin, Ralph P.   Cf. on Colossians.

Muller, Jac. J.   The Epistles of Paul to the Philippians and to Philemon (NIC).   Grand Rapids: Zondervan, 1955.

This is one of the finer works on Philippians and is also very helpful in Philemon. It is highly desirable.

O'Brien, Peter T.   Cf. on Colossians.

Vincent, M. R.   A Critical and Exegetical Commentary on Paul's Epistles to the Philippians and Philemon (ICC).   Edinburgh: T. & T. Clark, 1902.

Obtain this work for a detailed examination of the Greek text with good word studies.

Rees, Paul S.   Cf. on Philippians.

XVI. HEBREWS

Archer, Gleason L., Jr.   The Epistle to the Hebrews. A Study Manual.   Grand Rapids: Baker, 1957.

Archer aims to provide a well-organized, "handy guide" (p. 1) to a systematic exposition to help a pastor, Bible teacher or English Bible instructor in a college. Taking the central theme, Christ's superiority and its implications for victorious living, Archer follows the progression of the developing theme. He gives a 5-pp. outline at the outset, then writes the book in the form of his detailed outline, filling in verse by verse with key word meanings, related Old Testament passages, and brief help on problem passages such as 6:4-6 and 10:26-39 (he holds that those in view are professors though never genuinely saved). This is a very good brief survey compactly arranged.

Brown, Raymond.   Christ Above All. The Message of Hebrews.   Downers Grove: IVP, 1982.

A principal of Spurgeon's College, London did this in the refreshing Bible Speaks Today series, drawing on such greats as Bruce, Hughes and Westcott but keeping the exposition very readable and practical. Possibly Apollos wrote Hebrews in the early eighties. "Rest" in chapter 4 is a future reality on which we need to concentrate, yet is not attained by works but is God's gift (p. 90). Hebrews 6:4-6 and 10:26-31 are taken to refer to those who once had outward signs of being Christians but never were "genuinely born again by God's Spirit" (114). The penitent offender and weak backslider are not in view (cf. 189), yet Brown speaks confusingly of them as if once they really trusted in Christ. This is a stimulating, inviting exposition for laymen or Christian workers who want a book competent but easy to read.

Bruce, F. F.   The Epistle to the Hebrews (New International Commentary on the New Testament).   Grand Rapids: Eerdmans, 1990.

Before his death Bruce updated this outstanding evangelical work since it first appeared in 1964. The introduction does much to bring a reader abreast of the main facets related to the book. Bruce offers good discussion of how the epistle uses the Old Testament Scripture and the harmony with the gospel witness about Jesus (pp. 25-34). The commentary is excellent on detail about most verses, competent in Greek grammar, word study, background, etc. and lucid. It remains the best evangelical work on Hebrews.

Delitzsch, Franz.   Commentary on the Epistle to the Hebrews.   Edinburgh; T. & T. Clark, 1868-1870.   2 volumes.

Though somewhat technical, this work grapples seriously with the Greek text and stimulates thinking on the problems of the epistle. It is good on the Greek.

Demarest, Bruce.   A History of Interpretation of Hebrews 7:1-10 from the Reformation to the Present.   Tübingen: J. C. B. Mohr, 1976.

A 1973 University of Manchester dissertation which, as its title suggests, offers the reader interested in detail a competent account of how the Melchizedekian verses have been explained.

Greene, Oliver B.   The Epistle of Paul the Apostle to the Hebrews.   Greenville, SC: The Gospel Tour, Inc., 1965.

This evangelical commentary is made up of detailed radio messages that interact with some of the issues rather at length though popularly. Greene discusses certain problems in depth (as 6:4-6, where he believes that professors, not really saved, are the persons who fall away).

Guthrie, Donald.   Hebrews. An Introduction and Commentary (Tyndale New Testament Commentary).   Grand Rapids: Eerdmans, 1983.

This volume replaces Hewitt's in the series to meet new needs. Though vague, Guthrie apparently favors a date shortly before or after A. D. 70, leaving authorship open. The rest in chapter 4 is both present after conversion and future. The discussions of 6:4-6 and 10:26-31 do not appear to arrive at an unequivocal explanation of whether the really saved can actually lose salvation. A clearer taking of some stand would help. However, on many verses Guthrie is clear enough, though this is a concise commentary. I would not rate it near the top but about in the middle.

Hagner, Donald A. <u>Hebrews</u>. **2nd edition.** (**New International Biblical Commentary**). **Peabody, MA: Hendrickson, 1990. 296 pp.**

This work was originally in the <u>Good News Commentary</u> (San Francisco: Harper and Row, 1983). It is by a professor at Fuller Theological Seminary, evangelical, and fairly helpful at times, but not nearly in the range of Bruce, Lane, Morris, MacArthur, etc.

Hodges, Zane C. "Hebrews," in <u>Bible Knowledge Commentary</u>, **ed. John F. Walvoord and Roy B. Zuck, Volume II. Wheaton: Victor Books, 1985.**

A substantial commentary explaining Hebrews from the non-Lordship salvation viewpoint. Hodges takes passages such as the warnings in chapters 6 and 10 to relate to the saved guarding against failure to gain special reward, not the possibility of mere professors ending up unsaved. As in his commentary on the epistles of John in the BKC, he makes the distinction that the saved who are carnal will be in the kingdom but not possess it, will enter but not inherit, will be there but not be sons, etc. His views are further expounded in four of his books: <u>The Hungry Inherit</u> (Portland, OR: Multnomah Press, 1980, 143 pp.), <u>The Gospel Under Siege</u> (Dallas: Redencion Viva, 1985, 120 pp.), <u>Grace in Eclipse</u> (Dallas Redencion Viva, 1985, 120 pp.) and <u>Absolutely Free!</u> (Grand Rapids: Zondervan, 1989, 238 pp.) Another view, that salvation is entirely of God's grace, a free gift without any works or merit in any way, but manifests its reality in God-enabled fruit of obedience to God, is set forth in John MacArthur, <u>The Gospel According to Jesus</u> (Grand Rapids: Zondervan, 1988, 253 pp.). Cf. also an evaluation of the views and a favoring of the latter explanation in Richard P. Belcher, <u>A Layman's Guide to the Lordship Controversy</u> (Southbridge, MA: Crowne Publications, Inc., 1990, 123 pp.).

Hughes, Philip E. <u>A Commentary on the Epistle to the Hebrews</u>. **Grand Rapids: Eerdmans, 1977.**

A 623-page evangelical work by visiting Professor of New Testament at Westminster Theological Seminary. This, as his NICNT work on II Corinthians, is very good. He has a lengthy section on authorship, showing good awareness of scholarly discussion, finally leaning slightly to Barnabas over Apollos. He dates Hebrews before A. D. 70. The commentary is very readable and handles verses usually at length, with fine use of Greek (sometimes in lengthy notes). The special notes on problem areas are a help, as are the several Excursus sections on such subjects as Melchizedek, the blood of Jesus and his heavenly priesthood, etc. In a lengthy discussion of 6:4-6, he takes the view that some may prove never to have been truly saved to begin with despite their profession, benefit from contact with blessings, and witness as so-called Christians (pp. 206-22). The commentary is quite full and able to discuss ramifications where many even of the good commentaries are too general for some eager readers.

Kent, Homer A., Jr. The Epistle to the Hebrews: A Commentary. **Grand Rapids: Baker, 1972.**

A helpful evangelical commentary especially from the standpoint of clarity on the Greek where this is crucial to the interpretation, without being technical. It is also often helpful in discussing different main views and their support on problem passages (6:4-6, those who fall away; chapter 8, the new covenant, etc.). Dr. Kent has been Dean of the Seminary and also Professor of New Testament and Greek at Grace Theological Seminary.

Kistemaker, Simon J. Hebrews **(Hendriksen New Testament Commentary). Grand Rapids: Baker, 1984.**

The author has been going on with commentaries in the series William Hendriksen began. He writes from an evangelical, reformed perspective, providing diligently studied comments competent in aspects of the Greek, giving views and reasons, writing clearly, explaining most matters well.

Lane, William L. Hebrews, A Call to Commitment **(New International Biblical Commentary). Peabody, MA: Hendrickson, 1988. 184 pp.**

Lane, known among other things for his excellent work on Mark (NICNT), has written a fairly good briefer commentary on Hebrews, informed by scholarly awareness of the literature, views and arguments and skill in the Greek text and background. The work uses the NIV and is evangelical.

Lane, William L. Hebrews, **2 vols. (Word Biblical Commentary). Waco, TX: Word Books, 1987-1991.**

A work that has much to offer in details of the Greek text, exegesis, setting and bibliography. It will help readers be aware of a wealth of scholarly opinion and especially be helpful to teachers, preachers who study deeply, and Bible class leaders who are serious about their preparation. In bibliography it is of a high rating, in commentary not as good as the work by Bruce.

Lightfoot, Neil R. Jesus Christ Today, A Commentary on the Book of Hebrews. **Grand Rapids: Baker, 1976.**

An evangelical professor at Abilene Christian College (Texas) wrote this very readable, knowledgeable work, admittedly indebted much to A. B. Bruce, F. F. Bruce, and James Moffatt but also using a long list of other commentaries and literature in reference works and journals. Footnotes are frequent and often of helpful substance, drawn from sources. He concludes as Origen that only God knows who wrote Hebrews, ca. A. D. 65. He leans to the view that the "rest" in Hebrews 4 is future for Christians, that 6:4-6 refers to losing salvation at one time truly possessed, and that baptismal regeneration is correct (p. 122). On most verses he explains very well what most non-specialists but serious readers need to have explained. He uses the RSV.

MacArthur, John F., Jr. <u>Hebrews</u> **(MacArthur New Testament Commentary). Chicago: Moody, 1983. 466 pp.**

The forty studies centralize "The Preeminence of Jesus Christ." MacArthur wisely declines to guess the author but dates the book ca. A. D. 65 (p. x). He sees three groups: Hebrews who are truly saved, unsaved Hebrews who are intellectually persuaded but have not received Christ (2:1-3a; 6:4-6; 10:26ff.), and unsaved Hebrews who are not even convinced (9:14-15, 27-28). He is richly edifying on many passages, such as Christ's priesthood that encourages believers to come to him (4:15—5:10). The commentary flows lucidly and will stimulate pastors, Bible class teachers and any Christians. The sections on Hebrews 11 (aspects of faith) and 12 (disciplined living) are well-done.

MacDonald, Wm. <u>The Epistle to the Hebrews: From Ritual to Reality.</u> **Neptune, NJ: Loizeaux Brothers, 1971.**

A conservative exposition by a recent president of Emmaus Bible School (Plymouth Brethren). MacDonald gives fine-point outlines and explains verse by verse, understanding that the epistle is aimed at true Christians and professing Christians mingled among them. Hebrews 6:4-6 refers to professors who had not really been born again. Comments are brief.

Moffatt, James. <u>A Critical and Exegetical Commentary on the Epistle to the Hebrews</u> **(ICC). Edinburgh: T. & T. Clark, 1924.**

Some regard this work rather highly for its exegetical excellence at times in the Greek.

Morgan, G. Campbell. <u>The Triumphs of Faith: Expositions of Hebrews 11.</u> **Grand Rapids: Baker, 1973, reprint of 1934 ed.**

Preached expositions with good practical applications running through Hebrews 11. Some errors can agitate readers, e. g. having Moses' birth 64 years after Joseph's death, and the rejection of total depravity (p. 151). However, there is much to edify and to stimulate Christians, even to be suggestive for messages in a great chapter.

Morris, Leon. "Hebrews," in <u>Expositor's Bible Commentary</u>, **Volume 12, ed. Frank Gaebelein and J. D. Douglas. Grand Rapids: Zondervan, 1981.**

This is a substantial work (pp. 1-158) by a highly competent and prolific New Testament scholar in the evangelical realm. He is brief, aware of issues and arguments, sums things up well in several cases, and clear. For a shorter commentary this is a worthy effort which will be of service to teachers, preachers, Sunday School teachers and serious lay persons.

Morris, Leon. <u>Hebrews</u> **(Bible Study Commentary). Grand Rapids: Zondervan, 1983. 137 pp.**

A well-organized, lucid survey that gives synopses of sections and usually broad comment but dips into many of the verses for serious explanation, views on problems, and reasons. It is primarily of help to lay persons and pastors needing a concise but competent study. Longer, more detailed works ought to be used with it.

Murray, Andrew.   The Holiest of All.   Westwood, NJ: Revell, 1960.

One will find rich devotional reading here by an author with keen insight into spiritual truths. Such a work, though it does not deal with textual problems as exegetical books do, has value in that it stimulates the student along many rich lines of spiritual meditation.

Newell, William.   Hebrews Verse by Verse.   Chicago: Moody, 1947.

The student will find this a helpful volume on the English text much like Newell's valuable work on Romans. Newell was premillennial and dispensational. On Hebrew 6, Newell takes the stance that professors are in view.

Owen, John.   An Exposition of the Epistle to the Hebrews.   7 Volumes.   Grand Rapids: Baker, n. d.

Kregel in Grand Rapids has a 1-volume abridgement that makes the comments more manageable. Owen, a Puritan scholar, was voluminous on just about everything he wrote, and he did many masterful works. Here, the patient will meet with ponderous discussion of connections between New Testament fulfillments in Christ and Old Testament preparation for Him. Much is rich and worthwhile as one sorts through the laborious discussions to follow through to what he can use. Theologically Owen has a lot to contribute. He has many points and sees things from various sides, reasons through views and arguments, and often is very helpful to the person who begins his study early enough to devote the time it takes. In Hebrews 6 and 10, Owen decides reference is to mere professors who fall away or shrink back, never having been actually born again.

_____.   Hebrews: The Epistle of Warning.   One volume abridgement of his multi-volume set on the book.   Grand Rapids: Kregel, 1985.   283 pp.

Anytime one can get a book by Owen amounting only to 283 pages, he has made an unusual find. M. J. Tyron condensed the commentary yet retained the essence verse by verse. Owen wrestles well with such problem texts as 6:4-6 and, on several passages such as this is worth the time. His was one of the great theological minds of the Puritan tradition.

Perkins, William.   A Commentary on Hebrews 11, ed. J. H. Augustine.   NY: Pilgrim, 1991rp.   304 pp.

This originally appeared in 1609. It was an exposition on 11:1-12:1 preached at Cambridge in the 1590's and entitled "A Cloud of Faithful Witnesses." The book has four essays to introduce the exposition, setting the work in Perkin's life and ministry. His comments have much rich truth that solidly feeds the life as Perkins deals with different Old Testament characters, the witnesses in the line of faith.

Pfeiffer, Charles. <u>The Epistle to the Hebrews</u>. Chicago: Moody, 1962. Paperback.

In the <u>Everyman's Bible Commentary</u> series, this is a good brief study that deals with problems (as Hebrews 6:4-6) yet maintains the flow of thought well.

Pink, Arthur W. <u>An Exposition of Hebrews</u>. 2 volumes. Grand Rapids: Baker, 1963.

This is a rich study of the English text with many suggestive channels of thought which help the student in preparing messages or lessons. Though Pink's earlier writings reveal a dispensational belief, his later works such as this and <u>An Exposition of the Sermon on the Mount</u> show a switch-over to an amillennial concept.

Saphir, Adolph. <u>Lectures on Hebrews</u>. 2 volumes. NY: Gospel Publishing House (n.d.).

Careful insight into the text and fine articulation of the meaning by a Hebrew Christian.

Sauer, Erich. <u>In the Arena of Faith</u>. Grand Rapids: Eerdmans, 1955.

A fine study of Hebrews 12 with special value for its rich, detailed background behind the athletic terminology ("Let us run . . . ") here and in other New Testament passages. The well-organized material, written in a warming, heart-touching style, is helpful in preparing messages or Bible studies on passages dealing with athletic imagery. It grips the life.

Stedman, Ray C. <u>What More Can God Say? A Fresh Look at Hebrews</u>. Glendale, CA: G/L Publications, Regal Books, 1974.

A 247-pp. paperback giving a popular exposition by the late Pastor of Peninsula Bible Church, Palo Alto, California. The expositions of individual passages offer much that is enriching to general readers on a simple level in which practical application is rather quickly apparent. Sometimes readers can become confused as to how passages correlate consistently. For instance, those who do not hold fast to Christ in 3:6 reflect that they had never genuinely had faith in Christ (pp. 41-46), then 6:4-6 deals with Christians who do not go on to maturity, though there is some lack of clarity (81-91).

Stibbs, Alan M. <u>So Great Salvation</u>. London: Paternoster, 1970.

This is a good book on Hebrews from the standpoint of a capable brief survey that is well-organized and helpful in following the line of thought more quickly (than in Bruce, Delitzsch, etc.)

Thomas, W. H. Griffith. <u>Let Us Go On</u>. Grand Rapids: Eerdmans, 1961.

Expositional in nature, this book is often helpful to a degree on the English text. It is devotional in nature.

Turner, George Allen. The New and Living Way: An Exposition of the Epistle to the Hebrews. **Minneapolis: Bethany Fellowship, 1975.**

This work, by a conservative scholar from Asbury Theological Seminary who is Arminian in his theology, offers a good example of a serious effort to explain relevant texts in Hebrews in accordance with the belief that the truly saved can fall away and lose salvation (cf. his comments on such passages as Hebrews 3, 4, 6). Even if one is not of this conviction, it may be very helpful to see how Turner sets forth his case (cf. also the Beacon Bible Commentary for Arminian views).

Westcott, B. F. The Epistle to the Hebrews. **London: Macmillan and Company, 1889. Eerdmans reprint, 1950.**

This famous work discusses the Greek text and presents valuable studies on subjects related to it. Many have rated it as the best older commentary from the standpoint of dealing seriously with the Greek.

XVII. JAMES

Adamson, James. The Epistle of James **(NICNT). Grand Rapids: Eerdmans, 1976.**

This is one of the very best commentaries because it seriously tackles the issues verse by verse with a good use of the Greek and backgrounds and added detail on certain problems by the use of special excursuses (cf., for example, on anointing with oil and the prayer of a righteous man).

Blue, Ronald. "James," in Bible Knowledge Commentary, **ed. John F. Walvoord and Roy B. Zuck. Volume II. Wheaton: Victor Books, 1985.**

Blue offers a clear, concise study, well-organized, with attention given to some of the problem verses. He will not convince many with interpretations such as seeing the "crown" of 1:12 as relating to fullness of life now (p. 821). He does mention the view that reference is to eternal life for all believers, all of them loving God, and cites I John 4:8. He mentions two views on 2:14ff., and is somewhat confusing. In James 5:14-15, he takes the view that reference is to one who has grown weary (weak) morally and spiritually, not to a person with physical illness (834). He seems to see 5:20 as dealing with a saved person who needs restoration, not a professing believer who needs evangelism, yet presages this with a remark that the Greek planethe ("should wander") "suggests one who has missed his path and is hopelessly lost" (835). Despite some ambiguity, he apparently really holds the former idea. Some will be unsure about what he finally favors.

Criswell, W. A.   Expository Sermons on the Epistle of James.   Grand Rapids: Zondervan, 1975.

One of the great preachers of the 20th century (First Baptist, Dallas) gives 13 sermons expounding the epistle and illustrating with anecdotes, poetry, etc. The exposition is evangelical and popularly simple, geared for lay people.

Davids, Peter.   Commentary on James (NIGTC).   Grand Rapids: Eerdmans, 1982.

Davids is former Associate Professor of Biblical Studies at Trinity Episcopal School for Ministry in Ambridge, PA. He has done the finest recent critical work on James geared to be helpful to those who study the Greek text, showing a good grasp of technical points, critical matters, and old and new literature in English, German and French (a very long list). Davids writes in a style that often refreshes, and not only provides a verse by verse commentary that shows great awareness of literature and facets important to explain the text but in a special section develops seven themes of theology. These are suffering or testing, eschatology, Christ, poverty/piety, the law-grace-faith relationship ("Grace which has no outward result is not grace at all," p. 50), wisdom, and prayer. He did his Ph.D. thesis in 1974, "Themes in the Epistle of James that are Judaistic in Character" at Manchester. Davids favors an early date (between A. D. 40 and the Jerusalem Council) by James the Just, Brother of Jesus. Paul and James are essentially consistent with one another even if they have different emphases (pp. 50-51, 119-134).

Dibelius, M. and Greven, H.   James: A Commentary on the Epistle of James (Hermeneia).   11th revised edition.   Philadelphia: Fortress Press, 1976. 285 pp.

This is the English production of the German edition, Der Brief des Jakobus (1964). Abreast of much liberal scholarly thought, it is informative here as well as on research that elucidates the text. Dibelius was for thirty-two years Professor of the University of Heidelberg, Germany. Greven has updated the exhaustive bibliography and revised the commentary for the English. A long introduction (1-61) shows very instructive use of scholarly literature, with many notes. Dibelius reasons that the letter is pseudonymous, having attached the claim that James wrote it (1:1). He defends this as involving no fraudulent effort to deceive, saying it was a literary custom of that day (cf. 18-20, 65). Many will not be able to agree with his reasoning. The date, as he sees it, is around A. D. 80-130 (45). He interprets "twelve tribes" (1:1) as metaphorical, not denoting Jewish people per se but "the true Israel", in his mind Christians whatever their racial tie, who are scattered away from their true home, heaven (66). He says that 1:12 (crown of life, etc.) is an isolated saying separated from what precedes it in the text (71). That may persuade some but not satisfy others. His discussion of 2:14-26 is too often reasoned in such a manner that it is not easy to follow the logic, and perhaps only the extremely serious and skilled will stay with it.

Hiebert, D. E.   The Epistle of James: Tests of a Living Faith.   Chicago: Moody, 1979. 354 pp.

A lucid evangelical work that looks at every verse, discussing exegetical matters, views, supports, and the relevance to a practical spiritual life. The work delves into many of the issues in a knowledgeable manner and will be of value to teachers to some extent and to expositors, students and lay persons who want a fairly detailed but readable commentary.

Johnstone, R.   Lectures, Exegetical and Practical on the Epistle of James.   2nd edition.   Edinburgh: Oliphant, Anderson & Ferrier, 1888.

As on I Peter, Johnstone has produced a very helpful work for the English reader which is based to a large extent upon a sound knowledge of the Greek text.

Kent, Homer A., Jr.   Faith that Works, Studies in the Epistle of James.   Grand Rapids: Baker, 1986.   203 pp.

A writer of many commentaries and long-time faculty member at Grace Theological Seminary did this evangelical survey. Kent keeps summaries of the argument in view, shows connections between sections, deals helpfully with most verses, and is forthright in dealing with problems and stating reasons. This is a good, clear exposition that will assist preachers in places, and help Bible class teachers, Sunday School teachers and lay persons in general as in a series of Bible readings.

King, Guy.   A Belief that Behaves.   6th edition.   London: Marshall, Morgan & Scott, 1941.   Distributed in United States by Christian Literature Crusade, Fort Washington, PA.

This is a practical, expository development of James with creative chapter titles, illustrations and many other sermonic hints. King was a lucid writer and has given the reader much to think about in this provocative book based on the English. It is one of the better works to recommend to the layman and is good for the preacher or teacher's heart.

Kistemaker, Simon J.   James and I-III John (Hendriksen New Testament Commentary).   Grand Rapids: Baker, 1986.   425 pp.

This continues the Hendriksen commentary began in 1953. Hendricksen died in 1982. Using the NIV text, Kistemaker explains passages in scholarly competence and makes practical comments that are also usable to a pastor or any Christian. He makes things fairly clear in many cases but not with a constant citation of Greek or technical matters that some commentaries take up. He also does not show the relationship between sections as some do.

Laws, Sophie.   The Epistle of James (Harper's NTC).   New York: Harper, 1980. 273 pp.

A lecturer in New Testament at King's College, University of London, gives a 43 page introduction, then about 200-page translation and commentary. She decides that the epistle was not by James of Jerusalem but one using the honored name as a pseudonym after the death of James in A. D. 62 (41-42). She puts 1:12 (trial and crown) with verses 13-18 rather than with verses 2-11 on trials. The crown is eternal life itself (68). Many verses are explained rather fully and capably, out of a wide grasp of things. Some will feel that she fails to set things in a totally fair balance in making much of supposed differences between Paul in Romans 4 and James 2:14-26 (131-134). She has much of value, however, as in saying that what James means to contrast "is 'faith without works' and 'works inseparable from faith'" (13). On many matters the pertinent, clear and extended comments make this one of the most contributive commentaries on the epistle.

Martin, Ralph P.   James (Word Biblical Commentary).   Waco, TX: Word Books, 1988.   240 pp.

This work by a moderate evangelical shows broad awareness of scholarly opinions and lines of argument. This is true in the introduction and in the verse by verse commentary. Martin shows expertise in Greek details, relationships to other Scripture, and bibliography. Douglas Stuart seems to be overrating it by calling it "the best longer work on James" (A Guide to Selecting and Using Bible Commentaries. Dallas: Word, 1990, p. 126). Davids, Hiebert and Mitton all appear to be more generally helpful in a straight-forward way.

Mayor, Joseph B.   The Epistle of James.   3rd edition.   Grand Rapids: Kregel, 1990rp.   621 pp.

First issued in 1892, this commentary of more than 600 pages gives the reader almost 300 pages in introductory explorations about the identity of the writer James, the date (he says near the end of the A. D. 40's), the relations to other New Testament books, grammar and style, etc. It is a work of towering scholarship and exhaustive detail. From the standpoint of the Greek text it is one of the best on James.

This is a reprint of the 1910 edition with a 2-page Foreword by Cyril J. Barber, who wrote The Minister's Library. The massive 291-page introduction is a gold mine on facets of the study of the book. One learns much from Mayor's skillful assembling of relevant data on issues and verses, and he is rich in Scripture. Highly-regarded, it stands as one of the most helpful works on exegesis, views, arguments etc. even though it is not up to date on scholarly writings. Mayor died in 1916. Baker also has a 1978 reprint of it (460 pp.), and Zondervan had a 1954 publication of it (291 + 264 pp.).

Mitton, C. Leslie.   The Epistle of James.   Grand Rapids: Eerdmans, 1966.

This work by a more recent English scholar is in the Evangelical Bible Commentary series. The author is lucid, thorough, helpful on problems, and lists different viewpoints on debated matters.

Moo, Douglas J.   The Letter of James: An Introduction and Commentary (Tyndale New Testament Commentary).   Downers Grove: IVP, 1985.   191 pp.

Eerdmans published the same commentary in 1989. It is a concise, conservative, clear work adept in exegetical details from careful research by a member of the New Testament faculty at Trinity Evangelical Divinity School. It is helpful especially for teachers and preachers. Moo, who did the massive Volume I on Romans, also wrote "James" in The Evangelical Commentary on the Bible, ed. W. A. Elwell (Grand Rapids: Baker, 1989).

Motyer, J. Alec.   The Tests of Faith. The Message of James (Bible Speaks Today).   Downers Grove: IVP, 1985.   214pp.

Motyer (pronounced Ma-teer) attempts, with much unifying helpfulness, to show a tie-in between sections of James. He sees three keys in 1:26, 27: a controlled tongue, a compassion for those in need and helpless, and purity from worldly defilement. He sees the compassion developed in chapter 2, the tongue in chapter 3, and the purity in 4:1—5:6. James commences and ends with perseverance and prayer. The book is an asset on suggestive aspects of unity in carrying out themes.

Nieboer, Joe.   James: Practical Exposition.   NY: Loizeaux, 1950.

A lucid exposition with good illustrative material.

Reicke, Bo.   The Epistles of James, Peter and Jude (The Anchor Bible).   NY: Doubleday, 1964.

A reputed scholar from the University of Basel did this work favoring dating I Peter in the 60's, and the other three epistles in the 90's (James, brother of Jesus, did not actually write "James"). He sees expressions in the epistles which remind him of Qumran ideas, and in James sayings very close to Jesus' sayings as preserved in the Gospels. The actual verse by verse commentary often is quite helpful as to perspective but frequently very sparse and generalized on verses so that the reader looking for detail on word meanings or views has to go to Mayor, Mitten, Adamson and others to find help. Some sections (e. g. James 1:19-27) are treated in a somewhat general discussion, though individual verses are worked in briefly. Only 4 pages are devoted to James 2, about 4 1/2 to chapter 3, etc. Commentary on the other epistles likewise is brief, though at times offering quite helpful comments.

Robertson, A. T.   Studies in the Epistle of James.   Nashville: Broadman, 1959.

Here is another work helpful in the Greek text.

Ropes, J. H.   A Critical and Exegetical Commentary on the Epistle of St. James (ICC).   Edinburgh: T. & T. Clark, 1916.   319 pp.

In this liberal technical work, Ropes decides that the author was not James the Lord's brother but a teacher in Palestine between A. D. 75 and 125 (49). He devotes pp. 1-115 to introduction. His work is one of the better older ones on details of the Greek text and at times has fairly good input on what a phrase means, such as "the crown of life" in 1:12 (150-52). But Ropes fails to explain how reward as a crown, eternal life, is consistent with eternal life being entirely God's gift, not by works. At a number of points he is rather flat when he might be clearer.

Strauss, Lehman. *James Your Brother.* **NY:** **Loizeaux, 1956.**

Good on preaching material, evangelical and expositional.

Wolff, Richard. *The General Epistles of James and Jude.* **Wheaton:** **Tyndale House, 1969.**

The author explains the books very well in a brief way. Often he is quite helpful on citations from Jewish sources or other early channels. For brief discussion this is one of the best commentaries on the books in recent times.

Zodhiates, Spiros. *The Epistle of James and the Life of Faith.* **3 volumes.** **Grand Rapids:** **Eerdmans, 1959-60.**

Valuable mainly for good illustrations and its other choice sermonic material, this work is authored by a Greek who has been greatly used in soul-winning in Greece. It combines a thorough study of the text with a warmth in presentation, including many practical questions. It is one of the most enjoyable detailed works to read on James, and is of great value to the pastor.

XVIII. FIRST PETER

Barbieri, Louis. *First and Second Peter.* **Chicago:** **Moody, 1977.**

A 126-pp., brief exposition by a former professor of Bible at Dallas Seminary. Barbieri surveys with some reference to historical setting and awareness of Greek, dealing concisely with certain of the problem passages. The work is geared for devotional reading or a quick summation for lay Bible studies.

Beare, F. W. *The First Epistle of Peter: The Greek Text.* **Oxford:** **Blackwell, 1969.**

This is a liberal scholarly work offering some help for more skilled in-depth users. It mingles some contributions along practical lines. Beare shows broad awareness of issues and views gained by laborious study. He is against authorship by Peter, and argues for a late date.

Best, Ernest. *I Peter* **(New Century Bible Commentary).** **Grand Rapids:** **Eerdmans, 1982rp of 1971 ed.** **188 pp.**

Best taught at the universities of St. Andrews and Glasgow, retiring in 1982. He concludes that Peter did not write the letter but that it came from pseudonymous authorship in the Petrine school (p. 63) between A. D. 80-100 (64) from

Rome (65). Best has stimulating remarks on many verses, e. g. 1:5; 2:2, 3. His systematic and somewhat detailed comments on 3:19 conclude that Christ went prior to His resurrection to preach to angelic spirits in their prison a message of salvation which they possibly rejected (or else the passage is not clear as to the result), linking the text with bound angels in II Peter 2:4; Jude 6 and I Enoch. 10ff. This is at many points a good commentary even though rather brief in many instances. Many will not be able to follow his preferred view and defense of it on 4:6: Christ offered the Gospel to those who had physically died prior to His death, who never had the opportunity to hear it when they were alive. For that adds up to a "second chance," and Best's answers to objections appear to be rather lame.

Bigg, Charles. A Critical and Exegetical Commentary on the Epistles of St. Peter and St. Jude (ICC). London: T. & T. Clark, 1901. Reprint 1961.

This is probably the second best older study on I Peter from the standpoint of the Greek text. Selwyn is the other. As other ICC works, it deals with details of philology, grammar and possible views on problems.

Blum, Edwin. "I and II Peter," in Expositor's Bible Commentary. Volume 12, ed. Frank Gaebelein. Grand Rapids: Zondervan, 1981.

A perceptive evangelical work by a scholar who offers help on problem verses and explains much of the material in a worthy way.

Cranfield, C. E. B. First Epistle of Peter. London: SCM Press, 1950.

Cranfield is an outstanding exegete and offers comments of a critical, exegetical nature that are concise but helpful. One could wish so great a master had said more, as he does on Romans.

Davids, Peter H. The First Epistle of Peter (NICNT). Grand Rapids: Eerdmans, 1990.

Davids is known for his fine commentary on James. Here he has a 42-page introduction that reviews issues in an evangelical manner and discusses scholarly literature. A 266-page commentary follows, in which he capably handles the Greek and deals with the different views on problem passages.

Grudem, Wayne A. I Peter (Tyndale New Testament Commentary). Grand Rapids: Eerdmans, 1988. 239 pp.

An evangelical work which is at many points a good one, informative about views and helpful in the Greek. He holds to double predestination in 2:8, and says that God destined the stumbling and disobedience of the unsaved (p. 106). At 3:19-20, he believes the spirits in prison are unsaved humans of Noah's day, who are now in prison. He has a special appendix going into the "spirits" passage at some length. His work replaces the former contribution by A. M. Stibbs and Andrew Walls. He favors traditional conservative views or, in the "spirits" case, his 36-page discussion takes one of the conservative options.

Hiebert, D. E.   First Peter.   Chicago: Moody, 1984.   329 pp.

This book prints expositions from his series in Bibliotheca Sacra and Studia Missionalia. As in James, Heibert is vigorous in seeking to explain verses and sections, discuss views with an awareness of scholarly work, and use the Greek competently. It is a fairly good evangelical product.

Kelly, J. N. D.   A Commentary on the Epistles of Peter and of Jude (Harper's New Testament Commentary).   NY: Harper and Row, 1969.   Grand Rapids: Baker, 1981rp.   387 pp.

This is one of the better commentaries for the serious student, along with Beare, Bigg, Reicke, and Selwyn. Kelly shows good scholarship and insight, and usually is helpful on problems. He has taught at Oxford University. He posits a date of A. D. 64 for I Peter but is not firm on authorship by Peter. He feels that Peter did not author II Peter, but that it was written later (ca. 100-110). But he is excellent in exegesis of the text and grappling with issues and views. On many verses he has a lot to contribute.

Kistemaker, Simon J.   Peter and Jude (Hendriksen New Testament Commentary).   Grand Rapids: Baker, 1987.   441 pp.

A careful evangelical scholar in the reformed tradition carries on the Hendriksen series with good attention to exegesis, views, arguments and some practical application. It is quite readable for preacher or lay person.

Leighton, Robert.   Commentary Upon First Peter.   London: The Religious Tract Society (n. d.).

A thorough discussion of the texts with an exceptionally warm devotional spirit. Among older works it is easily one of the most helpful.

Luther, Martin.   Commentary on Peter and Jude.   Grand Rapids: Kregel, 1990.   303 pp.

The reader wanting to see how the great reformer handles these epistles will find a readable work with many judicious comments but one weak on some of the problems such as how to interpret the spirits in prison (3:19-21). Many commentaries are better overall.

Marshall, I. Howard.   I Peter (The IVP New Testament Commentary).   Downers Grove: IVP, 1991.   184 pp.

This launches a new series under the general editorship of Grant R. Osborne of Trinity Evangelical Divinity School. It aims to be brief, capture the message competently, and be practical for the church. Some of those who contribute to it are Darrell Bock (Luke), William Lane (Romans), Alan Johnson (I Corinthians), Gordon Fee (Philippians), Ray Stedman (Hebrews), and J. R. Michaels (Revelation). Marshall writes lucidly, refreshingly; he is aware of views on problems, reasons well usually, and crystallizes things helpfully. He has a five-point defense of authorship by Peter (pp. 22-23), a good list of nine points in Peter's theology. He has excellent remarks about trial in 1:6-7, a very instructive section on "Purity and Growth" (2:1-3), and a good list of views on 3:19-21, though some will wonder about his preference that Christ went to a prison in the heavens as He ascended and proclaimed His victory over evil supernatural beings. All in all, it is a very fine concise work which is bound to assist students who need a quick, well-informed review, and any Christian who uses it in a plan of daily readings.

Meyer, F. B.   Tried By Fire.   NY: Revell (n. d.).

The famous devotional writer of England has here dealt with I Peter in an expository way. He is very good on the subject of suffering. This is a very valuable devotional work to have.

Michaels, J. Ramsay.   I Peter (Word Biblical Commentary).   Waco, TX: Word Books, 1988.   337 pp.

Many view this as the current basic evangelical work in English. Michaels deals well with Greek details, is abreast of scholarly writings and gives helpful lists, wrestles with views and supports and often defends his view well. Differing from much thought, he thinks that Peter lived through persecution under Nero and authored the epistle in the A. D. 70's along with help from the church at Rome, despite evidence for death under Nero.

Mounce, Robert H.   A Living Hope [1 and 2 Peter].   Grand Rapids: Eerdmans, 1982.

Evidently meant to be a personal study guide, the book is really not very helpful. Mounce's comments are very brief and generally superficial. He begs many questions, calls the church the new Israel, and does not answer most "why?" or "how?" questions. His commentary on the Book of Revelation is at many points quite good. —Dan Phillips

A solid evangelical argues for authorship by Peter in the 60's and uses the NIV clause by clause, giving the rich Greek meaning and generously applying the points to today. The work is more useful for aggressive students, pastors and lay workers. Mounce could do far better to tie things together with synopses but he makes good contributions, at times verse by verse, meeting some issues fairly well.

Raymer, Roger.   "I Peter," in Bible Knowledge Commentary, ed. John F. Walvoord and Roy B. Zuck, Volume II.   Wheaton: Victor Books, 1985.

A concise evangelical entry that is backed by solid study and provides a lot of assistance on many of the problems as well as a capable job on the flow of thought and matters verse by verse.

Reicke, Bo.   The Epistles of James, Peter and Jude (Anchor Bible).   NY: Doubleday, 1964.

A competent treatment of the Greek text by a widely read liberal scholar. It is especially valuable on I Peter, the book in which the Basel scholar did his doctoral dissertation, "The Disobedient Spirits and Christian Baptism" (on 3:18ff.).

Reicke dates I Peter in the 60's, James and II Peter and Jude in the 90's. The commentary would be better if it discussed other views more often on difficult passages. Historical and social aspects are one of the stronger contributions.

Selwyn, E. G. The First Epistle of St. Peter. Grand Rapids: Baker, 1981, reprint.

This is one of the finest of all English scholarly liberal works on the Greek text. Selwyn gives detailed introduction material and exegesis plus 230 pages of further special notes. Though not up to date on scholarly literature and discussion, it still makes a great contribution.

Stibbs, A. M. The First Epistle General of Peter. Grand Rapids: Eerdmans, 1959.

Stibbs has done a thorough and discerning work. This is a very good commentary on the English but based on a careful study of the Greek.

Wuest, Kenneth S. First Peter in the Greek New Testament. Grand Rapids: Eerdmans, 1956.

Now available in paperback, this is one of Wuest's better works on a New Testament book. It is based on the Greek text though presented so that the English reader can have a lucid exposition. The word studies are sometimes good.

XIX. SECOND PETER

Bauckham, Richard J. Jude, 2 Peter (Word Biblical Commentary). Waco, TX: Word Books, 1983. 357 pp.

Some will not think the work evangelical. It has discussion looking at the Greek exegesis in some detail and with competence and showing a high familiarity with literature on the epistles as well as extra-biblical sources he feels pertains. In some cases he offers a spread of possibilities on views and arguments on problems. His bibliography is extensive. He will disturb many readers with his denial of authorship by Peter (he says the church at Rome produced it), and his view that the early readers would not disrespect it for being pseudonymous but take its message to heart as "a faithful mediator of the apostolic message" (pp. 161-62). Bauckham's view of inspiration is hazy, and he leaves students unsure whether he feels that any of the predictions or statements in the two epistles are objectively, actually true. In his thinking II Peter is dependent on Jude. The work is flawed in some of its doctrinal content but impressive in its help on exegesis and highly regarded in the academic community.

Barbieri, Louis. Cf. on I Peter.

Bigg, Charles. Cf. on I Peter.

Blum, Edwin. **Cf. on I Peter.**

Brown, John. <u>2 Peter 1: Parting Counsels</u> **(Geneva series).** **Carlisle, PA:** **Banner of Truth Trust, 1980rp of 1856 work.** **329 pp.**

Brown was minister of Broughton Place, Edinburgh (1829-58) at which post he died. He gives rich, solid comments verse by verse and can refresh any Christian in his devotional times or help a preacher pull together facets of truth and how they relate to life. To Brown, making the calling and election sure refers not to seeing to their existence but to the evidence of them (p. 53). Some, however, feel that they are saved when they are far from it (54). He is helpful on furnishing the virtues in verses 5-8. After 225 pages the rest of the book is given to other discourses on how Christians may have proper assurance of salvation, pray for the preacher (Ephesians 5:19), etc.

Clark, Gordon H. <u>II Peter: A Short Commentary</u>. **Nutley, NJ:** **Presbyterian and Reformed Publishing Co., 1972.**

This is a 78-page evangelical work that attempts to answer objections to the authenticity of II Peter (i. e., he believes that it was written indeed by the Apostle Peter) and to interpret the text according to the Greek grammar and textual evidence. There is a pronounced Calvinistic strain. It is a worthwhile book, and offers fresh help on such details as "daystar arise in your hearts" (1:19), "denying the Lord that bought them" (2:1), and "not willing that any should perish" (3:9).

Gangel, Kenneth. **"2 Peter," in** <u>Bible Knowledge Commentary</u>, **ed. John F. Walvoord and Roy B. Zuck, Volume II.** **Wheaton:** **Victor Books, 1985.**

A brief but often substantial tracing of the message verse by verse, dealing with problems fairly well or at least giving views. Gangel uses Greek word study (1:5, epichoregeō), feels the blind in 1:9 are carnal but saved, apparently favors saying that "they" in 2:20 refers to unstable, unsaved people who were "listeners" in verse 18, but gives four views, etc. He is premillennial in his "day of the Lord" concept in 3:10-13.

Green, Michael E. <u>The Second Epistle General of Peter and the General Epistle of Jude</u> **(Tyndale New Testament Commentary).** **Grand Rapids:** **Eerdmans, 1968.**

An articulate evangelical commentary, upholding the Petrine authorship after a careful weighing of evidence, then explaining the text carefully though concisely. It rates as one of the best overall works.

Hiebert, D. E. <u>Second Peter and Jude</u>. **Greenville, SC:** **Unusual Publications, 1989.** **324 pp.**

He takes conservative positions, even seeing Jude as following Peter's second epistle. He usually has something clarifying on a verse and displays considerable awareness of views and issues. Preachers and lay readers will find his present work worth the time.

Kelly, J. N. D.   Cf. on I Peter.

Lloyd-Jones, D. M.   Expository Sermons on Peter.   Carlisle, PA: Banner of Truth Trust, 1983.   263 pp.

> The book gives 25 sermons preached in 1946-47, the preacher's first series through a book of Scripture. He delivered the messages at Westminster Chapel, London. He usually includes 1-4 verses in a sermon and moves through the epistle. One is soon aware that Lloyd-Jones has much insight, explaining the essentials of the text adeptly and developing how it has vital force for living in this world. The book is a primer for expositors and refreshing for Christians in general.

Mayor, J. B.   The Epistles of Jude and Second Peter: The Greek Text with Introduction, Notes and Comments.   Grand Rapids: Baker, 1979.

> This is quite a good older work on the Greek exegesis by the man who did an outstanding commentary on James. Mayor is more for serious students who know the Greek and are ready to read more technical detail on verses without being overcome.

Mayor, Joseph.   The Second Epistle of St. Peter and the Epistle of St. Jude.   NY: Macmillan, (n. d.).

> Along with Bigg, this is a detailed study of the Greek text which the student will want to have.

Mounce, Robert H.   Cf. on I Peter.

Reicke, Bo.   Cf. on James.

Wuest, Kenneth S.   In These Last Days: Studies in the Greek Text of II Peter, John and Jude For the English Reader.   Grand Rapids: Eerdmans, 1957.

> This work is recommended as a very good book to give to a layman to stimulate his study. It is also good for the pastor and Sunday school teacher because it deals with the Greek word meanings verse-by-verse and has a warm devotional strain.

XX. THE JOHANNINE EPISTLES

Barclay, William.   Letters of John and Jude.   Philadelphia: Westminster, 1961.

> This is a lucid and well-organized exposition of the epistles with many helpful lists on different facets of truth John can have in mind at different points as on "light" and "darkness" in I John 1:5. There is stimulating background material and warm application.

Brooke, A. H.   The Johannine Epistles (ICC).   Edinburgh: T. & T. Clark.

This ICC work rates with Westcott as one of the top two detailed older commentaries of a technical nature based on the Greek text.

Brown, Raymond.   The Epistles of John (Anchor Bible).   Garden City, NY: Doubleday, 1982.   840 pp.

Many rate this as the best work on these epistles in view of its extensive discussion of issues and the skill in which the famous Roman Catholic scholar handles so many aspects. He is highly-informed exegetically, full in consideration of views and lines of reasoning, and has a tone of respect for the truthfulness and relevance of the message. If the expositor, teacher or lay person wants a commentary that looks at just about every side of a matter in a readable manner and with authoritative grasp of the literature, he will consult this work. The same is true of Brown's detailed commentary on the Gospel of John. Brown, however, will not always agree with a reader's convictions, as when he favors John the Presbyter as the author. The sheer length will not please some, but the diligent and serious will find the source very useful.

Bruce, F. F.   The Epistles of John.   Grand Rapids: Eerdmans, 1970.

A verse-by-verse evangelical commentary of 160 pp. intended for the general reader and using the R.V. Bruce, as usual, has much to offer, even though briefly here. The brevity removes it from being among the better commentaries to explain the text, which has problems requiring at times more than he gives. Footnotes, sometimes substantial, go into some points for readers who wish to pursue things a bit.

Bultmann, Rudolf.   The Johannine Epistles (Hermeneia series).   Translated by R. P. O'Hara with L. C. McGaughy and R. W. Funk, ed. by R. W. Funk. Philadelphia: Fortress Press, 1973.

A detailed commentary with Bultmann's use of the RSV, which he alters according to his radical view of the text. Included in the work is a list of best-known commentaries and other literature relating to these letters issued in this century, combined with the main scholarly studies during the last century, provided by E. J. Epp and J. W. Dunky. These are only the works these scholars consider to be scholarly, from their liberal perspective and circle of learning.

Burdick, Donald.   The Epistles of John.   Chicago: Moody Press, 1970.

A part of the Everyman's Bible Commentary series, this work by a careful evangelical New Testament scholar from Denver Seminary is quite perceptive on problems and good as a brief commentary.

Burdick, Donald W.   The Letters of John the Apostle. An In-Depth Commentary. Chicago: Moody, 1985.   488 pp.

This is far more detailed in getting at issues than his Everyman's Commentary effort of 1970. It is a diligent conservative product on Greek syntax, word meaning and theology, and follows the line of thought through the epistles well. The introduction (pp. 3-92) takes up the background, authorship, date, place, recipients, occasion, purpose, character and content of I John. Later, he also has introductions to II and III John. He believes that I John gives grounds for assurance, tests of practice that can provide valid assurance (cf. pp. 81-82). Though copious in aspects of grammar that open up the books, Burdick is more lucid than Westcott's helpful exegetical work of the past, and probably the best now on the Greek. At some points one ought to go to longer discussions of views and issues in Brown, and also consult Brooke, Marshall, Plummer, Smalley etc. on technical matters, Marshall and Smalley also for more on studies of recent years.

Candlish, R. S. A Commentary on I John. 2 volumes in 1, Geneva Series of Commentaries, 2nd ed. London: Banner of Truth Trust, 1973.

Here is an 1870 work by a noted Scottish preacher. It is one of the better older commentaries on I John and has much good comment on the epistle, though it is not as valuable as a number of the later works. It is penetrating in its devotional depths which search the reader's heart. Spurgeon said in his day that a man hardly needed anything on I John beyond Candlish.

Findlay, G. G. Fellowship in the Life Eternal. London: Hodder and Stoughton, 1909. Eerdmans reprint.

Based on the Greek text, this work is one of the great commentaries on the three epistles from more than three quarters of a century ago.

Findlay, George G. Studies in John's Epistles. Grand Rapids: Kregel, 1989rp of 1925 edition from lectures in 1909. 477 pp.

This is another production of Findlay's above work.

Hodges, Zane C. "I, II and III John," in Bible Knowledge Commentary, ed. John F. Walvoord and Roy B. Zuck, Volume II. Wheaton: Victor Books, 1985.

Cf. the comment on Hodges' work in the Hebrews section. The same non-Lordship salvation view is championed here in a lucid and capable way. Passages given Hodges' turns will surprise and dismay many from an exegetical standpoint (cf. 3:4-10; 3:15; 4:7, 8; 5:13 etc.).

King, Guy. The Fellowship. Fort Washington, PA: Christian Literature Crusade, 1963.

Only 127 pages long, this book is like King's other expositions in that it is rich in phraseology, sermonic ideas and illustrations. It is a good, brief work to recommend to laymen and also good for the preacher or teacher's heart.

Kistemaker, Simon J. Cf. on James.

Marshall, I. Howard. <u>The Epistles of John</u> (NICNT). Grand Rapids: Eerdmans, 1978.

Like Ryrie and Stott, Marshall has keen ability to follow the thought of a book and articulate it with clarity. He often is helpful on stating views gleaned from the literature and is up-to-date. His use of the Greek, good footnotes, and detail on many of the problem verses make this a very good evangelical commentary by one of the best New Testament scholars in the British Isles (he is head of the New Testament Department at King's College, University of Aberdeen, Scotland).

Morris, Leon. "1, 2, 3 John" in <u>New Bible Commentary Revised</u>, ed. D. Guthrie et al. Grand Rapids: Eerdmans, 1970.

This is a brief study (pp. 1259-73) by a top evangelical exegete. Some of the passages are dealt with rather well despite the terseness, and the expositor or any Christian can receive help at certain points.

Plummer, Alfred. <u>The Epistles of John</u> (Cambridge Bible). Cambridge: University Press, 1906.

Though old, this is a good study from the Greek text which will be helpful in any serious study of the epistles. There are other works more highly recommended, however.

Ryrie, Charles C. "I, II and III John." <u>The Wycliffe Bible Commentary</u>. Chicago: Moody, 1962.

This is a brief study based on the English text. The author's rare ability to state truth precisely and concisely enables him to say a lot in these verse-by-verse studies. His work is recommended as a good survey discussion, and it includes unusually lucid homiletical outlines of the epistles.

Smalley, Stephen S. <u>1, 2, 3 John</u> (Word Biblical Commentary). Waco, TX: Word Books, 1984. 420 pp.

This ranks high with Brown, Burdick and Marshall in recent years. Smalley is excellent in helping the reader be up on views and arguments from recent years, drawn from massive research, and is second only to Brown in this regard. He is usually quite full in discussing issues so that he offers much help on verses, and does so with clarity, directness and confidence. He delves into changes in tense, many of the syntactical aspects, and doctrine. He sees the author of II and III John as John the presbyter, a Christian in the Johannine circle, and this same man may also have written I John, all in the A. D. 90's. Smalley often makes good choices on views, and tends to give definite reasons for them. He sees <u>charisma</u> (2:20, 27) as both the Spirit and the Word; 3:4-10 relates to a potential state without sin, but in practice Christians do sin (1:8-2:2). Sin in 5:16-17 is apostasy, wilful disobedience, etc.

Stott, John R. W.   The Epistles of John (Tyndale NTC).   2nd edition.   Grand Rapids: Eerdmans, 1988.   234 pp.

Here is a recent lucid, stimulating work by a gifted writer who has served as rector of the All Souls (Anglican) Church, Langham Place, London. Several New Testament scholars have hailed it as an outstanding commentary from the standpoint of exegesis, exposition and warm application. It was listed among 22 "Choice Evangelical Books of 1964" in Christianity Today (February 12, 1965, p. 16). Stott displays a vast breadth of reading in the best conservative works on the Johannine epistles. This 1988 version updates the 1964 original.

Vine, W. E.   Epistles of John.   Grand Rapids: Zondervan, 1965.

This is a concise but carefully stated work very helpful in getting at the interpretation. There is often a reference to Greek tenses which is helpful.

Westcott, B. F.   The Epistles of John.   Cambridge and London: Macmillan, 1883.

This work has long been ranked by many as the best older effort on the Greek text. It is detailed, thorough, and very useful for its incisive, definitive statements on problem areas as well as grammatical matters.

White, R. E. O.   An Open Letter to Evangelicals.   Grand Rapids: Eerdmans, 1964.

A Baptist minister presents both a commentary with deep insight and some penetrating applications to spiritual life, ethics, and other particulars. It is a verse-by-verse devotional and homiletical exposition which also deals with problems including the difficult passage in 3:4-10.

Wuest, Kenneth S.   Cf. on II Peter.

XXI. JUDE

Barclay, William.   Cf. Johannine Epistles.

Bauckham, Richard J.   Jude, 2 Peter (Word Bible Commentary).   Waco: Word, 1983.

Provides a rich source of exegetical material, closely examining the Greek text and displaying thorough familiarity with the literature, as well as with extra-Biblical material. Sure to become a standard; unsatisfactory, however, from an evangelical viewpoint, in that the author denies Petrine authorship of 2 Peter and sees a great deal of use of apocryphal and apocalyptic sources. The author's understanding of inspiration is very foggy, and one is not certain whether he believes that any of the predictions or statements in the two epistles are objectively and actually true. Thus, little direct help for some doctrinal concerns, but great help in the detailed work of exegesis; theologically disappointing but academically extremely impressive. —Dan Phillips.

Bigg, Charles. Cf. on I Peter.

Blum, Edwin. "Jude," in <u>Expositor's Bible Commentary</u>, Volume 12, ed. Frank Gaebelein. Grand Rapids: Zondervan, 1981.

A worthy evangelical work which, though brief, argues well and knowledgeably, helping on the verses.

Coder, Maxwell. <u>The Acts of the Apostates</u>. Chicago: Moody, 1958.

This work grew out of a Th. M. thesis at Dallas Theological Seminary and a series of articles in <u>Moody Monthly</u>. It is a verse-by-verse study of the epistle.

Green, Michael E. Cf. on II Peter.

Hiebert, D. E. Cf. on II Peter.

Jenkyns, William. <u>An Exposition Upon The Epistle of Jude</u>. Minneapolis: James & Klock, 1976. Reprint of 1863 work.

An exceptionally thorough analysis of the Greek text and its theological and practical import. A student looking for detail laying out the progression of thought will certainly find it here.

Kelly, J. N. D. Cf. under I Peter.

Kistemaker, Simon J. Cf. on I Peter.

Lawlor, George L. <u>The Epistle of Jude</u>. Nutley, NJ: Presbyterian and Reformed Publishing Co., 1972.

The author, a graduate of Grace Theological Seminary where he studied under Alva J. McClain, Herman A. Hoyt and Homer A. Kent, Sr., was Professor of Greek and New Testament at Cedarville College in Ohio when he wrote this commentary. The interpretation verse by verse is detailed, lucid, handles the Greek well, discusses problems at length, and uses good scholarly sources which he documents carefully. This is one of the most helpful recent works on Jude.

Luther, Martin. Cf. on I Peter.

MacArthur, John F., Jr. <u>Beware the Pretenders</u>. Wheaton: Scripture Press/ Victor Books, 1980.

One of the earlier MacArthur expositions, following the verses of Jude and pointing out the relevance of the truths to being on guard against error today.

Manton, Thomas. <u>Commentary on Jude</u>. London: 1655, reprinted by The Sovereign Grace Publishers.

Though a very old work, it is good.

Mayor, Joseph.   <u>The Second Epistle of St. Peter and the Epistle of St. Jude</u>.   NY: Macmillan (n. d.).

Cf. on II Peter.

Plummer, Alfred.   <u>The General Epistles of St. James and St. Jude</u> (Expositor's Bible).   NY: Hodder & Stoughton (n. d.).

This is a good study in the Greek text.

Reicke, Bo.   Cf. on James.

Wolff, Richard.   <u>A Commentary on the Epistle of Jude</u>.   Grand Rapids: Zondervan, 1960.

This is a thorough and scholarly verse-by-verse exposition which shows a good breadth of reading. It is conservative and recommended.

Wuest, Kenneth S.   Cf. on II Peter.

XXII. REVELATION

<u>Alford's Greek Testament</u> (premillennial) is fairly good on The Revelation. In addition:

Barclay, William.   <u>Letters to the Seven Churches</u>.   London: S. C. M. Press Ltd., 1957.

He is good on the seven churches from the standpoint of philology and explaining historical customs which illumine many statements found here. A major weakness is that he does not document his sources so that it becomes difficult to check up on him.

Barnhouse, Donald Grey.   <u>Revelation</u>.   Grand Rapids: Zondervan, 1971.

Devotional, popular-level commentary incorporating illustrations, word studies, and broad scriptural comparison. He is premillennial and pretribulational, using a fairly literal interpretation. He was a great preacher and Bible teacher in the latter first half and middle of this century.

Beasley-Murray, G. R.   <u>The Book of Revelation</u> (New Century Bible).   Greenwood, SC: Attic Press, 1974.

A well-outlined, competent work that explains many facets rather well verse by verse but shows no use of certain great commentators as Beckwith, a total absence of dispensational works such as by Walter Scott, J. B. Smith, and John Walvoord. He is unable to reach a conclusion as to which man by the name of John wrote the book, but favors the traditional date around A. D. 95. His willingness to devote lengthy or at least pertinent discussion on some problem verses makes his work often helpful, e. g. 1:4, seven spirits; 1:10, Lord's day; 1:20, seven stars; 6:2, white horse rider; 7:4-8, the 144,000; 11:3, 4, the two witnesses (but do they represent the church as he says?); 12:4, the dragon stood before the woman to devour the child as soon as he was born; 13:18, the 666; 19:7-9, the bride and the guests, etc. One may need to read him several times on Revelation 20 to decide where he really believes the "thousand years" fit into the scheme of things.

Beckwith, Isbon T. The Apocalypse of John. NY: Macmillan, 1919.

This is often a highly-rated commentary. There is an excellent introduction, detail, and the fact that Beckwith does justice to the Jewish flavor of the book.

Beckwith, Roger T. and Wilfred Stott. This is The Day, The Biblical Doctrine of the Christian Sabbath in its Jewish and Early Christian Setting. Greenwood, SC: Attic Press, 1978.

The "Lord's Day" is Sunday in Revelation 1:10 in the early church, not Easter Day, Day of the Lord, etc. A competent, well-researched and argued book with many good footnotes arranged by chapters at the end.

Bruce, F. F. "The Revelation," in The International Bible Commentary, ed. F. F. Bruce. 1 volume.

A brief survey by one of the foremost New Testament scholars of the past nearly half century. Most of Bruce's works have been in books in which he did not need to show much of his viewpoint about eschatological matters. Here one can see how he deals with the Revelation.

Bullinger, E. W. The Apocalypse. 3rd edition. London: 1935.

The Greek student will find this a very good commentary generally, but will have to watch Bullinger on chapters 2-3 where his ultra-dispensational conclusions are not really valid. It is almost impossible to find a copy, except in some libraries.

Caird, G. B. A Commentary on The Revelation of St. John the Divine. NY: Harper & Row, 1966.

He is not sure whether the Apostle John wrote it though he leaves this open and dates the book ca. A. D. 95. As a brief commentary this does a fair job, but skipping verses (as 1:10) is disconcerting to some as is covering some key sections so fast (as 1:12ff.). The 144,000 are the whole band of the saved, and he also equates them with the great throng of 7:9ff. He holds, curiously, that the birth of the child in 12:2-5 is not the Nativity but the Cross; fleeing of the woman (he says she is the church) is handled with exceeding vagueness, but apparently related to the entire present age. One has difficulty respecting his awareness of things when on p. 235 he sweepingly claims that until Daniel the Jewish people had no expectation of an afterlife, a liberal notion widely held but often refuted by evangelicals. To him "All the evidence we have is against . . . a literal interpretation" of resurrection in 20:5 (p. 254). Though at times vague in regard to the millennium, he appears to see it as a state before the eternal state, with many questions left hanging. He is often quite helpful in bringing in possible background from Jewish apocalyptic literature. It is a fair commentary, quite good in many places but mystifying in some.

Campbell, Donald K. and Jeffrey L. Townsend, eds. A Case for Premillennialism. A New Consensus. Chicago: Moody, 1992.

Fourteen scholars wrote chapters reasoning out how the view makes the best hermeneutical sense in different parts of the Bible. Some of these are: Genesis (Robert Chisholm), Psalm 89 (Ron Allen), Jeremiah (Walt Kaiser), Daniel (Ken Barker), Matthew (David Lowery), Acts (Darrell Bock), Revelation (Harold Hoehner). The "Case" will be much-discussed and of substantial help to many pastors, Bible teachers, and lay people.

Charles, R. H. The Revelation of St. John (ICC). 2 volumes. Naperville, IL: Allenson, 1959.

This is a voluminous work on critical and exegetical matters. The serious student who is laboring in the Greek will want to use this commentary even though he may not agree with many of the liberal conclusions.

Chilton, David. The Days of Vengeance. An Exposition of the Book of Revelation. Fort Worth, TX: Dominion Press, 1987. 721 pp.

A learned advocacy of a postmillennial view. Cf. also Chilton's first book on eschatology, Paradise Restored: A Biblical Theology of Dominion (Fort Worth: Dominion Press, 1985). Gary North in the "Publisher's Preface" (p. xv) says that what Chilton generalized in the first book, "is now supported with chapter and verse—indeed, lots and lots of chapters and verses." He asserts that Chilton has, at long last among commentators, found the secret key that unlocks the code of the Book of Revelation (xvi).

Clark, David S. The Message from Patmos: A Postmillennial Commentary on the Book of Revelation. Grand Rapids: Baker, 1989. 148 pp.

A more succinct effort than Chilton's to support the postmillennial interpretation.

Cohen, Gary. Understanding Revelation. Chicago: Moody Press, 1978.

A premillennial, pretribulational work that deals at length with several main subjects rather than being a commentary. Cohen deals systematically with such topics as whether Revelation 2, 3 gives periods of church history, the chronology of Revelation 21, 22, etc., presenting different views and arguing for his own. This is in some ways a helpful book on orientation, as is M. C. Tenney's Interpreting Revelation.

Cohen, Gary and Kirban Salem. <u>Revelation Visualized</u>. Chicago: Moody Press, 1972.

This is an effort by a Christian Jew (Cohen, the comments) and a Christian Arab (Salem, the background) to provide pictures of many things deemed to be like those mentioned in the text, interspersed with commentary. The outlook is premillennial and pretribulational. The commentary does not explore issues very far past surface considerations (as on the twenty-four elders, 4:4) but seems dogmatically to give popularly-held views. However, if a basically literal time of tribulation is intended in the Apocalyptic descriptions, there are many pictures and details here that help the student visualize something of what it might be like in practical terms.

Colclasure, Chuck. <u>The Overcomers</u>. Nashville: Thomas Nelson, 1981.

This 206-pp. book develops the view that all Christians are overcomers by faith, and pulls together from all of the Apocalypse spiritual lessons pertaining to salvation and spiritual victory, hope, comfort, and encouragement. It is more topical than expository, and reflects an amillennial perspective in various key passages.

Coleman, Robert E. <u>Songs of Heaven</u>. Old Tappan, NJ: Revell, 1980.

Fourteen meditations on songs in the Apocalypse, using exposition, illustration, reference to hymns we know today, and a devotional thrust that warms and refreshes.

Ellul, Jacques. <u>Apocalypse: The Book of Revelation</u>. Translated by G. W. Schreiner. NY: Seabury Press, 1977.

Ellul is a famous theologian of the Reformed Church of France and Professor of Law and History, University of Bordeaux. He sees apocalyptic as not allowing a literal interpretation of prophecy, and writes so much in a philosophical train of thought that the reader is often vague as to what is going on or what is being really explained in any definite sense. Rather than rescuing the Apocalypse from improper treatment (and indeed it has had plenty of that!), Ellul only plunges it again into a fog for many readers.

Epp, Theodore. <u>Practical Studies in the Revelation</u>. 2 volumes. Lincoln, NE: Back to the Bible Broadcast, 1969.

This includes several simple studies with a clear perspective on the pattern of events to take place according to a more literal understanding of biblical prophecy. The chapters would be quite readable for laymen and less advanced students of Scripture. At many points Epp includes spiritual lessons and challenges that show the practicality of the Book of Revelation to experience today.

Erdman, Charles R.   The Revelation of John.   Grand Rapids: Baker, 1987rp. 181 pp.

Erdman did a commentary of 17 volumes on the entire New Testament. He is quite concise in surveying books, and very clear in his writing. Here he distinctly shows his amillennial view in Revelation 20, for example (pp. 155-56), although he does not defend it in the length that William Hendriksen does (More Than Conquerors, this list).

Feinberg, Charles L.   "The Book of Revelation," in the Liberty Bible Commentary, ed. Jerry Falwell et al.   Nashville, TN: Thomas Nelson Publishers, 1983. 2,721 pp.

Feinberg, an outstanding voice for premillennialism in the dispensational pattern and a Jewish Christian, was allowed pp. 2,652-2,721 for a work of brevity. He has a detailed outline, treats many of the problems, giving views of his own and reasons. He believes that 1:19 is the key verse; 1:20 refers to ministers of local churches, not celestial beings; there are five crowns for believers and they may win one or more of these as special reward (cf. on 2:10); 4:4 supports a pre-tribulational rapture since the elders represent the church in heaven after chapters 1-3 (even many dispensationalists do not agree with his seven reasons); the 144,000 in chapter 7 are Israelites, not the church saints; the locusts are literal but supernatural beings; etc.

Fiorenza, Elizabeth S.   Invitation to the Book of Revelation: A Commentary on the Apocalypse with Complete Text From the Jerusalem Bible.   Garden City, NY: Doubleday, 1981.

This 223-page work is by a professor of Biblical Theology at the University of Notre Dame. Two other Catholic women have written recognized commentaries on the Revelation (Josephine M. Ford, Anchor Bible, 1975, also on Notre Dame faculty; and Adela Yarbro Collins, 1979). Fiorenza is also scheduled to come out with a more definitive commentary on Revelation in the Hermeneia series (Fortress Press). She is against source-critical theories on the composition and takes a futurist scheme of interpretation. Yet she is very different from the futurist views of Premillennialists. She does not take the Apostle John as author. The "five who have fallen" (chapter 17) are emperors in the first century, Caesar, Caligula, Nero and Domitian (p. 166) (she does not mention a fifth!). The first seal deals with the conquest by the Roman Empire (Babylon); the 144,000 are the Church; the thousand years refer to an earthly Messianic Kingdom as Jesus hoped for, not the "spiritual" interpretation common in Roman Catholic circles and among many Protestants (amillennialism).

Ford, Josephine.   Revelation (Anchor Bible).   Garden City, NY: Doubleday, 1975.

The very liberal author was Professor of New Testament Studies at Notre Dame University. Her viewpoint is that Revelation is by multiple authors in the mid-first century. Chapters 4-11 are by John the Baptist or his disciples,

Chapters 12-22 by unknown writers. Ford gives a new translation but comments in general on sections, not verse by verse. The bibliography is helpful if one wishes to consult liberal authors and have an extensive list, but evangelical writers are missing. There is little help exegetically to put the book together in a meaningful way for conservative readers. One can waste much time here.

Hailey, Homer. **Revelation: An Introduction and Commentary.** **Grand Rapids: Baker, 1977.**

Hailey, amillennial like William Hendriksen (More Than Conquerors), goes so far as to contend that all of Revelation 1-19 was fulfilled in pre-Constantine times, before ca. 235. Even the "thousand years" are symbolic of the period from Constantine until Satan is released. Only 20:7ff. is clearly yet future. Armageddon took place in the subduing of the Roman Empire. The four horsemen of Chapter 6 are Christ going with the gospel, persecution of saints, problems in the economic situation, and judgments on Christ-rejecters (186-93). The great tribulation is the 240 years of Roman-Christian struggle; the two witnesses the church; the woman of chapter 12 the people of God; the coming of the warrior in 19:1lff. is not Jesus' Second Advent but a picture of victory over the world's sinful forces; Gog and Magog denote trends such as atheism, materialism, humanism, communism (397). The work is a clear presentation of one amillennialist's handling of the Revelation.

Hemer, Colin J. **The Letters to the Seven Churches of Asia in Their Local Setting.** **Sheffield, England:** **Department of Biblical Studies, University of Sheffield/Journal for Study of the Old Testament Press, 1986.** **338 pp.**

This is based on Hemer's Ph.D thesis under F. F. Bruce at the University of Manchester. It is an exegetical study of the seven letters with much research into the local setting (manners and customs as on the white stone) that helps readers grasp what was meant in that culture. The work is very helpful for one teaching or preaching in one or all of the letters, and well-documented in ancient sources.

Hendriksen, William. **More Than Conquerors.** **Grand Rapids:** **Baker, 1982rp of 1940 edition (Tyndale Press).** **216 pp.**

An evangelical but amillennial approach to the Apocalypse. Some will doubt that this is one of Hendriksen's better works, but premillennial readers will profit from following how an amillennialist can explain his view. The work is quite readable, and Hendriksen often provides several arguments to support his view, which he has thought through carefully.

Hoeksema, Herman. **Behold, He Cometh!** **Grand Rapids:** **Reformed Free Publishing Association, 1969.**

A 726-page work, result of a lifetime of study, posthumously published from a preached series given in the magazine The Standard Bearer. It is done with warmth and simple amillennial explanation on a popular basis by a noted writer on Reformed Dogmatics. The seven seals depict "the main aspects and larger currents of the history of this dispensation . . . " (p. 186). The woman of Chapter 12 is the Church; the millennium is the whole present age, etc.

Kuyper, Abraham. <u>The Revelation of St. John.</u> **Translated by J. H. de Vries. Grand Rapids: Eerdmans, 1963.**

This is the larger part of the fourth volume in Dr. Kuyper's Dutch work on "The Consummation of the World," his last work, begun at age 76 seven years before his death. He takes what he thinks best in Augustine's view and in an idealist position. In history and on the current scene the things the visions depict repeat themselves. Numbers here, to Kuyper, are not literal. The work is not verse by verse but set up in general chapters: "The Mysticism of Numbers," "The Seven Churches," "The Transition to the Prophetical Part" (at 4:1), "The Seven Seals," etc. Kuyper divides the Revelation into Chapters 1, 2-3, 4:1-22:6, and 22:7ff. The twenty-four elders are believers in Christ who will dwell on the new earth, including even Old Testament believers who join those before Pentecost (p. 61). Kuyper wonders if the fourth seal events have already come (p. 76). The trumpets come from the last seal and the vials from the last trumpet (p. 84). The trumpet and vial judgments are God's acts upon a world after the day of grace ends. The judgments, as in 8:7ff., are taken apparently as actual physical calamities on the earth, on nature and on people (p. 90). The blood mingled with hail and fire is a material substance especially prepared by God in heaven. The great star that falls is a meteor shower (94, 95). The locust-like hosts picture military invaders. He understands the "thousand years" (chapter 20) as symbolic of the abundant fullness of God's action in bringing judgment on Satan to consummation (277), and much vagueness attaches to Kuyper's work here.

Hughes, Philip E. <u>The Book of the Revelation.</u> **Grand Rapids: Eerdmans, 1990. 242 pp.**

A renowned New Testament scholar and Anglican clergyman provides an amillennial work (cf. p. 211, the thousand years are today). He is clear and lucid, but not outstanding in exegesis. He has a very good commentary on the second epistle to the Corinthians and a fairly good one on Hebrews.

Johnson, Alan F. "Revelation," in <u>Expositor's Bible Commentary,</u> **Volume 12, ed. Frank Gaebelein. Grand Rapids: Zondervan, 1981.**

A faculty member of the Wheaton College did this fairly-well documented study in a premillennial manner, grappling with views on issues, displaying wide reading and awareness.

Johnson, Alan F. <u>Revelation</u> **(Bible Study Commentary). Grand Rapids: Zondervan, 1983. 220 pp.**

This is a less-documented work articulating the essence of Johnson's views. Even here he often mentions different views and concisely states some reasons, and is usually clear, often thought-provoking. He is not always convincing as when he sees the 144,000 of chapter 7 as the whole elect people of God. He distinguishes a millennial kingdom in chapter 20 from the eternal state after this (21:1ff.), surveys views, and gives his reasoning. Pages 218-20 list commentaries under four basic views on the Revelation.

Karleen, Paul S.   The Pre-Wrath Rapture of the Church—Is it Biblical? Langhorne, PA: BF Press, 1991. 102 pp.

A graduate of Yale University, Dallas Seminary and University of Pennsylvania (Ph.D. in Linguistics of Ancient Greek) has a well organized and penetrating evaluation of Marvin Rosenthal's The Pre-Wrath Rapture of the Church (cf. in this section). He takes up several issues Rosenthal raised and devotes a chapter to each, pointing out what he regards as flaws in the Rosenthal case. In essence Karleen defends a pre-tribulational rapture. A boiled down version of his book appears in "Evaluating the Pre-wrath Rapture of the Church," Voice, An Independent Church Journal (IFCA), Volume 70, No. 1, Grandville, MI: January-February, 1991, pp. 9-13. An even longer work arguing for a Rosenthal-type view is Robert Van Kampen, The Sign (Wheaton: Crossway Books, 1992, 538 pp., with fold-out map).

Ladd, George.   A Commentary on the Revelation of John.   Grand Rapids: Eerdmans, 1972.

A premillennial but not pretribulational effort to interpret the apocalypse. Ladd shows keen awareness of issues and is competent in his comments, though sometimes too brief. It is a very fine evangelical work in general, one of the best.

La Haye, Tim.   Revelation Illustrated and Made Plain.   Grand Rapids: Zondervan, 1973.

A popularly-written book (and easy to follow) with a pretribulational stance, which follows some popular pretribulational views. His belief that the seven churches depict seven basic periods of church history (p. 16 etc.) is not acceptable to some even within that basic theological group and most outside it. The same is true at other points (e. g., his explanation of being blotted from the book of life, 3:5 etc., his view that the rapture of the church is pictured in 4:1, 2, etc.). But for pretribulational rapture people, the work overall will be helpful to lay readers.

Landels, William.   The Victor's Sevenfold Reward: Being Discourses on the Promises of Our Lord to the Seven Churches.   London: James Nisbet & Co. 1878.

Very good, well-organized, perceptive discussion on aspects of reward, quite picturesque, eloquent, and suggestive with word pictures. Quite stimulating when one is preparing a series or wants a book to speak in some detail on an aspect of reward.

Larkin, Clarence. <u>The Book of Revelation</u>. Philadelphia: The Clarence Larkin Estate, 1959.

A famous older-type dispensational work especially helpful at times from the standpoint of its many line drawings, charts and maps, but too cluttered in some.

Loane, Marcus. <u>They Overcame. An Exposition of Revelation 1-3</u>. Grand Rapids: Baker, 1971.

A well-written evangelical book more in the stimulating practical line that helps a reader see points of relevance to churches today. Along with the work by Stott this is one of the better popular-style books on the seven churches in recent years.

Mauro, Philip. <u>Things Which Soon Must Come to Pass</u>. Swengel, PA: Reiner Publications, 1974.

A 623-page amillennial work reprinted. Along with works by Hendriksen and Hoeksema, etc., one can see how an interpreter develops an amillennial view in the Revelation. Beckwith, Lenski and Mounce do, and Colclasure, Erdman and Morris have brief treatments. Hendriksen is the best in general, on most areas.

Morgan, G. Campbell. <u>The Letters of Our Lord</u>. London: Pickering and Inglis, 1945. This also carries the title <u>First Century Messages to Twentieth Century Believers</u>.

A 112-page study, this book deals with expositions on the seven churches in chapters 2-3. When one is studying this portion of the Apocalypse he will find Morgan helpful, along with Barclay, Landels, Loane, Ramsay, Seiss, Stott and Trench.

Morris, Leon. <u>The Book of Revelation. An Introduction and Commentary</u> (Tyndale NTC). Grand Rapids: Eerdmans, 1987, revised, updated. 256 pp.

Morris concisely comments on verses in an amillennial vein, as on Revelation 20. He is frequently helpful on views and information from his wide reading. Noteworthy here and there, the work does not rank high as do his commentaries on John, Romans and the Thessalonian Epistles.

Morris, Henry M. <u>The Revelation Record</u>. Wheaton: Tyndale; and San Diego: Creation-Life, 1983.

A 521-pp. premillennial, pretribulational work by a writer who has specialized in hydrology and geology and desires to help with the many references to natural phenomena. His perspective is full verbal inspiration, and a literal interpretation in the futuristic vein. At times things are rather artificially blocked off — chapters 4-11 cover the first half of the seven-year tribulation period, chapters 12-19 the second half (p. 27). Morris holds that the 24 elders are men, the locust-like beings of chapter 9 are demonic spirits, the two witnesses of chapter 11 are Enoch and Elijah who have waited in heaven in their natural bodies since departing this earth. Babylon in chapters 17-18 is the literal, rebuilt city of Babylon on the Euphrates as a world center of trade, communications, education, etc. (pp. 348-49), the rider on the white horse of 6:2 is Christ who is on the white horse in 19:11, etc. Morris is fairly thorough in taking things literally and gives his reasons, but allows for symbolism, e. g. the woman (12:1), the white horse (6:2; 19:11), the two-edged sword, etc. There is sometimes an indefiniteness (lack of clarity) in who the "overcomer" is, at times sounding like some more faithful among the saved (p. 59) but sometimes every redeemed person (pp. 227, 443).

Mounce, Robert.   The Book of Revelation (NICNT).   Grand Rapids: Eerdmans, 1977.

This is a very well-written, fine commentary based on exceptional awareness of views and literature. Tentatively Mounce accepts authorship by John the Apostle, son of Zebedee, and a date of ca. A. D. 95-96. Mounce holds that there can be elements of various views—preterist, historicist, futurist, idealist—but that John's predictions, stated in forms from his own culture, will receive a final, total realization in the last days of history. He furnishes a clear, detailed outline (pp. 47-49), an excellent bibliography of commentaries, journal articles, and other works (49-60), and very knowledgeable comments verse by verse showing awareness of main views on problems and giving good detail to many issues, whatever view he finally favors. He holds that the 144,000 are the new Israel, the church and the number is symbolic of completeness (168-69). The references to other Jewish literature with similar-sounding descriptions is often evident, but one is not always sure a verse in the Revelation has been really explained after all the sincere effort, as the great mountain burning with fire, 8:8, 9 (pp. 186-87). His conviction about the thousand years seems to be finally influenced by Beckwith's amillennial concept: John taught a literal millennium—gave it in that form—but the realization may be not in an actual era of political social history but in a different form, a life of highest union with God in a non-temporal sense (p. 359). His discussion of the millennium in general has a number of turns many premillennialists cannot easily figure, but he gathers choice citations in ancient Jewish writings about the length of a temporary reign.

Newell, William R.   The Book of Revelation.   Chicago: Moody, 1935.

This is a premillennial, dispensational study which takes a thorough-going literal approach to the book. It is good on the English text and will have its main usefulness in some points for lay people. Read Ironside to maintain a balance in a lighter dispensational work.

Ramsay, William.   The Letters to the Seven Churches of Asia.   Grand Rapids: Baker, 1985rp of 1905 ed. and reprint in 1963.   446 pp.

This is the outstanding older work on the historical background of the churches in chapters 2-3. The student will obtain much rich detail here to lend colorful vividness to his preaching and teaching. He takes the preterist point of view on the book. Colin Hemer's 1986 work now surpasses this in updating on scholarly discussion and discovery and in comments on some details. Until Hemer and Yamauchi, this was the outstanding work.

Rosenthal, Marvin. The Pre-Wrath Rapture of the Church. Nashville: Thomas Nelson, 1990. 319 pp.

A frequent speaker at Bible conferences on prophecy, Rosenthal was for thirty years a firm pre-tribulationalist but here shows in detail his arguments for turning to a new view. He reasons that the church will not escape all of the oppression in the future tribulation period by being raptured to heaven, but will be taken out of the earth when the wrath begins during the second half of the seven years. His view requires re-defining many aspects of prophecy and 20 chapters to expound. Cf. Karleen (this list) for an evaluation by a pre-tribulationalist.

Ryrie, Charles C. Revelation. Chicago: Moody, 1968.

This work is included because it offers a quick yet competent study of Revelation in a well-organized way. It lays out the various parts of the book in a simple fashion and the comments are brief and to the point, yet offer solutions to many of the difficult problems of exposition. It would help the average church member gain a perspective of prophecy as taught in the final book of Scripture, and then he could go on to more detailed study. Ryrie is dispensational.

Scott, Walter. Exposition of the Revelation of Jesus Christ. Westwood, NJ: Revell (n. d.).

A helpful older premillennial work that is at some points lucid in expounding the meaning.

Seiss, J. A. Lectures on the Apocalypse. 3 volumes. Grand Rapids: Zondervan, 1957. Reprint in one volume.

An expository older premillennial work of great detail on units of the book.

Thomas, Robert L. Revelation 1-7, An Exegetical Commentary (Wycliffe Exegetical Commentary). Chicago: Moody Press, 1992. xxvii + 524 pp.

Thomas has a second volume yet to come in this most exegetically detailed yet premillennial effort. The field is one of his specialties since his Th. D. dissertation, "The Argument of The Book of Revelation." He brings more than thirty years of Greek teaching expertise to the task. He argues for authorship by the Apostle John (pp. 2-19) and a date of ca. A. D. 95 (20-23). His wide interaction looks at issues fairly and carefully. A good section explores hermeneutics for interpreting the Apocalypse (29-39). He employs his own translation verse by verse. He deals in considerable detail with many interpretive issues, gives reasons for views, is clear, and follows a detailed outline. He favors seeing the Lord's day (1:10) as Sunday, sees in 1:19 a three-fold division of the book due to grammar, opts for human messengers in 1:20, and sees a mixed group in the churches (some genuinely saved, others only professors). He looks penetratingly at views on Nicolaitans (2:6), sees "the overcomer" as applicable to all genuinely saved persons, reasoning this out with awareness of relevant factors, and prefers taking "crown of life" in 2:10 as a genitive of apposition, "crown which is (eternal) life," understood as received through grace and not merit. Thomas favors a pre-tribulational removal of the church in 3:10, devoting six pages to an appraisal of arguments for views. The twenty-four elders are exalted celestial beings. The white horse rider of 6:2 is decided, after a long evaluation of views, to personify a movement or force working against the Messiah's interests in the future tribulation period. He defends the view that the 144,000 in chapter 7 are distinctively certain men of Israel, not the church, etc.

Tickle, J.   The Book of Revelation. A Catholic Interpretation of the Apocalypse. Liguori, MO: Liguori Publications, 1983.   143 pp.

The Rector of the Immaculate Heart of Mary Cathedral, Los Cruces, New Mexico gives a Roman Catholic interpretation of the symbols and the message.

Trench, R. C.   Commentary on the Epistles to the Seven Churches.   NY: Macmillan, 1861.

This is another work which will be profitable in a study of chapters 2-3. Trench is helpful in the Greek, and also on customs and detail about older views, many of which are still held today.

Walvoord, John F.   The Revelation of Jesus Christ.   Chicago: Moody, 1966.

Written by one of the foremost modern-day articulators of premillennial dispensationalism, this book is a lucid exposition of the Revelation which combines textual exposition with theological orientation. Walvoord shows awareness of wide reading, gives various views, is fair, and deals with problems as they arise. It is the best broad dispensational work to appear in recent years, and Robert Thomas has the best detailed technical work so far, through chapter 7.

Walvoord, John F.   "Revelation," in Bible Knowledge Commentary, ed. John F. Walvoord and Roy B. Zuck, Volume II.   Wheaton: Victor Books, 1985.

This is a condensed statement of views Walvoord develops in his larger work, The Revelation of Jesus Christ. It is, then, premillennial and dispensational.

Wilcock, Michael.   I Saw Heaven Opened: The Message of Revelation (Bible Speaks Today).   Downers Grove: IVP, 1975.   223 pp.

A work that lucidly explains symbolism here and favors an amillennial view.

Yamauchi, Edwin M.   The Archaeology of the New Testament Cities in Western Asia Minor.   Grand Rapids: Baker, 1980.

A respected evangelical scholar has researched at length on Ephesus, Pergamus, Sardis and Laodicea. The expositor planning a message or series in this part of Scripture will find substantial background help here, as in Ramsay and Hemer.

130238

NOTES

NOTES